Meaning

BLACKWELL READINGS IN PHILOSOPHY

Series Editor: Steven M. Cahn

Blackwell Readings in Philosophy are concise, chronologically arranged collections of primary readings from classical and contemporary sources. They represent core positions and important developments with respect to key philosophical concepts. Edited and introduced by leading philosophers, these volumes provide valuable resources for teachers and students of philosophy, and for all those interested in gaining a solid understanding of central topics in philosophy.

Meaning

Edited by
Mark Richard

Blackwell
Publishing

350 Main Street, Malden, MA 02148-5018, USA
108 Cowley Road, Oxford OX4 1JF, UK
550 Swanston Street, Carlton South, Melbourne, Victoria 3053, Australia
Kurfürstendamm 57, 10707 Berlin, Germany

First published 2003 by Blackwell Publishing Ltd

Library of Congress Cataloging-in-Publication Data

Meaning / edited by Mark Richard.
    p. cm.—(Blackwell readings in philosophy; 5)
  Includes bibliographical references and index.
  ISBN 0-631-22222-7 (alk. paper)—ISBN 0-631-22223-5 (pbk.: alk. paper)
  1. Language and languages—Philosophy. 2. Meaning (Philosophy) I. Richard, Mark. II. Series.

B840 .M445 2002
121'.68—dc21

2002066432

A catalogue record for this title is available from the British Library.

Set in 10/12.5pt Palatino
by Kolam Information Services Pvt. Ltd, Pondicherry, India
Printed and bound in the United Kingdom
by MPG Books Ltd, Bodmin, Cornwall

For further information on
Blackwell Publishing, visit our website:
http://www.blackwellpublishing.com

For Michael and Eleanor

Contents

viii *Contents*

Acknowledgments

The editor and publisher gratefully acknowledge the permission granted to reproduce the copyright material in this book:

Chapter 1: Gottlob Frege, "On Sense and Reference," pp. 56–78 from Peter Geach and Max Black (eds.), *Translations from the Philosophical Writings of Gottlob Frege*. Oxford: Basil Blackwell, 1970. Reproduced by permission of Blackwell Publishing and Rowman and Littlefield Inc.

Chapter 2: Saul A. Kripke, extracts from *Naming and Necessity*, pp. 22–144. Cambridge, Mass.: Harvard University Press, 1980. © 1972, 1980 by Saul A. Kripke. Reproduced by permission of Blackwell Publishing and Harvard University Press.

Chapter 3: Hilary Putnam, "Meaning and Reference," pp. 699–711 from *Journal of Philosophy* 70: 19 (November 8, 1973). © 1973 The Journal of Philosophy, Inc. Reproduced by permission of the journal and the author.

Chapter 4: Mark Wilson, "Predicate Meets Property," pp. 549–89 from *The Philosophical Review* 91: 4 (October 1982). © 1982 Sage School of Philosophy of Cornell University. Reprinted by permission of the publisher and the author.

Chapter 5: Paul Horwich, extracts from *Meaning*, pp. 43–99. Oxford: Clarendon Press, 1998. © Paul Horwich 1998. Reprinted by permission of Oxford University Press.

Chapter 6: W. V. Quine, extract from "Ontological Relativity," pp. 185–206 in *Journal of Philosophy* 65: 7 (April 4, 1968). © 1968 The Journal of

Philosophy, Inc. Reproduced by permission of the journal and the author's estate.

Chapter 7: Scott Soames, extracts from "The Indeterminacy of Translation and the Inscrutability of Reference," pp. 321–57 in *Canadian Journal of Philosophy* 29: 3 (September 1999).

Chapter 8: Jody Azzouni, "Individuation, Causal Relations, and Quine." Written especially for this volume. © 2003 by Jody Azzouni.

Chapter 9: Donald Davidson, "Radical Interpretation," pp. 125–39 (chapter 9) from Donald Davidson, *Inquiries into Meaning and Truth*. Oxford: Clarendon Press, 1984. © Donald Davidson 1984. Reprinted by permission of Oxford University Press.

Chapter 10: Scott Soames, "Semantics and Semantic Competence," pp. 575–96 from *Philosophical Perspectives* 3 (1989). Reproduced by permission of Blackwell Publishing.

Chapter 11: James Higginbotham, "Truth and Understanding," pp. 3–16 from *Philosophical Studies* 65: 3 (1992). Reproduced with kind permission from Kluwer Academic Publishers.

Chapter 12: John Perry, extracts from "Indexicals and Demonstratives," pp. 586–612 (chapter 23) in Bob Hale and Crispin Wright (eds.), *A Companion to the Philosophy of Language*. Oxford: Blackwell Publishers, 1997. Reproduced by permission of Blackwell Publishing.

Chapter 13: W. V. Quine, "Two Dogmas of Empiricism," pp. 20–46 (chapter 2), reproduced by permission of the publisher from W. V. Quine, *From a Logical Point of View*, second edition (revised). Cambridge, Mass.: Harvard University Press, 1980. © 1953, 1961, 1980 by the President and Fellows of Harvard College, renewed 1989 by W. V. Quine.

Chapter 14: Frank Jackson, "Armchair Metaphysics," pp. 154–76 (chapter 11) from Frank Jackson, *Mind, Method and Conditionals*. London and New York: Routledge, 1998. Reproduced by permission of Taylor and Francis Ltd.

Every effort has been made to trace copyright holders and to obtain their permission for the use of copyright material. The publisher apologizes for any errors or omissions in the above list and would be grateful if notified of any corrections that should be incorporated in future reprints or editions of this book.

Introduction: Conceptions of Meaning

Mark Richard

We use language to represent the world to ourselves; we interpret the speech of others and thereby discover what they think about the world. Philosophical work on meaning tries to explain what underlies linguistic representation and interpretation. The essays which follow are representative of important philosophical work on meaning over the last 100 years. This introduction provides some of its philosophical context.

1   Most twentieth-century work on meaning is in one way or another a reaction to Gottlob Frege's work; to understand the former one needs some familarity with the latter.

At the center of Frege's work in philosophy of language is his distinction between sense and reference. The reference of a name is its bearer; 'Al Gore,' for example, refers to Al Gore. Frege extended the notion of reference to all meaningful expressions. In particular, the reference of a predicate (such as 'is a Democrat') is the collection of things of which the predicate is true (here, the set of Democrats); the reference of a sentence (such as 'Al Gore is a Democrat') is its truth value.[1] Reference could be said to be a *kind* of meaning (Frege's term for reference, *bedeutung*, is normally translated into English as "meaning"). Frege argues that there's more to meaning than reference. The sentences

1   Mary loves Mark Twain.
2   Mary loves the author of *Huck Finn*.

are the same, except (1) has 'Mark Twain' where the other has 'the author of *Huck Finn*.' So they are the same as far as reference goes. But they seem to mean different things, as witnessed by the fact that one could understand both while finding one informative or interesting, the other neither.

"On Sense and Reference" (chapter 1) begins by puzzling over the question "How can sentences which differ only by terms with the same reference differ in how informative they are?" Frege's answer is that words and sentences not only have reference but *sense*. The sense of an expression is a "way of thinking" or "mode of presentation" of its reference. There are, of course, many ways to conceptualize an individual: one may, for example, think of Twain as the author of *Huck Finn* or as Hartford's most famous resident. Given that it is the sense of a sentence which determines how informative it is, and that to each reference there correspond many senses, we have the elements of a solution to Frege's puzzle.

Frege assigns sense a number of tasks which one would expect the notion of meaning to discharge. Senses are anchors of linguistic competence: understanding a language requires "grasping" the senses of its expressions. Sense determines reference: one *explains* how a name comes to pick out an individual, a predicate to be true of a particular class of objects, by adverting to the expression's sense. In the case of names, the mechanism of reference is apparently descriptive: Frege's examples in "On Sense and Reference" suggest that a name's sense is a descriptive condition (e.g., the sense of 'Aristotle' might be *the student of Plato and teacher of Alexander the Great*). Such a condition determines or "presents" an individual; for 'Aristotle' to refer to Aristotle is for the sense of 'Aristotle' to present Aristotle.

In these respects, sense is meaning-like; in other respects, it is not. The senses of sentence uses – *thoughts*, as Frege calls them – are what are believed, doubted, asserted, and communicated; it is thoughts which are in the first instance true or false. These properties of thoughts make them poor candidates for sentence meanings. A sentence is not ambiguous because it contains a context sensitive word like 'I.' But such a sentence – e.g., 'I am a woman' – expresses different thoughts when uttered by Simone and I, since it is false when uttered by me, but true when uttered by Simone. Thus we cannot in general identify the meaning of a sentence with the thought(s) its literal utterance would express, even granting that there is an intimate relation between sense and linguistic meaning.

2   Sense for Frege was objective and mind-independent. If it were not, Frege argues in "Thoughts" (Frege, 1918), thought would be subjective (it would be constituted by "ideas"), and it would not be possible for two people to think the same thing. Nonetheless, sense (and thus, on Frege's view, reference and meaning) seem to reflect speakers' psychological

states. Sense is a way of *thinking* of a reference, apparently a way of *conceptualizing* it. Frege himself allows that the sense of a name like 'Aristotle' may vary across thinkers, just as the ways those thinkers think of Aristotle vary. The sense of an expression, as used by a particular individual, is fixed by that individual's *grasping* the sense and associating it with the expression. Whatever it is to grasp a sense, it is something one does in virtue of one's mental states.

These aspects of Frege's views have been subjected to intense criticism. We saw that Frege's examples suggest that the sense of a proper name is generally given by a definite description the speaker associates with the name, one which expresses the "mode of presentation" the speaker associates with the name. Saul Kripke argues in "Naming and Necessity" (chapter 2) that on any remotely plausible hypothesis about the descriptions speakers associate with the names of which they have command, such a view makes obviously incorrect predictions about the semantic and epistemic properties of sentences.

Suppose, for example, the sense of 'Simone' for Miriam is that of 'the author of *The Second Sex*.' Imagine Miriam utters

1 Simone wrote nothing.
2 The author of *The Second Sex* wrote nothing.

If I say, referring to what Miriam says in uttering (1), 'that could have been true,' I speak truly, for Beauvoir might have written nothing. But if, referring to what Miriam's utterance of (2) says, I say 'that could have been true,' I speak falsely: it's impossible that an author write nothing.[2] Thus, contrary to a Fregean view, the sentences don't say the same thing. (A simliar point can be made about the epistemic properties of the claims the two sentences make: only one can be known *a priori* to be false.) Frege's view also requires far too much of speakers, in order that they be able to refer. Suppose Justin is somewhat confused, thinking that Beauvoir wrote both *The Second Sex* and *The Feminine Mystique*, so that the sense of 'Simone de Beauvoir' for him is that of 'the author of *The Second Sex* and *The Feminine Mystique*.' Then Justin's use of 'Simone de Beauvoir' won't refer, since his sense for the name presents nothing.[3]

Hilary Putnam's "Meaning and Reference" (chapter 3) begins with a well-known criticism of Fregean accounts of the semantics of "natural kind" terms – nouns such as 'water,' 'gold,' and 'electricity' which (intuitively) pick out kinds that are appropriate objects of study for natural science. Putnam's criticisms apply to any account that, like Frege's, holds both

(A)   Meaning is determined by a speaker's psychological state, narrowly construed (i.e., is determined by the facts about her brain and nervous system);

(B)   the reference of a word is determined by its meaning.

Putnam asks us to imagine individuals whose environments and histories are as much alike as possible, save that the "underlying natures" of some kind in their environments differ: perhaps the first individual is you here on earth, where water is composed of H_2O; the second is your "twin" on a distant planet qualitatively indistinguishable from Earth, but where the stuff that fills oceans, comes from the tap, and so on is a quite different substance, XYZ. Since the differences between the two individuals are all "outside of them," in their environments, they will be molecule for molecule duplicates.[4] Since their psychologies, narrowly construed, are identical, by (A) they mean the same thing by the word 'water.' By (B), the extensions of 'water,' as each uses it, are the same. But this is obviously wrong, says Putnam: when you use 'water,' you're talking about water – i.e., about H_2O – not about the substance XYZ, with which you presumably have had no causal interaction whatsoever; when your twin uses 'water,' on the other hand, she is talking about XYZ, not H_2O.

Both Kripke and Putnam sketch positive accounts of how the references of expressions are determined. (These accounts, along with the account of indexicals and demonstratives in Kaplan (1989), are sometimes lumped together under the heading 'the new theory of reference.') On each account, a term's reference is in large part determined by the relations of speakers to their environment and by historical facts about how speakers acquire vocabulary items. According to Kripke, the reference of a proper name is initially determined by a "baptism" of one sort or another – one fixes on an object perceptually, or perhaps describes it, and tags it with a name. The name is then passed from speaker to speaker, preserving its reference so long (roughly) as the person acquiring the term intends to preserve it. On such a view, the "way of thinking" a speaker associates with a name is by and large irrelevant to what the name names: that Justin has many false beliefs about Beauvoir associated with 'Simone de Beauvoir' does not prevent him from referring to Beauvoir with the name.

Putnam suggests that associated with a kind term (in virtue of its use) is a collection of "good samples" of what it applies to, as well as a *genus*, or kind of kind. Associated with 'water,' for example, are (something like) the contents of oceans, lakes, and rivers, as well as what comes out of the tap and clouds; the associated *genus* is *liquid*. Associated with 'gnu' are creatures that "authorities" (naturalists and such) have labeled 'gnu'; the associated *genus* is *animal*. Now, under a *genus* there will fall various kinds. Under *liquid*, for example, fall particular kinds of liquids (H_2O, kerosene, alcohol, and so on); under *animal* fall particular kinds of animals (gnus, baboons, human beings, etc.). In happy cases, when a kind term k is associated with a set S of samples and *genus* G, there will be exactly one kind K such that (a) K falls under G, and (b) all or most of the members of S are Ks. In this case, the extension of k is the collection of all those things, be they among the samples or not, which are of kind K. Thus, since ("give or take impurities," as Putnam puts it in Putnam (1973)) pretty much all of the things we take to be good examples of what 'water' applies to are samples of H_2O (and not samples of any other liquid), 'water' is true of samples of H_2O.

3 In the *Philosophical Investigations*,[5] Wittgenstein claims that what underlies the use of 'game' is a "complicated network of similarities overlapping and criss-crossing." We "extend our concept of [a game, or other concepts, such as that of a number] as in spinning a thread we twist fibre on fibre." The concept of a game (and thus the meaning of 'game') is such that "the extension of the concept is not closed by a frontier. . . . For how is the concept of a game bounded? What still counts as a game and what no longer does? Can you give the boundary? No." To the objection

> But if the concept "game" is uncircumscribed like that, you don't really know what you mean by a "game."

comes the response

> When I give you the description "The ground was quite covered with plants" – do you want to say that I don't know what I am talking about until I can give a definition of a plant?

Wittgenstein's view of meaning and reference seems strikingly different from both Frege's and Putnam's. For the latter, the meaning of a noun, adjective, or verb determines ("in advance," as it were) to what the word can be correctly applied. It does this, in effect, by "unifying" the predicate's extension. The things to which a term whose semantics is Putnamian apply are all alike in being of a single kind. And the extension of an expression with a Fregean sense is the set of exactly those things which are correctly conceptualized in a certain way. Wittgenstein, on the other hand, insists that whatever constitutes the meaning of 'game' (or 'plant,' or 'number,' or, one suspects, just about any noun) need not, and generally does not, determine how the word is to be used in novel cases. What constitutes this meaning – my "concept" of a game, if you like – is "completely expressed in the various explanations I could give.... That is, in my describing examples of various kinds of game; shewing how all sorts of other games can be constructed on the analogy of these; saying that I should scarcely include this or this among games; etc." (Wittgenstein, 1953, § 75).

Mark Wilson's "Predicate Meets Property" (chapter 4) critically discusses Putnam's (and other) accounts from a broadly Wittgenstinian perspective. Wilson assumes that claims about the semantics of a predicate as used by a particular group at a particular time can be justified only in terms of the way the group applies the predicate. Suppose, for example, that isolated Druids apply 'bird' to ambient birds, but have never seen (or imagined) anything like an airplane or balloon. Whether they will apply 'bird' to airplanes is not determined simply by their use of 'bird': if they first observe planes in the sky (and it seems natural at the moment to call them 'birds'), they will apply 'bird' to planes; if they are introduced to planes in another way (say, technology gradually encoaches upon the island), they won't. Since we cannot predict how Druids will react to planes independently of how things go in the future – current use *alone* does not here determine future use – we have "no warrant for *choosing* either [the set of birds] or [the set of things which fly] as *the* correct extension for 'bird'" (Wilson, see chapter 4, p. 98).

How, then, should we assign extensions to predicates? Wilson begins by comparing speakers with measuring devices such as scales and thermometers. The latter detect physical properties, but only for a circumscribed range of objects (mercury thermometers work poorly at the bottom of the sea) and when appropriately confronted with an object (spectrometers can't measure an object's spectrum if the object isn't illuminated). Likewise, a competent user of a predicate P is a property detector, but only for an appropriately circumscribed range of application and "mode of presentation." If, for example, we restrict the range of application of 'water' to proximate samples of liquids "presented normally," English speakers are detectors of the presence of H_2O. For generally speaking, if a speaker were confronted with a liquid and asked 'is this water?', she would answer 'yes' iff it were a sample of H_2O. Say that when a predicate P, as used by a speaker, bears such a relation to a physical property, the property *indexes* the predicate in the speaker's language. Then, says Wilson, the extension of P is the set of objects (be they in the speaker's environment or not) which have any property which indexes the predicate (see p. 96). Neither the set of birds nor the set of flying things is "*the* correct extension for [Druid] 'bird', since [a choice of one as the extension of the term] is tantamount to predicting how Druids will classify aircraft in the cosmopolitan world. These two sets are *interchangeable* within the range of application parameter appropriate to pristine Druids. . . . The properly conservative linguist will hedge . . . by stressing a limited range of applicability: 'bird' in parochial Druid dialect has extension [the set of birds] with a range of applicability limited to objects similar to those found in the environs of the Druid isle" (see p. 98).

The primary issue Wilson's paper raises, of course, is whether the facts about predicate extensions are tied, as Wilson says they must be, to the facts about speaker dispositions to apply the predicates. Suppose the Druids have developed very rudimentary locks which they use to secure cattle pens. They would not recognize electronic locks as 'locks' and would not apply 'lock' thereto, if they were spirited to modern lands. Does this mean that 'lock' in Druid does not apply to modern locks? On natural fleshings out of the example, one wants to say the Druid term does apply. Perhaps this is because we are confident that any normal person *if* given enough information and a rudimentary concept of lock could, as Wilson puts it, be "brought around" to seeing modern locks as such. But here we are allowing Druid 'lock' to apply to modern locks in virtue of Druid usage *combined* with information about "the underlying nature" of modern locks. Wouldn't something similar establish that Druid 'bird' is definitely false of airplanes? The issues here are closely tied to issues concerning the determinancy of meaning and reference, taken up in sections 5 and 6 below.[6]

4 Paul Horwich's *Meaning*, from which his contribution to this anthology is taken (chapter 5), also takes a broadly Wittgenstinian approach to meaning, in so far as Horwich undertakes to develop and defend Wittgenstein's idea, that "meaning is use."

Horwich takes meanings to be abstract entities ('concepts'); an account of meaning needs to explain what makes it the case that a word or sentence expresses the concept it in fact expresses. What constitutes a word's expressing a particular concept, says Horwich, is "a relatively small and simple body" of principles concerning the "circumstances in which certain specified sentences containing the word are accepted" by its users. Which princples, exactly? Those "which (in conjunction with other factors and with the basic properties of other words) explain total linguistic behavior with respect to that word" – which explain, that is, the totality of a speaker's dispositions to verbal behavior. Horwich's examples of such acceptance properties are themselves simple verbal dispositions: the disposition, for example, to apply 'red' to and only to things which are (observed to be) clearly red; the disposition to accept *p and q* when and only when one is disposed to accept both *p* and *q*.

Horwich's account is coupled with a "deflationist" attitude towards semantic notions such as truth and reference. Many philosophers suppose that there is a "substantial" account to be given of the notions of truth and reference – that (for example), it is in principle possible to provide illuminating necessary and sufficient conditions for what it is for a proper name to refer to an object, or for a sentence to be true. Some philosophers even hold that it is possible to give an account of truth and reference in purely naturalistic terms, and that reference and truth are thus useful notions for explanatory purposes.[7] Given, for example, a naturalistic account of truth and an account of representation in terms of truth conditions, it would be possible to give a naturalistic explanation of what it is for an organism to have a belief.

According to the deflationist, notions such as truth and reference are simply not substantial in this way; the idea that reference and truth can bear explanatory weight is mistaken. On Horwich's version of the view, truth and reference are "formal" concepts: for example, we have a concept of truth only because it makes it possible for us to assert generalizations about propositions (e.g., that none of the Pope's pronouncements about abortion are true). For one to have the concept of truth, it suffices that one has a predicate *T* in one's vocabulary such that, for any claim *p*, one is disposed to ascribe *T* to *p* when only one is disposed to assert *p*. To have the notion of reference (for one's own language, at any rate) is simply to be disposed to accept any sentence of the form *the reference of the name 'n' (in my language) is n.*

If there is nothing substantial to say about truth and reference, there cannot be anything substantial to say about how meaning determines truth and reference. However, Horwich holds that meaning determines reference in the weak sense that (context sensitivity set aside) expressions with the same meaning cannot differ in reference (see p. 130). And he holds that use – that is, those ("explanatorily basic") principles which suffice to explain dispositions to accept sentences – determines meaning. Anyone moved by Putnam's Twin Earth example is unlikely to be happy with the upshot, that use determines reference. Suppose that Smith is pregnant with identical twins, but that only one can survive to term. In world *a*, twin A is aborted so that B may survive; in world *b*, B is aborted so that A may survive; otherwise, the worlds are as much alike as is possible. In particular, the child born to Smith on July

4 is named 'Carla' in each world. Since 'Carla' has a different reference in each world, the explanatorily basic principles which suffice for explaining the dispositions of users to accept sentences in which 'Carla' occur must differ across worlds. But is this so? We can explain the linguisitic dispositions of speakers, with respect to each world, by invoking the fact that speakers are disposed to apply 'Carla' to the child born to Smith on July 4, "in conjunction with other factors and with the basic properties of other words." For example, we explain why speakers in world *a* are disposed to accept 'Carla is wearing a red dress' when they observe A wearing a red dress (roughly) so:

> *a*-speakers are disposed to apply 'Carla' to the child born to Smith on July 4.
> (In *a*) A is the child born to Smith on July 4.
>
> *a*-speakers are disposed to apply 'is wearing a red dress' to things they observe wearing a red dress.

But exactly the same explanation, modulo changes in the non-linguistic facts to which we appeal, suffices for explaining why *b*-speakers are disposed to accept 'Carla is wearing a red dress' when they observe B wearing a red dress:

> *b*-speakers are disposed to apply 'Carla' to the child born to Smith on July 4.
> (In *b*) B is the child born to Smith on July 4.
>
> *b*-speakers are disposed to apply 'is wearing a red dress' to things they observe wearing a red dress.

The upshot seems to be that 'Carla,' on Horwich's view, means the same in both worlds. If so, then there are important aspects of meaning – those which determine reference and truth – not captured by use in Horwich's sense.[8]

5   Wilson's objections to Putnam were fueled by the complaint that current usage underdetermines facts about reference and meaning. Few would deny that there are cases in which reference (and thus meaning) is indeterminate. Newton had no notion of a difference between rest mass and relativistic mass. He would have been completely befuddled as to which was "meant" by his use of 'mass'; some of his central beliefs about mass are true of both rest and relativistic; some are true only of rest mass;

some only of relativistic. It seems there is just no saying of exactly what Newton's use of 'mass' was true.[9]

What is the scope of the indeterminancy of meaning and reference? W. V. Quine argues that indeterminancy's scope is devastatingly large (chapter 6). Even in the case of humdrum "observational" predicates such as English's 'rabbit' and French's 'lapin,' there is "no fact of the matter" as to how to translate them from one language to another. According to Quine, though we find the hypothesis

(H1)   the French are talking about rabbits, when they use 'lapin,'

more natural than the hypothesis

(H2)   The French are talking about undetached rabbit parts (henceforth *urp*s), when they use 'lapin,'

there is nothing to justify a preference for one hypothesis over the other; Nannette's use of 'lapin' is no more determinate than Newton's use of 'mass.' Quine infers in "Ontological Relativity" that our ordinary talk of reference and meaning is, as he puts it, "nonsense." We can sensibly employ relativized notions: We can, for example, speak of what a word refers to relative to an arbitrarily chosen "translation manual." But since the choice of manual is arbitrary, this assimilates the claim, that Nannette is talking about rabbits with 'lapin,' to the claim that it pleases me to fancy that Nannette is talking about rabbits with 'lapin.'

Quine gives several arguments that translation and reference are indeterminate; here is the most discussed.[10] (1) Since language is learned by observing verbal behavior, facts about linguistic meaning (and thus about synonymy and reference) must be determined by (observable) facts about dispositions to verbal behavior. (2) Such facts do not decide between radically divergent accounts of meaning and reference. For example, they do not decide between (H1) and (H2). For the situations in which it is appropriate to say 'there goes a rabbit' are precisely the situations in which it's appropriate to say 'there goes an urp.' So, (3) What facts there are about meaning and reference are not sufficient to decide between radically divergent accounts of meaning and reference. There just is no fact of the matter, as to whether Nannette is talking about rabbits or their undetached parts.[11]

A natural reaction questions the argument's first premiss. Why, one wants to ask, don't causal relations fix meaning and reference? Why don't facts about reference along with facts about the psychological roles of words justify translating 'vache' as 'cow,' and not 'undetached cow part'? That there is a "causal chain" connecting Nanette's use of 'Nantes' with a christening of the city Nantes with 'Nantes' is not an observable fact about behavioral dispositions; that the underlying nature of what elicts her exclamation 'le vache ris!' is bovine, not porcine, is not *simply* a fact about behaviorial dispositions. Likewise, the fact (supposing that it is a fact) that all of us come to language learning with an innate, if rudimentary, propensity to classify in certain ways is not such a fact.

Quine's position is that even if such facts were relevant, they would not suffice to remove the indeterminancy of meaning and reference. And in fact, it is not immediately clear how appeal to causal relations is of any help with referential indeterminancy, since causal relations presumably come in collections: for each causal relation R which you bear to rabbits there is, one might well suggest, a causal relation R' to urps such that you bear R to a rabbit when and only when you bear R' to some urps of the rabbit. What makes it R, and not R', that settles the reference of 'rabbit'? And if Nanette's 'lapin' and our 'rabbit' suffer from referential indeterminancy, we cannot obviously appeal to the fact that the words have similar, or even isomorphic psychological roles to justify translating one by the other. Similarity of psychological role is not sufficient for sameness of meaning; one needs to add referential identity before one has a sufficient condition. This, after all, is the point which underlies Putnam's Twin Earth example.

6   Scott Soames argues that Quine's argument for indeterminancy risks equivocating on 'determines' (chapter 7). Think of the argument so:

1   The physical facts determine all the facts.
2   The physical facts don't determine facts about meaning and reference. So,
3   Meaning and reference aren't determined by anything.

Soames considers a number of possible meanings for *the set F of facts (or claims) determines the set G of facts (claims)*:

(a)   It's metaphysically impossible that F obtain but G does not.
(b)   That G obtains is an *a priori* consequence of F's obtaining.
(c)   That G obtains is an *a priori* consequence of F and theoretical identifications.
(d)   That G obtains is an *a priori* consequence of F and necessarily true theoretical identifications.

According to Soames, Quine gives no reason to think that (2) is true if 'determines' is defined as in (a): how could situations differ in no physical way while in one Nannette's 'lapin' refers to rabbits, in the other to urps? Using (b) to define 'determines' leaves (1) questionable: why think that every fact is *a priori* determined by physical facts? Soames argues that (c) renders (2) trivially false. As for understanding 'determines' along the lines of (d), Soames claims it renders (1) dubious, since it seems to commit us to there being a finite, necessary equivalent to such predicates as 'refers' expressible in the language of physics.

Soames is right that the plausibility of Quinean arguments for indeterminacy rests on what is meant by 'determines.' But there seem to be options he doesn't consider. Suppose I am a physicalist. I hold that any relation relates what it relates in virtue of physical properties, processes, and relations which 'underlie' it. Now, suppose someone alleges that there is a relation R which relates A to A' alone, B to B' alone, and so on. However, every account she gives, of the physical processes which underlie R, is either one on which the proposed underlying mechanism is not discriminating enough to explain R (the mechanism relates A to A', B', C', and so on), or seems arbitrary, in the sense that while the mechanism proposed does relate A to A' alone and so on, there are other mechanisms, just as plausible as candidates for the physical mechanism underlying R, which have R relating A not to A', but to other things. My physicalism justifies me in thinking that talk about R is highly indeterminate. Note that my worry would not be one about supervenience (determination in Soames' (a) sense); neither is it a worry about some *a priori* relation between the physical facts and the R-facts.

But this is just the situation the Quinean alleges obtains with reference. Dispositions to verbal behavior are just too anemic, to decide whether 'lapin' refers to rabbits or urps. Causal relations can do the job of underlying the reference relation only if there is something which isolates some among the profusion of causal relations our terms and behavior bear to the objects in our environment as the mechanisms of reference. If, as suggested above, causal relations run in packs (so that for each relation a word bears to a rabbit, there is one the word bears to urps), it is not clear that causal relations can underwrite reference. And psychological similarity between speakers can determine translation relations only if reference is already determinate.[12]

To show that there are no serious grounds for skepticism about the determinacy of semantic relations, we need to be shown that *something* – unremarked verbal dispositions, special causal relations, or the like – can be resonably held to eliminate the threat of indeterminacy. In his contribution, Jody Azzouni sets out to show just this (chapter 8). Azzouni observes that there is a large family of "temporally extended" causal relations associated with the use of a term. Not only do we *see* rabbits (an interaction which typically lasts a short while), we hunt them, cook them, keep them as pets. Azzouni argues that by appeal to such relations, we can eliminate deviant accounts of 'lapin's' reference, such as those on which it refers to urps. Azzouni claims that we can *see* that when the French are, for example, hunting, feeding, and domesticating rabbits, it is *rabbits*, not (proper) undetached parts of the rabbit, to which they are causally related. Since it is relations to rabbis (not urps) which are associated with their use of 'lapin,' rabbits, but not urps, are genuine candidates for the reference of 'lapin.'

Azzouni is surely correct that Quine's (and subsequent) discussions of referential indeterminacy have tended to ignore the rich store of causal relations which are potentially relevant to assigning reference to terms, concentrating on relatively simple visual encounters with potential referents. Skeptics will continue to wonder whether multiplying causal relations can eliminate Quinean indeterminacy. For one thing, one might wonder if we can be said to *observe* that Nanette is *hunting the rabbit*. We can, let us agree, observe that Nannette is doing something which is caused by her having an intention which she voices with 'Je prendrai un lapin,' and that she won't rest content until she has a whole rabbit in her bag. Whether she is *hunting a rabbit*, as opposed to, say, *endeavouring to entrap some urps* would seem to turn on what intention she voices with her sentence. This, of course, can be determined only once we have assigned reference to 'lapin' and 'prendre.' Apparently, we are thrown back on the multitude of causal relations, between Nanette and her neighborhood, which constitue her present activity, as well as all of her other rabbity activities. But this is surely a mixed bag of relations, many of which are relations to rabbits, many of which are relations to urps. It is not at all obvious that sifting through this bag (and the bags associated with Nanette's other verbs) will provide a compelling reason to interpret 'prendre' as a relation to rabbits. Perhaps the appropriate conclusion is that it is not yet clear, whether there is a compelling case for or against Quinean skepticism.

7   On almost anyone's view, a central aspect of linguistic competence is the ability to correctly interpret other speakers – to be able to tell what it is that a speaker is saying, when she utters a sentence. Suppose that such an ability is not simply *a* central component of linguistic understanding, but *the* central component thereof. Then to explain what knowledge and

abilities are necessary or sufficient for interpretation is to explain what is necessary or sufficient "to know the meanings of the sentences of a language." One might reasonably propose that giving such an explanation is the central task of a philosophical theory of meaning. In a remarkably influential series of papers, Donald Davidson has argued (roughly put) that knowledge of a "Taskian theory of truth" for a language is sufficient for having the ability to interpret its speakers, and therefore constructing such a theory is discharging the central task of a philosophical theory of meaning.[13]

In order to understand Davidson's proposal, as well as the qualms many philosophers have had about it, one needs some understanding of Tarski's work on truth.[14] Tarski showed how to define "is a true sentence of language L," for a broad class of languages; significantly, his approach enables one to define 'true in L' in *non-semantic* terms. How does one go about doing this? First of all, one defines the notion of reference for the language one is interested in. The definition is a brute force affair. For example, if the language L in which we are interested contains just the names 'Mark Twain' and 'Mary Gaitskill,' our definition of reference will look like this:

> A name n refers in L to x iff: n is 'Mark Twain' and x is Mark Twain, or n is 'Mary Gaitskill' and x is Mary Gaitskill.

Secondly, one defines what it is for a simple predicate to be true of an individual or series of individuals. Again, the definition is a brute force affair. Suppose L contains just the predicates 'is an author,' 'is a woman,' and 'admires.' Then our definition would go as follows:

> A one place predicate P is true in L of x iff: P is 'is an author' and x is an author, or P is 'is a woman' and x is a woman.

> A two place predicate P is true in L of the pair of x and y iff P is 'admires' and x admires y.

Note that the definitions of 'refers' and 'true of' don't involve any semantic notions whatsoever. For example, the definition we give of 'refers in L' mentions only Twain, Gatiskill, their names, and the relation of identity.[15]

We next give principles which specify the conditions under which a sentence is true in terms of the semantic properties of its parts. Sample principles are:

A sentence consisting of a name *n* followed by a predicate *P* is true in *L* iff *P* is true in *L* of what *n* names in *L*.

A sentence consisting of a name *n* followed by a verb *V* followed by a name *m* is true in *L* iff *V* is true in *L* of the pair, of what *n* names in *L* and what *m* names in *L*.

A sentence of the form *A and B* is true in *L* iff *A* is true in *L* and *B* is true in *L*.[16]

How do we know that such a theory correctly characterizes truth for *L*? Tarski requires that, for each sentence *S* of the language *L*, the theory imply a sentence of the form

(T)   *s* is true in *L* iff *p*,

where *s* names the sentence *S* and *p* translates *S* into the language of the theory. If *p translates S*, then, of course, *p* and *S* are true under exactly the same conditions, and so such a sentence (a "T-sentence", as it is often called) says exactly the right thing about the conditions under which *S* is true. So, if the theory implies instances of (T) for all of *L*'s sentences (and is consistent), it will correctly characterize truth. Note if *L* is part of the language of truth theory, and if we use quotation names to name sentences of *L*, this requirement boils down to the requirement that, for each sentence *S* of *L*, the theory imply a sentence of the form

'*S*' is true in *L* iff *S*.

And in fact the principles above (given trivialities such as " 'Mary Gaitskill' is a name") imply T-sentences such as

'Mary Gaitskill is an author and Mary Gaitskill admires Mark Twain' is true in *L* iff Mary Gaitskill is an author and Mary Gaitskill admires Mark Twain.

8   Tarski's work showed that the notion *is a true sentence of L* could be characterized without making use of any semantic notions, such as 'refers to' or 'is true of'. He did not require that his definition "capture the meaning" of 'true' in any sense other than providing such a characterization. In fact, a little reflection will show that Tarski's definition does not explicate what we mean by ascribing truth to a sentence; someone could

know a Tarskian definition of truth for a language without having the least idea under what conditions its sentences are true (in the ordinary meaning of 'true') or what its sentences mean.[17]

In "Radical Interpretation" (chapter 9), Davidson suggests that what suffices for understanding a language is, not that one knows a Tarskian truth theory for it, but that one know a theory with the *form* of a Tarskian theory, in which the notion of 'truth' is taken as primitive. If one also knows that the theory has certain properties, then, when the theory implies

Sentence S is true in the language iff p

one is justified, says Davidson, in interpreting a speaker of the language who assertively utters S as having said (what is said in the language of the theory by) p.

What are these properties? Roughly, that one could arrive at the theory by means of "radical interpretation," a process similar to the "radical translation" which underlies one of Quine's arguments for the indeterminacy of translation. In such a process, one takes the fact that

Speakers "hold true" the sentence 'that is a rabbit' when and only when there is a rabbit being demonstratived

as evidence for the claim that

A use of 'that is a rabbit' is true in the speaker's language iff the speaker is demonstrating a rabbit.

Supposing that this is evidence of truth conditions guides one in constructing the rudiments of a theory, with the form of a Tarskian truth theory, confirmed by speaker behavior. One extends the theory to cover the whole language by assuming that speakers' beliefs are by and large true (by the theorist's lights), looking for principles about the reference of speaker's names and predicates which, coupled with those which one already has, will make the natives, by and large, true believers.

Davidson holds that the notion of reference is "theoretical": what decides whether principles such as

(R1)   'rabbit' is true (in English) of something iff it is a rabbit

are to be accepted is, in the main, whether the principles allow us to assign appropriate truth conditions to English sentences. Those unimpressed by Quine's arguments for the indeterminancy of reference will of course find this aspect of Davidson's views objectionable. But even if this sort of worry is waived, many find Davidson's account objectionable. A persistent criticism is that truth conditions are not strong enough to determine meaning. One way of making this point – due originally to John Foster (1976) and discussed in Scott Soames' "Semantics and Semantic Competence" (chapter 10) – is to observe that it is perfectly possible for someone who uses a correct theory of truth for a language to misinterpret its speakers. Since it is a mathematical, and thus necessary, truth that there are infinitely many primes, a truth theory for English based upon (R1) is necessarily equivalent to a theory based upon

(R2)   'rabbit' is true (in English) of something iff it is a rabbit and there are infinitely many primes;

any empirical support for the one theory is support for the other. But if one uses the latter theory to interpret an utterance of 'Peter is a rabbit,' one would interpret it as the claim that Peter is a rabbit and there are infinitely many primes. But the utterance just doesn't mean that.

Though (R2) is true, one doesn't need to know it to understand an English speaker; one needs to know (R1). Suppose we collect all the facts about the reference and truth conditions of English expressions, which one needs to know in order to understand English. Call this set of facts R. Would knowing R (or some finite theory from which R straightforwardly follows) suffice for understanding English? No, for one could know R *and* believe that (R2) is something that English speakers are expected to know. This belief might lead one to believe that 'Peter is a rabbit' means that Peter is a rabbit and there are infinitely many primes. Suppose, however, we added to R the claim that it exhausts the things which one has to know, in order to understand English. The mistaken inference about the meaning of 'Peter is a rabbit' is now blocked: if one doesn't need to know (R2) to understand 'Peter is a rabbit,' that sentence can't mean that Peter is a rabbit and there are infinitely many primes.

What determines what one needs to know, to understand the speakers of a language? Surely this is in good part socially determined: one needs to know those things about the language which everyone expects everyone to know (and expects everyone to expect everyone to know, and expects . . .). Putting all this together, we arrive at the proposal made in James Higginbotham's contribution to the present collection (chapter 11): to understand a language – and thus in one good sense of 'know the meaning' to know the meanings of its expressions – is to know what its speakers are expected to know about the reference and truth conditions of its expressions – and that that is all that they are expected to know. Knowledge of meaning, as Higginbotham puts it, "reduces to the norms of knowledge of reference."

Higginbotham's suggestion apparently presupposes that there is some *one* body of knowledge one is expected to acquire to become a competent speaker. One might wonder whether this is so. One might count as a competent user of 'jazz' if one knows that 'jazz' is true of music like *this* (play a few bars of "So what"); and one might count as competent if one knows that 'jazz' is true of music like *this* (play a few bars of "Bitches Brew"). Arguably, to be a competent user of 'jazz' requires *some* identificatory ability. If no *particular* ability is required, however, there need be no general expectation included in the norms the community shares. Neither need there be a disjunctive expectation held by all: if you have never heard Miles play "So what," then (your life thus far is impoverished and) you can hardly expect that speakers are supposed to recognize either this (play a few bars of "So what") or this or . . . this as jazz.

One might respond that to understand a language, it suffices simply to know one set of facts, about reference and truth for the language, as well as to know that knowing those facts suffices for understanding. But this suggestion runs afoul of variations of Foster's point. Suppose it is sufficient, to understand 'jazz,' to know that 'jazz' is true of music like 'So what.' If Sonny knows this, and knows that knowing this is sufficient, what is to stop him from thinking that 'Mary likes jazz' means that Mary likes music like 'So what'?

9   At the core of Davidson's view is the idea that understanding a sentence is knowing its truth conditions. A related idea is that we can identify the meaning of a sentence with its truth conditions. Such an identification has struck many as too crude, for reasons related to those underlying Foster's objection to Davidson: on most any account of truth conditions, necessarily equivalent sentences (e.g., 'Peter is a rabbit,' 'Peter is a rabbit and there are infinitely many primes') have the same truth conditions, but different meanings.

A natural thought is that what a sentence means is closely related to what the sentence (when used literally) says; a sentence's meaning, so the idea goes, is a rule which assigns to a context or situation what a use of the sentence would say therein. Frege's notion of sense provides one way of cashing out the notion of what is said: what is asserted, according to Frege, is a sentence's sense, a thought. For reasons brought to the fore in section 2, Frege's view is problematic. But what can we put in its place?

A currently fashionable answer is that we should think of what is said – let us use the term *proposition* for the object of assertion – as being "constructed" out of the objects and properties the assertion is about. If I say 'Twain is a man,' you say 'Clemens is a man,' and Twain says 'I am a man,' we all ascribe the same property to the same object, and thus express the same proposition; if I say 'Jim bought an ophidian' and you say 'Jim purchased a snake,' we ascribe one relation to an object (Jim) and a property (being a snake), and thus express the same proposition. That we may associate different ways of conceptualizing Twain or the ophidan with our words is neither here nor there. Propositions, on this view, don't involve ways of thinking of objects and properties; they contain just the objects and properties themselves. They are *singular* with respect to the objects and properties they concern.

That what we say and think is thus singular is variously called 'Russellianism,' 'Millianism,' and 'Referentialism.' One virtue of this view is that it squares with the data to which Kripke and Putnam pointed, in their objections to Frege. It also squares with the way we report assertions. If I utter 'Twain is a man,' you can report me as having said that Clemens is a man, even if you and I associate different senses with 'Twain' and 'Clemens.' This is what we would expect, given Russellianism and the principle, that *x said that S* simply reports a relation between *x* and the proposition expressed by *S*.[18]

Sentence meaning is constituted by what a sentence can be used to say. What a sentence says can be believed or doubted, known or desired. Our beliefs and desires, in turn, motivate and explain our behavior. All this suggests that an account of sentence meaning should cohere with our practice of explaining behavior by ascribing beliefs and desires. And here, it has been argued, singular propositions are inadequate. Suppose Rupert has a desire 'to shake Twain's hand' as well as a belief that 'this man is in front of me.' Unbeknowst to Rupert, the man in front of him is Twain. Despite his desire, Rupert doesn't stick out his hand. Why? Because he didn't realize that *this man* (imagine I point at Twain) is Twain. But if the proposition that *this man* is Twain *is* the proposition that Twain is Twain, then Rupert *did* realize that *this man* is Twain, for of course he knew that Twain is Twain. It seems that either we can't explain Rupert's behavior by ascribing his beliefs and desires to him, or we can't individuate propositions as the Russellian does.[19]

Much of John Perry's contribution to the present volume is concerned with this problem (chapter 12). Perry develops an idea, of Hans Reichenbach and Arthur Burks, that the meanings of indexicals and demonstratives – words such as 'I,' 'now,' 'this,' and 'those,' whose reference and content varies systematically with the situation of their user – are "token reflexive." According to Reichenbach, utterances of sentences in which such words occur make claims about the word tokens uttered: "The word 'I', for instance" wrote Reichenbach, "means the same as 'the person who utters this token'" (Reichenbach, 1947, p. 284). Perry argues that 'I' and 'the person who utters this token' can't be synonymous. However, he suggests, we can think of the meaning of words like 'I' as given by a rule which tells us what relation an object must bear to its utterance in order to be its referent. The meaning of 'I' is something like the rule

An utterance u of 'I' refers to x just in case x is the person who produced u;

the meaning of 'I am tired' is something like the rule

An utterance of 'I am tired' is true iff the person who produced its subutterance of 'I' is (at the time of utterance) tired.

Suppose, now, that I utter 'I am tired'; call my utterance of 'I' u. According to Perry, there are (at least) two things which might be said to be the content of my utterance. There is the singular proposition, that I, Mark Richard, am tired, which Perry calls the utterance's "official content." But there is also the proposition which one obtains if one "plugs my utterance into its meaning" – that is, the proposition that the person who produced u is (at the time of utterance) tired. Perry calls this the utterance's "content$_M$." Perry suggests that we can resolve puzzles, like that involving Rupert and Twain, by recognizing that sentences have these two sorts of content.

How exactly does this help? Perry tells us that to explain behavior "we must specify the modes of presentation that are actually involved in cognition and the ways they are linked in the mind" (see p. 290). When we give such an explanation, of course, we do so with a background of assumptions, mostly tacit, about the mental life of the explanation's subject. Relative to such a background, we can often achieve our explanatory goals simply by ascribing belief in singular propositions. Consider a (more or less normal) situation in which Rupert fears that Twain, the man in front of him, is about to shoot him. Given that Twain is in front of Rupert, that Rupert sees him, and that Rupert doesn't want to die, we explain Rupert's hitting Twain by saying 'Rupert thought that Twain was going to shoot him.' Given that it's not at issue, how Rupert might name

Twain, the explanation tells us enough, given background assumptions, about how Rupert's mental processes were linked to his action.

But when "there is something in the context of explanation that suggests that the ordinary links [between mental states, the sentences which express them, and action] might be broken," an adequate explanation requires that we specify in more detail the modes of presentation which actually motivate the actor. According to Perry, we can do this by invoking the second sort of content mentioned above. Suppose, for example, that Rupert wants to shake the hand of Twain, the man in front of him. Rupert will say 'I'd like to shake your hand,' not '*Rupert* would like to shake your hand,' even though the two utterances express the same proposition. "If we ask what [Rupert] hoped to accomplish...we might say that [Rupert] wanted to make [Twain] aware that [he] wanted to shake his hand.... This would be accurate, but incomplete.... The content$_M$ of [Rupert's] utterance is the key to [Rupert's] plan [to get Twain to shake his hand. That uttering 'Rupert wants to shake your hand' wouldn't have the desired effect] comes out at the level of content$_M$" (see chapter 12, p. 285).

Perry is undoubtedly correct, that sentences have content$_M$, and that we must often appeal to it in order to make sense of linguistic behavior. His proposal does, however, raise a number of questions. (a) Suppose Rupert says 'I'd like to shake your hand' and Twain in response sticks out his hand. I explain Twain's behavior by saying 'Twain thought Rupert wanted to shake his hand.' What is the relation between what I actually *say* that Twain thought and the token reflexive content, that the person who produced Rupert's utterance wanted to shake Twain's hand? It is not very plausible that I literally say that Twain believes the latter, for pretty much those reasons which Perry gives for saying that our "offical notion of content" is (more or less) that given by the referentialist (Perry, see chapter 12, pp. 285–7). But if I am not literally saying this, how exactly does it come about that my utterance is explanatory?

(b) Can Perry's token reflexive contents carry the explanatory role he assigns them? In many cases in which singular propositions seem inadequate to explaining behavior, content$_M$ cannot play an explanatory role, simply because no one is uttering anything. When Rupert hits Twain to prevent Twain from shooting him, Rupert doesn't *utter* anything, and so nothing involved in the causation of Rupert's behavior *has* content$_M$.

Of course, one can envision various generalizations of content$_M$. If Rupert thinks that Twain is about to shoot him, there is, we may suppose, a token event, t, of Rupert's so thinking. And this will have something like content$_M$ – it will have the content that Twain is about to shoot the person who is having *this* thought (i.e., thought *t*). But is this sort of content at all relevant to the causation or explanation of behavior?

Suppose a dog, a 5-year-old child, and a philosopher are confronted with a banana. Each sees the banana, wants to eat it, and is thus moved to reach for it; the child and the philosopher, let us suppose, each thinks to herself 'that is a banana in front of me.' It is utterly implausible to suppose that the dog could have a thought whose "official content" is a token reflexive thought, such as the thought that *this* thought which I (Fido the dog) am having now is one of a banana. For it is utterly implausible to suppose that the dog has the cognitive wherewithall to have such a thought. The dog (we may suppose) has a representation of the banana which helps realize the thought, that *that* looks tasty. It is this thought, not one whose official content makes it a thought *about* the representation, which guides the dog's action. This is not to say that the dog's thought does not have content$_M$: *we* could, if we knew enough of the semantics of the dog's "language of thought," state rules which would assign to Fido's believings their content$_M$. But this aspect of the thought's content would be conceptually unavailable to Fido.

Given this, it seems quite implausible that appeal to a token reflexive content – that *this* thought which I (Fido the dog) am having now is one of a banana – should be of much help in explaining the dog's behavior. If the dog is unable to have a thought whose official content is thus reflexive, it cannot "conceptualize" or "be presented with" the banana as a thing which is picked out by its current representations. But then how does the fact that the dog's thought have such content help us to "specify the modes of presentation that are actually involved in cognition and the ways they are linked in the mind," which Perry thinks we can do by appeal to content$_M$?

Much the same worry can be raised concerning the child and the philosopher. The child thinks 'that's a banana,' thereby thinking about what is in front of her, not about token representations; it is that thought which produces her action. Even supposing that the child has the ability to entertain a thought about its own representations, there is no reason to think token reflexive "modes of presentation are...actually involved in [its] cognition." Why should we think that anything different is true of the philosopher? In the case of both the child and the philosopher, what represents the banana is, or involves, a linguistic token which refers to the banana. And each, we may suppose, knows some things which, if she reflected upon them, would lead her to connect the banana and the representation in various ways: the content$_M$ of their thoughts *could* become articulate in their thoughts. But it is not clear how this fact does or could enter into what we are doing, when we explain that the child and the philosopher are fighting because each of them wants the banana.

Exactly the same sort of thing should be said about examples involving utterances. We can agree that a linguistically competent speaker's use of 'that' is somehow governed by a rule like

(T)   An utterance of 'that' accompanied by a demonstration of x refers to x.

It just doesn't follow that the motivational properties of sentences in which 'that' occurs, or of thoughts naturally expressed by such sentences, have very much to do with claims about tokenings of the word 'that.' (T) governs my behavior (roughly) if I have a strong disposition to look in the direction the speaker is pointing when I hear 'that,' taking the object I see to be the subject of discourse. Doing this, I think about that object. And I do it "by means of" a token of 'that.' But why think that I think *about* the token of 'that'?

10   Linguistic meaning has often been held to be "epistemologically transparent": if, for example, the nouns A and B are synonymous, the speaker who understands them both knows that they are so, or is at least in a position to determine that without further research. If the noun A means what's meant by the phrase B *which is* C, the competent speaker knows (or is at least in a position to determine without further research) that the sentence *no A fails to be a B* is true.

An *analytic* sentence is one, knowledge of whose truth is underwritten simply by what the competent speaker knows when she understands it. It seems obvious that there are such sentences: logical truths, "definitional" truths ('a bachelor is an unmarried man'), "species/genus" truths ('red is a color,' 'ants are insects') are common examples. Analyticity has been important in a variety of philosophical projects. Since knowledge of analytic truths seems non-empirical (after all, it might be said, we just *stipulate* what our words mean), analytic sentences have been thought to provide an example of *a priori* knowledge amenable to the most hard-nosed empiricist. And since whatever is *a priori* is presumably necessary (after all, it might be said, if I can know S true without looking at the world, then S must be true no matter how the world might be), analyticity also provides a benign notion of necessity. There is a strong current in twentieth century philosophy which would identify the *a priori* and the necessary with the analytic.

Quine's wildly influential "Two Dogmas of Empiricism" (chapter 13) can be understood as arguing that there is not, and could not be, any such thing as an analytic sentence, or, for that matter, a sentence whose truth was (relative to what the competent speaker knows) *a priori*. Quine's article is in part polemical. He argues that extant accounts of what it is to be analytic are either obviously wrong or empty; he provides a picture of language use (roughly, as a "tool" for anticipating and systematizing experience) in which the idea of an analytic sentence has no place. Perhaps the most compelling consideration against analyticity suggested by "Two Dogmas" is this: no matter what sentence you might consider, it seems that you could – given the right "recalcitrant experience" – rationally reject the sentence's truth without feeling that, in doing so, you were giving the sentence a new meaning. But if so, the sentence couldn't be analytic: if it were, you'd know, simply by understanding it, that it was true.[20]

"Two Dogmas" tries to discredit Frege's notion of analyticity, on which an analytic sentence is one which can be turned into a logical truth by replacing synonyms with synonyms. One might wonder how Quine could possibly hold that such sentences are impossible. As Paul Bogohossian (1996) notes in a recent defense of the notion of analyticity, Quine seems to concede the possibility of synonymy, and thus analyticity, since he seems to concede the possibility of stipulating that phrases mean the same. Bogohossian thinks the best argument against the synonymy needed for Fregean analytic truths runs thus: the meaning of a word depends upon all of the inferential practices and beliefs of its users. But then, since different words will almost invariably differ in their inferential properties, it is practically impossible that two words be synonyms. So it is practically impossible that sentences (other than perhaps logical truths) be Frege analytic. As Bogohossian notes, such an argument doesn't show that analyticity is impossible. It is also only as plausible as the radical holism which is its major premiss. Bogohossian further argues that one can't accept Quine's skepticism about analyticity while resisting the indeterminancy of translation: how could there be a fact of the matter, whether one word translates another, if it is impossible for a sentence to be "Frege analytic"?

Many Quineans will insist that Quine's skepticism about analyticity does not depend upon "meaning holism," on which revising one's opinion about the validity of *any* inference, including inductive ones, constitutes a change of meaning. Quine holds (on the basis of the "recalcitrant experience" argument mentioned above) that there is no principled way to distinguish between those inferences involving a word which are meaning constitutive (that is, ones such that to cease to judge them valid is to change the word's meaning) and those which, though mundane and obvious, aren't meaning constitutive.[21] Suppose Quine is right that there just is no distinction to be drawn here. Then there isn't any inference determinately such that one can know its validity *simply* on the basis of knowing the meaning of the words involved. It will, for example, be indeterminate whether what the competent speaker knows suffices to underwrite the validity of 'Frances is a vixen; thus she is a fox.' (This, of course, is **not** to say that it is indeterminate whether the inference is valid.)

It does not follow that meaning is particularly holistic, since there might be any number of inferences which were determinately *not* meaning constitutive. For example, one could hold that it is indeterminate whether the inferences *Frances is a vixen; so she is a fox* and *Frances is a vixen; so she is smaller than a star* **are** meaning constitutive for 'vixen,' although many inferences, such as *Frances is a vixen; thus she cannot do differential equations* are determinately **not** meaning constitutive. One can quite consistently hold Quine's "no principled distinction" doctrine, while holding that it is perfectly determinate that the validity or invalidity of ever so many inferences cannot be justified by appeal simply to what the competent speaker knows.[22]

What of the claim, that the skepticism of "Two Dogmas" about analyticity threatens to saddle us with indeterminancy of meaning? Here it is perhaps relevant to note that nothing in "Two Dogmas" implies that *reference* is indeterminate. One might agree with the conclusions of "Two Dogmas" while holding that translation from one natural language to another is an objective matter because (a) it is an objective matter what the extensions (and possible worlds intensions) of natural language expressions are; (b) it is an objective matter whether a translation manual would allow speakers to communicate with one another in a way which seemed to them to be one on which they understood one another; (c) a translation manual is objectively correct iff it is based upon a mapping of the vocabulary of one language into the other's which preserves ex- (and in-) tensions and allows communication. Quine's skepticism about translation may be prefigured in "Two Dogmas," but it is not entailed by it.

11   The primary targets of Quine's attack in "Two Dogmas of Empiricism" were the logical positivists, many of whom held that the necessary truths are the *a priori* ones, the *a posteriori* truths (i.e., those knowable only on the basis of experience) the contingent ones, and that the realm of the *a priori* is exhausted by truths which can be known simply by grasping interconnections among our concepts and their linguistic mirrors, word meanings. A quite different kind of attack on these views, one in no way skeptical about the objectivity of meaning or the *a priori*, occurs in Kripke's *Naming and Necessity* (see chapter 2).

Kripke observes that the semantics of proper names (such as 'Quine' and 'nine') differ from those of definite descriptions (such as 'the author of *Word and Object*' and 'the number of observed planets') in an important way. The sentence

(1)   It could have been that the number of observed planets was even

is, on its most natural reading, true, as we might have observed just eight planets; the sentence

(2)   It could have been that nine was even

is simply false. Why this difference, given that nine is the number of observed planets?

Kripke's explanation employs the idea of a "possible world," a way the universe might have been. According to Kripke, the way we use a term like 'nine' or 'the number of observed planets' determines what the term refers to, not just in the actual world but relative to other possible worlds. The description 'the number of observed planets,' given its meaning, refers at a possible world w to the number of planets which, at w, have been observed. Since we could have observed just eight planets, the description doesn't always have the same reference; it isn't "rigid."

Proper names, Kripke argues, are used differently. Whether a sentence containing a name expresses something which could have been true is a function of what the name in fact refers to, and how *it* might have been. According to Kripke, the falsity of (2) is a matter of (i) 'nine' picking out, at any world, the number nine, along with (ii) the fact that that number, nine, could not be even. Thus, on Kripke's view, the falsity of (2) rests upon a semantic fact – that a proper name's reference is determined to be, at any world, what it in fact refers to – along with a metaphysical one – that numbers, if actually odd, are necessarily so.

Kripke uses the term 'rigid designator' for expressions which are like names, in that they invariably pick out ("designate") the same thing at any possible world. Suppose that a and b are, like 'Hesperus' and 'Phosphorus,' rigid designators of a single thing x. Whether the sentences a *is F* and b *is F* express something possible or necessary then turns simply on whether x could be *F*. Thus both sentences are necessary if either is; substituting one rigid designator of x for another can't turn a necessity into a non-necessity.[23] But it is a necessary truth that a thing is identical with itself, and thus $a = a$ is necessary. Thus, $a = b$ is also necessary. But a true sentence of the form $a = b$, Kripke claims, generally expresses an *a posteriori* truth. It was, after all, an empirical discovery that Hesperus was Phosphorus. Thus, the idea that all necessary truth is *a priori* truth is simply wrong. According to Kripke, the same sort of argument shows that many *a posteriori* theoretical identifications, such as 'Water is H_2O' and 'Heat is molecular motion,' are necessary, since kind terms such as 'water' and 'heat' are rigid designators of kinds and phenomena. 'Water,' for example, rigidly designates that liquid which is colorless, odorless, drunk by humans, is in bottles labeled 'Perrier,' freezes when cold, etc. But this substance, H_2O, is rigidly designated by 'H_2O.' Thus 'water is H_2O' is necessary, but *a posteriori*.

Kripke's views seem to presuppose that there are different sorts of necessity. There would seem to be *some* sense in which it is possible that water not be H_2O: take all that we can know via conceptual and linguistic analysis, and all that we can derive from all of this via logic; add, if you like, all mathematical truths. One won't, it seems, derive that water is H_2O; water's being something else is a logical – if you like, conceptual – possibility. That water is H_2O is a "metaphysical necessity." The necessity here is to be traced back, not simply to facts about relations among the meanings of words, but to something about the substances, or things, to which the words refer.

It is worth pointing out the distance between Kripke's and Quine's views on necessity and analyticity. Simplifying somewhat, it was Quine's view that the best hope of making sense of talk of necessity was in terms of analyticity, with all necessities being analytic truths. (See, for instance, Quine, 1953.) Rejecting the notion of analyticity, Quine rejected the cogency of necessity. Kripke is no skeptic about analyticity, and this already marks a significant difference between him and Quine. But quite apart from necessities which might be explicable in terms of analyticity, Kripke allows for the existence of necessities (that nine is odd, that water is H_2O, that Jean Eustache is a man) which are not to be understood as "merely verbal necessities," and which are not discoverable *a priori*. Rather, in some interesting sense, such necessities are *a posteriori* and "rooted in the nature of things."

Frank Jackson's "Armchair Metaphysics" (chapter 14) evinces a sort of skepticism about the necessary *a posteriori* and arguably flirts with a picture of the relation among necessity, analyticity, and the *a priori* reminiscent of that held by the positivists. "[I]t is a mistake," writes Jackson, "to hold that the necessity possessed by 'Water = H_2O' is different from that possessed by 'Water = water' ... '" If so, and the necessity that water is water is conceptual, so is the necessity that water is H_2O. Thus, Jackson claims, if facts about the distribution of fundamental particles and forces necessitate all the facts, there *is* a conceptual or analytic connection between physical claims and claims about meaning, belief, and consciousness: "the physicalist must have *some* story to tell; otherwise how the purely physical makes psychological statements true is rendered an impenetrable mystery."

Jackson acknowledges the necessity of the claim that water = H_2O; he also acknowledges there is something *a posteriori* here: namely, that the *sentence* 'Water is H_2O' expresses a necessity. Here, Jackson appeals to ideas cognate to those to which John Perry appeals, in Perry's attempt to reconcile "Millian" accounts of propositions with our intuitions about cognitive significance. Perry observed that what a competent speaker knows about a sentence such as 'I am tired' is not what it says (after all, what the sentence says depends upon who is using it), but instead how to get from facts about the context of its use to what it says. Jackson claims that this sort of thing is true quite generally. According to Jackson, to understand a sentence such as 'there is water on the floor' is not (necessarily) to know what it says – we may suppose that what constitutes our understanding it is what constitutes understanding it on Twin Earth. Rather, to understand the sentence one must understand how to get from facts "about context" to what it says.

Appreciating this, Jackson claims, helps us see how claims about water and heat can be analytically tied to ones about H_2O and molecular kinetic energy. To understand 'water' is to know that it (rigidly) designates whatever substance in fact is colorless and odorless, drunk by humans, is in bottles labeled 'Perrier,' freezes when cold, etc. This sort of knowledge is *a priori*, and so we know *a priori*

(3)   Water is the substance which is colorless and odorless, drunk by humans, is in bottles labeled 'Perrier,' freezes when cold, etc.

But now the "facts about context" which make it the case that it is H_2O which has these properties are (if physicalism is true) all physical facts. Thus, the claim

(4) H_2O is the substance which is colorless and odorless, drunk by humans, is in bottles labeled 'Perrier,' freezes when it is cold, etc.

is a physical claim "about context" which determines what is said by sentences in which 'water' occurs. So there is an *a priori* connection between physical facts and facts about water. For example, it is *a priori* that conjoining

(5) There is H_2O on the floor

with (4) implies

(6) There is water on the floor,

for (3) is *a priori*, and (6) follows *a priori* from (3) through (5). The same sort of thing, if physicalism is true, will be true of claims about reference, desire, and conscious experience.

It is rather implausible that there is an *a priori* connection between facts about quarks and the weak force and ones about what it is like to feel jealous. So if Jackson's arugment is sound, physicalism is rather implausible. But one might well wonder whether physicalists must take on the commitments Jackson suggests they must. For example, Jackson's argument requires that (4) – the claim which "gives the context" which determines that 'water' names H_2O – itself is either a physical claim (i.e., one simply about the distribution of fundamental forces and particles) or is *a priori* dervivable from such a claim. It's obviously not the former; it's puzzling why we are supposed to believe the latter if we do not already accept Jackson's view. After all, (3) involves talk of intentional actions (bathing, bottling), referential relations (labeling), and phenonmenal experience (being colorless, odorless); it's the *a priori* derivability of just such talk which is at issue.[24]

One can grant this, but still wonder if Jackson doesn't have a point. Certainly it is unsatisfactory *simply* to be told that facts about reference and the mental are determined by the physical facts, in the sense that it's impossible that the former should vary without the latter varying. Shouldn't we be able to say *how* the physical determines the semantic and pyschological, giving for reference and regret what (3) gives for water? To do this would not, of course, be to give an (*a priori*!) physical reduction of regret or reference, for we would speak of intentional and semantic relations, just as (3) itself does. But, it might be said, if physicalism is true, we ought to be able illuminate *a priori* what common sense properties and relations make it the case that our words refer to that to which they refer. That it is so hard to give an illuminating and convincing account of this is, in part, what makes skeptical positions such as Quine's so persistently tempting to the naturalistically minded philosopher.[25]

Notes

1   Strictly speaking, Frege took the reference of a predicate to the rule which assigns an object truth or falsity, depending on whether the predicate is true or false of the object.

2   Strictly speaking, the argument needs to be stated a bit more fussily, since (2) is (arguably) ambiguous, with a reading on which it is true if no one wrote *The Second Sex*. This problem is evaded by fronting each of the sentences with 'Exactly one person wrote *The Second Sex*, and.'

3   Further discussion of Kripke's *Naming and Necessity* – in particular, of Kripke's use of the notions of a possible world and of a rigid designator – occurs below, in section 11.

4   Actually, this can't be true if XYZ plays the role, on "twin earth," that H_2O plays on earth, since we are mostly made up of water! But Putnam's point can be made with other examples which don't have this feature.

5   Sections 65–78. The citations come from sections 66–8 and section 70.

6   We ought to raise the question as to whether Wilson's proposal in fact predicts the alleged indeterminacy of the Druid's 'bird,' or that of mundane uses of 'water' before the advent of modern chemistry. Note, first of all, Wilson misrepresents his view when he says that 'bird' in parochial Druid doesn't have a single correct extension. Presumably there is a most appropriate range of application for the word – roughly, the collection of things (perceptually similar to those) on the island. Thus, there is a fixed set of physical properties which index the predicate in Druid – those properties **P** such that, were an object x from the range of application be presented to a Druid, he would classify x with 'bird' iff x had **P**. *The* extension of 'bird' in Druid is the set of those objects which have at least one such **P**. Since, as Wilson stresses, both **being a bird** and **being a flying thing** index the predicate, it turns out that the Druid's 'bird' is true of airplanes after all.

Note, second of all, that Wilson makes two uses of the notion of a predicate's range of application. The range of application of a predicate provides a set of samples which one uses, along with speaker dispositions, to fix what properties index the predicate (and thereby to fix an extension for the predicate). Wilson also uses a predicate's range of application to limit the significance of talk about the predicate's extension: if one says that set S is the extension of predicate P, one should use P's range of application as a hedge. Presumably, there is no semantic significance to x's being in a predicate's extension unless x is also in the predicate's range of applicability.

Suppose, however, that the Druids have heard of a place in America called 'Logan' but are innocent of airplanes (and thus these are outside of the range of application of 'bird' for them). A Druid conjectures 'there are birds at Logan.' If airplanes are in the extension of parochial Druid's 'bird' – which, as we have seen, they are – then the conjecture is true (even if only airplanes, not birds, are to be found at Logan). How is the fact that 'bird' is true of airplanes of no semantic significance?

One might respond that the extension of a predicate ought, on Wilson's view, be limited to the set *of those things in the predicate's range of applicability* which have some property which indexes the predicate. It is altogether unclear, however, that we can non-arbitrarily exclude such things as airplanes from the range of application of 'bird.' Airplanes are similar to things on the Druid island in ways that are relevant to Druid classification. Druids (let us imagine) are good at telling when something is made of metal, as good as are we. Presumably the airplane is similar enough to Druid metal artifacts that it should be in the range of applicability of 'metal.' It's very similar (we may suppose) to a vehicle, as well, in ways which one would think make it a candidate for the range of applicability of Druid's 'vehicle.' If the appropriate range of applicability for Druid predicates consists of the "objects similar to those found in the environs of the Druid isle," airplanes seem to qualify for admission to the range. One could, I suppose, simply banish everything absent from the Druid's immediate environment from the extension of their predicates; the reader may judge whether this is a tolerable response.

7 To give a naturalistic account of a property or relation is, roughly, to explain, using only concepts from natural sciences such as physics, chemistry, and biology, under just what conditions objects have the property or stand in the relation.

8 Alternative explanations for the linguistic behavior of a- and b-speakers are available. We could use the principles

(P) a-speakers are disposed to apply 'Carla' to A
b-speakers are disposed to apply 'Carla' to B

to explain a- and b-behavior. This should be of no solace to anyone who thinks that 'Carla' as used at world a means something different from what it means as used at b. For if the explanations we give of verbal behavior using

(Q) a-speakers are disposed to apply 'Carla' to the child born to Smith on July 4.
b-speakers are disposed to apply 'Carla' to the child born to Smith on July 4.

are *as good* as those we give using (P), it would seem that the right conclusion to draw, from Horwich's perspective, is that it is *indeterminate* whether 'Carla' means the same in the two worlds. Indeed, the explanations *of speaker dispositions to verbal behavior* involving (Q) are arguably *better* than those using (P). For there is a strong intuition that in Twin Earth examples the verbal behavior of the Earthian (who reaches for water when thirsty) and the Twin Earthian (who reaches for XYZ when thirsty) are to be explained in the same way. In so far as we moved by this intuition, we have reason to prefer theories which explain *a*- and *b*-speakers' dispositions to verbal behavior in the same way to ones which do not.

There are a number of subtleties involved in the example which deserve further discussion. I have formulated the explanatory principles to be used in explaining *a*- and *b*-speakers' behavior using 'apply'; one might well wonder what 'apply' means here. Horwich is not entitled to invoke principles which make use of the notion of *referring* to Carla in any substantial sense of reference, given his "deflationary" attitude to the notions of truth and reference. Application of a name must thus be cashed out in terms of dispositions, to accept sentences in which the name occurs, in certain situations. This, I suspect, undercuts the idea that a principle such as

a-speakers are disposed to apply 'Carla' to A

could be "explanatorily basic" in Horwich's sense.

9   The example is Hartry Field's; see Field (1974, 209–10).

10   What follows is a simplified version of an argument in Chapter 2 of Quine (1960); the argument is present in the first half of "Ontological Relativity." A second argument, involving "proxy functions," surfaces in the second half of "Ontological Relativity;" it receives some discussion in the contribution by Azzouni. Yet another line of argument is presented in Quine (1971).

11   Argument is of course needed for premiss (2). One might grant Quine that if we limit our attention to very simple observation sentences such as 'there goes a rabbit,' verbal dispositions will not suffice to determine a unique translation. But once we invoke the apparatus of counting, identity, and quantification, we *can* eliminate bizarre hypotheses such as (H2). (Note, for instance, that the situations in which it's appropriate to say 'there go two rabbits' are obviously *not* the situations in which it's appropriate to say 'there go two urps.')

Quine is well aware of this. He argues at length at the beginning of "Ontological Relativity" that there is no reason to think that the apparatus of quantification, counting, and identity is any less subject to indeterminacy than the likes of 'lapin.' And as Quine tries to show, given the right interpretation of the French idioms of quantification and counting, it is possible to translate 'il y a deux lapins' (which is conventionally translated as 'there are two rabbits') so that it is about urps, but is assertable exactly when there are two rabbits.

12   What, then, is the Quinean argument? One might put it so: it would be arbitrary (for example) to identify the physical relations which explain why 'rabbit' refers to whatever it does in English with relations which make it refer to rabbits, instead of with relations which make it refer to urps. But reference (and thus meaning) is determinate only if this sort of thing is not arbitrary.

The second premiss here reflects Quine's physicalism, requiring a physical explanation for why any (purported) relation relates the things it (purportedly) relates. With the notion of one fact making a second fact, the case is to be understood in explanatory terms: F makes F' the case when a correct explanation of F is given by pointing out that F'.

For an account of Quinean arguments for inscrutability and their import which differs from Soames', see Richard (1998).

13 These papers are collected in Davidson (2001). Davidson, to my knowledge, does not endorse the idea that knowing such a theory is the only route to linguistic competence, nor does he endorse the empirical hypothesis that our linguistic competence is based on such knowledge. Followers of Davidson have not been so cautious. For example, Richard Larson and Gabriel Segal's widely read text (Larson and Segal, 1995), argues for the hypothesis that linguistic competence in humans is, in part, realized by their implicit knowledge of a truth theory for their language.

14 This work is in "The Concept of Truth in Formalized Languages," reprinted in Tarski (1983).

15 I am simplifying a lot here. For example, what I say about defining 'true of' ignores complex predicates (e.g., 'is a woman and an author'). Tarski's approach applies to languages in which such constructions are possible. In fact, what Tarski did was show how to directly define 'true of' for such languages, and to define 'true' in terms of this.

16 Part of Tarski's technical accomplishment was figuring out how to give such a principle for sentences involving the quantifiers 'some' and 'all.'

17 Consider a very simple language. Seven-month-old Baby B's linguistic repertoire consists of 'hama' ("momma's here") and 'kama' ("kitty's here"). Let P be the property a sentence S has iff (S is 'hama' and B's mother is in his vicinity, or S is 'kama' and B's kitty is in his vicinity). P *is* the property a Tarskian truth theory for B's language defines. Someone could know that the sentence 'hama' had property P without having any idea what 'hama' means, or under what conditions it is true. (This is because, though *in fact* P coincides with truth in B's language, the co-incidence is completely accidental. Suppose 'hama' had meant 'Daddy's here,' and that Mommy, but not Daddy, was in B's vicinity. Then 'hama' would have had P, but it wouldn't have been true in B's language.) Because of the "brute force" nature of the definitions of 'refers in L' and 'true of in L,' precisely the same point applies to Tarskian definitions of truth for more complex languages.

The point is kindred to that which underlies John Foster's objection to Davidson discussed below. For discussion, see Soames (1999, chapter 4).

18 David Kaplan's work on demonstratives and indexicals is the fountainhead of contemporary enthusiasm for this sort of view; see Kaplan (1989). A collection of seminal articles on the topic is Salmon and Soames (1988).

19 The literature on this and allied problems is vast indeed. A small sample: Salmon (1986) defends a Russellian view of what is said against its counterintuitive consequences; Evans (1982) gives a "neo-Fregean" account of the contents of utterances and thoughts; Richard (1990) argues that the individuation of content is a highly contextual matter.

20   Quine infers the premiss here from "confirmation holism," the view (roughly) that what experiments confirm or disconfirm are not a theory's individual claims, but theories as wholes. One might observe that the premiss doesn't follow from confirmation holism: what gets confirmed or disconfirmed, one might say, is the *synthetic* (i.e., non analytic) part of a theory. Quine's response is (in part) to point out that even logical laws can be brought into question given weird enough experimental data.

21   A defender of analyticity might suggest that *x is a vixen; so x is a female* is among the meaning constitutive for 'vixen,' while *x is a vixen, so x is not the size of a star* is merely obvious, not meaning constitutive.

22   Note further that if Quine's views are as I have suggested, he is not committed to the view that meaning is even "locally holistic," in the sense that there are some inferences (involving, say, 'vixen') such that, were one to cease to hold them valid, one would thereby change the meanings of some of the words in which they occur. If it is simply indeterminate whether the validity of *x is a vixen; so x is a fox* is underwritten by principles about meaning, then if someone ceases to accept this inference, it is just indeterminate whether he is using 'vixen' with the same meaning.

23   This needs to be qualified in various ways – for example, the term in question can't be governed by a verb such as 'believes.' The relevant qualifications are irrelevant here.

24   This point is forcefully made by Alex Byrne (1999).

25   Thanks to Jody Azzouni, Nancy Bauer, David Braun, and Jeff King for helpful comments.

References

Bogohossian, Paul A. 1996. Analyticity Reconsidered. *Noûs* 30, 360–91.

Byrne, Alex 1999. Cosmic Hermeneutics. In J. Tomberlin (ed.), *Philosophical Perspectives 13*. Oxford: Blackwell.

Davidson, D. 2001. *Inquiries into Meaning and Truth*, 2nd edn. Oxford: Oxford University Press.

Evans, G. 1982. *The Varieties of Reference*. Oxford: Oxford University Press.

Field, H. 1974. Quine and the Correspondence Theory. *The Philosophical Review 83*, 200–28.

Foster, J. 1976. Meaning and Truth Theory. In Gareth Evans and John McDowell (eds.), *Truth and Meaning*. Oxford: Oxford University Press, pp. 3–32.

Frege, Gottlob 1918. Der Gedanke. In Frege (1984).

Frege, Gottlob 1984. *Collected Papers on Mathematics, Logic, and Philosophy*, ed. by B. McGuinness. Oxford: Blackwell.

Kaplan, D. 1989. Demonstratives: An essay on the semantics, logic, metaphysics, and epistemology of demonstratives and other indexicals. In J. Almog, J. Perry, and H. Wettstein (eds.), *Themes from Kaplan*. New York: Oxford University Press, pp. 481–563.

Larson, R. and Segal, G. 1995. *Knowledge of Meaning*. Cambridge, Mass.: MIT Press.

Putnam, H. 1973. The Meaning of 'Meaning'. In Hilary Putnam, *Mind, Language, and Reality*, vol. 2. Cambridge: Cambridge University Press, pp. 215–71.

Quine, W. V. 1953. Three Grades of Modal Involvement. In Quine (1966).

Quine, W. V. 1960. *Word and Object*. Cambridge, Mass.: MIT Press.

Quine, W. V. 1966. *The Ways of Paradox and Other Essays*. Cambridge, Mass.: Harvard University Press.

Quine, W. V. 1971. On the Reasons for the Indeterminacy of Translation. *Journal of Philosophy 67*, 178–83.

Reichenbach, H. 1947. *Elements of Symbolic Logic*. New York: Free Press.

Richard, M. 1990. *Propositional Attitudes*. Cambridge: Cambridge University Press.

Richard, M. 1998. Inscrutability. In Ali Kazmi (ed.), *Meaning and Reference*. Calgary: University of Calgary Press, pp. 165–209.

Salmon, N. 1986. *Frege's Puzzle*. Cambridge, Mass.: MIT Press.

Salmon, N. and Soames, S. (eds.) 1988. *Propositions and Attitudes*. Oxford: Oxford University Press.

Soames, S. 1999. *Understanding Truth*. Oxford: Oxford University Press.

Tarski, A. 1983. *Logic, Semantics, Metamathematics*, 2nd edn. Trans by J. H. Woodger. Indianapolis: Hackett.

Wittgenstein, L. 1953. *Philosophical Investigations*. Trans by G. E. M. Anscombe. Oxford: Basil Blackwell.

1

On Sense and Reference

Gottlob Frege

Equality[*] gives rise to challenging questions which are not altogether easy to answer. Is it a relation? A relation between objects, or between names or signs of objects? In my *Begriffsschrift*[1] I assumed the latter. The reasons which seem to favour this are the following: $a = a$ and $a = b$ are obviously statements of differing cognitive value; $a = a$ holds *a priori* and, according to Kant, is to be labelled analytic, while statements of the form $a = b$ often contain very valuable extensions of our knowledge and cannot always be established *a priori*. The discovery that the rising sun is not new every morning, but always the same, was one of the most fertile astronomical discoveries. Even to-day the identification of a small planet or a comet is not always a matter of course. Now if we were to regard equality as a relation between that which the names 'a' and 'b' designate, it would seem that $a = b$ could not differ from $a = a$ (i.e. provided $a = b$ is true). A relation would thereby be expressed of a thing to itself, and indeed one in which each thing stands to itself but to no other thing. What is intended to be said by $a = b$ seems to be that the signs or names 'a' and 'b' designate the same thing, so that those signs themselves would be under discussion; a relation between them would be asserted. But this relation would hold between the names or signs only in so far as they named or designated something. It would be mediated by the connexion of each of the two signs with the same designated thing. But this is arbitrary. Nobody can be forbidden to use any arbitrarily producible event or object as a sign for something. In that case the sentence $a = b$ would no longer refer to the subject matter, but only to its mode of designation; we would express no proper knowledge by its

[*] I use this word in the sense of identity, and understand '$a = b$' to have the sense of 'a is the same as b' or 'a and b coincide.'

means. But in many cases this is just what we want to do. If the sign '*a*' is distinguished from the sign '*b*' only as object (here, by means of its shape), not as sign (i.e. not by the manner in which it designates something), the cognitive value of $a = a$ becomes essentially equal to that of $a = b$, provided $a = b$ is true. A difference can arise only if the difference between the signs corresponds to a difference in the mode of presentation of that which is designated. Let *a*, *b*, *c* be the lines connecting the vertices of a triangle with the midpoints of the opposite sides. The point of intersection of *a* and *b* is then the same as the point of intersection of *b* and *c*. So we have different designations for the same point, and these names ('point of intersection of *a* and *b*,' 'point of intersection of *b* and *c*') likewise indicate the mode of presentation; and hence the statement contains actual knowledge.

It is natural, now, to think of there being connected with a sign (name, combination of words, letter), besides that to which the sign refers, which may be called the reference of the sign, also what I should like to call the *sense* of the sign, wherein the mode of presentation is contained. In our example, accordingly, the reference of the expressions 'the point of intersection of *a* and *b*' and 'the point of intersection of *b* and *c*' would be the same, but not their senses. The reference of 'evening star' would be the same as that of 'morning star,' but not the sense.

It is clear from the context that by 'sign' and 'name' I have here understood any designation representing a proper name, which thus has as its reference a definite object (this word taken in the widest range), but not a concept or a relation, which shall be discussed further in another article.[2] The designation of a single object can also consist of several words or other signs. For brevity, let every such designation be called a proper name.

The sense of a proper name is grasped by everybody who is sufficiently familiar with the language or totality of designations to which it belongs;[*] but this serves to illuminate only a single aspect of the reference, supposing it to have one. Comprehensive knowledge of the reference would require us to be able to say immediately whether any given sense belongs to it. To such knowledge we never attain.

---

[*] In the case of an actual proper name such as 'Aristotle' opinions as to the sense may differ. It might, for instance, be taken to be the following: the pupil of Plato and teacher of Alexander the Great. Anybody who does this will attach another sense to the sentence 'Aristotle was born in Stagira' than will a man who takes as the sense of the name: the teacher of Alexander the Great who was born in Stagira. So long as the reference remains the same, such variations of sense may be tolerated, although they are to be avoided in the theoretical structure of a demonstrative science and ought not to occur in a perfect language.

The regular connexion between a sign, its sense, and its reference is of such a kind that to the sign there corresponds a definite sense and to that in turn a definite reference, while to a given reference (an object) there does not belong only a single sign. The same sense has different expressions in different languages or even in the same language. To be sure, exceptions to this regular behaviour occur. To every expression belonging to a complete totality of signs, there should certainly correspond a definite sense; but natural languages often do not satisfy this condition, and one must be content if the same word has the same sense in the same context. It may perhaps be granted that every grammatically well-formed expression representing a proper name always has a sense. But this is not to say that to the sense there also corresponds a reference. The words 'the celestial body most distant from the Earth' have a sense, but it is very doubtful if they also have a reference. The expression 'the least rapidly convergent series' has a sense but demonstrably has no reference, since for every given convergent series, another convergent, but less rapidly convergent, series can be found. In grasping a sense, one is not certainly assured of a reference.

If words are used in the ordinary way, what one intends to speak of is their reference. It can also happen, however, that one wishes to talk about the words themselves or their sense. This happens, for instance, when the words of another are quoted. One's own words then first designate words of the other speaker, and only the latter have their usual reference. We then have signs of signs. In writing, the words are in this case enclosed in quotation marks. Accordingly, a word standing between quotation marks must not be taken as having its ordinary reference.

In order to speak of the sense of an expression 'A' one may simply use the phrase 'the sense of the expression "A"'. In reported speech one talks about the sense, e.g., of another person's remarks. It is quite clear that in this way of speaking words do not have their customary reference but designate what is usually their sense. In order to have a short expression, we will say: In reported speech, words are used *indirectly* or have their *indirect* reference. We distinguish accordingly the *customary* from the *indirect* reference of a word; and its *customary* sense from its *indirect* sense. The indirect reference of a word is accordingly its customary sense. Such exceptions must always be borne in mind if the mode of connexion between sign, sense, and reference in particular cases is to be correctly understood.

The reference and sense of a sign are to be distinguished from the associated idea. If the reference of a sign is an object perceivable by the senses, my idea of it is an internal image,[*] arising from memories of sense impressions which I have had and acts, both internal and external, which I have performed. Such an idea is often saturated with feeling; the clarity of its separate parts varies and oscillates. The same sense is not always connected, even in the same man, with the same idea. The idea is subjective: one man's idea is not that of another. There result, as a matter of course, a variety of differences in the ideas associated with the same sense. A painter, a horseman, and a zoologist will probably connect different ideas with the name 'Bucephalus.' This constitutes an essential distinction between the idea and the sign's sense, which may be the common property of many and therefore is not a part or a mode of the individual mind. For one can hardly deny that mankind has a common store of thoughts which is transmitted from one generation to another.[†]

In the light of this, one need have no scruples in speaking simply of *the* sense, whereas in the case of an idea one must, strictly speaking, add to whom it belongs and at what time. It might perhaps be said: Just as one man connects this idea, and another that idea, with the same word, so also one man can associate this sense and another that sense. But there still remains a difference in the mode of connexion. They are not prevented from grasping the same sense; but they cannot have the same idea. *Si duo idem faciunt, non est idem.* If two persons picture the same thing, each still has his own idea. It is indeed sometimes possible to establish differences in the ideas, or even in the sensations, of different men; but an exact comparison is not possible, because we cannot have both ideas together in the same consciousness.

The reference of a proper name is the object itself which we designate by its means; the idea, which we have in that case, is wholly subjective; in between lies the sense, which is indeed no longer subjective like the idea, but is yet not the object itself. The following analogy will perhaps clarify these relationships. Somebody observes the Moon through a telescope. I compare the Moon itself to the reference; it is the object of the observation, mediated by the real image projected by the object glass in the interior of the telescope, and by the retinal image of the observer.

---

[*] We can include with ideas the direct experiences in which sense-impressions and acts themselves take the place of the traces which they have left in the mind. The distinction is unimportant for our purpose, especially since memories of sense-impressions and acts always go along with such impressions and acts themselves to complete the perceptual image. One may on the other hand understand direct experience as including any object, in so far as it is sensibly perceptible or spatial.

[†] Hence it is inadvisable to use the word 'idea' to designate something so basically different.

The former I compare to the sense, the latter is like the idea or experience. The optical image in the telescope is indeed one-sided and dependent upon the standpoint of observation; but it is still objective, inasmuch as it can be used by several observers. At any rate it could be arranged for several to use it simultaneously. But each one would have his own retinal image. On account of the diverse shapes of the observers' eyes, even a geometrical congruence could hardly be achieved, and an actual coincidence would be out of the question. This analogy might be developed still further, by assuming A's retinal image made visible to B; or A might also see his own retinal image in a mirror. In this way we might perhaps show how an idea can itself be taken as an object, but as such is not for the observer what it directly is for the person having the idea. But to pursue this would take us too far afield.

We can now recognize three levels of difference between words, expressions, or whole sentences. The difference may concern at most the ideas, or the sense but not the reference, or, finally, the reference as well. With respect to the first level, it is to be noted that, on account of the uncertain connexion of ideas with words, a difference may hold for one person, which another does not find. The difference between a translation and the original text should properly not overstep the first level. To the possible differences here belong also the colouring and shading which poetic eloquence seeks to give to the sense. Such colouring and shading are not objective, and must be evoked by each hearer or reader according to the hints of the poet or the speaker. Without some affinity in human ideas art would certainly be impossible; but it can never be exactly determined how far the intentions of the poet are realized.

In what follows there will be no further discussion of ideas and experiences; they have been mentioned here only to ensure that the idea aroused in the hearer by a word shall not be confused with its sense or its reference.

To make short and exact expressions possible, let the following phraseology be established:

A proper name (word, sign, sign combination, expression) *expresses* its sense, *stands for* or *designates* its reference. By means of a sign we express its sense and designate its reference.

Idealists or sceptics will perhaps long since have objected: 'You talk, without further ado, of the Moon as an object; but how do you know that the name 'the Moon' has any reference? How do you know that anything whatsoever has a reference?' I reply that when we say 'the Moon,' we do not intend to speak of our idea of the Moon, nor are we satisfied with the sense alone, but we presuppose a reference. To assume that in the sentence 'The Moon is smaller than the Earth' the idea of the Moon is in question, would be flatly to misunderstand the sense. If this is what the speaker wanted, he would use the phrase 'my idea of the Moon.' Now we can of course be mistaken in the presupposition, and such mistakes have indeed occurred. But the question whether the presupposition is perhaps always mistaken need not be answered here; in order to justify mention of the reference of a sign it is enough, at first, to point out our intention in speaking or thinking. (We must then add the reservation: provided such reference exists.)

So far we have considered the sense and reference only of such expressions, words, or signs as we have called proper names. We now inquire concerning the sense and reference for an entire declarative sentence. Such a sentence contains a thought.* Is this thought, now, to be regarded as its sense or its reference? Let us assume for the time being that the sentence has reference. If we now replace one word of the sentence by another having the same reference, but a different sense, this can have no bearing upon the reference of the sentence. Yet we can see that in such a case the thought changes; since, e.g., the thought in the sentence 'The morning star is a body illuminated by the Sun' differs from that in the sentence 'The evening star is a body illuminated by the Sun.' Anybody who did not know that the evening star is the morning star might hold the one thought to be true, the other false. The thought, accordingly, cannot be the reference of the sentence, but must rather be considered as the sense. What is the position now with regard to the reference? Have we a right even to inquire about it? Is it possible that a sentence as a whole has only a sense, but no reference? At any rate, one might expect that such sentences occur, just as there are parts of sentences having sense but no reference. And sentences which contain proper names without reference will be of this kind. The sentence 'Odysseus was set ashore at Ithaca while sound asleep' obviously has a sense. But since it is doubtful whether the name 'Odysseus,' occurring therein, has reference, it is also doubtful whether the whole sentence has one. Yet it is certain, nevertheless, that anyone who seriously took the sentence to be true or false would ascribe to the name 'Odysseus' a reference, not merely a sense; for it is of the reference of the name that the predicate is affirmed or denied. Whoever does not admit the name has reference can

---

* By a thought I understand not the subjective performance of thinking but its objective content, which is capable of being the common property of several thinkers.

neither apply nor withhold the predicate. But in that case it would be superfluous to advance to the reference of the name; one could be satisfied with the sense, if one wanted to go no further than the thought. If it were a question only of the sense of the sentence, the thought, it would be unnecessary to bother with the reference of a part of the sentence; only the sense, not the reference, of the part is relevant to the sense of the whole sentence. The thought remains the same whether 'Odysseus' has reference or not. The fact that we concern ourselves at all about the reference of a part of the sentence indicates that we generally recognize and expect a reference for the sentence itself. The thought loses value for us as soon as we recognize that the reference of one of its parts is missing. We are therefore justified in not being satisfied with the sense of a sentence, and in inquiring also as to its reference. But now why do we want every proper name to have not only a sense, but also a reference? Why is the thought not enough for us? Because, and to the extent that, we are concerned with its truth value. This is not always the case. In hearing an epic poem, for instance, apart from the euphony of the language we are interested only in the sense of the sentences and the images and feelings thereby aroused. The question of truth would cause us to abandon aesthetic delight for an attitude of scientific investigation. Hence it is a matter of no concern to us whether the name 'Odysseus,' for instance, has reference, so long as we accept the poem as a work of art.* It is the striving for truth that drives us always to advance from the sense to the reference.

We have seen that the reference of a sentence may always be sought, whenever the reference of its components is involved; and that this is the case when and only when we are inquiring after the truth value.

We are therefore driven into accepting the *truth value* of a sentence as constituting its reference. By the truth value of a sentence I understand the circumstance that it is true or false. There are no further truth values. For brevity I call the one the True, the other the False. Every declarative sentence concerned with the reference of its words is therefore to be regarded as a proper name, and its reference, if it has one, is either the True or the False. These two objects are recognized, if only implicitly, by everybody who judges something to be true – and so even by a sceptic. The designation of the truth values as objects may appear to be an arbitrary fancy or perhaps a mere play upon words, from which no profound consequences could be drawn. What I mean by an object can

---

* It would be desirable to have a special term for signs having only sense. If we name them, say, representations, the words of the actors on the stage would be representations; indeed the actor himself would be a representation

be more exactly discussed only in connexion with concept and relation. I will reserve this for another article.[3] But so much should already be clear, that in every judgment,[*] no matter how trivial, the step from the level of thoughts to the level of reference (the objective) has already been taken.

One might be tempted to regard the relation of the thought to the True not as that of sense to reference, but rather as that of subject to predicate. One can, indeed, say: 'The thought, that 5 is a prime number, is true.' But closer examination shows that nothing more has been said than in the simple sentence '5 is a prime number.' The truth claim arises in each case from the form of the declarative sentence, and when the latter lacks its usual force, e.g., in the mouth of an actor upon the stage, even the sentence 'The thought that 5 is a prime number is true' contains only a thought, and indeed the same thought as the simple '5 is a prime number.' It follows that the relation of the thought to the True may not be compared with that of subject to predicate.

Subject and predicate (understood in the logical sense) are indeed elements of thought; they stand on the same level for knowledge. By combining subject and predicate, one reaches only a thought, never passes from sense to reference, never from a thought to its truth value. One moves at the same level but never advances from one level to the next. A truth value cannot be a part of a thought, any more than, say, the Sun can, for it is not a sense but an object.

If our supposition that the reference of a sentence is its truth value is correct, the latter must remain unchanged when a part of the sentence is replaced by an expression having the same reference. And this is in fact the case. Leibniz gives the definition: '*Eadem sunt, quae sibi mutuo substitui possunt, salva veritate.*' What else but the truth value could be found, that belongs quite generally to every sentence if the reference of its components is relevant, and remains unchanged by substitutions of the kind in question?

If now the truth value of a sentence is its reference, then on the one hand all true sentences have the same reference and so, on the other hand, do all false sentences. From this we see that in the reference of the sentence all that is specific is obliterated. We can never be concerned only with the reference of a sentence; but again the mere thought alone yields no knowledge, but only the thought together with its reference, i.e. its truth value. Judgments can be regarded as advances from a thought to a truth value. Naturally this cannot be a definition. Judgment is something

---

[*] A judgment, for me, is not the mere comprehension of a thought, but the admission of its truth.

quite peculiar and incomparable. One might also say that judgments are distinctions of parts within truth values. Such distinction occurs by a return to the thought. To every sense belonging to a truth value there would correspond its own manner of analysis. However, I have here used the word 'part' in a special sense. I have in fact transferred the relation between the parts and the whole of the sentence to its reference, by calling the reference of a word part of the reference of the sentence, if the word itself is a part of the sentence. This way of speaking can certainly be attacked, because the whole reference and one part of it do not suffice to determine the remainder, and because the word 'part' is already used in another sense of bodies. A special term would need to be invented.

The supposition that the truth value of a sentence is its reference shall now be put to further test. We have found that the truth value of a sentence remains unchanged when an expression is replaced by another having the same reference: but we have not yet considered the case in which the expression to be replaced is itself a sentence. Now if our view is correct, the truth value of a sentence containing another as part must remain unchanged when the part is replaced by another sentence having the same truth value. Exceptions are to be expected when the whole sentence or its part is direct or indirect quotation; for in such cases, as we have seen, the words do not have their customary reference. In direct quotation, a sentence designates another sentence, and in indirect quotation a thought.

We are thus led to consider subordinate sentences or clauses. These occur as parts of a sentence complex, which is, from the logical stand-point, likewise a sentence – a main sentence. But here we meet the question whether it is also true of the subordinate sentence that its reference is a truth value. Of indirect quotation we already know the opposite. Grammarians view subordinate clauses as representatives of parts of sentences and divide them accordingly into noun clauses, adjective clauses, adverbial clauses. This might generate the supposition that the reference of a subordinate clause was not a truth value but rather of the same kind as the reference of a noun or adjective or adverb – in short, of a part of a sentence, whose sense was not a thought but only a part of a thought. Only a more thorough investigation can clarify the issue. In so doing, we shall not follow the grammatical categories strictly, but rather group together what is logically of the same kind. Let us first search for cases in which the sense of the subordinate clause, as we have just supposed, is not an independent thought.

The case of an abstract[4] noun clause, introduced by 'that,' includes the case of indirect quotation, in which we have seen the words to have their indirect reference coinciding with what is customarily their sense. In this case, then, the subordinate clause has for its reference a thought, not a truth value; as sense not a thought, but the sense of the words 'the thought, that...,' which is only a part of the thought in the entire complex sentence. This happens after 'say,' 'hear,' 'be of the opinion,' 'be convinced,' 'conclude,' and similar words.[*] There is a different, and indeed somewhat complicated, situation after words like 'perceive,' 'know,' 'fancy,' which are to be considered later.

That in the cases of the first kind the reference of the subordinate clause is in fact the thought can also be recognized by seeing that it is indifferent to the truth of the whole whether the subordinate clause is true or false. Let us compare, for instance, the two sentences 'Copernicus believed that the planetary orbits are circles' and 'Copernicus believed that the apparent motion of the sun is produced by the real motion of the Earth.' One subordinate clause can be substituted for the other without harm to the truth. The main clause and the subordinate clause together have as their sense only a single thought, and the truth of the whole includes neither the truth nor the untruth of the subordinate clause. In such cases it is not permissible to replace one expression in the subordinate clause by another having the same customary reference, but only by one having the same indirect reference, i.e. the same customary sense. If somebody were to conclude: The reference of a sentence is not its truth value, for in that case it could always be replaced by another sentence of the same truth value; he would prove too much; one might just as well claim that the reference of 'morning star' is not Venus, since one may not always say 'Venus' in place of 'morning star.' One has the right to conclude only that the reference of a sentence is not *always* its truth value, and that 'morning star' does not always stand for the planet Venus, viz. when the word has its indirect reference. An exception of such a kind occurs in the subordinate clause just considered which has a thought as its reference.

If one says 'It seems that...' one means 'It seems to me that...' or 'I think that...' We therefore have the same case again. The situation is similar in the case of expressions such as 'to be pleased,' 'to regret,' 'to approve,' 'to blame,' 'to hope,' 'to fear.' If, toward the end of the battle of Waterloo,[5] Wellington was glad that the Prussians were coming, the basis for his joy was a conviction. Had he been deceived, he would have been no less pleased so long as his illusion lasted; and before he became so convinced he could not have been pleased that the Prussians

---

[*] In 'A lied in saying he had seen B,' the subordinate clause designates a thought which is said (1) to have been asserted by A (2) while A was convinced of its falsity.

were coming – even though in fact they might have been already approaching.

Just as a conviction or a belief is the ground of a feeling, it can, as in inference, also be the ground of a conviction. In the sentence: 'Columbus inferred from the roundness of the Earth that he could reach India by travelling towards the west,' we have as the reference of the parts two thoughts, that the Earth is round, and that Columbus by travelling to the west could reach India. All that is relevant here is that Columbus was convinced of both, and that the one conviction was a ground for the other. Whether the Earth is really round and Columbus could really reach India by travelling west, as he thought, is immaterial to the truth of our sentence; but it is not immaterial whether we replace 'the Earth' by 'the planet which is accompanied by a moon whose diameter is greater than the fourth part of its own.' Here also we have the indirect reference of the words.

Adverbial final clauses beginning 'in order that' also belong here; for obviously the purpose is a thought; therefore: indirect reference for the words, subjunctive mood.

A subordinate clause with 'that' after 'command,' 'ask,' 'forbid,' would appear in direct speech as an imperative. Such a clause has no reference but only a sense. A command, a request, are indeed not thoughts, yet they stand on the same level as thoughts. Hence in subordinate clauses depending upon 'command,' 'ask,' etc., words have their indirect reference. The reference of such a clause is therefore not a truth value but a command, a request, and so forth.

The case is similar for the dependent question in phrases such as 'doubt whether,' 'not to know what.' It is easy to see that here also the words are to be taken to have their indirect reference. Dependent clauses expressing questions and beginning, with 'who,' 'what,' 'where,' 'when,' 'how,' 'by what means,' etc., seem at times to approximate very closely to adverbial clauses in which words have their customary references. These cases are distinguished linguistically [in German] by the mood of the verb. With the subjunctive, we have a dependent question and indirect reference of the words, so that a proper name cannot in general be replaced by another name of the same object.

In the cases so far considered the words of the subordinate clauses had their indirect reference, and this made it clear that the reference of the subordinate clause itself was indirect, i.e. not a truth value but a thought, a command, a request, a question. The subordinate clause could be regarded as a noun, indeed one could say: as a proper name of that thought, that command, etc., which it represented in the context of the sentence structure.

We now come to other subordinate clauses, in which the words do have their customary reference without however a thought occurring as sense and a truth value as reference. How this is possible is best made clear by examples.

Whoever discovered the elliptic form of the planetary orbits died in misery.

If the sense of the subordinate clause were here a thought, it would have to be possible to express it also in a separate sentence. But this does not work, because the grammatical subject 'whoever' has no independent sense and only mediates the relation with the consequent clause 'died in misery.' For this reason the sense of the subordinate clause is not a complete thought, and its reference is Kepler, not a truth value. One might object that the sense of the whole does contain a thought as part, viz. that there was somebody who first discovered the elliptic form of the planetary orbits; for whoever takes the whole to be true cannot deny this part. This is undoubtedly so; but only because otherwise the dependent clause 'whoever discovered the elliptic form of the planetary orbits' would have no reference. If anything is asserted there is always an obvious presupposition that the simple or compound proper names used have reference. If one therefore asserts 'Kepler died in misery,' there is a presupposition that the name 'Kepler' designates something; but it does not follow that the sense of the sentence 'Kepler died in misery' contains the thought that the name 'Kepler' designates something. If this were the case the negation would have to run not

Kepler did not die in misery

but

Kepler did not die in misery, or the name 'Kepler' has no reference.

That the name 'Kepler' designates something is just as much a presupposition for the assertion

Kepler died in misery

as for the contrary assertion. Now languages have the fault of containing expressions which fail to designate an object (although their grammatical form seems to qualify them for that purpose) because the truth of some sentence is a prerequisite. Thus it depends on the truth of the sentence:

> There was someone who discovered the elliptic form of the planetary orbits

whether the subordinate clause

> Whoever discovered the elliptic form of the planetary orbits

really designates an object or only seems to do so while having in fact no reference. And thus it may appear as if our subordinate clause contained as a part of its sense the thought that there was somebody who discovered the elliptic form of the planetary orbits. If this were right the negation would run:

> Either whoever discovered the elliptic form of the planetary orbits did not die in misery or there was nobody who discovered the elliptic form of the planetary orbits.

This arises from an imperfection of language, from which even the symbolic language of mathematical analysis is not altogether free; even there combinations of symbols can occur that seem to stand for something but have (at least so far) no reference, e.g. divergent infinite series. This can be avoided, e.g., by means of the special stipulation that divergent infinite series shall stand for the number 0. A logically perfect language (*Begriffsschrift*) should satisfy the conditions, that every expression grammatically well constructed as a proper name out of signs already introduced shall in fact designate an object, and that no new sign shall be introduced as a proper name without being secured a reference. The logic books contain warnings against logical mistakes arising from the ambiguity of expressions. I regard as no less pertinent a warning against apparent proper names having no reference. The history of mathematics supplies errors which have arisen in this way. This lends itself to demagogic abuse as easily as ambiguity – perhaps more easily. 'The will of the people' can serve as an example; for it is easy to establish that there is at any rate no generally accepted reference for this expression. It is therefore by no means unimportant to eliminate the source of these mistakes, at least in science, once and for all. Then such objections as the one discussed above would become impossible, because it could never depend upon the truth of a thought whether a proper name had a reference.

With the consideration of these noun clauses may be coupled that of types of adjective and adverbial clauses which are logically in close relation to them.

Adjective clauses also serve to construct compound proper names, though, unlike noun clauses, they are not sufficient by themselves for this purpose. These adjective clauses are to be regarded as equivalent to adjectives. Instead of 'the square root of 4 which is smaller than 0,' one can also say 'the negative square root of 4.' We have here the case of a compound proper name constructed from the expression for a concept with the help of the singular definite article. This is at any rate permissible if the concept applies to one and only one single object.*

Expressions for concepts can be so constructed that marks of a concept are given by adjective clauses as, in our example, by the clause 'which is smaller than 0.' It is evident that such an adjective clause cannot have a thought as sense or a truth value as reference, any more than the noun clause could. Its sense, which can also be expressed in many cases by a single adjective, is only a part of a thought. Here, as in the case of the noun clause, there is no independent subject and therefore no possibility of reproducing the sense of the subordinate clause in an independent sentence.

Places, instants, stretches of time, are, logically considered, objects; hence the linguistic designation of a definite place, a definite instant, or a stretch of time is to be regarded as a proper name. Now adverbial clauses of place and time can be used for the construction of such a proper name in a manner similar to that which we have seen in the case of noun and adjective clauses. In the same way, expressions for concepts bringing in places, etc., can be constructed. It is to be noted here also that the sense of these subordinate clauses cannot be reproduced in an independent sentence, since an essential component, viz. the determination of place or time, is missing and is only indicated by a relative pronoun or a conjunction.†

In conditional clauses, also, there may usually be recognized to occur an indefinite indicator, having a similar correlate in the dependent clause. (We have already seen this occur in noun, adjective, and adverbial

---

* In accordance with what was said above, an expression of the kind in question must actually always be assured of reference, by means of a special stipulation, e.g. by the convention that 0 shall count as its reference, when the concept applies to no object or to more than one.

† In the case of these sentences, various interpretations are easily possible. The sense of the sentence, 'After Schleswig-Holstein was separated from Denmark, Prussia and Austria quarrelled' can also be rendered in the form 'After the separation of Schleswig-Holstein

clauses.) In so far as each indicator refers to the other, both clauses together form a connected whole, which as a rule expresses only a single thought. In the sentence

If a number is less than 1 and greater than 0, its square is less than 1 and greater than 0

the component in question is 'a number' in the conditional clause and 'its' in the dependent clause. It is by means of this very indefiniteness that the sense acquires the generality expected of a law. It is this which is responsible for the fact that the antecedent clause alone has no complete thought as its sense and in combination with the consequent clause expresses one and only one thought, whose parts are no longer thoughts. It is, in general, incorrect to say that in the hypothetical judgment two judgments are put in reciprocal relationship. If this or something similar is said, the word 'judgment' is used in the same sense as I have connected with the word 'thought,' so that I would use the formulation: 'A hypothetical thought establishes a reciprocal relationship between two thoughts.' This could be true only if an indefinite indicator is absent;[*] but in such a case there would also be no generality.

If an instant of time is to be indefinitely indicated in both conditional and dependent clauses, this is often achieved merely by using the present tense of the verb, which in such a case however does not indicate the temporal present. This grammatical form is then the indefinite indicator in the main and subordinate clauses. An example of this is: 'When the Sun is in the tropic of Cancer, the longest day in the northern hemisphere

---

from Denmark, Prussia and Austria quarrelled.' In this version, it is surely sufficiently clear that the sense is not to be taken as having as a part the thought that Schleswig-Holstein was once separated from Denmark, but that this is the necessary presupposition in order for the expression 'after the separation of Schleswig-Holstein from Denmark' to have any reference at all. To be sure, our sentence can also be interpreted as saying that Schleswig-Holstein was once separated from Denmark. We then have a case which is to be considered later. In order to understand the difference more clearly, let us project ourselves into the mind of a Chinese who, having little knowledge of European history, believes it to be false that Schleswig-Holstein was ever separated from Denmark. He will take our sentence, in the first version, to be neither true nor false but will deny it to have any reference, on the ground of absence of reference for its subordinate clause. This clause would only apparently determine a time. If he interpreted our sentence in the second way, however, he would find a thought expressed in it which he would take to be false, beside a part which would be without reference for him.

* At times an explicit linguistic indication is missing and must be read off from the entire context.

occurs.' Here, also, it is impossible to express the sense of the subordinate clause in a full sentence, because this sense is not a complete thought. If we say: 'The Sun is in the tropic of Cancer,' this would refer to our present time and thereby change the sense. Just as little is the sense of the main clause a thought; only the whole, composed of main and subordinate clauses, has such a sense. It may be added that several common components in the antecedent and consequent clauses may be indefinitely indicated.

It is clear that noun clauses with 'who' or 'what' and adverbial clauses with 'where,' 'when,' 'wherever,' 'whenever' are often to be interpreted as having the sense of conditional clauses, e.g. 'who touches pitch, defiles himself.'

Adjective clauses can also take the place of conditional clauses. Thus the sense of the sentence previously used can be given in the form 'The square of a number which is less than 1 and greater than 0 is less than 1 and greater than 0.'

The situation is quite different if the common component of the two clauses is designated by a proper name. In the sentence:

Napoleon, who recognized the danger to his right flank, himself led his guards against the enemy position

two thoughts are expressed:

1 Napoleon recognized the danger to his right flank
2 Napoleon himself led his guards against the enemy position.

When and where this happened is to be fixed only by the context, but is nevertheless to be taken as definitely determined thereby. If the entire sentence is uttered as an assertion, we thereby simultaneously assert both component sentences. If one of the parts is false, the whole is false. Here we have the case that the subordinate clause by itself has a complete thought as sense (if we complete it by indication of place and time). The reference of the subordinate clause is accordingly a truth value. We can therefore expect that it may be replaced, without harm to the truth value of the whole, by a sentence having the same truth value. This is indeed the case; but it is to be noticed that for purely grammatical reasons, its subject must be 'Napoleon,' for only then can it be brought into the form of an adjective clause belonging to 'Napoleon.' But if the demand that it be expressed in this form be waived, and the connexion be shown by 'and,' this restriction disappears.

Subsidiary clauses beginning with 'although' also express complete
thoughts. This conjunction actually has no sense and does not change
the sense of the clause but only illuminates it in a peculiar fashion.* We
could indeed replace the concessive clause without harm to the truth of
the whole by another of the same truth value; but the light in which the
clause is placed by the conjunction might then easily appear unsuitable,
as if a song with a sad subject were to be sung in a lively fashion.

In the last cases the truth of the whole included the truth of the
component clauses. The case is different if a conditional clause expresses
a complete thought by containing, in place of an indefinite indicator, a
proper name or something which is to be regarded as equivalent. In the
sentence

If the Sun has already risen, the sky is very cloudy

the time is the present, that is to say, definite. And the place is also to be
thought of as definite. Here it can be said that a relation between the truth
values of conditional and dependent clauses has been asserted, viz. such
that the case does not occur in which the antecedent stands for the True
and the consequent for the False. Accordingly, our sentence is true if the
Sun has not yet risen, whether the sky is very cloudy or not, and also if
the Sun has risen and the sky is very cloudy. Since only truth values are
here in question, each component clause can be replaced by another of
the same truth value without changing the truth value of the whole. To be
sure, the light in which the subject then appears would usually be
unsuitable; the thought might easily seem distorted; but this has nothing
to do with its truth value. One must always take care not to clash with the
subsidiary thoughts, which are however not explicitly expressed and
therefore should not be reckoned in the sense. Hence, also, no account
need be taken of their truth values.†

The simple cases have now been discussed. Let us review what we
have learned.

The subordinate clause usually has for its sense not a thought, but only
a part of one, and consequently no truth value as reference. The reason
for this is either that the words in the subordinate clause have indirect
reference, so that the reference, not the sense, of the subordinate clause is

---

* Similarly in the case of 'but,' 'yet.'
† The thought of our sentence might also be expressed thus: 'Either the Sun has not risen
yet or the sky is very cloudy' – which shows how this kind of sentence connexion is to be
understood.

a thought; or else that, on account of the presence of an indefinite indicator, the subordinate clause is incomplete and expresses a thought only when combined with the main clause. It may happen, however, that the sense of the subsidiary clause is a complete thought, in which case it can be replaced by another of the same truth value without harm to the truth of the whole – provided there are no grammatical obstacles.

An examination of all the subordinate clauses which one may encounter will soon provide some which do not fit well into these categories. The reason, so far as I can see, is that these subordinate clauses have no such simple sense. Almost always, it seems, we connect with the main thoughts expressed by us subsidiary thoughts which, although not expressed, are associated with our words, in accordance with psychological laws, by the hearer. And since the subsidiary thought appears to be connected with our words of its own accord, almost like the main thought itself, we want it also to be expressed. The sense of the sentence is thereby enriched, and it may well happen that we have more simple thoughts than clauses. In many cases the sentence must be understood in this way, in others it may be doubtful whether the subsidiary thought belongs to the sense of the sentence or only accompanies it.* One might perhaps find that the sentence

Napoleon, who recognized the danger to his right flank, himself led his guards against the enemy position

expresses not only the two thoughts shown above, but also the thought that the knowledge of the danger was the reason why he led the guards against the enemy position. One may in fact doubt whether this thought is merely slightly suggested or really expressed. Let the question be considered whether our sentence be false if Napoleon's decision had already been made before he recognized the danger. If our sentence could be true in spite of this, the subsidiary thought should not be understood as part of the sense. One would probably decide in favour of this. The alternative would make for a quite complicated situation: We would have more simple thoughts than clauses. If the sentence

Napoleon recognized the danger to his right flank

were now to be replaced by another having the same truth value, e.g.

Napoleon was already more than 45 years old

---

* This may be important for the question whether an assertion is a lie, or an oath a perjury.

not only would our first thought be changed, but also our third one. Hence the truth value of the latter might change – viz. if his age was not the reason for the decision to lead the guards against the enemy. This shows why clauses of equal truth value cannot always be substituted for one another in such cases. The clause expresses more through its connexion with another than it does in isolation.

Let us now consider cases where this regularly happens. In the sentence:

Bebel fancies that the return of Alsace-Lorraine would appease France's desire for revenge

two thoughts are expressed, which are not however shown by means of antecedent and consequent clauses, viz.:

(1)   Bebel believes that the return of Alsace-Lorraine would appease France's desire for revenge
(2)   the return of Alsace-Lorraine would not appease France's desire for revenge.

In the expression of the first thought, the words of the subordinate clause have their indirect reference, while the same words have their customary reference in the expression of the second thought. This shows that the subordinate clause in our original complex sentence is to be taken twice over, with different reference, standing once for a thought, once for a truth value. Since the truth value is not the whole reference of the subordinate clause, we cannot simply replace the latter by another of equal truth value. Similar considerations apply to expressions such as 'know,' 'discover,' 'it is known that.'

By means of a subordinate causal clause and the associated main clause we express several thoughts, which however do not correspond separately to the original clauses. In the sentence: 'Because ice is less dense than water, it floats on water' we have

(1)   Ice is less dense than water;
(2)   If anything is less dense than water, it floats on water;
(3)   Ice floats on water.

The third thought, however, need not be explicitly introduced, since it is contained in the remaining two. On the other hand, neither the first and third nor the second and third combined would furnish the sense of our sentence. It can now be seen that our subordinate clause because ice is less dense than water

expresses our first thought, as well as a part of our second. This is how it comes to pass that our subsidiary clause cannot be simply replaced by another of equal truth value; for this would alter our second thought and thereby might well alter its truth value.

The situation is similar in the sentence

If iron were less dense than water, it would float on water.

Here we have the two thoughts that iron is not less dense than water, and that something floats on water if it is less dense than water. The subsidiary clause again expresses one thought and a part of the other.

If we interpret the sentence already considered

After Schleswig-Holstein was separated from Denmark, Prussia and Austria quarrelled

in such a way that it expresses the thought that Schleswig-Holstein was once separated from Denmark, we have first this thought, and secondly the thought that at a time, more closely determined by the subordinate clause, Prussia and Austria quarrelled. Here also the subordinate clause expresses not only one thought but also a part of another. Therefore it may not in general be replaced by another of the same truth value.

It is hard to exhaust all the possibilities given by language; but I hope to have brought to light at least the essential reasons why a subordinate clause may not always be replaced by another of equal truth value without harm to the truth of the whole sentence structure. These reasons arise:

(1)   when the subordinate clause does not stand for a truth value, inasmuch as it expresses only a part of a thought;
(2)   when the subordinate clause does stand for a truth value but is not restricted to so doing, inasmuch as its sense includes one thought and part of another.

The first case arises:

(a)   in indirect reference of words
(b)   if a part of the sentence is only an indefinite indicator instead of a proper name.

In the second case, the subsidiary clause may have to be taken twice over, viz. once in its customary reference, and the other time in indirect reference; or the sense of a part of the subordinate clause may likewise be a component of another thought, which, taken together with the thought directly expressed by the subordinate clause, makes up the sense of the whole sentence.

It follows with sufficient probability from the foregoing that the cases where a subordinate clause is not replaceable by another of the same value cannot be brought in disproof of our view that a truth value is the reference of a sentence having a thought as its sense.

Let us return to our starting point.

When we found '$a = a$' and '$a = b$' to have different cognitive values, the explanation is that for the purpose of knowledge, the sense of the sentence, viz., the thought expressed by it, is no less relevant than its reference, i.e. its truth value. If now $a = b$, then indeed the reference of 'b' is the same as that of 'a,' and hence the truth value of '$a = b$' is the same as that of '$a = a$.' In spite of this, the sense of 'b' may differ from that of 'a', and thereby the thought expressed in '$a = b$' differs from that of '$a = a$.' In that case the two sentences do not have the same cognitive value. If we understand by 'judgment' the advance from the thought to its truth value, as in the above paper, we can also say that the judgments are different.

Translator's Notes

1   The reference is to Frege's *Begriffsschrift, eine der arithmetischen nachgebildete Formelsprache des reinen Denkens* (Halle, 1879).
2   See his 'Über Begriff und Gegenstand' (*Vierteljahrsschrift für wissenschaftliche Philosophie* XVI [1892], 192–205).
3   See his 'Über Begriff und Gegenstand' (*Vierteljahrsschrift für wissenschaftliche Philosophie* XVI [1892], 192–205).
4   A literal translation of Frege's 'abstracten Nennsätzen' whose meaning eludes me.
5   Frege uses the Prussian name for the battle – 'Belle Alliance.'

2

From *Naming and Necessity*

Saul A. Kripke

Lecture I: January 20, 1970

...What's the difference between asking whether it's necessary that 9 is greater than 7 or whether it's necessary that the number of planets is greater than 7?...The answer to this might be intuitively 'Well, look, the number of planets might have been different from what it in fact is. It doesn't make any sense, though, to say that nine might have been different from what it in fact is'. Let's use some terms quasi-technically. Let's call something a *rigid designator* if in every possible world it designates the same object, a *nonrigid* or *accidental designator* if that is not the case. Of course we don't require that the objects exist in all possible worlds. Certainly Nixon might not have existed if his parents had not gotten married, in the normal course of things. When we think of a property as essential to an object we usually mean that it is true of that object in any case where it would have existed. A rigid designator of a necessary existent can be called *strongly rigid*.

One of the intuitive theses I will maintain in these talks is that *names* are rigid designators. Certainly they seem to satisfy the intuitive test mentioned above: although someone other than the US President in 1970 might have been the US President in 1970 (e.g., Humphrey might have), no one other than Nixon might have been Nixon. In the same way, a designator rigidly designates a certain object if it designates that object wherever the object exists; if, in addition, the object is a necessary existent, the designator can be called *strongly rigid*. For example, 'the President of the US in 1970' designates a certain man, Nixon; but someone else (e.g., Humphrey) might have been the President in 1970, and Nixon might not have; so this designator is not rigid.

In these lectures, I will argue, intuitively, that proper names are rigid designators, for although the man (Nixon) might not have been the President, it is not the case that he might not have been Nixon (though he might not have been *called* 'Nixon')....

Above I said that the Frege – Russell view that names are introduced by description could be taken either as a theory of the meaning of names (Frege and Russell seemed to take it this way) or merely as a theory of their reference. Let me give an example, not involving what would usually be called a 'proper name,' to illustrate this. Suppose someone stipulates that 100 degrees centigrade is to be the temperature at which water boils at sea level. This isn't completely precise because the pressure may vary at sea level. Of course, historically, a more precise definition was given later. But let's suppose that this were the definition. Another sort of example in the literature is that one meter is to be the length of *S* where *S* is a certain stick or bar in Paris. (Usually people who like to talk about these definitions then try to make 'the length of' into an 'operational' concept. But it's not important.)

Wittgenstein says something very puzzling about this. He says: 'There is one thing of which one can say neither that it is one meter long nor that it is not one meter long, and that is the standard meter in Paris. But this is, of course, not to ascribe any extraordinary property to it, but only to mark its peculiar role in the language game of measuring with a meter rule.'[1] This seems to be a very 'extraordinary property', actually, for any stick to have. I think he must be wrong. If the stick is a stick, for example, 39.37 inches long (I assume we have some different standard for inches), why isn't it one meter long? Anyway, let's suppose that he is wrong and that the stick is one meter long. Part of the problem which is bothering Wittgenstein is, of course, that this stick serves as a standard of length and so we can't attribute length to it. Be this as it may (well, it may not be) is the statement 'stick *S* is one meter long', a necessary truth? Of course its length might vary in time. We could make the definition more precise by stipulating that one meter is to be the length of *S* at a fixed time t_0. Is it then a necessary truth that stick *S* is one meter long at time t_0? Someone who thinks that everything one knows *a priori* is necessary might think: 'This is the *definition* of a meter. By definition, stick *S* is one meter long at t_0. That's a necessary truth.' But there seems to me to be no reason so to conclude, even for a man who uses the stated definition of 'one meter'. For he's using this definition not to *give the meaning* of what he called the 'meter', but to *fix the reference*. (For such an abstract thing as a unit of length, the notion of reference may be unclear. But let's suppose it's clear enough for the present purposes.) He uses it to fix a reference. There is a certain length which he wants to mark out. He marks it out by an accidental property, namely that there is a stick of that length. Someone else might mark out the same reference by another accidental property. But in any case, even though he uses this to fix the reference of his standard of length, a meter, he can still say, 'if heat had been applied to this stick S at t_0, then at t_0 stick S would not have been one meter long.'

Well, why can he do this? Part of the reason may lie in some people's minds in the philosophy of science, which I don't want to go into here. But a simple answer to the question is this: Even if this is the *only* standard of length that he uses,[2] there is an intuitive difference between the phrase 'one meter' and the phrase 'the length of S at t_0'. The first phrase is meant to designate rigidly a certain length in all possible worlds, which in the actual world happens to be the length of the stick S at t_0. On the other hand 'the length of S at t_0' does not designate anything rigidly. In some counterfactual situations the stick might have been longer and in some shorter, if various stresses and strains had been applied to it. So we can say of this stick, the same way as we would of any other of the same substance and length, that if heat of a given quantity had been applied to it, it would have expanded to such and such a length. Such a counterfactual statement, being true of other sticks with identical physical properties, will also be true of this stick. There is no conflict between that counterfactual statement and the definition of 'one meter' as 'the length of S at t_0', because the 'definition', properly interpreted, does *not* say that the phrase 'one meter' is to be *synonymous* (even when talking about counterfactual situations) with the phrase 'the length of S at t_0', but rather that we have *determined the reference* of the phrase 'one meter' by stipulating that 'one meter' is to be a *rigid* designator of the length which is in fact the length of S at t_0. So this does *not* make it a necessary truth that S is one meter long at t_0. In fact, under certain circumstances, S would not have been one meter long. The reason is that one designator ('one meter') is rigid and the other designator ('the length of S at t_0') is not.

What then, is the *epistemological* status of the statement 'Stick S is one meter long at t_0', for someone who has fixed the metric system by reference to stick S? It would seem that he knows it *a priori*. For if he used stick S to fix the reference of the term 'one meter', then as a result of this kind of 'definition' (which is not an abbreviative or synonymous definition), he knows automatically, without further investigation, that S is one meter long. On the other hand, even if S is used as the standard of a meter, the *metaphysical* status of 'S is one meter long' will be that of a contingent statement, provided that 'one meter' is regarded as a rigid designator: under appropriate stresses and strains, heatings or coolings, S would have had a length other than one meter even at t_0. (Such statements as 'Water boils at 100°C at sea level' can have a similar status.) So in this sense, there are contingent *a priori* truths. More important for present purposes, though, than accepting this example as an instance of the contingent *a priori*, is its illustration of the distinction between 'definitions' which fix a reference and those which give a synonym.

In the case of names one might make this distinction too. Suppose the reference of a name is given by a description or a cluster of descriptions. If the name *means the same* as that description or cluster of descriptions, it will not be a rigid designator. It will not necessarily designate the same object in all possible worlds, since other objects might have had the given properties in other possible worlds, unless (of course) we happened to use essential properties in our description. So suppose we say, 'Aristotle is the greatest man who studied with Plato'. If we used that as a *definition*, the name 'Aristotle' is to mean 'the greatest man who studied with Plato'. then of course in some other possible world that man might not have studied with Plato and some other man would have been Aristotle. If, on the other hand, we merely use the description to *fix the referent* then that man will be the referent of 'Aristotle' in all possible worlds. The only use of the description will have been to pick out to which man we mean to refer. But then, when we say counterfactually 'suppose Aristotle had never gone into philosophy at all', we need not mean 'suppose a man who studied with Plato, and taught Alexander the Great, and wrote this and that, and so on, had never gone into philosophy at all', which might seem like a contradiction. We need only mean, 'suppose that *that man* had never gone into philosophy at all'.

It seems plausible to suppose that, in some cases, the reference of a name is indeed fixed *via* a description in the same way that the metric system was fixed. When the mythical agent first saw Hesperus, he may well have fixed his reference by saying, 'I shall use "Hesperus" as a name of the heavenly body appearing in yonder position in the sky.' He then fixed the reference of 'Hesperus' by its apparent celestial position. Does it follow that it is part of the *meaning* of the name that Hesperus has such and such position at the time in question? Surely not: if Hesperus had been hit earlier by a comet, it might have been visible at a different position at that time. In such a counterfactual situation we would say that Hesperus would not have occupied that position, but not that Hesperus would not have been Hesperus. The reason is that 'Hesperus' rigidly designates a certain heavenly body and 'the body in yonder position' does not—a different body, or no body might have been in that position, but no other body might have been Hesperus (though another body, not Hesperus, might have been *called* 'Hesperus'). Indeed, as I have said, I will hold that names are always rigid designators.

Frege and Russell certainly seem to have the full blown theory according to which a proper name is not a rigid designator and is synonymous with the description which replaced it. But another theory might be that this description is used to determine a rigid reference. These two alternatives will have different consequences for the questions I was asking before. If 'Moses' *means* 'the man who did such and such', then, if no one did such and such, Moses didn't exist; and maybe 'no one did such and such' is even an *analysis* of 'Moses didn't exist'. But if the description is used to fix a reference rigidly, then it's clear that that is *not* what is meant by 'Moses didn't exist', because we can ask, if we speak of a counterfactual case where no one did indeed do such and such, say, lead the Israelites out of Egypt, does it follow that, in such a situation, Moses wouldn't have existed? It would seem not. For surely Moses might have just decided to spend his days more pleasantly in the Egyptian courts. He might never have gone into either politics or religion at all; and in that case maybe no one would have done any of the things that the Bible relates of Moses. That doesn't in itself mean that in such a possible world Moses wouldn't have existed. If so, then 'Moses exists' means something different from 'the existence and uniqueness conditions for a certain description are fulfilled'; and therefore this does not give an analysis of the singular existential statement after all. If you give up the idea that this is a theory of meaning and make it into a theory of reference in the way that I have described, you give up some of the advantages of the theory. Singular existential statements and identity statements be-tween names need some other analysis.

Frege should be criticized for using the term 'sense' in two senses. For he takes the sense of a designator to be its meaning; and he also takes it to be the way its reference is determined. Identifying the two, he supposes that both are given by definite descriptions. Ultimately, I will reject this second supposition too; but even were it right, I reject the first. A descrip-tion may be used as synonymous with a designator, or it may be used to fix its reference. The two Fregean senses of 'sense' correspond to two senses of 'definition' in ordinary parlance. They should carefully be distinguished.

I hope the idea of fixing the reference as opposed to actually defining one term as meaning the other is somewhat clear. There is really not enough time to go into everything in great detail. I think, even in cases where the notion of rigidity versus accidentality of designation cannot be used to make out the difference in question, some things called definitions really intend to fix a reference rather than to give the meaning of a phrase, to give a synonym. Let me give an example. π is supposed to be the ratio of the circumference of a circle to its diameter. Now, it's something that I have nothing but a vague intuitive feeling to argue for: It seems to me that here this Greek letter is not being used as *short for* the phrase 'the ratio of the circumference of a circle to its diameter' nor is it even used as short for a cluster of alternative definitions of π, whatever that might mean. It is used as a *name* for a real number, which in this case is necessarily the ratio of the circumference of a circle to its diameter. Note that here both 'π' and 'the ratio of the circumference of a circle to its diameter' are rigid designators, so the arguments given in the metric case are inapplicable. (Well, if someone doesn't see this, or thinks it's wrong, it doesn't matter.)

Let me return to the question about names which I raised.... [T]here is a popular modern substitute for the theory of Frege and Russell; it is adopted even by such a strong critic of many views of Frege and Russell, especially the latter, as Strawson.[3] The substitute is that, although a name is not a disguised description it either abbreviates, or anyway its reference is determined by, some cluster of descriptions. The question is whether this is true.... [T]here are stronger and weaker versions of this. The stronger version would say that the name is simply *defined*, synonymously, as the cluster of descriptions. It will then be necessary, not that Moses had any particular property in this cluster, but that he had the disjunction of them. There couldn't be any counterfactual situation in which he didn't do any of those things. I think it's clear that this is very implausible. People *have* said it – or may be they haven't been intending to say that, but were using 'necessary' in some other sense. At any rate, for example, in Searle's article on proper names:

> To put the same point differently, suppose we ask, 'why do we have proper names at all?' Obviously to refer to individuals. 'Yes but descriptions could do that for us'. But only at the cost of specifying identity conditions every time reference is made: Suppose we agree to drop 'Aristotle' and use, say, 'the teacher of Alexander', then it is a necessary truth that the man referred to is Alexander's teacher – but it is a contingent fact that Aristotle ever went into pedagogy (though I am suggesting that it is a necessary fact that Aristotle has the logical sum, inclusive disjunction, of properties commonly attributed to him).[4]

Such a suggestion, if 'necessary' is used in the way I have been using it in this lecture, must clearly be false. (Unless he's got some very interesting essential property commonly attributed to Aristotle.) Most of the things commonly attributed to Aristotle are things that Aristotle might not have done at all. In a situation in which he didn't do them, we would describe that as a situation in which *Aristotle* didn't do them. This is not a distinction of scope, as happens sometimes in the case of descriptions, where someone might say that the man who taught Alexander might not have taught Alexander; though it could not have been true that: the man who taught Alexander didn't teach Alexander. This is Russell's distinction of scope. (I won't go into it.) It seems to me clear that this is not the case here. Not only is it true *of* the man Aristotle that he might not have gone into pedagogy; it is also true that we use the term 'Aristotle' in such a way that, in thinking of a counterfactual situation in which Aristotle didn't go into any of the fields and do any of the achievements we commonly attribute to him, still we would say that was a situation in which *Aristotle* did not do these things. Well there are some things like the date, the period he lived in, that might be more imagined as necessary. Maybe those are things we commonly attribute to him. There are exceptions. Maybe it's hard to imagine how he could have lived 500 years later than he in fact did. That certainly raises at least a problem. But take a man who doesn't have any idea of the date. Many people just have some vague cluster of his most famous achievements. Not only each of these singly, but the possession of the entire disjunction of these properties, is just a contingent fact about Aristotle; and the statement that Aristotle had this disjunction of properties is a contingent truth.

A man might know it *a priori* in some sense, if he in fact fixes the reference of 'Aristotle' as the man who did one of these things. Still it won't be a necessary truth for him. So this sort of example would be an example where a prioricity would not necessarily imply necessity, if the cluster theory of names were right. The case of fixing the reference of 'one meter' is a very clear example in which someone, just because he fixed the reference in this way, can in some sense know *a priori* that the length of this stick is a meter without regarding it as a necessary truth. Maybe the thesis about a prioricity implying necessity can be modified. It does appear to state some insight which might be important, and true, about epistemology. In a way an example like this may seem like a trivial counterexample which is not really the point of what some people think when they think that only necessary truths can be known *a priori*. Well, if the thesis that all *a priori* truth is necessary is to be immune from this sort of counterexample, it needs to be modified in some way. Unmodified it leads to confusion about the nature of reference. And I myself have no idea how it should be modified or restated, or if such a modification or restatement is possible.

...

Lecture III: January 29, 1970

...

[A]n identity statement between names, when true at all, is necessarily true, even though one may not know it *a priori*. Suppose we identify Hesperus as a certain star seen in the evening and Phosphorus as a certain star, or a certain heavenly body, seen in the morning; then there may be possible worlds in which two different planets would have been seen in just those positions in the evening and morning. However, at least one of them, and maybe both, would not have been Hesperus, and then that would not have been a situation in which Hesperus was not Phosphorus. It might have been a situation in which the planet seen in this position in the evening was not the planet seen in this position in the morning; but that is not a situation in which Hesperus was not Phosphorus. It might also, if people gave the names 'Hesperus' and 'Phosphorus' to these planets, be a situation in which some planet other than Hesperus was called 'Hesperus'. But even so, it would not be a situation in which Hesperus itself was not Phosphorus.[5]

Some of the problems which bother people in these situations, as I have said, come from an identification, or as I would put it, a confusion, between what we can know *a priori* in advance and what is necessary. Certain statements – and the identity statement is a paradigm of such a statement on my view – if true at all must be necessarily true. One does know *a priori*, by philosophical analysis, that *if* such an identity statement is true it is necessarily true....

...I want to go on to the more general case, which I mentioned in the last lecture, of some identities between terms for substances, and also the properties of substances and of natural kinds. Philosophers have, as I've said, been very interested in statements expressing theoretical identifications; among them, that light is a stream of photons, that water is H_2O, that lightning is an electrical discharge, that gold is the element with the atomic number 79.

To get clear about the status of these statements we must first maybe have some thoughts about the status of such substances as gold. What's gold? I don't know if this is an example which has particularly interested philosophers. Its interest in financial circles is diminishing because of increased stability of currencies. Even so gold has interested many people. Here is what Immanuel Kant says about gold. (He was a wealthy speculator who kept his possessions under his bed.) Kant is introducing the distinction between analytic and synthetic judgements, and he says: 'All analytic judgements depend wholly on the law of contradiction, and are in their nature *a priori* cognitions, whether the concepts that supply them with matter be empirical or not. For the predicate of an affirmative analytic judgement is already contained in the concept of the subject, of which it cannot be denied without contradiction.... For this very reason all analytic judgements are *a priori* even when the concepts are empirical, as, for example, "Gold is a yellow metal"; for to know this I require no experience beyond my concept of gold as a yellow metal. It is, in fact, the very concept, and I need only analyze it without looking beyond it.'[6] I should have looked at the German. 'It is in fact the very concept' sounds as if Kant is saying here that 'gold' just *means* 'yellow metal'. If he says that, then it's especially strange, so let's suppose that that is not what he's saying. At least Kant thinks it's a *part* of the concept that gold is to be a yellow metal. He thinks we know this *a priori*, and that we could not possibly discover this to be empirically false.

Is Kant right about this? First, what I would have wanted to do would have been to discuss the part about gold being a metal. This, however, is complicated because first, I don't know too much chemistry. Investigating this a few days ago in just a couple of references, I found in a more phenomenological account of metals the statement that it's very difficult to say what a metal is. (It talks about malleability, ductility, and the like, but none of these exactly work.) On the other hand, something about the periodic table gave a description of elements as metals in terms of their valency properties. This may make some people think right away that there are really two concepts of metal operating here, a phenomenological one and a scientific one which then replaces it. This I reject, but since the move will tempt many, and can be refuted only after I develop my own views, it will not be suitable to use 'Gold is a metal' as an example to introduce these views.

But let's consider something easier—the question of the yellowness of gold. Could we discover that gold was not in fact yellow? Suppose an optical illusion were prevalent, due to peculiar properties of the atmosphere in South Africa and Russia and certain other areas where gold mines are common. Suppose there were an optical illusion which made the substance appear to be yellow; but, in fact, once the peculiar proper-ties of the atmosphere were removed, we would see that it is actually blue. Maybe a demon even corrupted the vision of all those entering the gold mines (obviously their *souls* were already corrupt), and thus made them believe that this substance was yellow, though it is not. Would there on this basis be an announcement in the newspapers: 'It has turned out that there is no gold. Gold does not exist. What we took to be gold is not in fact gold.'? Just imagine the world financial crisis under these condi-tions! Here we have an undreamt of source of shakiness in the monetary system.

It seems to me that there would be no such announcement. On the contrary, what would be announced would be that though it appeared that gold was yellow, in fact gold has turned out not to be yellow, but blue. The reason is, I think, that we use 'gold' as a term for a certain *kind* of thing. Others have discovered this kind of thing and we have heard of it. We thus as part of a community of speakers have a certain connection between ourselves and a certain kind of thing. The kind of thing is *thought* to have certain identifying marks. Some of these marks may not really be true of gold. We might discover that we are wrong about them. Further, there might be a substance which has all the identifying marks we commonly attributed to gold and used to identify it in the first place, but which is not the same kind of thing, which is not the same substance. We would say of such a thing that though it has all the appearances we initially used to identify gold, it is not gold. Such a thing is, for example, as we well know, iron pyrites or fool's gold. This is not another kind of gold. It's a completely different thing which to the uninitiated person looks just like the substance which we discovered and called gold. We can say this not because we have changed the *meaning* of the term gold, and thrown in some other criteria which distinguished gold from pyrites. It seems to me that that's not true. On the contrary, we *discovered* that certain properties were true of gold in addition to the initial identi-fying marks by which we identified it. These properties, then, being characteristic of gold and not true of iron pyrites, show that the fool's gold is not in fact gold.

. . .

So far I've only been talking about what we could find out. I've been saying we could find out that gold was not in fact yellow, contrary to what we thought. If one went in more detail into the concept of metals, let's say in terms of valency properties, one could certainly find out that though one took gold to be a metal, gold is not in fact a metal. Is it necessary or contingent that gold be a metal? I don't want to go into detail on the concept of a metal – as I said, I don't know enough about it. Gold apparently has the atomic number 79. Is it a necessary or a contingent property of gold that it has the atomic number 79? Certainly we could find out that we were mistaken. The whole theory of protons, of atomic numbers, the whole theory of molecular structure and of atomic structure, on which such views are based, could *all* turn out to be false. Certainly we didn't know it from time immemorial. So in that sense, gold could turn out not to have atomic number 79.

Given that gold *does* have the atomic number 79, could something be gold without having the atomic number 79? Let us suppose the scientists have investigated the nature of gold and have found that it is part of the very nature of this substance, so to speak, that it have the atomic number 79. Suppose we now find some other yellow metal, or some other yellow thing, with all the properties by which we originally identified gold, and many of the additional ones that we have discovered later. An example of one with many of the initial properties is iron pyrites, 'fool's gold.' As I have said, we wouldn't say that this substance is gold. So far we are speaking of the actual world. Now consider a possible world. Consider a counterfactual situation in which, let us say, fool's gold or iron pyrites was actually found in various mountains in the United States, or in areas of South Africa and the Soviet Union. Suppose that all the areas which actually contain gold now, contained pyrites instead, or some other substance which counterfeited the superficial properties of gold but lacked its atomic structure.[7] Would we say, of this counterfactual situation, that in that situation gold would not even have been an element (because pyrites is not an element)? It seems to me that we would not. We would instead describe this as a situation in which a substance, say iron pyrites, which is not gold, would have been found in the very mountains which actually contain gold and would have had the very properties by which we commonly identify gold. But it would not be gold; it would be something else. One should *not* say that it would still be gold in this possible world, though gold would then lack the atomic number 79. It would be some other stuff, some other substance. (Once again, whether people counterfactually would have *called* it 'gold' is irrelevant. *We* do not describe it as gold.) And so, it seems to me, this would not be a case in which possibly gold might not have been an element, nor can there be such a case (except in the epistemic sense of 'possible'). Given that gold *is* this element, any other substance, even though it looks like gold and is found in the very places where we in fact find gold, would not be gold. It would be some other substance which was a counterfeit for gold. In any counterfactual situation where the same geographical areas were filled with such a substance, they would not have been filled with gold. They would have been filled with something else.

So if this consideration is right, it tends to show that such statements representing scientific discoveries about what this stuff *is* are not contingent truths but necessary truths in the strictest possible sense. It's not just that it's a scientific law, but of course we can imagine a world in which it would fail. Any world in which we imagine a substance which does not have these properties is a world in which we imagine a substance which is not gold, provided these properties form the basis of what the substance is. In particular, then, present scientific theory is such that it is part of the nature of gold as we have it to be an element with atomic number 79. It will therefore be necessary and not contingent that gold be an element with atomic number 79. (We may also in the same way, then, investigate further how color and metallic properties follow from what we have found the substance gold to be: to the extent that such properties follow from the atomic structure of gold, they are necessary properties of it, even though they unquestionably are not part of the *meaning* of 'gold' and were not known with *a priori* certainty.)

. . .

Notes

1 Ludwig Wittgenstein, *Philosophical Investigations*, translated by G. E. M. Anscombe, Macmillan, 1953, § 50.
2 Philosophers of science may see the key to the problem in a view that 'one meter' is a 'cluster concept'. I am asking the reader hypothetically to suppose that the 'definition' given is the *only* standard used to determine the metric system. I think the problem would still arise.
3 P. F. Strawson, *Individuals*, Methuen, London, 1959, Ch. 6.
4 John R. Searle, 'Proper Names', in Caton (ed.), *Philosophy and Ordinary Language*, University of Illinois Press, Urbana, 1963, p. 160.
5 Recall that we describe the situation in our language, not the language that the people in that situation would have used. Hence we must use the terms 'Hesperus' and 'Phosphorus' with the same reference as in the actual world. The fact that people in that situation might or might not have used these names for different planets is irrelevant. So is the fact that they might have done so using the very same descriptions as we did to fix their references.
6 *Prolegomena to Any Future Metaphysics*, Preamble Section 2.b. (Prussian Academy edition, p. 267). My impression of the passage was not changed by a

subsequent cursory look at the German, though I can hardly lay claim to any real competence here.

7   Even better pairs of ringers exist; for example, some pairs of elements of a single column in the periodic table which resemble each other closely but nevertheless are different elements.

3

Meaning and Reference[*]

Hilary Putnam

Unclear as it is, the traditional doctrine that the notion "meaning" possesses the extension/intension ambiguity has certain typical consequences. The doctrine that the meaning of a term is a concept carried the implication that meanings are mental entities. Frege, however, rebelled against this "psychologism." Feeling that meanings are *public* property – that the *same* meaning can be "grasped" by more than one person and by persons at different times – he identified concepts (and hence "intensions" or meanings) with abstract entities rather than mental entities. However, "grasping" these abstract entities was still an individual psychological act. None of these philosophers doubted that understanding a word (knowing its intension) was just a matter of being in a certain psychological state (somewhat in the way in which knowing how to factor numbers in one's head is just a matter of being in a certain very complex psychological state).

Secondly, the timeworn example of the two terms 'creature with a kidney' and 'creature with a heart' does show that two terms can have the same extension and yet differ in intension. But it was taken to be obvious that the reverse is impossible: two terms cannot differ in extension and have the same intension. Interestingly, no argument for this impossibility was ever offered. Probably it reflects the tradition of the ancient and medieval philosophers, who assumed that the concept corresponding to a term was just a conjunction of predicates, and hence that the concept corresponding to a term must *always* provide a necessary and sufficient condition for falling into the extension of the term. For philosophers like Carnap, who accepted the verifiability theory of meaning, the concept corresponding to a term provided (in the ideal case, where the term had "complete meaning") a *criterion* for belonging to the extension (not just in the sense of "necessary and sufficient condition," but in the strong sense of *way of recognizing* whether a given thing falls into the extension or not). So theory of meaning came to rest on two unchallenged assumptions:

1　That knowing the meaning of a term is just a matter of being in a certain psychological state (in the sense of "psychological state," in which states of memory and belief are "psychological states"; no one thought that knowing the meaning of a word was a continuous state of consciousness, of course).

2　That the meaning of a term determines its extension (in the sense that sameness of intension entails sameness of extension).

I shall argue that these two assumptions are not jointly satisfied by *any* notion, let alone any notion of meaning. The traditional concept of meaning is a concept which rests on a false theory.

Are meanings in the head?

For the purpose of the following science-fiction examples, we shall suppose that somewhere there is a planet we shall call Twin Earth. Twin Earth is very much like Earth: in fact, people on Twin Earth even speak *English*. In fact, apart from the differences we shall specify in our science-fiction examples, the reader may suppose that Twin Earth is *exactly* like Earth. He may even suppose that he has a *Doppelganger* – an identical copy – on Twin Earth, if he wishes, although my stories will not depend on this.

Although some of the people on Twin Earth (say, those who call themselves "Americans" and those who call themselves "Canadians" and those who call themselves "Englishmen," etc.) speak English, there are, not surprisingly, a few tiny differences between the dialects of English spoken on Twin Earth and standard English.

One of the peculiarities of Twin Earth is that the liquid called "water" is not H_2O but a different liquid whose chemical formula is very long and complicated. I shall abbreviate this chemical formula simply as XYZ. I shall suppose that XYZ is indistinguishable from water at normal temperatures and pressures. Also, I shall suppose that the oceans and lakes and seas of Twin Earth contain XYZ and not water, that it rains XYZ on Twin Earth and not water, etc.

If a space ship from Earth ever visits Twin Earth, then the supposition at first will be that 'water' has the same meaning on Earth and on Twin Earth. This supposition will be corrected when it is discovered that "water" on Twin Earth is XYZ, and the Earthian space ship will report somewhat as follows.

"On Twin Earth the word 'water' means XYZ."

Symmetrically, if a space ship from Twin Earth ever visits Earth, then the supposition at first will be that the word 'water' has the same meaning on Twin Earth and on Earth. This supposition will be corrected when it is discovered that "water" on Earth is H_2O, and the Twin Earthian space ship will report:

"On Earth the word 'water' means H_2O."

Note that there is no problem about the extension of the term 'water': the word simply has two different meanings (as we say); in the sense in which it is used on Twin Earth, the sense of water$_{TE}$, what *we* call "water" simply isn't water, while in the sense in which it is used on Earth, the sense of water$_E$, what the Twin Earthians call "water" simple isn't water. The extension of 'water' in the sense of water$_E$ is the set of all wholes consisting of H_2O molecules, or something like that; the extension of water in the sense of water$_{TE}$ is the set of all wholes consisting of XYZ molecules, or something like that.

Now let us roll the time back to about 1750. The typical Earthian speaker of English did not know that water consisted of hydrogen and oxygen, and the typical Twin-Earthian speaker of English did not know that "water" consisted of XYZ. Let Oscar$_1$ be such a typical Earthian English speaker, and let Oscar$_2$ be his counterpart on Twin Earth. You may suppose that there is no belief that Oscar$_1$ had about water that Oscar$_2$ did not have about "water." If you like, you may even suppose that Oscar$_1$ and Oscar$_2$ were exact duplicates in appearance, feelings, thoughts, interior monologue, etc. Yet the extension of the term 'water' was just as much H_2O on Earth in 1750 as in 1950; and the extension of the term 'water' was just as much XYZ on Twin Earth in 1750 as in 1950. Oscar$_1$ and Oscar$_2$ understood the term 'water' differently in 1750 *although they were in the same psychological state*, and although, given the state of science at the time, it would have taken their scientific communities about fifty years to discover that they understood the term 'water' differently. Thus the extension of the term 'water' (and, in fact, its "meaning" in the intuitive preanalytical usage of that term) is *not* a function of the psychological state of the speaker by itself.[1]

But, it might be objected, why should we accept it that the term 'water' had the same extension in 1750 and in 1950 (on both Earths)? Suppose I point to a glass of water and say "this liquid is called water." My "ostensive definition" of water has the following empirical presupposition: that the body of liquid I am pointing to bears a certain sameness relation (say, x *is the same liquid as* y, or x *is the* same$_L$ *as* y) to most of the stuff I and other speakers in my linguistic community have on other occasions called "water." If this presupposition is false because, say, I am – unknown to me – pointing to a glass of gin and not a glass of water, then I do not intend my ostensive definition to be accepted. Thus the ostensive definition conveys what might be called a "defeasible" necessary and sufficient condition: the necessary and sufficient condition for being water is bearing the relation same$_L$ to the stuff in the glass; but this is the necessary and sufficient condition only if the empirical presupposition is satisfied. If it is not satisfied, then one of a series of, so to speak, "fallback" conditions becomes activated.

The key point is that the relation same$_L$ is a *theoretical* relation: whether something is or is not the same liquid as *this* may take an indeterminate amount of scientific investigation to determine. Thus, the fact that an English speaker in 1750 might have called XYZ "water," whereas he or his successors would not have called XYZ water in 1800 or 1850 does not mean that the "meaning" of 'water' changed for the average speaker in the interval. In 1750 or in 1850 or in 1950 one might have pointed to, say, the liquid in Lake Michigan as an example of "water." What changed was that in 1750 we would have mistakenly thought that XYZ bore the relation same$_L$ to the liquid in Lake Michigan, whereas in 1800 or 1850 we would have known that it did not.

Let us now modify our science-fiction story. I shall suppose that molybdenum pots and pans *can't* be distinguished from aluminum pots and pans save by an expert. (This could be true for all I know, and, *a fortiori*, it could be true for all I know by virtue of "knowing the meaning" of the words *aluminum* and *molybdenum*.) We will now suppose that molybdenum is as common on Twin Earth as aluminum is on Earth, and that aluminum is as rare on Twin Earth as molybdenum is on Earth. In particular, we shall assume that "aluminum" pots and pans are made of molybdenum on Twin Earth. Finally, we shall assume that the words 'aluminum' and 'molybdenum' are *switched* on Twin Earth: 'aluminum' is the name of *molybdenum*, and 'molybdenum' is the name of *aluminum*. If a space ship from Earth visited Twin Earth, the visitors from Earth probably would not suspect that the "aluminum" pots and pans on Twin Earth were not made of aluminum, especially when the Twin Earthians *said* they were. But there is one important difference between the two cases. An Earthian metallurgist could tell very easily that "aluminum" was molybdenum, and a Twin Earthian metallurgist could tell equally easily that aluminum was "molybdenum." (The shudder quotes in the preceding sentence indicate Twin Earthian usages.) Whereas in 1750 no one on either Earth or Twin Earth could have distinguished water from "water," the confusion of aluminum with "aluminum" involves only a part of the linguistic communities involved.

This example makes the same point as the preceding example. If Oscar$_1$ and Oscar$_2$ are standard speakers of Earthian English and Twin Earthian English, respectively, and neither is chemically or metallurgically sophisticated, then there may be no difference at all in their psychological states when they use the word 'aluminum'; nevertheless, we have to say that 'aluminum' has the extension *aluminum* in the idiolect of Oscar$_1$ and the extension *molybdenum* in the idiolect of Oscar$_2$. (Also we have to say that Oscar$_1$ and Oscar$_2$ mean different things by 'aluminum'; that 'aluminum' has a different meaning on Earth than it does on Twin Earth, etc.) Again we see that the psychological state of the speaker does *not* determine the extension (*or* the "meaning," speaking preanalytically) of the word.

Before discussing this example further, let me introduce a *non-*science-fiction example. Suppose you are like me and cannot tell an elm from a beech tree. We still say that the extension of 'elm' in my idiolect is the same as the extension of 'elm' in anyone else's, viz., the set of all elm trees, and that the set of all beech trees is the extension of 'beech' in *both* of our idiolects. Thus 'elm' in my idiolect has a different extension from 'beech' in your idiolect (as it should). Is it really credible that this difference in extension is brought about by some difference in our *concepts*? My *concept* of an elm tree is exactly the same as my concept of a beech tree (I blush to confess). If someone heroically attempts to maintain that the difference between the extension of 'elm' and the extension of 'beech' in *my* idiolect is explained by a difference in my psychological state, then we can always refute him by constructing a "Twin Earth" example – just let the words 'elm' and 'beech' be switched on Twin Earth (the way 'aluminum' and 'molybdenum' were in the previous example). Moreover, suppose I have a *Doppelganger* on Twin Earth who is molecule for molecule "identical" with me. If you are a dualist, then also suppose my Doppelganger thinks the same verbalized thoughts I do, has the same sense data, the same dispositions, etc. It is absurd to think *his* psychological state is one bit different from mine: yet he "means" *beech* when he says "elm," and I "mean" *elm* when I say "elm." Cut the pie any way you like, "meanings" just ain't in the *head*!

A sociolinguistic hypothesis

The last two examples depend upon a fact about language that seems, surprisingly, never to have been pointed out: that there is *division of linguistic labor*. We could hardly use such words as 'elm' and 'aluminum' if no one possessed a way of recognizing elm trees and aluminum metal; but not everyone to whom the distinction is important has to be able to make the distinction. Let us shift the example; consider *gold*. Gold is important for many reasons: it is a precious metal; it is a monetary metal; it has symbolic value (it is important to most people that the "gold" wedding ring they wear *really* consist of gold and not just *look* gold); etc. Consider our community as a "factory": in this "factory" some people have the "job" of *wearing gold wedding rings*; other people have the "job" of selling gold wedding rings; still other people have the job of *telling whether or not something is really gold*. It is not at all necessary or efficient that every one who wears a gold ring (or a gold cufflink, etc.), or discusses the "gold standard," etc., engage in buying and selling gold. Nor is it necessary or efficient that every one who buys and sells gold be able to tell whether or not something is really gold in a society where this form of dishonesty is uncommon (selling fake gold) and in which one can easily consult an expert in case of doubt. And it is *certainly* not necessary or efficient that every one who has occasion to buy or wear gold be able to tell with any reliability whether or not something is really gold.

The foregoing facts are just examples of mundane division of labor (in a wide sense). But they engender a division of linguistic labor: every one to whom gold is important for any reason has to *acquire* the word 'gold'; but he does not have to acquire the *method of recognizing* whether something is or is not gold. He can rely on a special subclass of speakers. The features that are generally thought to be present in connection with a general name – necessary and sufficient conditions for membership in the extension, ways of recognizing whether something is in the extension, etc. – are all present in the linguistic community *considered as a collective body*; but that collective body divides the "labor" of knowing and employing these various parts of the "meaning" of 'gold'.

This division of linguistic labor rests upon and presupposes the division of *non*linguistic labor, of course. If only the people who know how to tell whether some metal is really gold or not have any reason to have the word 'gold' in their vocabulary, then the word 'gold' will be as the word 'water' was in 1750 with respect to that subclass of speakers, and the other speakers just won't acquire it at all. And some words do not exhibit any division of linguistic labor: 'chair', for example. But with the increase of division of labor in the society and the rise of science, more and more words begin to exhibit this kind of division of labor. 'Water', for example, did not exhibit it at all before the rise of chemistry. Today it is obviously necessary for every speaker to be able to recognize water (reliably under normal conditions), and probably most adult speakers even know the necessary and sufficient condition "water is H_2O," but only a few adult speakers could distinguish water from liquids that superficially resembled water. In case of doubt, other speakers would rely on the judgment of these "expert" speakers. Thus the way of recognizing possessed by these "expert" speakers is also, through them, possessed by the collective linguistic body, even though it is not possessed by each individual member of the body, and in this way the most *recherché* fact about water may become part of the *social* meaning of the word although unknown to almost all speakers who acquire the word.

It seems to me that this phenomenon of division of linguistic labor is one that it will be very important for sociolinguistics to investigate. In connection with it, I should like to propose the following hypothesis:

Hypothesis of the universality of the division of linguistic labor: Every linguistic community exemplifies the sort of division of linguistic labor just described; that is, it possesses at least some terms whose associated "criteria" are known only to a subset of the speakers who acquire the terms, and whose use by the other speakers depends upon a structured cooperation between them and the speakers in the relevant subsets.

It is easy to see how this phenomenon accounts for some of the examples given above of the failure of the assumptions (1 and 2). When a term is subject to the division of linguistic labor, the "average" speaker who acquires it does not acquire anything that fixes its extension. In particular, his individual psychological state *certainly* does not fix its extension; it is only the sociolinguistic state of the collective linguistic body to which the speaker belongs that fixes the extension.

We may summarize this discussion by pointing out that there are two sorts of tools in the world: there are tools like a hammer or a screwdriver which can be used by one person; and there are tools like a steamship which require the cooperative activity of a number of persons to use. Words have been thought of too much on the model of the first sort of tool.

Indexicality and rigidity

The first of our science-fiction examples – 'water' on Earth and on Twin Earth in 1750 – does not involve division of linguistic labor, or at least does not involve it in the same way the examples of 'aluminum' and 'elm' do. There were not (in our story, anyway) any "experts" on water on Earth in 1750, nor any experts on "water" on Twin Earth. The example *does* involve things which are of fundamental importance to the theory of reference and also to the theory of necessary truth, which we shall now discuss.

Let W_1 and W_2 be two possible worlds in which I exist and in which this glass exists and in which I am giving a meaning explanation by pointing to this glass and saying "This is water." Let us suppose that in W_1 the glass is full of H_2O and in W_2 the glass is full of XYZ. We shall also suppose that W_1 is the *actual* world, and that XYZ is the stuff typically called "water" in the world W_2 (so that the relation between English speakers in W_1 and English speakers in W_2 is exactly the same as the relation between English speakers on Earth and English speakers on Twin Earth). Then there are two theories one might have concerning the meaning of 'water':

(1)   One might hold that 'water' was *world-relative* but *constant* in meaning (i.e., the word has a constant relative meaning). On this theory, 'water' means the same in W_1 and W_2; it's just that water is H_2O in W_1, and water is XYZ in W_2.

(2)   One might hold that water is H_2O in all worlds (the stuff called "water" in W_2 isn't water), but 'water' doesn't have the same meaning in W_1 and W_2.

If what was said before about the Twin Earth case was correct, then (2) is clearly the correct theory. When I say "*this* (liquid) is water," the "this" is, so to speak, a *de re* "this" – i.e., the force of my explanation is that "water" is whatever bears a certain equivalence relation (the relation we called "*same$_L$*" above) to the piece of liquid referred to as "this" *in the actual world*.

We might symbolize the difference between the two theories as a "scope" difference in the following way. On theory (1), the following is true:

(1′)   (For every world W) (For every x in W) (x is water $\equiv x$ bears *same$_L$* to the entity referred to as "this" in W)

while on theory (2):

(2′)   (For every world W) (For every x in W) (x is water $\equiv x$ bears *same*$_L$ to the entity referred to as "this" *in the actual world W_1*)

I call this a "scope" difference because in (1′) 'the entity referred to as "this"' is within the scope of 'For every world W' – as the qualifying phrase 'in W' makes explicit – whereas in (2′) 'the entity referred to as "this"' means "the entity referred to as 'this' *in the actual world*," and has thus a reference *independent* of the bound variable 'W'.

Kripke calls a designator "rigid" (in a given sentence) if (in that sentence) it refers to the same individual in every possible world in which the designator designates. If we extend this notion of rigidity to substance names, then we may express Kripke's theory and mine by saying that the term 'water' is *rigid*.

The rigidity of the term 'water' follows from the fact that when I give the "ostensive definition": "*this* (liquid) is water," I intend (2′) and not (1′).

We may also say, following Kripke, that when I give the ostensive definition "*this* (liquid) is water," the demonstrative 'this' is *rigid*.

What Kripke was the first to observe is that this theory of the meaning (or "use," or whatever) of the word 'water' (and other natural-kind terms as well) has startling consequences for the theory of necessary truth.

To explain this, let me introduce the notion of a *cross-world relation*. A two-term relation R will be called *cross-world* when it is understood in such a way that its extension is a set of ordered pairs of individuals *not all in the same possible world*. For example, it is easy to understand the relation *same height as* as a cross-world relation: just understand it so that, e.g., if x is an individual in a world W_1 who is 5 feet tall (in W_1) and y is an individual in W_2 who is 5 feet tall (in W_2), then the ordered pair x,y belongs to the extension of *same height as*. (Since an individual may have different heights in different possible worlds in which that same individual exists, strictly speaking, it is not the ordered pair x,y that constitutes an element of the extension of *same height as*, but rather the ordered pair x-*in-world-W_1, y-in-world-W_2*.)

Similarly, we can understand the relation *same*$_L$ (same liquid as) as a cross-world relation by understanding it so that a liquid in world W_1 which has the same important physical properties (in W_1) that a liquid in W_2 possesses (in W_2) bears *same*$_L$ to the latter liquid.

Then the theory we have been presenting may be summarized by saying that an entity x, in an arbitrary possible world, is *water* if and only if it bears the relation *same*$_L$ (construed as a cross-world relation) to the stuff *we* call "water" in the actual world.

Suppose, now, that I have not yet discovered what the important physical properties of water are (in the actual world) – i.e., I don't yet know that water is H_2O. I may have ways of *recognizing* water that are successful (of course, I may make a small number of mistakes that I won't be able to detect until a later stage in our scientific development), but not know the microstructure of water. If I agree that a liquid with the superficial properties of "water" but a different microstructure *isn't really water*, then my ways of recognizing water cannot be regarded as an analytical specification of what *it is to be* water. Rather, the operational definition, like the ostensive one, is simply a way of pointing out a standard – pointing out the stuff *in the actual world* such that, for x to be water, in *any* world, is for x to bear the relation $same_L$ to the *normal* members of the class of *local* entities that satisfy the operational definition. "Water" on Twin Earth is not water, even if it satisfies the operational definition, because it doesn't bear $same_L$ to the *local* stuff that satisfies the operational definition, and local stuff that satisfies the operational definition but has a microstructure different from the rest of the local stuff that satisfies the operational definition isn't water either, because it doesn't bear $same_L$ to the *normal* examples of the local "water."

Suppose, now, that I discover the microstructure of water – that water is H_2O. At this point I will be able to say that the stuff on Twin Earth that I earlier *mistook* for water isn't really water. In the same way, if you describe, not another planet in the actual universe, but another possible universe in which there is stuff with the chemical formula XYZ which passes the "operational test" for *water*, we shall have to say that that stuff isn't water but merely XYZ. You will not have described a possible world in which "water is XYZ," but merely a possible world in which there are lakes of XYZ, people drink XYZ (and not water), or whatever. In fact, once we have discovered the nature of water, nothing counts as a possible world in which water doesn't have that nature. Once we have discovered that water (in the actual world) is H_2O, *nothing counts as a possible world in which water isn't H_2O.*

On the other hand, we can perfectly well imagine having experiences that would convince us (and that would make it rational to believe that) water *isn't* H_2O. In that sense, it is conceivable that water isn't H_2O. It is conceivable but it isn't possible! Conceivability is no proof of possibility.

Kripke refers to statements that are rationally unrevisable (assuming there are such) as *epistemically necessary*. Statements that are true in all possible worlds he refers to simply as necessary (or sometimes as "metaphysically necessary"). In this terminology, the point just made can be restated as: a statement can be (metaphysically) necessary and epistemically contingent. Human intuition has no privileged access to metaphysical necessity.

In this paper, our interest is in theory of meaning, however, and not in theory of necessary truth. Words like 'now', 'this', 'here' have long been recognized to be *indexical*, or *token-reflexive* – i.e., to have an extension which varies from context to context or token to token. For these words, no one has ever suggested the traditional theory that "intension determines extension." To take our Twin Earth example: if I have a *Doppelganger* on Twin Earth, then when I think "I have a headache," *he* thinks "I have a headache." But the extension of the particular token of 'I' in his verbalized thought is himself (or his unit class, to be precise), while the extension of the token of 'I' in *my* verbalized thought is *me* (or my unit class, to be precise). So the same word, 'I', has two different extensions in two different idiolects; but it does not follow that the concept I have of myself is in any way different from the concept my Doppelganger has of himself.

Now then, we have maintained that indexicality extends beyond the *obviously* indexical words and morphemes (e.g., the tenses of verbs). Our theory can be summarized as saying that words like 'water' have an unnoticed indexical component: "water" is stuff that bears a certain similarity relation to the water *around here*. Water at another time or in another place or even in another possible world has to bear the relation $same_L$ to *our* "water" *in order to be water*. Thus the theory that (1) words have "intensions," which are something like concepts associated with the words by speakers; and (2) intension determines extension – cannot be true of natural-kind words like 'water' for the same reason it cannot be true of obviously indexical words like 'I'.

The theory that natural-kind words like 'water' are indexical leaves it open, however, whether to say that 'water' in the Twin Earth dialect of English has the same *meaning* as 'water' in the Earth dialect and a different extension – which is what we normally say about 'I' in different idiolects – thereby giving up the doctrine that "meaning (intension) determines extension," or to say, as we have chosen to do, that difference in extension is *ipso facto* a difference in meaning for natural-kind words, thereby giving up the doctrine that meanings are concepts, or, indeed, mental entities of *any* kind.[2]

It should be clear, however, that Kripke's doctrine that natural-kind words are rigid designators and our doctrine that they are indexical are but two ways of making the same point.

We have now seen that the extension of a term is not fixed by a concept that the individual speaker has in his head, and this is true both because extension is, in general, determined *socially* – there is division of linguistic labor as much as of "real" labor – and because extension is, in part, determined *indexically*. The extension of our terms depends upon the actual nature of the particular things that serve as paradigms, and this actual nature is not, in general, fully known to the speaker. Traditional semantic theory leaves out two contributions to the determination of reference – the contribution of society and the contribution of the real world; a better semantic theory must encompass both.

Notes

* Presented at an APA Symposium on Reference, December 28, 1973. Commentators were Charles Chastain and Keith S. Donnellan; for Donnellan's paper, see *Journal of Philosophy*, vol. 70, no. 19, pp. 711–12; Professor Chastain's comments are not available.

A very much expanded version of this paper appeared in volume 7 of Minnesota Studies in the Philosophy of Science (*Language, Mind, and Knowledge*, edited by Keith Gunderson), under the title "The Meaning of 'Meaning'."

1 See note 2 below, and the corresponding text.

2 Our reasons for rejecting the first option – to say that 'water' has the same meaning on Earth and on Twin Earth, while giving up the doctrine that meaning determines reference – are presented in "The Meaning of 'Meaning'." They may be illustrated thus: Suppose 'water' has the same meaning on Earth and on Twin Earth. Now, let the word 'water' become phonemically different on Twin Earth – say, it becomes 'quaxel'. Presumably, this is not a change in meaning per se, on any view. So 'water' and 'quaxel' have the same meaning (although they refer to different liquids). But this is highly counterintuitive. Why not say, then, that 'elm' in my idiolect has the same meaning as 'beech' in your idiolect, although they refer to different trees?

4

Predicate Meets Property[1]

Mark Wilson

I

When we speak of a predicate's *extension*, we intend to delineate the class of objects of which it is true.[2] Unfortunately, in some common situations the proper ground for determining whether a predicate is true of a particular individual becomes uncertain or ambiguous. One kind of situation in which this can happen – the kind of situation I will be particularly concerned with in this paper – is one in which the linguistic community is unaware of the existence of kinds of objects to which a predicate might be thought to apply. It is frequently indeterminate whether such unexpected objects should be assigned to the extension or to the counter-extension of the predicate. This common phenomenon suggests deeper issues concerning the rationale for our intuitive extension assignments. I shall discuss some real life examples of this phenomenon, but it will be convenient to begin with a simple fictional case.

I once saw a movie (*Island of Lost Women*) in which a colony of Druids drifted in ancient times to a South Sea island, where they were subsequently terrorized by cavemen and out-takes from *One Million BC*. Their descendents, naturally, were able to speak a variety of English, albeit with miscellaneous archaic features. A B-52 full of regular American types landed on their uncharted island and the Druids exclaimed, "Lo, a great silver bird falleth from the sky." Aside from the local avian population, this bomber was the first flying device the Druids had ever seen.[3] During the course of the movie at least, the Druids were notably loath to learn new vocabulary like "airplane" and we can imagine that this syntactic conservativism persisted through their eventual integration into the modern world. Airplanes, helicopters and dirigibles are now called "birds" in the Druidic dialect and true *aves* are specially denoted by compound phrases like "feathered birds." It is clear that the extension of the predicate "is a bird" for the cosmopolitan Druidese is something like the set of flying devices (including animal varieties).

The crucial question for our purposes is what extension should a covert linguist have assigned to the Druid predicate "is a bird" in the colony's *pre*-B-52 days? Should it be {x/x is a member of *aves*} or {x/x is a flying device}? A definitive answer will seem quite problematic, given a bit more background on the Druids. Let us assume that our pre-B-52 natives also possessed the following dispositional trait. If the hapless aviators had crashed in the jungle unseen and were discovered by the Druids six months later as they camped discontently around the bomber's hulk, their Druid rescuers would have proclaimed, "Lo, a great silver house lieth in the jungle." This appellation might stick and the later, globe-trotting Druids would persist in calling all forms of aviation "flying houses," to be distinguished from "stationary houses" and "earthbound but mobile houses." Here airplanes are no longer held to be "birds." If this history had obtained, the extension in cosmopolitan Druidese for "is a bird" would be {x/x is a member of *aves*} and for "is a house," roughly, {x/x is a man-made enclosure}. Which extension should be assigned to "bird" in cosmopolitan Druidese thus depends upon the *history* of the introduction of B-52's to the island (other possible initiations into the modern world might have induced yet other extensions for "bird"). In our first scenario, the B-52 clearly belongs to the extension of "bird" in cosmopolitan Druidese, but our alternative possible development suggests that we should not uncritically assign this same extension to the word in its earlier employment. So here we have a predicate ("bird" in parochial Druidese) and a rather hefty unexpected object (the B-52) which cannot be happily counted within the extension or without.

The traditional response to our problem is to seek the "concept," "sense," or "universal" the prebomber Druids had associated with "bird" and study the extension determined by this intervening entity. A consequence of this account is that the Druids in one or both of our alternative histories must have "changed the meaning" of "bird" – i.e., switched its associated universal. However the Druids themselves needn't feel that they have modified or extended the meaning of "bird" when they apply it to aircraft, for that classification appears spontaneously natural to them in the circumstances. Upon reflection, post-bomber Druids might admit that *if* they had seen the plane first in the jungle, they would have called it a "house" and not a "bird," yet cheerfully and consistently avow that they had not altered "bird"'s meaning when they classified bombers as "birds." And the "house"-favoring

Druids of our alternate history might make exactly symmetrical claims. Although such Druid contentions may seem perverse or unpalatable, we shall find that we make precisely analogous declarations about the developmental history of our own language all the time!

An alternative response to our dilemma is to modify our notion of "extension." The classical treatment demands a choice between $\{x/x$ is a member of $aves\}$ and $\{x/x$ is a flying device$\}$, but such a selection seems tantamount to a prediction about how the Druids will come to classify aircraft. The "semantical facts" about prebomber Druids do not seem to warrant such extrapolation. If we complicate our "extensions" somewhat, we can hedge against these forecasts. Accordingly Hartry Field[4] and others have suggested an assignment of a set of "partial denotations" to predicates – i.e., a *class* of classical extension sets for each predicate. Thus both of our candidate extensions will be "partial denotations" for "bird." My own proposal in this paper represents a variation on this strategy, employing "implicit parameters" to tie the various "partial denotations" together.[5]

Articulation of a precise formal device, however, is not the primary interest of this essay, which is instead to probe the grounds for its employment. The Druids may have been likewise unacquainted with kiwis, ostriches and other nonstandard specimens of *aves* and will not be inclined to call them "birds" upon first acquaintance. It is an anthropological fact[6] that labeling an ostrich a "bird" will strike the natives as more of a distortion of meaning than any bomber dubbing. Nonetheless, our inclination is to assign the various avian oddities to parochial "bird," despite native truculence. Do we possess *systematic standards* for deciding whether an unexpected object can be fitted into a simple extension (as the kiwi) or instead mandate assignment of more complicated "partial denotations" (as the bomber)?

Although an acceptable criterion can be adduced for the present case, I do not believe that all of our intuitive hunches about the "proper extensions" of various predicates ultimately follow any simple pattern. Instead they seem to be the product of a tangled web of incompatible descriptive aims. Unfortunately acceptance of a traditional theory of meaning (as outlined in Section II) has blinded us to these disparate purposes. My method for dealing with this situation will be as follows: after study of the related but simpler locution "device m can detect the property P," I shall extract a core notion of "extension" that captures in a crisp and systematic manner a *portion* of the empirical utility of the preanalytic notion. In particular, I shall insure that my reconstruction meets the following rough adequacy condition:

The evidence for assignment of an extension to a predicate should be limited to such linguistic behavior as can be reasonably extrapolated from the community's contemporaneous practice and should not reflect accidental features of the society's later history.

For example, the fortuitous mode of bomber arrival was responsible for the later Druid classificatory behavior, which should not be adduced as evidence about the proper extension of parochial "bird." On the other hand, study of pristine Druids may allow us to predict that they will eventually come round on the kiwi question and thus legitimate their assignment to the extension. Finally, in Section X, we shall study the prospects for *extending* my core treatment of "extension" consistent with this adequacy condition.

This program for building up, by degrees, an empirically sound notion of "extension" will be disdained as "operationalist" by many, especially those who view extension assignments as "theoretically determined" relationships. However, the history of science has seen many instances when a notion has improved in scientific utility through a bit of "theoretical" disfranchisement. For example, consider the term "species" in zoology. Naturalists from Aristotle to Linnaeus regarded specieshood as a primitive theoretical property, assuming that it is manifest in nature when two animals belong to the same "natural kind" (although it may require diligent dissection to discover the hidden essential characteristics). However, actual difficulties in classification forced elucidation of a complicated and detailed set of criteria for specieshood, a list which is under continual revision. Although these standards are intended to reflect facts about the genetic nature and phylogenetic development of the animals classified, it nonetheless remains a strictly taxonomic notion and no biologist believes that specieshood means *that* much on a genetic level (i.e., dogs don't carry little messages "I am a *Canis Familiaris*" in their DNA). "Species" remains a central and indispensible concept in modern biology, but this theory does not free it from the need for criterial explication. The cry "don't be operationalist about 'species'" would have led to stagnation in biology, for it would have protected the "natural kinds" picture of animal life and obscured the variety of quite different mechanisms which produce genetic isolation in nature.[7] The traditional theory of "extension" accords the term a relatively lofty status, free from much need for critical examination. However, I believe that this theory is mistaken and leads us to overlook many fundamental aspects of linguistic evolution. If "extension" is to survive as a useful taxonomic tool in linguistics, it will greatly benefit from some further explication and correction. I hope this essay will prove a useful start in that direction.

On the other hand, if the reader is currently inclined to accept the traditional view (or some appropriate modification thereof), my reconstruction may nonetheless have value as a vehicle for uncovering unnoticed facts about language. Einstein's methodology in "The Electrodynamics of Moving Bodies"[8] may be profitably viewed from this vantage. His alleged "definition" of "simultaneity" actually consisted in the introduction of a *new* notion, *simultaneity with respect to an inertial frame*, whose classificatory utility in low velocity situations closely resembles that of the Newtonian *absolute simultaneity*. Since his new notion was explained by appeal to the behavior of light signals and since he misleadingly wrote of *defining* "simultaneity," he has frequently been read as an operationalist *à la* Percy Bridgeman. The true motivation for his apparent "operationalism" was instead to delineate an empirical arena where classical theory was untested by experiment and to indicate the *minimal* conception of time order a rival theory requires to save the familiar facts about apparent simultaneity. Einstein would have readily admitted that such "analysis" would have proved completely sterile if his hunch about the infirmities of classical theory had not born empirical fruit. My reconstructed "extension" is likewise designed to mark both the strengths and weaknesses of its classical original. In Section XI, we shall examine certain uncomfortable aspects of the traditional account in light of the data encountered *en route*.

My central idea is to tie sets to predicates by treating the term's employers as *imperfect measuring instruments* for a property with that extension. Motivation for this approach will occupy us until Section V, whereupon my actual proposal and its attendant case studies will follow.

II

In this section, I shall briefly sketch the classical account of extension, drawn from the works of Frege and Russell (their many differences in detail do not affect our present concerns). They held that an intermediate entity exists which forges a bond between predicate and set. These Platonic go-betweens were called "senses" by Frege and "universals" by Russell. A predicate "P" will alledgedly denote a universal A, which in turn fixes the set $\{x/x$ falls under $A\}$. The correlation of attribute and language performs two functions:

1 The speaker's "grasp" of the universal provides a necessary condition for his understanding of the predicate. The attribute represents what he shares in common with other speakers of the language with respect to the particular bit of syntax.

2 On its own, the attribute determines a set of objects in the world as extension.

This account intends to encompass a rich variety of linguistic data, such as a speaker's alleged "intuitions" of synonymy, ambiguity and informativeness. However, insofar as I can determine, the classical explanations of these phenomena do not require attributes to determine extensions at all.[9] Rather, the sets are grafted onto language largely as a measure of the speaker's ability to *apply* the predicate to the world, as witnessed by an ability to classify objects under the predicate. The extension of a predicate consists of the objects that the intervening universal *should* lead one to positively classify.[10] Unfortunately, classical theorists are rather unforthcoming about the process that ultimately connects the attribute with the resulting activity. In fact, the invocation of attributes can be viewed in two ways:

(I) The attribute plays a causal role in guiding human classification, rather as a template steers the activity of a machine. The attribute thus constitutes part of the *explanation* of human classificatory skills.[11]

(II) The association of attribute with predicate is not intended to explain the speaker's ability to use the word (which must await better understanding of brain mechanics) but simply as a salient means for cataloging the ability. This I call the *taxonomic* view of the attribute–predicate linkage.[12]

The tension between these two readings can be seen if we examine a recent critique of the classical view, Hilary Putnam's.[13] He doubts whether any entity can perform the dual tasks [(1) and (2)] the classical theory requires. In particular, concepts regarded as "ideas in the head," cannot completely determine extensions, because two speakers could conceivably share the same "ideas" with respect to a pair of predicates that intuitively possess quite different extensions. However, a true-born Fregean might remain unimpressed since universals were never supposed to dwell "in the head," but rather in an extraterrestrial "third realm." An allowable "indexicality" in the speaker's mental state might produce a link to distinct concepts in the Platonic stratosphere.

Putnam is obviously insisting on something like (I) in his interpretation of classical theory, whereas his opponent has retreated to (II). But as long as the explanatory function of the universals is minimized and their value as ideal standards for cataloging behavior is emphasized, then the suggested response seems cogent. As an analogy, consider the relationship between human manipulation with numerals and the addition function of mathematics. That various of our calculations with small numerals approximately correspond to values of the addition function *in itself* justifies association of the human activity to the divine rule. Putnam's objections are in order only if we require the function to be "in our head" or suggest that some quasi-mechanical, although supersensible, interaction with the function *guides* our calculation. Treating the attribute–predicate link as merely an external, "black box" *measure* of a speaker's ability to employ the predicate may be an exceedingly minimal construal of classical theory, but it indicates the direction I wish to follow.

But given that subjects often make mistakes in the employment of a predicate, how should we correlate "grasp" of an attribute with linguistic behavior? Paraphrasing a remark of Michael Dummett's, the tightest link we might expect is that "the correct application of a predicate to an object x involves the possibility in principle that this classification should be or should have been recognized as correct by a being – not necessarily a human being – who grasps the universal associated with the predicate and is appropriately situated and with sufficient perceptual and intellectual powers."[14] This treats the "ideal observer" as a sort of *perfect detection device* for the "universal" in question. Dummett correctly stresses that a Fregean is reluctant to improve upon this rather vague counterfactual, perhaps excusing his taciturnity by appeal to the specially postulated nature of universals. However, in the philosophy of science, we know ways to convert loose attributions of "ideal" measurement capacities into statements of greater precision. I believe this analogy provides a valuable clue for the empirical reexamination of "extension." By following its lead, I shall develop a concrete bond between usage and "attribute" (and, derivatively, sets) that achieves some of the goals of traditional theory, yet at the same time delineates its limitations. Perhaps this one-strand analysis of "extension" will prove too limited to serve as a fully satisfactory surrogate for the traditional notion, but the facts we note in working it out should persuade the Fregean to amplify *his* account. A first step towards progress is to scrutinize the notion of "attribute" more carefully.

III

Recently some philosophers have recognized that two quite distinct motivations for positing attributes have historically been confused.[15]

A As in the Frege–Russell theory, concepts are hypothesized to explain *common linguistic* understanding so that if Gary and Danny understand the same thing by "*P*," they must have each grasped the same attribute ϕ and assigned it to "*P*." Such attributes will be identical only if they represent the same idea or concept. I shall reserve the term *concept* for these linguistically motivated entities.

B "Attributes" constitute the range of physical traits which objects might be discovered to possess. A scientific theory will articulate this realm of potential traits through its specification of which systems are physically permissible. The nature of this collection and its associated identity conditions are to be discovered empirically through the development of physics and is completely independent of the linguistic motivations of the "concept" view. Employment of this use of "property" is clearly displayed, for example, in the general contentions about "physical quantities" revealed in the Poisson bracket or commutation relations of classical and quantum physics. These relationships would make no sense if the range of the quantifications includes concepts derived from alien physical theories – e.g. it is nonsense to seek the Poisson bracket of classical energy with Aristotlean impetus. Attributes so construed I shall call *physical properties* (or simply *properties* when no confusion would acrue).

The *predicates* (= open sentences) of a physical theory T denote typical specimens of the physical properties postulated by T.[16] Thus the predicates of current scientific theory represent our "best guesses" so far as to the realm of physical traits in the universe. From this point of view, there is absolutely no reason to hold that the predicates of a discarded scientific theory, such as "contains caloric," correspond to properties at all. Only confusion with the linguistic motivations of the concept view could make us think otherwise; as we have just seen, such assimilation would make hash of the typical property quantifications of science. For clarity, I shall adopt the following notation: *P* shall name the physical property (if any) corresponding to a given predicate "P." †P† will represent its correlated concept (if it exists), and "P" indicates the linguistic expression itself.

In this essay, I shall comprehend the attribute–predicate link in a purely taxonomic (i.e., nonexplanatory) way, but claim that we should employ *physical properties* rather than concepts as the appropriate middle terms. If members of a linguistic community can independently agree in most of their attempts to classify objects under a predicate, this unanimity of results is to be *partially* explained by *objective* features of the objects catalogued. In parallel fashion, the fact that a variety of instrumentation (mercury, gas and resistance thermometers) supply approximately equal numerical values over the same range of objects partially rests upon objective thermal traits of the objects tested. Roughly speaking, my purpose is to codify such objective features into a so-called *property index* for the predicate and then relate our intuitive assignments of extensions to these indices. This procedure, I believe, represents a tolerably accurate first approximation to our preanalytic method of assigning extensions to predicates. Part of my motivation in following this nonstandard course is that I believe the "concept" notion to be a child of confusion, whose unhappy parentage cannot be redeemed through postulation.

In this regard, it is worth pointing out that Hilary Putnam[17] and Saul Kripke[18] have already proposed a physical property linkage for a limited class of "natural kind predicates." On their account, an unspecified causal relationship is established between a "natural kind" attribute in the physical world and a predicate *via* an initial baptism ceremony and this tie is inherited by the descendent linguistic community. The extension of the predicate becomes simply the set of objects possessing the natural kind in question. The salient aspect of this account, from the present viewpoint, is that natural kinds must constitute a genus of *physical property*, rather than concept, for the attached "natural kinds" are *not* intended to represent the speakers' conception of the predicate in question.[19] Thus *contains largely H_2O* will be the natural kind index of "is water," even for speakers who have no conception of molecular chemistry.

I find the assumption of a subcategory of "natural kinds" and unique causal chains physically unpersuasive (*cf.* Section IX). Nor do I understand the limitation to "natural kind predicates." It may be suggested that competent English speakers *intend* "is gold" to correlate with a "natural kind," whereas they lack similar designs upon "is a chair," but I find such a thesis incoherent or empirically false. As long as no pretence is made, however, that the intervening properties represent the speaker's *conception* of his predicate or its *meaning*, there is no reason to limit this account to "natural kind" predicates. "Is a chair" can be indexed by the complex physical properties which lead us to classify chairs as such (insofar as our classifications depend upon such traits, rather than the nomenclatural whim of the manufacturer)[20] and the aboriginal *gavagai* can be assigned the property *belongs to family *Leporidae** without thereby implying that the native has any notion of biological families or even normal physical objects. The many features which distinguish the natives' use of *gavagai* from our own "is a rabbit" must be brought out by the linguist using other varieties of linguistic description than my bald property assignment. The dream of traditional linguistic theory has been to collapse all of these descriptive tasks into a unitary assignment of a "concept index," a goal I regard as chimerical.

IV

In this section, I shall briefly discuss attributions of *measurement capabilities to instrumentation*, as when we say that a thermometer is capable of measuring temperature. This digression is important for our purposes because it will illustrate (a) why we must distinguish concepts from physical properties, (b) why a reasonable explication of "extension" needs to proceed in stages, and (c) how to abstract from the linguistic mistakes of speakers.

Let m be a concrete piece of laboratory apparatus such as a common mercury thermometer. The knowledge that "m can measure the physical quantity *temperature**" provides certain useful information about the *internal* construction of m. Admittedly this knowledge is rather abstract; roughly, we learn that m has some means of coupling with the gas so that a correlated modification in the state of m will be amplified to an observable level. In a thermometer, its entering into equilibrium with the gas produces an observable alteration in the length of the mercury column. If m is a "black box" and we know nothing about m except that it can measure the temperature of gases, then there are a host of quite different mechanisms which may be housed inside m, one of which is the workings of a mercury thermometer. On the other hand, if we discover that m cannot measure the percentage of oxygen in the gas, we learn other information about m, although this data is hardly as salient as a positive measurement capability. Let us call the assignment of property to instrumentation a *property index* of the device.

These attributions are *idealized* in the sense that m can correctly be accredited with a temperature recognition capability, yet nonetheless in many circumstances give wrong answers or no answers at all. Moreover they are *objective* in the sense that if "Q" is another name for the physical property *P*, then *m* must be capable of measuring *Q* as well. So *if*[21] *temperature*equals*mean kinetic energy per degree of freedom*, the thermometer *m* must be capable of measuring mean kinetic energy as well. However, it is important to recognize that sometimes predicates which do not pick out physical properties in our sense are associated with measuring instruments; granting the Devil his due, such attributions may be called *concept indices*.

For example, consider the sentence "Apparatus *m* (allegedly) measures the property †contains orgone†." This claim is of a quite different order than those considered above, for little information about *m*'s internal structure is conveyed, but a historical fact is attributed to *m*; roughly, "*m* is built according to specifications left by Wilhelm Reich or his followers, who thought devices of this type could measure the presence of a fictitious substance they called 'orgone.'" There is little question of classifying arbitrary apparatus, historically unconnected with Reicheans, as potential "orgone" detectors – the theory of orgone is sufficiently incoherent and out of step with modern science that we wouldn't know how to carry out the classification.

Similarly, one can apply the concept †measures gain or loss of caloric† to the antique calorimeters employed by Lavoisier and his associates, as well as the objective attribution *measures gain or loss of heat energy*. However, it seems inappropriate to classify more modern and sophisticated calorimeters as †capable of measuring caloric loss or gain† since these devices typically operate according to principles at variance with caloric theory. If one accepts caloric theory, it becomes quite difficult to explain why these modern devices behave as they do or what it is that they measure. "Concept indices" do not proceed upon systematic principles and contrast sharply with the objective property attributions. In the latter, a mechanical device can be decided to be a measuring instrument for *P* simply on the basis of its *internal* structure.[22]

It is apparent that the two types of attribute indices are founded upon quite different criteria, although they frequently become muddled in practice. Moreover it would be quite difficult, if not impossible, to give a *unitary* account of all these attributions of measurement capacity. Sorting out the disparate motivations for "concept indices" would be quite messy, but the typical objective, physical property indexing procedure is amenable to a fairly simple treatment. The key to its unraveling lies in the fact that such assignments require physical properties and transpire against a background of implicit assumptions (or *parameters*, as I shall call them). Except in trivial cases, almost no universal detection devices exist; instruments which can detect the presence or absence of *P* in *any* object whatsoever in any context. A mercury thermometer will not function properly in an environment full of shock waves or if applied to objects at extremely high or low temperatures. When we claim that the thermometer measures temperature, we tacitly limit our claim that it will accurately transmit temperature information to a range of appropriate conditions. If we hope to define *"m* can measure property *P"* rigorously, such background conditions must be made explicit in the form of extra parameters. For example, consider a calibrated spring balance m^1 (such as a household bathroom scale) and a beam balance m^2 (such as Justice carries) with a set of standard weights. Typically, we are willing to claim that both devices can measure not only the *mass* of an object, but its *impressed gravitational force* ("weight") as well. In other words, the readings of the instruments can be regarded indifferently as reports about either the mass or "weight" of the object measured. If used in suitable conditions, a value of "2 lbs." in either instrument serves to detect the property *has a mass of .9 kg.* as well as *is under an impressed gravitational force of 9 nts.*. But these remarks hold only if the range of m^1 and m^2's application is limited to the earth's surface. If we instead enlarge the field of applicability to the moon, then the beam balance will register only mass and the spring balance only impressed gravitational force. If the range of application is further expanded to include objects found in space stations or in radically nonhomogeneous gravitational fields, then neither m^1 nor m^2 will measure either of the properties mentioned (although there are properties of a more complicated description which they continue to detect).

The moral is that a *range of application* is required as an implicit parameter in our definition of property indexing. Within these limitations, a given device may be expected to measure *many* distinct physical properties simultaneously – some of which may be simple from a theoretical point-of-view (*mass*) or more complicated (e.g., *impressed gravitational force plus centripetal pseudoforce*). Such properties will be said to be *interchangeable* with respect to the implicit parameters. Typically, instruments detect "simple" properties only within a relatively narrow arena of application.

When we pay sufficient attention to these details, we are frequently surprised to find that many common attributions of measurement capability are mistaken. Consider again the familiar mercury thermometer and its alleged ability to measure temperature. In fact, thermometers do not give correct answers about the temperature of gases in ordinary sunlight. This is because their readings depend as much upon the radiant energy reflected from the nearby solids as the absolute temperature of the air. The thermometer is actually responding to some complicated average of temperature plus reflected radiation rather than simple gas temperature alone. Meteorologists actually employ a device consisting of a thermometer inside a complicated housing to measure true temperature. When one learns it is "90°F in the shade," one is thereby given the true air temperature measured by this device, rather than the misleading reading of an ordinary thermometer, which in this situation is not measuring temperature at all. The phrase "in the shade" really means "true temperature" and does not refer to fictitious differential in air temperature between a shady spot and direct sunlight. A thermometer can correctly be said to measure temperature only when such radiation effects are not extreme; if this reference class is enlarged to include sunlit gases, it is no longer accurate to say that it measures simple temperature.

In the appendix, I describe more fully the range of parameters needed to make our account of property indexing for measuring devices precise. The net result of the analysis is:[23]

A device m (of general type M) can detect P (with range of application R, method of application A and "yes" answer T) if and only if it is a law of nature that if x is any device of type M, v is an object meeting R, and x is applied to y at t in manner A, then x will assume the property T at a time subsequent to t if and only if y has P at t.

This treatment applies only to completely reliable instruments, but the possibility of error within the range of application can be introduced by techniques (involving the ensemble *M*) described in the appendix.

The notion of property indexing just defined cannot be happily regarded as a "meaning analysis" (in the traditional sense) of the original locution. After all, we *do* talk about the measurement capabilities of orgone boxes! My definition certainly captures some of the *empirical basis* that underlies our talk of measuring devices, but it would be hard to specify when this account shades from *explication* into *critique* of vernacular use. Moreover, in ascribing a given measurement capability, we seldom attend to the underlying implicit parameters, although they are clearly necessary. Why is this so? In the first place, we are often totally incapable of specifying them, even if we are relatively confident that m is objectively measuring a certain property in familiar use. In particular, the fact that devices of a certain type act *as if* they detect a physical property may provide good evidence that various undiscovered laws or structural facts about those devices are at hand. For example, the early inventors of the thermometer possessed no valid theories about how their devices worked; their efforts towards design improvement were motivated largely by considerations of repeatability of results in an ever increasing class of thermal apparatus employing different working substances. This collusion of instrumentation provided strong evidence that they were all roughly measuring an important new physical property called "temperature," but the physical processes underlying the transfer of information from object measured to thermometer reading remained largely unknown. Moreover, the implicit parameters limiting valid applicability of their thermal devices were not well understood either; there were few standards for judging the temperature of substances except by thermometer. Contemporary evidence thus justified early theorists in making claims like "this thermometer measures temperature" and "this calorimeter measures caloric gain or loss," even though only the former proved to be correct. Even if the working principles and implicit parameters of a given device are presently understood, a working scientist may have no interest in these factors beyond the truth of "m can detect property P." An industrial chemist will probably be quite ignorant of the theory of his NMR machine; he will be content to read in its instruction manual that, under suitable programming, it can detect a given trait and it won't occur to him to wonder how it might operate in bizarre environments.

These pragmatic considerations explain why in practice apparently objective property indices may drift into becoming "concept indices" of the historically derived variety. In the absence of an objective capability, the claim that "thermometer m measures temperature" may persevere because of our ongoing tendency to treat temperature as whatever a thermometer measures. Thus the average citizen's attributions of measurement capacities typically reflect a motley of motivations. Nonetheless, property indexing clearly constitutes the central *empirical core* of our talk of measuring abilities, from which the various looser forms of measurement talk exude as a confusing exhalation. I think that similar tangled purposes have led to the "concepts" and "extensions" of traditional theory. In the following section, I shall isolate a notion that I believe serves as the empirical backbone for our intuitive talk of "extensions."

V

If we accept a need for implicit parameters, we can bind properties to predicates in the manner of the last section.

Property Q indexes predicate "P" in S's language (with range of application R, method of application A, S's general type being M) if and only if it generally holds that for any person x of type M, any object y meeting R, then if x interacts with y at t in manner A, x will assent to the sentence "Is this P?" at some time subsequent to t if and only if y is Q at t.[24]

The transition to a type of "extension" is immediate:

Predicate "P" has (timeless) extension α in S's language (with range of application R, method of application A, S's general type being M) if and only if $(\exists \phi)$ (ϕ indexes "P" in S's language (with respect to R, A, M) and $\alpha = \{x/x \text{ is } \phi \text{ at some t}\}$).[25]

Roughly speaking, a property *Q* will be assigned to predicate "P" (as used by S) in those cases where the counterfactual "if speaker S were confronted with objects of type Q, S would classify them as 'P'" will be true. Instead of appealing to an "ideal observer," extra parameters have been introduced to convert this somewhat vague counterfactual into a straightforward, albeit complex, scientific claim about what will transpire when the given system (the object to be classified) interacts with an external detection system (human being *cum* measuring devices). Classificatory error or incompetence on the part of a particular observer *a* is to be factored out through a judicious selection of appropriate parameters (especially the ensemble M).

Thanks to Putnam's and Kripke's work, we have learned that the practical assignment of extension to a predicate like "is gold" often requires an initial isolation of those objective properties (of the objects catalogued) that are "responsible" for the term's successful employment. On the other hand, the Frege–Russell account holds that when a child learns a predicate and grasps its associated universal, this "concept" correlates with the child's preparedness to use the term. Our reflections on thermometers *et al.* have shown how the Putnam–Kripke objective features can be understood as *measures* of the speakers' internal "preparation" relevant to the predicate's use. Our "adequacy condition" was imposed precisely so that these indices properly reflect this linguistic prescience. In this way, our new approach is brought into partial alignment with the old "concept" story. The restriction in my definitions to the native employment of simple combinations of the predicate with indexicals, which might otherwise appear to be errant operationalism, rests upon the premise that the external traits which underlie simple classificatory behavior also serve to underwrite the successful employment of sentences of a more complicated grammatical form as well. The advantage of the simple indexical sentences is that "traits responsible for their successful employment" can be unpacked in a fairly elementary fashion. However this working assumption is only approximately correct, for a community's use of sentences of a more complicated grammatical type (*e.g.*, with quantifiers) can properly influence our ultimate choice of extension assignment. I ignore these factors at present because I believe that most of our preanalytic extension assignments are based upon simple classificatory skills and that the typical "corrections" to these ascriptions often introduce unsystematic violations of our adequacy condition. We shall return to these matters in Section X.

My treatment of "extension" can be easily extended to a theory of truth for L in the manner of Hartry Field or Kit Fine. However, I find the ascription of truth-value to a language, especially of a primitive tribe, to be a quite complicated affair. I doubt that the simple modifications of Tarski proposed by Field and Fine neatly capture any familiar valuation of native assertion. *Pace* Donald Davidson, we can possess a good feel for the extension of a predicate in the absence of a developed truth-theory for L. In the Karam language of New Guinea, the "color" word *pk* is applied in different color ranges for different classes of object, e.g., foliage and fruit versus human skin. The class of objects of which *pk* is true – its extension – can be approximately delineated as $\{x/(x$ reflects light in Munsell range 2.5–5 YR 4–5/4–6 & x is human skin) $\bigvee$ (x reflects light in range 5YR–5Y 6–8/7–8, otherwise)$\}$[26] But once we voyage beyond simple classificatory sentences into the dark heart of *pk*'s taboo structure (and the sentences which express it), my own sense of Karam truth and falsity begins to wither. So I propose tabling the question of native "truth" for independent study.

Qua measures of classificatory ability, I hold set and property indices on a par (although the latter typically embodies a little extra information). If it can be assumed that all of a predicate's potential positive instances will actually be examined and classified by a portion of the linguistic community (as happens for predicates like "is Bix Biederbecke"), then intervening properties may not be needed to delineate an appropriate extension. The set can be simply collated from the actual classifications. Properties are needed mainly to support the *counterfactual* "If speaker S were to examine a, S would classify it as 'F'" for predicates with open-ended application.[27]

VI

Our implicit parameters were introduced as a hedge against the complications introduced by unexpected objects. In this section, I shall illustrate their use in the Druid example.[28]

We saw that a linguist studying the semantics of parochial Druid has no warrant for *choosing* either {x/x is a member of *aves*} or {x/x is a flying device} as *the* correct extension for "bird," since such a choice is tantamount to predicting how Druids will classify aircraft in the cosmopolitan world. These two sets are *interchangeable* within the range of application parameter appropriate to pristine Druids. A prediction about how they will classify when placed in circumstances outside of that range of application is not warranted by any linguistic facts about prelanding Druids, since later behavior depends as much on the subsequent accidents of history (how B-52's came to the island) as their prior linguistic training. The properly conservative linguist will hedge this prediction by stressing a limited range of applicability; " 'bird' in parochial Druid dialect has extension {x/x is a member of *aves*} with a range of applicability limited to objects similar to those found in the environs of the Druid isle." She prudently demurs from making any univocal prediction via her extension assignments about how Druids will react to B-52's. Of course, the linguist may make some predictions on this score – it surely reflects a "semantic" feature of Druidese that a plane appearing in the sky will be dubbed a "bird" if it is the first piece of aviation spied – but these predictions must be described *directly* and cannot be encoded in a single property or extension-index.

Contrast the Druid term "bird" with their term "water." In English, "water" possesses more "borderline" cases than "bird;" it is uncertain why sugar water counts as "water" but lemon-lime soda pop does not. Naturally we expect that the Druids may disagree with us on these "borderline" classifications, although we expect that they should consider them quasi-conventional as well. Nonetheless, no likely *history of introduction* to our modern world should materially affect how the Druids divide the bulk of earthly furniture into "water" and "nonwater" – usually they will agree with the average American speaker on these matters. So whatever constitutes the complicated physical property that the various hunks of stuff we call "water" share, it can serve to index Druid "water" equally well. Hence, the field linguist may leave the range of application tacit in her property indexing, since there is essentially only one way the Druids will adapt to the contemporary world *vis à vis* this predicate.

Somewhat intermediate is the ostrich and kiwi case. Previously we assumed that when the Druids eventually embrace modern science, they will override their initial rejection of these creatures as "birds." If a linguist can confidently predict this reversal, then she is warranted in allowing "bird"'s range of application to include kiwis. The linguistic data needed will not require discovery of the true Druid "meaning" of "bird," but study of the tribe's general receptivity towards neologism and linguistic borrowing. If other vocabulary can be readily manufactured to cover zoology's needs, Druid "bird" may forever exclude the kiwis, but in a syntactically conservative society scientific requirements will overpower these original tendencies.[29] If we cannot predict, with reasonable certainty, a unique evolution, then the range of application parameter must exclude nonstandard fowl and both *is a member of aves* and *aves not of order Struthioniformes, Rheiformes, Casuariformes or Apterygiformes* should be among the interchangeable indices for "bird."

Such nonunique linguistic development seems an *unavoidable* facet of human behavior. As such, implicit parameter limitations will be required if we expect extension assignments to meet our earlier adequacy condition. None of this entails that the predicates in question have "changed their meaning" during their "evolution." I have already stressed that the Druids themselves won't feel that they have altered the sense of "bird" when they apply it to the aircraft. The willingness to dub it "bird" occurs spontaneously to all members of Druid society and their surprise at encountering this unexpected object may be no greater than the shock of meeting the stuff in Lake Erie, likewise unreservedly called "water" despite its unexpectedly awful characteristics. From the Druids' own point of view, the meaning of "bird" has not altered, nor is there reason for the field linguist to describe matters in this fashion either. Attribution of change of meaning seems best tied to *recognition* by the linguistic community of a need for conventional decision and, *ex hypothesis*, this is not the case here.

VII

Real life examples of the Druid phenomenon occur in virtually every case of enlargement of our world view through scientific progress. Should the extension of "electron" in 1900 English include positrons? Its extension in present day English does not, but easily could have if the phrase "positive electron" had prevailed in common use. In short, the present day extension of "electron" was partially settled by a matter of phonetic convenience. What then was the term's extension when positrons were totally unconceived? The answer is that the extension indexing of "electron" in 1900 English needs to be limited by a range of applicability (roughly, nonrelativistic quantum effects).

The term "Grant's zebra" was originally (*circa* 1820) applied to a strain of zebras native to Kenya. A set of morphologically distinct animals from Rhodesia was likewise called "Chapman's zebra." Later exploration showed that the two animals interbred near the Zambezi River and constituted one species *Equus burchelli*. Thus the term "Grant's zebra" in present day English is indexed by *belongs to E. burchelli grant*. On the other hand, if zoological exploration of Africa had begun instead near the Zambezi, "Grant's zebra" would have naturally evolved to become a vernacular title for the *entire species*, with property index *belongs to E. burchelli*. In discussing the original 1820 semantics of "Grant's zebra" it seems inappropriate to choose between these two indices and their corresponding extensions. These attributions should rather be limited by the parameter *found outside the Zambezi region*. Examples of this nature are rife in any taxonomic science.[30]

Consider the phrase "weighs 2 lb." in the English of 1600, when the peculiar behavior of spring and beam balances on the moon was unknown. Should the property index of "weighs 2 lb." have been *has mass .9 kg.* or *is under an impressed gravitational force of 9 nt.*? Again the range of applicability must be restricted, here to objects located near the surface of the earth (in which case both property-indexes are interchangeable). Unlike the previous cases, we have no resolution in present-day English, since there are actually two official English systems of weights and measures in which the pound is a measure of *mass* and of *force* respectively (the latter system is generally preferred however). If semantics attributes the mass property or the gravitational force property *tout court* to 1600 "weighs 2 lb.," it has outstripped the sort of predictions warranted by considerations of English speakers' linguistic preparation in 1600.

If my argument is correct, almost no predicate of English possessing any property index at all is immune to *multiple* property-indices which coincide only within a restricted range of application. Apparently stalwart predicates like "is water" or "is red" differ only in requiring discussion of more extraordinary environments to elicit this feature, and thus seem mere "science fiction" to the skeptic.[31] However, at the present day "is red" *may* be close to demonstrating the "weighs 2 lbs" behavior. Consider the beautiful colored pictures of microbes found in textbooks and assume that these are natural and are not due to staining (as is usually the case). In point of fact, these photos have all been taken in ultraviolet light because visible light cannot be focused at such small diameters. Should we say that (1) a given bacillus is *red* because all of its photos show it to *look* red on ultraviolet film, (2) it is *green* because it reflects visible frequency "white" light strongly in the "green" middle spectrum (although we cannot obtain a clear image in this color due to resolution problems), or (3) it has no true color at all? I don't know whether biologists consistently pursue one of these three policies of color talk. However, if all microscopists routinely employ a standardized ultraviolet film, the first alternative will possess immediate classificatory utility. But it seems clear enough that, in appropriate framing circumstances, any of these three courses of action could be pursued without any *awareness* on the part of biologists that they had settled upon a new "convention" for ascribing color to microbes. Nonetheless, a linguist assigning an extension to "is red" in 1850 English should not allow his indexing to reflect just one of the three possibilities outlined, because that is tantamount to predicting what varieties of ultraviolet film will be marketed in future years!

VIII

Let us now peruse effects of the second implicit parameter for property indexing – the traits which form the ensemble of permissible classifiers. Consider the phrase "weighs 2 lb." in present-day English. Should its index now be *mass* or *impressed gravitational force*? For most of us, our daily usage of the term is totally indifferent to any choice between the two physical properties, because in our comings and goings with the butcher and the health spa, we seldom need to measure nongravitational forces. In this regard, our daily employment of "weighs 2 lb." closely resembles that of Elizabethan Englishmen. It is true that we have all read accounts of the peculiar effects that happen away from the surface of the earth (and are more in tune with the mysteries of the world than the citizens of 1600), but most of us have never faced these features in daily life and our discussions of other-worldly "weight" remain charmingly contradictory. Consider, for example, the assertion, "An astronaut in a space station is weightless (weighs 0 lbs), but if she doesn't eat her rations for a week, she'll lose 5 lbs." Admittedly, we never assert such a sentence in one breath, but most of us have uttered such inconsistencies in more widely separated breaths. *Serious* confrontation (say, through frequent space travel) with the novel environment away from the earth would *force* us to repair these inconsistencies and nothing in present-day English absolutely determines how usage should be improved. Present-day physical practice prefers to understand the pound as a unit of *force*, but I predict that the average American would likely wind up employing the term as a measure of *mass* in his interplanetary trips to butcher and health-spa. In this sense, the semantics of "weighs 2 lb." for most of us differs somewhat, and is partially independent of, that for physicists. Thus if the ensemble M *excludes* the physics experts, "weighs 2 lb." will permit the noted double-indexing even in present-day English, whereas if M includes mainly physics experts, *has a mass of .9 kg.* drops out as a possible index. The odd facts about the usage of "weighs 2 lb." encapsuled in this complicated array of indices clearly belongs to the domain of "semantics" for present-day English.

The term "is 90°F" demonstrates this behavior in an even more unusual manner. As I remarked above, the true temperature of the air in the sun and under a shady tree are approximately the same, but thermometers read different values in the two locales and it certainly feels cooler in the shade (as every fixit man knows). For most of us, "is 90°F" does not denote a temperature proper, but rather a complicated average of true air temperature plus the radiant energy available in that air from other sources. The linguist can capture this interesting behavior in English by stating which property indices are justifiable when the ensemble of human types includes the experts, and when it does not. This odd fact about English is as much in the proper province of the semanticist as the fact that a certain term in Eskimo denotes male siblings and seals. This example shows that discussion in English of the semantics of English language predicates is not always trivial. It also suggests qualifications to Putnam's "Principle of the Division of Linguistic Labor."[32] We can meaningfully ascribe an extension (with certain implicit parameters) to the everyday use of "is 90°F" which differs from that appropriate to the temperature experts in our society. There is a natural temptation to claim that the experts assign a somewhat different *meaning (or sense) to "is 90°F"* than the rest of us. The fact that "is 90°F" corresponds to two fairly clearcut *ranges of application* represents an interesting aspect of English linguistics, but this common phenomenon should be regarded as *sui generis* and not lumped with ambiguities of "meaning" such as the word "bank" displays. Intuitive talk of the "varying senses" of "is 90°F" is unexceptionable if understood merely as a description of the double range of application, but it should not mislead us into supposing that the experts "grasp" a distinct *concept* (especially when physicists employ the term in the same way as the rest of us in ordinary conversation with no sense of disharmony with their laboratory practice).

IX

Successful application of the foregoing model requires a certain *stability* in classificatory behavior with respect to the predicate indexed. Human beings, unlike thermometers, are *self-correcting* measurement devices with memories. Any such device, mechanical or biological, is affected by the *history* of its earlier classifications. A sophisticated, self-correcting egg candling machine might accept eggs a and b and reject c if presented in the order $\langle a, b, c \rangle$, yet accept b and c and reject a if presented in the order $\langle c, b, a \rangle$. The utility of our extension assignments (which are modeled upon thermometer type cases) require that almost all objects within an appropriate range of application will be eventually classifiable as "P" or not *irrespective of the order in which they are tested*. As an example which lacks this "stability," consider the 1780 employment of "has lost 1 BTU of caloric." Within a suitably limited range of application, can we profitably assign this predicate a property-index, e.g., *has lost 1 BTU of thermal energy*? The task is to find a reasonable account of this range, which is not as easily produced as in the foregoing cases. The difficulty is simply that cannon boring and other mechanical sources of heat (Rumford's classic work in overthrowing caloric theory centered around such observations) constitute fairly unavoidable thermal events. Serious reflection on these phenomena will totally confuse anyone about how to apply the predicate "has lost one BTU of caloric" (granted that classical caloric theory postulated that caloric loss can be determined by both temperature loss *and* change in specific heat capacity). Accordingly, prior observations of cannon boring will generally affect the determination of caloric content one might otherwise make on other physical systems. Thus there is no reasonable range of application in which the use of "caloric" will be stable.

The problem is even more pronounced in the case of "contains orgone." Although Reicheans classified an odd variety of objects as pure orgone (e.g., the reflection mirages seen on a warm highway), it seems impossible to find a suitable range of application or ensemble of nonexperts to satisfy our model. Only over-zealous Duhemians doubt that serious study by rational agents of quite humdrum objects in hopes of determining their orgone content will lead instead to a rejection of the theory. Here the only reasonable extension for "is orgone" is the null set, because we can predict that, in time, further organic research will lead to the term's abandonment. General philosophic practice agrees that "caloric" and "orgone" should be assigned empty extensions. However, in related cases our "intuitions" are less clear and closely connected with problems of classificatory error. As indicated above, an object *a* classified as "P" by subject *S* should not be reckoned in "P"'s extension, if *a* would not be so classified by other members of *S*'s ensemble or if *S* could be led to change his mind through permissible scientific and technological developments. Often, however, observation of an unexpected object will radically affect the society's linguistic behavior, possibly in a quite unpredictable sort of way. Imagine a primitive tribe that believes all large objects which move through the sky in apparent disregard of gravitational influences do so because of a special kinematic ability correlated with wings. They employ a term *oneymey* to apply to some of these objects, in particular, all birds and the sun. How will they react when some visiting pedagog exposes them to the telescope and more detailed ornithological observations? The natives may stop calling the sun an *oneymey* or they may continue in their labeling, yet with a chastened sense of kinematics. Such enlightened natives would employ *oneymey* as we would if we had an atomic predicate meaning "is a bird or the sun." Recognition of new scientific fact alone needn't force alteration of classificatory behavior, as long as the misleading implications of that practice can be somehow defused. (We continue to employ "weighs 5 lbs." in a jolly, 1600 sort of way, despite our heightened appreciation of the difference between force and mass.) If the range of applicability and permissible technological development is explicitly limited to the stable range appropriate to Iron Age peoples, *oneymey* can be granted the extension $\{x/x$ is a bird or the Sun$\}$, but within a wider compass we may possess no rationale for assigning an extension at all if it cannot be predicted whether the enlightened tribe will continue to apply *oneymey* to birds and the sun, restrict it to birds only or abandon its use altogether.

If I understand correctly, the Kripke–Putnam view discussed in Section III would probably maintain that the only proper extension for *oneymey* should be $\{x/x$ is a member of *aves*$\}$. The preference for this class rests upon a doctrine of natural kinds. I have never fully grasped what these are supposed to be; presumably they are physical properties (in my sense) which are somehow prominent or privileged in nature. My understanding is that *is a member of *aves** constitutes such a kind, whereas the disjunctive *is a member of *aves* or the sun** does not. I lack space to discuss this metaphysical (or epistemological?) view here, but I firmly believe that such notions are indefensible and based upon naïveties about the complexity of the physical world. Certainly the class of stuff we call "water" is not a "simple" category at all – I challenge the natural kinds enthusiast to clearly explain why a glass of Lake Erie belongs to the same "natural kind" as distilled water, whereas a glass of celery juice or soda pop (which usually contains more H_2O by volume) does not.

In any case, Hilary Putnam presents a view like the following:[33]

> Predicate "P" denotes property Q in L if and only if "P" was introduced into L by the baptism " 'P' will henceforth denote whatever property is causally responsible for *this* physical behavior" and Q is the natural kind responsible for the behavior indicated.

Thus Fahrenheit could have pointed to his thermometer and said, "Henceforth, 'is 5°F' will denote whatever property of an object is causally responsible for making my device read '5'."[34] According to Putnam, this singles out a certain thermal property which becomes the denotation of the predicate. The "natural kind" doctrine makes the *uniqueness* of this property seem more likely than is reasonably plausible (in fact, concepts of "temperature" bifurcate according to the variety of Gibbsian ensembles to which the system under study may be assigned). Such unanalyzed appeal to the notion of a property being "causally responsible for certain behavior" should be viewed with some suspicion. In philosophy of science, phrases like this occur most naturally in the context of measurement interactions and the present paper grew (like Topsy) from musings on the justification for such locutions within purely physical contexts. Almost no measurement instrument can succeed in responding to only one physical property and there is little reason to suppose that we, as hydrocarbon detection devices, can isolate physical attributes by our classificatory predicates either. But measuring implements work perfectly well even if they are not universal and human beings may use language perfectly comfortably even if their predicates don't correspond uniquely to physical properties – as long as both stay within their appropriate ranges of applicability.

The "natural kind" picture, while commendably pointing to the *predictive* aspects of extension assignments, overstates its case by neglecting the complicated phenomena associated with our implicit parameters and postulating far too many unique linguistic evolutions. Within our own language, its presumptions of univocal development are encouraged by a peculiar form of historical parochialism due to a faulty association of extension with intuitive "meaning." Putnam has quite rightly and wisely stressed that there is little reason to hold that "weighs 2 lbs," "has momentum 2 kg-m/sec" or "is an electron" have changed their *meaning* during their respective terms of scientific employment, for the utility of "meaning" talk does not lie in this direction. However, one should not conclude from this "meaning" invariance that the predicates' extensions have remained likewise constant. In truth, the *implicit parameters* appropriate to these predicates will have widened enormously over the past four centuries and no linguist could have legitimately predicted how their application was to be extended in the new circumstances. We observed this earlier for "weight" and "electron"; the same moral holds for "momentum" as well. Given this change of parameters, it becomes misleading to say that the *extensions* of these predicates haven't changed over time (although it is equally inappropriate to claim that they have).

Like anachronism surrounds popular conceptions of the extension of "gold" in, e.g., Locke's usage. The idea that all Au-atoms should indubitably belong to this set ignores many of the complexities and viccisitudes in the history of "element." Given the complicated intertwining of "chemical" (combination properties) and "physical" (optical and mass spectroscopy) experiments in our actual scientific development, our final identification of "element" with atomic number was perhaps historically inevitable.[35] However I fail to see that this scheme is the only rational one. Certainly proof of its uniqueness would require a more careful study of alternate historical developments than "natural kïnd" proponents typically provide. Neutrons are often best regarded as excited (isospin) states of protons. The transition from Pa^{234} to U^{234} through β-emission can thus be viewed as the collapse of an "element" into a lower energy state. In fact, older writers wrote this decay as "Uranium X_{II} → Uranium II + β" and this old-fashioned terminology does not represent a simple "mistake." Moreover if chemical behavior is the key criterion for elementhood, why couldn't the rare earths be labeled as one "element"? So while we can safely assign samples of the stable isotope of Au to Locke's "gold," there is no reason to insist that the twelve radioactive forms of Au be so apportioned. For classificatory convenience, we will prefer to assign *is Au* to Locke's "gold" because that particular property, among all its interchangeable indices, has the shortest label in present-day English. But the convenience of this description should not bewitch us into historical parochialism.

X

Thus far we have restricted our attention to the community's employment of sentences like "this is P." However, within a linguistic community there are many predicates "P" which are not used to classify *anything* positively as "P," simply because the relevant objects are too small, too large or otherwise unapproachable to be easily "presentable" through available technology. Consider the predicate "is an atom" as employed by Daltonians *circa* 1840. Certainly it seems appropriate to assign {x/x is an atom}, understood in the modern sense. On the other hand, consider Newton's "is a (single) light corpuscle." No object was ever classified as such by Newtonians. Rather, beams of light and so forth were classified as "*aggregates* of light corpuscles" and it seems permissible to correlate the latter term with the property *is a collection of photons with energies in the visible range*[36] and its analogous extension. Yet it does not seem so appropriate to index "is a single light corpuscle" by *is a photon with an energy in the visible region*. Our simple model of property indexing fails in this case and requires supplementation if we are to discuss property-indexing for such predicates. A wide range of other examples exhibit this same character: "contains 10 BTU's of caloric" (*total* amount of caloric in a substance was never determined), "is a Mendelian gene" (as opposed to "this plant *expresses* a Mendelian gene"), "is a Thompson electron" and so forth. A better understanding of when such predicates can be profitably indexed by nonnull properties would be desirable.

The fact that the community holds more complicated sentences true suggests a strategy. The atomistic tenets of kinetic theory justify a certain mathematical treatment of macroscopic gases. As long as the mathematics seems appropriate and fruitful in application, the scientific community will cling to the sentence "gases are composed of molecules, which don't interact strongly except on collision, etc." "Molecule" can then be assigned an extension consisting of whatever partitioning of the gas allows that mathematical treatment to work. It is this sort of consideration which underlies many of Putnam's remarks. It remains a challenge to develop such examples into a clear model on a par with that we have supplied for classificatory behavior. By combining these various factors, we may obtain a better reconstruction of the intuitive notion of "extension."[37]

However we might proceed to extend our model to cover such predicates, we must be careful to insure that our adequacy condition is met. Otherwise we cannot guarantee that our extension assignments have much connection with the current linguistic competence of the speakers, as seems necessary for the subject of semantics. Although most of us are inclined to assign Newton's "is a light corpuscle" the null extension, I wager that if Einstein, in tribute to Newton, had resurrected this phrase in lieu of "photon," then we would presently be more willing to grant

Newton's "light corpuscle" an extension consisting of the things we call "photons." Obviously a system of extension assignments designed to reflect only facts warranted by a Newtonian speaker's linguistic training in the 1700's should not be dependent upon this later action of Einstein's. Hence, any development of the present theory of property-indexing must avoid smuggling in appeals to unsystematic intuitions of the "light corpuscle"–*photon* sort.

Such temptations towards semantic myopia are so prevalent that we must proceed with considerable care for rigor if we seek to extend our one-strand explication of "extension" in further ways. We have already seen that we must likewise be circumspect in our "correction" of extension assignments to native languages in connection with classificatory error. In a rough characterization of a native predicate, we shall employ the most convenient of its inter-changeable English labelings, but this selection should not be canonized into a mythology of "natural kinds." In these ways, this paper is content to disagree somewhat with common "intuitions" about the *correct* extensions for various specimen predicates. Hence if this paper errs towards the "operational," it is only because the Scylla of anachronism represents a vastly more imminent danger.

However our model is extended, implicit parameters will still be required as prophylactics against unwarranted linguistic prediction. In the molecule case, the underlying mathematics works profitably only for dilute gases and forces no decision as to what a "molecule" should represent in a typical solid (where present practice is rather unpredictable).

XI

For most physical quantities ϕ, at most historical moments in time, it is extremely unlikely that a linguistic community should be *prepared*, even collectively, to recognize all proper objects possessing ϕ. This follows, I believe, as a corollary to the general difficulty of constructing measuring instruments to correctly detect the presence of ϕ in all circumstances. Frege's hope for a "logically perfect language," where the application of every predicate is well determined, must represent an impossible dream; a society's best preparation against unexpected classifications is a detailed scientific account of the world.

There are two major factors which lead to underestimation of this underdetermination. First, a schedule of linguistic training can easily minimize the psychological surprise (and subsequent linguistic disruption) occasioned by the discovery of an unexpected object, so that its essential novelty may pass unnoticed. The Druids, for example, believe that virtually everything they will discover can be classified appropriately as a "bird" or not, without significant qualms or need for conventional legislation by a Druid kingpin. We possess the same sanguine attitude towards our own "bird," "is red," etc. This optimism helps explain why the Druids and ourselves often glide smoothly through delicate periods like B-52 landings without linguistic tremor. Indeed the genuine novelty of a previously unmet object will typically be recognized only long after linguistic practices concerning its classification have ossified in the language. In Wittgensteinian fashion, we should accordingly distinguish two senses in which linguistic indoctrination can *determine* the subsequent classification of an object *a*. 1) The speakers in the society generally agree, when *a* is ultimately confronted, whether it is "F" or not. 2) It can be *predicted* from knowledge of the initial training alone, without data about the intervening history of the speakers, how this classification will proceed. Our case studies illustrate how these two senses of "determine" often diverge.

Generally, a society will be satisfied with a linguistic training just in case it determines$_1$ classificatory behavior. Bombers were not upsetting to the Druids in this regard. Nonetheless, it was not determinate$_2$ that a B-52, however presented, was a "bird," but this lack of foresight did not bother the Druids in the least. Confusion of these two senses makes "determination$_2$" appear a more common feature of language than it really is.[38]

Second, we will sometimes grant that a particular object *a* is determined$_2$ to lie in the extension of "P," although none of the "P"'s employers will in fact be able to so classify *a*, for much the same reasons that similar allowances are provided for the "mistakes" of measuring instruments. The positive theory of this paper has tried to delineate reasonable guidelines for this exculpation of "mistakes." Whether one fully acquiesces in the details of this analysis or not, our case studies clearly show that all lack of determination$_2$ should not be pardoned as a linguistic "mistake." The fundamental distortions of the traditional theory of meaning, it seems to me, lie in this direction. Certainly, talk of "concepts" in itself can be harmless, as when we absolve speaker S from a routine "misclassification" by the description "S possesses the correct concept for 'P,' but doesn't know how to test *a* for this trait." But we are led to a mystifying view of language if we demand (as Fregean theory does) that such "concept" talk be applicable in more extreme linguistic situations. As an example of how a parallel form of description can be pushed beyond its useful limits, consider an automated ore gathering device which can be programmed via a punched card to select specimens of an assigned mass. Thus the current *program* of our machine might express: "Gather samples of mass 1 kg." Occasionally, the machine will *misclassify* stones according to this program, either because of machine misfunction or oddities in the ore tested. But if we ship our apparatus to the moon, without changing its card, it will routinely gather stones of considerably larger mass. Is the machine *now* "misclassifying" the lunar rocks "relative to its program?" The question seems peculiar, because the assumed stability of environment which underlies fruitful "programming" talk has been transgressed.

Likewise, if one attempts to depict the Druid classifications in terms of the idiom of traditional theory – i.e., delineate the "concepts" which the Druids at various points in our various histories have assigned to "bird" – one is led to implausible and strained descriptions of the phenomena. I won't run through the alternatives in detail, but the upshot will attribute quite peculiar mental states to the Druids (e.g., spells of mass amnesia or ineffable meanings for "bird"). In this way, Putnam's "Twin Earth" argument against Fregean theory can be reconstructed based on the data of linguistic evolution presented here.

Classical theories of meaning must represent the Druid classifications as freakish and aberrant behavior, whereas there is every reason to suppose that theirs is the *normal way* we should expect a linguistic community to function in a novel environment. One should accordingly beware of inflating innocent "concept" talk into a theory which attempts to explain all major aspects of language learning and use in terms of "grasp" of a special entity called a "sense" or "concept." The relevant difference between the Druids and ourselves is that they are more ignorant of the world's variety than we. Fregean theory attempts to distill this ignorance into a distinct concept-index for "bird." In truth, the only way we can recapture for ourselves the blissful frame of mind the Druids enjoyed when they employed the term "bird" in pre-B-52 days is to forget a lot of what we know about the world. Entertaining a novel concept does not make one ignorant, but forgetfulness is the only possible route to employing a predicate with the same "semantical" properties as Druidese "bird." In short, we don't need to *acquire* something here (a novel concept); we need to *lose* something (general knowledge). Nor is it useful, in the absence of other peculiar features in Druid society, to suppose that the Druids possess a different "conceptual scheme" from us – a phrase which often conveys a very misleading picture of the difference between cultures. The Druids don't think in any mysterious way; they are simply unaware of machinery.

The purpose of this essay has been twofold: to uncover data inimical to Fregean theory and, through construction of a simplified model, show that the undeniable utility of extension assignments can be retained while abandoning the rigid guidance of language, independent of historical happenstance, required by the traditional theory. That view conceives of language rather as a railway line designed by a corps of engineers (the advance party sent out at the "setting up" of the language) and the process of employing it consists in sitting in the observation car and remarking upon the scenery passed en route. I advocate thinking instead of those comical locomotives in children's literature which unroll their tracks before them as they move through a terrain. In the short run, the path of the train responds to the hills and gullies of the landscape virtually as well as the better designed line and the view from the observation car may seem practically identical. In the words of the old song, "she gets there just the same," partially because the passengers are along only for the ride and have no clear conception of a long term destination anyhow.[39]

Appendix: Further Remarks on Measurements

To simplify discussion, I introduce the notion of a *detection device*, an instrument which will correctly answer "yes" or "no" whether the object tested has the property P or not. A measurement device, on the other hand, typically supplies a numeral which has some correlation with the degree to which the measured object possesses a physical quantity Q. Many detection devices (e.g., a thermostat) are not measuring devices, but every measuring instrument constitutes a family of detection devices, depending upon which numeral is selected as the "yes" answer. Thus a centigrade thermometer can detect the properties* is 5°C*, * is 6°C*, etc., by selecting *the mercury rests on the '5'*, * the mercury rests on the '6'*, and so on, as a "yes" answer. The notion of a detection device is simpler to analyze, because there are a variety of ways in which a scale of measurement may reflect facts about the relationships of the objects measured, as indicated by an associated transformation group. The reader may easily erect a suitable theory of measurement indices based on the following and standard literature on scales of value.[40] It is worth remarking that the knowledge that a device *m* can measure a given physical quantity supplies much more information about *m* than the simple fact that it can detect a related physical property. A somewhat richer theory of indexing by physical quantities in language can be evolved along these lines, but we shall not pursue the matter further.

The four parameters our theory requires are:

1   *Range of Applicability* (R).   This is illustrated in the text by the fact
    that a beam balance detects mass and "weight" properties indiffer-
    ently if used on earth.
2   *Manner of Application* (A).   This parameter is closely related to the
    foregoing and probably cannot be sharply distinguished from it. A
    medicinal thermometer may measure internal body temperature,
    but only if the device is inserted in the proper orifice and not,
    e.g., balanced on the top of the subject's head. Under this heading
    the various standing conditions necessary to the measuring instru-
    ment's proper functioning may be placed. In foundational studies,
    such problems of application are often simplified by assuming the
    measuring instrument and its objective are initially closed, nonin-
    teracting systems which come to interact in time via the definite
    process M, and I have tacitly made a similar assumption in the
    language case. Our understanding of this parameter could be much
    improved.
3   *The "yes" answer* (Y).   We have already noted that a thermometer
    may serve as a detection device for many distinct properties,
    depending upon which numeral is selected for the "yes" answer.
    I have allowed the absence of a "yes" answer to be a "no" answer,
    but other approaches are possible here.
4   *General type of the device* (M).   The production of a correct "yes" or
    "no" answer in *m* for P must not be the result of accidental coinci-
    dence; rather the measurement event should be, in principle,
    repeatable. In the jargon of the physicists, this requires reference
    to an *ensemble* of devices. We cannot require simply that *m* give
    repeated answers under repeated trials, because many common
    testing devices may be employed only once. We ask instead that
    devices of the same type as *m* provide statistically regular answers
    under exactly similar test conditions. Hence we need to know the
    properties which determine the general "type" of *m* as a fourth
    implicit parameter for property-indexing. In practice, we usually
    allow a broader class of instrumentation to count as the "same
    type" as *m* beyond the narrow class of devices macroscopically
    indistinguishable from *m*. For example, we are inclined to credit
    some of the early "thermoscopes" with the ability to measure
    temperature (rather than, e.g., barometric pressure) because we
    allow the *family* of thermometers to include these devices and the
    group as a whole reliably indicates temperature. In such cases, the

attribution "*m* detects P" really doesn't tell us much about the internal structure of a device *m*, but only about the internal structure of most of the systems macroscopically similar to *m*. So wide tolerances about the type of a machine may allow us to claim that a particular instrument *m* can detect a certain property P even though *m* usually gives wrong answers! Perhaps this example depends upon casting our ensemble net too widely, but this problem can theoretically surface no matter how narrowly we restrict the type of *m* – a possibility always remains that *m* is an unrepresentative member of the ensemble and lacks the internal characteristics of the others (*vide* the analogous properties of "temperature" analyzed in Gibb's fashion). Thus a slight cavil must attach to our claim that property indexing always indicates structural information about the device indexed; it may only convey such information about most members of *m*'s ensemble.

Although our definition strictly applies only to completely reliable instruments, error may be accommodated by appeal to the ensemble M. Roughly, *m* can detect P with 90% accuracy with respect to M if and only if for every suitable test object x, 90% of M-devices give correct "yes" or "no" answers on x. (We will not pursue the standard problems of applying percentages to infinite ensembles). When an ensemble ranges over a developmental history (as in most linguistic cases and the thermometer/thermoscope example), it is natural to weigh the contribution of the latter members of M more heavily. As pointed out in the text, the utility of the objective property indexing format breaks down if M lacks suitable stability to provide a natural standard of weighting.

P and Q will be *interchangeable* as indices if and only if no device in the ensemble M can discriminate P objects meeting R from Q objects meeting R. The most typical case is where it is a law of nature that any object fulfilling R will have P if and only if it has Q. Thus *has mass .9.kg* and *is under an impressed gravitational force of 9 nts.* are interchangeable with respect to the parameter *is located on the surface of the earth*.

Notes

1   This paper is partially intended as a commentary upon Hilary Putnam's "The Meaning of Meaning" (in his *Mind, Language and Reality*, Cambridge University Press, Cambridge, 1975), to which I am deeply indebted. Thanks

also to George Wilson for extensive discussions essential to the paper's development and to Bob Pippin and an anonymous referee for their helpful comments.

2   Actually there are several related types of extension: the set of things presently P, things which are P at some time or other, spacetime slices of things while they are P, etc. I ignore these distinctions here and the problem of making these notions relativistically acceptable!

3   I ignore the pterodactyls present in the original movie. Also, by fiat, insects, boomerangs, etc., are not to be considered "flying devices."

4   *Journal of Philosophy* 70, August 16, 1973. See also Kit Fine, "Vagueness, Truth and Logic," *Synthese* 30, 1975. There is some overlap in spirit between the Field piece and my own, although his motivating examples are drawn entirely from Kuhnian "scientific revolutions." As J. Earman and A. Fine point out in "Against Indeterminacy," *Journal of Philosophy* (Sept. 1977), the subsequent employment of a term like "mass" is usually uniquely predictable from its prior usage in such cases (partially because the new equations of motion are derived through explicit ties to the old). My focus is rather on the *silent* linguistic evolutions which may transpire in the course of the most humdrum scientific research. Kit Fine's examples are all of the "borderline" case type.

It is quite important to distinguish sharply between the *expected vagueness* of a term like "red" where one has been taught (as part of one's linguistic training) to anticipate the "borderline cases" and the *unexpected vagueness* studied here. I think the two phenomena have quite distinct places within semantics (which manifests itself clearly when one provides a semantic justification for the derivation roles of a language). I hope to discuss these matters on another occasion.

5   Formal analogy: *extension* is to *implicit parameter* as *scale of measurement* is to *transformation group*.

6   For some interesting data on this very matter, see R. Bulmer's "Why is the Cassowary not a Bird?" *Man*, vol. 2, no. 1, March 1967.

7   "The rigidity of zoological nomenclature forces the taxonomist to record borderline forms either as subspecies or as species. An outsider would never realize how many interesting cases of evolutionary intermediacy are concealed by the seeming definiteness of the species and subspecies designations." – E. Mayr, *Populations, Species and Evolution*, Harvard (Cambridge, 1970), p. 286.

8   Reprinted in Lorentz, Einstein *et al.*, *The Principle of Relativity*, Dover (New York, 1952).

9   An example of a classical theory without extensions might be a Katzian account of "semantic markers." I do not intend this division of explanatory role to be very precise.

10   Vague predicates like "is red" are best treated in the classical mold as follows: the concept intermediary for the predicate is likewise imprecise,

yet *conceptually* linked to a nonvague relation such as... *is redder than - - -*. This associated ordering will provide a measure *r* (not necessarily numerical) of a's nearness to a core. From this measure, a "fuzzy set" of pairs <a,r> can be assigned to "is red." Thus Dummett's ideal observer should be able to assign borderline cases of "is red" to an appropriate ordering from her grasp of the correlated relation.

11 Wittgenstein's discussion of "following a rule" can be profitably viewed as an attack on this submerged explanatory aspect of classical theory. Incidently, I feel that much of this paper, especially the treatment of "determine" in Section XI, bears close ties to Wittgenstein's views, but since the *Investigations* have so often served as a Rorschach pattern to elicit the most diverse philosophic opinions, I won't press the point further.

12 To explain the taxonomy/explanation distinction further: measuring devices can be segregated according to the properties they detect. Such attributions represent a pure taxonomy of measuring instruments, for they provide no explanation at all of how the devices, *qua* "blackboxes," work. Nonetheless, such facts can prove valuable parts of other explanations, e.g., "Scott found his way back to camp, because he had a device which could detect magnetic north."

13 *Op. cit.*, pp. 223–27. This is his well-known "Twin Earth" argument. We shall visit these basic themes again in Section XI, purged of "ideas in the head" identifications or kriptic appeals to "indexicality."

14 This is a paraphrase, altered from sentences to predicates, of a remark in "The Justification of Deduction" in *Truth and Other Enigmas*, Harvard University Press (Cambridge, 1978) p. 314.

15 *Cf.* Hilary Putnam's "On Properties" in his *Mathematics, Matter and Method*, Cambridge University Press (Cambridge, 1975) or my "Physical Properties," forthcoming in *Philosophia*. D. M. Armstrong's *A Theory of Universals*, Cambridge University Press (Cambridge, 1978), also adopts this basic tack, although I am less happy with the details.

16 Predicates will denote physical properties if they can be "reduced" to purely physical notions. Thus we can expect the special vocabulary of chemistry, biology and so forth to constitute "physical property predicates."

17 "Explanation and Reference" in *Mind, Language and Reality, op. cit.*

18 Saul Kripke, *Naming and Necessity*, Harvard University Press (Cambridge, 1980).

19 At least this is how I shall interpret the natural kind theory, although the originals are not entirely explicit. Putnam views "reference" (the connection between predicate and set) as irreducibly "theoretical," without clear warrant.

20 However adequate understanding of such examples would require a lengthy discussion of definability in physics, which I will not pursue here. *Cf.*, my forthcoming "What is this Thing Called 'Pain'?"

21 It isn't!

22   The requirement that a measurement attribution reflects only the internal composition of the device is the analogue of our earlier adequacy condition for extension assignments.

23   For an explanation of the switch from "measure" to "detect," *cf.* the appendix. In Nelson Goodman's terminology, "relevant conditions" are needed to convert a counterfactual into a straightforward statement of scientific law (*cf. Fact, Fiction and Forecast*, Bobbs-Merrill (Indianapolis, 1965), p. 5). My implicit parameters can be viewed as appropriate "relevant conditions" for the rather vague counterfactual "if *m* were applied to object *n*, *m* would answer 'yes' if and only if *n* has P."

24   Some predicates should be indexed by entities which are not true properties in the sense of "Physical Properties," *op. cit.*, but rather ordered n-tuples of a relational property plus particular physical objects. *Is Earthbound* is a case in point. The above definition can be easily expanded to fit these situations, as can the earlier account for detection devices. Except in English, we require a *translation* of "Is this P?"

25   If *a* associates "P" with a relational predicate "T" then "P" can be granted a "fuzzy" extension α (w.r.t. R, A, M, "T") if ($\exists\beta$) (β is the timeless extension for "T" (w.r.t. R, A, M) and α is any directed set determined by β). *Cf.* note 10. Objects in the "fuzzy" portion of a "fuzzy" extension I call *expectedly vague*; objects outside the range of application parameter *R* are *unexpectedly vague*.

26   Data drawn (with slight simplification) from R. Bulmer, "Karam Color Categories," *Kivung* (November, 1968). The normal dictionary entry for *pk* is "red," but *pk*'s extension is clearly not $\{x/x$ is red$\}$. This suggests that the relationship between a predicate's "translation" (in the sense of a dictionary entry) and its extension is not always straightforward.

27   A predicate like "is a chair," whose instances we may assume will be manufactured by humans, probably represents a mixed case. Its extension, in so far as it is determinate, will consist roughly of those objects possessing objective traits of resemblance to what will happen to be labeled "chairs" by their designers.

28   Throughout this paper, I will suppress the method of application parameter A (*cf.* appendix), by assuming that the examining agent x is brought from infinity into object y's spatial vicinity at t with whatever collection of apparatus x might have at hand in his society. This parameter merits more rigorous scrutiny, however.

29   For a fascinating study of these divergent tendencies with respect to terms like "salt," "acid," and "butter," *cf.* M. P. Crosland, *Historical Studies in the Language of Chemistry*, Dover (New York, 1978). It seems to me that the long vexed problem of whether color properties can be properly *identified* with quantum structural traits is intimately tied to these considerations. The only legitimate notion of "property" I accept is that of a physical property, but a predicate like "is red" or "weighs 5 lbs." can be insulated from the pressures to align with a unique physical property through a variety of compensative linguistic factors.

30 Example derived from L. Mettler and T. Gregg, *Population Genetics and Evolution*, Prentice-Hall (Englewood Cliffs, 1969), pp. 15–17.

31 To provide an example for "water": Macroscopic "heavy water" (fluids containing large concentrations of D_2O) will not quench thirst or otherwise satisfy biological needs. If, contrary to fact, heavy water had been known since antiquity to occur in natural pools, such stuff would probably not be considered "(macroscopic) water" now, but instead some form of "fool's water" (although D_2O *molecules* might still be considered "water molecules").

32 "The Meaning of Meaning," *op. cit.*, pp. 227–9.

33 "Explanation and Reference," *op. cit.*, p. 200. In fairness, it is unclear that Putnam himself accepts the "natural kinds" doctrine sketched here.

34 Actually Fahrenheit's "5" was in the wrong place, but Putnam's theory can be clarified to handle this. On the other hand, his account apparently supplies no reason why "has lost 1 BTU of caloric" should fail to denote a property, since presumably some "natural kind" will have been responsible for the physical behavior present at its baptism.

35 For a history of the dispute, see H. R. Post, "Atomism 1900," *Physics Education*, vol. 3, 1968.

36 Thus a compound term may possess an extension, although some of its components do not. *Cf.*, Philip Kitcher, "Theories, Theorists and Theory Change," *Philosophical Review* (October, 1978), on "phlogiston" versus "dephlogistonated air."

37 A fairly pure example of such reasoning would be E. T. Whittaker's contention that "caloric" in Carnot's usage "denoted" entropy. *Cf.*, *From Euclid to Eddington*, Dover (New York, 1958) p. 77.

38 Suppose that the rubies on Pluto are such that their present environment permits a peculiar crystaline structure which reflects the ambient low intensity "white" light strongly in the "green." Bombarding the rubies with sufficient radiation to activate the cones in our eyes alters the molecular arrangement to the familiar terrestial forms. If asked "what *color* are the rubies presently on Pluto?" we might say, "well, I can't decide on the basis of your description of the case whether they are red or not, but we would be able to tell when we get there." Our overwhelming tendency to respond to science fiction cases in this manner is worth noting – it is an expression of our confidence that our training determines$_1$ our classificatory behavior. In truth, we are not awaiting further subtle facts about the objects *per se* (my description supplied all relevant facts about the rubies' scientific behavior) but for a *history of our approach* to the rubies. Thus if they are first discovered by a Plutonaut turning her light upon them, the practice of considering them "red" will probably arise, whereas they will [be] treated henceforth as "green" if they are instead first uncovered via a time exposure at low temperatures! What, on the concept view, explains why we adopt this peculiar "wait and see" attitude?

39   Either Wittgenstein or railroad nostalgia inspired Barry Stroud, quite independently, to like imagery. The points of our similar similes are different
however. *Cf.* his "Wittgenstein on Logical Necessity," *Philosophical Review* 74,
October, 1965.

40   E.g., S. S. Stevens, "On the Theory of Scales of Measurement" in A. Danto
and S. Morgenbesser, ed., *Philosophy of Science*, Meridian (Cleveland, 1961).

5

From *Meaning*

Paul Horwich

What I shall be calling "the use theory of meaning" is intended to answer the question: in virtue of which of its underlying properties does a word come to possess the particular meaning it has? The theory I am going to articulate bears certain affinities to ideas in the works of Wittgenstein, Sellars, Field, Harman, Block, Peacocke, Brandom, Cozzo, and other philosophers whose views could reasonably be labelled *use* theories of meaning.[1] But when I deploy this term I will be referring to my own specific version of the approach. My plan for this chapter is to sketch the main features of this account, to supply several arguments in its favour, to compare it with alternative theories, and to clarify and defend the proposal by responding to a large collection of old and new objections.

A Sketch of the Theory

The picture I intend to develop involves three principal claims.

(I) *Meanings are concepts.* A word or phrase – whether it be spoken, written, signed, or merely thought (i.e. an item of 'mentalese') – expresses a 'concept', which is an abstract entity from which beliefs, desires, and other states of mind are composed. Thus, what a linguistic expression *means* – what it gives us reason to regard as present in the mental state of the speaker – is a concept. For example, the property of believing one has a dog consists in standing in the belief relation to the concept, I HAVE A DOG, i.e. to the meaning of "I have a dog".[2] And such concepts, expressed by sentences, are somehow engendered by the concepts expressed by words. Thus the concept, I HAVE A DOG, is made in part from the concept DOG, which is the meaning of "dog". I would argue, moreover, that one can identify *properties* with predicative concepts (that, for example, DOG = doggyness); but this further suggestion will play little role in what follows.

(II)   *The overall use of each word stems from its possession of a basic acceptance property.*   For each word there is a small set of simple properties which (in conjunction with other factors and with the basic properties of other words) explain total linguistic behaviour with respect to that word. These explanatorily basic properties fall into various kinds – the so-called phonological, syntactic, semantic, and pragmatic – where each such kind is defined by the distinctive form of its members and by the range of phenomena they are needed to account for. The present theory is focused on the *semantic* feature of a word. The distinctive form of that feature is that it designates the circumstances in which certain specified sentences containing the word are accepted; and the primary explanatory role of a word's acceptance property is to account for the acceptance of other sentences containing the word. For example, it may be that

(a)   the acceptance property that governs a speaker's overall use of "and" is (roughly) his tendency to accept "p and q" if and only if he accepts both "p" and "q";
(b)   the explanatorily fundamental acceptance property underlying our use of "red" is (roughly) the disposition to apply "red" to an observed surface when and only when it is clearly red;
(c)   the acceptance property governing our total use of the word "true" is the inclination to accept instances of the schema 'the proposition *that p* is true if and only if p'.

Thus for each word, w, there is a regularity of the form

All uses of w stem from its possession of acceptance property $A(x)$,

where $A(x)$ gives the circumstances in which certain specified sentences containing w are accepted. Think of all the facts regarding a person's linguistic behaviour – the sum of everything he will say, and in what circumstances. The thesis is that this constellation of data may be unified and explained in terms of a relatively small and simple body of factors and principles including, for each word, a basic use regularity. Statements (a), (b), and (c) indicate (to a first approximation) the sort of generalizations I have in mind. It is not implausible that something like these regularities are what explain our overall use of the words "and", "red", and "true".[3]

(III)   *Two words express the same concept in virtue of having the same basic acceptance property.*   Thus w expresses the same concept as "dog" – hence w means DOG – because a certain acceptance property is responsible for the overall use of w: namely, the one that is responsible for the overall use of "dog". Therefore the meaning property of a word is constituted by its having a certain basic acceptance property (or, in other words, by its conforming to the regularity, 'All uses of w stem from such-and-such acceptance property'). For example, the properties, 'x means AND', 'x means RED', and 'x means TRUE' are constituted by something like the use properties described in (II). Note that the thesis is not that meanings are uses; nor is it even that meaning properties are identical to use properties. The proposal is rather that meaning properties are constituted by use properties of roughly the sort just illustrated. The relevant notion of 'constitution' is quite familiar. . . . Just as 'being water' is constituted by 'being made of H_2O molecules' and 'being red' is constituted by 'emitting light of such-and-such a wavelength', so 'meaning AND' is constituted by the property characterized in (a) above.

These three theses form the core of the theory of meaning that I want to propose. I will elaborate them in the course of giving various reasons for believing the theory and in responding to a series of twenty-four objections.

Seven Arguments in Favour of the Use Theory of Meaning

1   *The univocality-of-"meaning" argument*

. . . [O]ne thing to be said on behalf of the use theory – especially the first component of it – is that it accommodates our ordinary way of speaking of *meanings* as a species of entity to which words stand in the relation 'x means y'. Moreover it makes do with the familiar, non-semantic use of the word "means". When we say, for example, that black clouds mean it will rain, or that the expression on his face means that he is sad, we are deploying a notion of *means* which is, roughly speaking, the notion of *indication*. To say, in this sense, that x means y, is to say, roughly, that x provides a good reason to believe in the presence of y. Now, according to the above theory, when we specify the meaning of a word, we are claiming that someone's use of the word would provide a good reason to expect the occurrence in his mental state of a certain concept. Thus, according to this account, the notion of meaning we deploy in connection with language – in speaking of the meanings of words – is exactly the same as the notion we deploy in non-semantic contexts. It is a virtue of this account that it respects the relational appearance of meaning attributions and that it calls for no special, *ad hoc* assumption about the meaning of "means" in semantic contexts.

2   *The explanation argument*

One of the properties of meaning that we recognize pretheoretically is that what people say is due, in part, to what they mean. For example, I assent to "That's red", when I do, partly because of what I mean by the word "red". And this explanatory feature of meaning is immediately accounted for by the use theory. For the central component of that theory is that the property which constitutes a word's having the meaning it does is that its use is governed by a certain explanatorily fundamental acceptance property. And it is indeed quite clear (as we have just seen) how the total use of a word might be derived, in light of circumstantial factors, from a basic 'law' of use – whereas it is relatively unclear how any other sort of property of a word (such as a reference, a normative characteristic, or some neurological correlate) would constrain its overall use.

Notice, by the way, that there is no conflict between my proposal to reduce meaning properties to use properties and the present observation that meaning explains use. For the aspect of use to which meaning properties reduce is quite different from the aspects of use that meaning properties explain. The former are generalizations to the effect that every use of a given word stems from a specified acceptance property; the latter are particular uses of that word. So it is perfectly natural to explain one in terms of the other. The generalizations about use explain particular utterances; therefore the theory that meaning properties are constituted by such generalizations accommodates the intuition that the things we say may be explained, in part, by reference to what we mean.

3   *The meaning-attribution argument*

Another strong argument in favour of the use theory is that it rationalizes our practice of meaning attribution: it squares with the procedures we actually follow to arrive at judgements about the meanings of words. For clearly we do establish what is meant by a word by observation of how it is used – more specifically, by recognizing an appropriate similarity between its use and the use of one of our already understood terms.

Thus we judge that the Italian "cane" means DOG on the basis of discovering an appropriate similarity in the use of "cane" and our use of "dog". Such 'appropriate' similarity does not preclude divergences in use – just as long as they can be explained away as resulting from circumstantial differences. For example, the fact that someone accepts "It is true that God exists" while someone else denies it, is not taken to show that they mean different things by "true", because this difference in their use of the word is explained by the fact that one of them accepts "God exists" while the other does not. Similarly, a disagreement about whether to apply "red" to the colour of some unexamined tomatoes in the fridge would not suggest any variation in what is meant by that word. For again the divergence in use is plausibly explained away as the product of differences that are unrelated to what the speakers mean. On the other hand, if someone assents to the sentence "Even though it is true that God exists, nevertheless God does not exist", we might well conclude that he does not mean what we do by the word "true". And if someone applies the word "red" to a surface that is obviously green, we will be inclined to think that his understanding of the word differs from ours.

These sentiments are exactly what one would expect in light of the use theory. For the way we are deciding whether the use of one word is 'appropriately' similar to the use of another is by determining whether the divergence in their use can be explained away, i.e. reconciled with there being an identity in the basic regularity that governs them. That is, their uses are regarded as 'appropriately' similar just in case they are governed by same basic regularity. When this is thought to hold of some foreign term w and one of our words "f", then we conclude (as the use theory predicts) that the concepts expressed by w and "f" are identical – hence (since trivially "f" expresses the concept F) that w expresses the concept F – or, in other words, that w means F. . . .

4   The synonymy argument

A further piece of evidence derives from the fact that synonyms are pretty freely substituted for one another. Suppose that terms w and v belong to the same language and have the same meaning. In that case speakers of the language, when they are prepared to accept something containing w, will usually be just as prepared to accept the sentence derived from it by replacing w with v. And this fact about synonyms calls for explanation. What account of the nature of meaning properties will explain that if two terms have the same one then they are 'co-accepted' in this way? Notice that if understanding a predicate were simply a matter of knowing what it is true of, this phenomenon would remain unexplained. For one might perfectly well know of some object both that w is true of it and that v is true of it, yet not be aware that those words are true of the same thing. The use theory, on the other hand, provides a natural answer; for the co-acceptance of synonyms is exactly what one should expect if the meaning property of a word is constituted by whatever explains the assertive utterances in which it figures – that is, by the fact that a certain basic regularity governs its use. For if w and v are governed by the same *basic* regularity, then, provided that all the other factors influencing the deployment of those words are the same – as they will be for a single person at a single time – the overall dispositions for their use by a given person at a given time will be the same, and so they will indeed be co-accepted. Thus the use theory derives a good measure of confirmation from the co-acceptance of synonyms.

5   The implicit definition argument

A fifth source of support for the theory lies in the phenomenon of implicit definition. One may introduce a new term, "f", and give it a meaning, simply by accepting a body of postulates, "#f", containing the term. This is how the non-observation vocabulary of a scientific theory is typically defined. But there is a question as to how such 'definitions' could work. What does meaning have to be like in order for there to be a possibility of conferring it in such a way? And it is hard to think of a plausible alternative to the answer that

   "f" means what it does

is constituted by the fact that

   The basic acceptance property of *"f"* is that *"#f"* is regarded as *true*.

Thus *"f"* means what it does in virtue of possessing the property that accounts for its overall use. . . .

6   The translation argument

The way in which we operate with manuals of translation (i.e. mappings that preserve meaning) is explained – and can only be explained – by means of the use theory of meaning. To see this, notice that a translation manual T (which maps our words, w_1, w_2,..., into foreign words $T(w_1)$, $T(w_2)$,..., and vice versa) is an instrument intended to enable us to manage successfully in a foreign community. To that end it is used as a device of 'expectation replacement': when we are abroad, instead of asserting *our* sentences, we assert the translations of them, supposing that this will generate the same relevant expectations in the audience as our sentences would at home. Conversely, when a foreigner says some-thing, we are to have the expectations normally associated with the translation of what he said. What this suggests is that our expectations at home are engendered by an implicit psychological – behavioural theory, $\$[w_1, w_2,...]$, specifying the uses of our words, w_1, w_2,..., in relation to one another and to environmental and other circumstances; and that our deployment of translation manual T in a foreign community consists in our operating there with the same implicit theory, but trans-formed by T. That is, we operate abroad with $T(\$)$, i.e. with $\$[T(w_1)$, $T(w_2)$,...]. And this is useful if $T(\$)$ is as good at enabling accurate predictions there as $\$$ is here – which will be the case if and only if $T(\$)$ is as true as $\$$. But the difference between $\$$ and $T(\$)$ is merely that the theory structure, $\$(x_1, x_2,...)$, is occupied on the one hand by our words and on the other hand by the associated foreign words. That is to say, the property of w_1 that any adequate translation of w_1 must also have, is $(\exists x_2)$ $(\exists x_3)...\$(x_1, x_2, x_3,...)$ – which specifies a basic regularity of use. Thus the function of translation manuals (as devices of expectation replace-ment) is explained by the theory that a good translation manual preserves the basic explanatory roles of words – i.e. by the theory that meanings consist in basic regularities of use....

7   *The pragmatic argument*

A related point in favour of the theory is that, in so far as it explains why we should seek manuals of translation, it explains, *a fortiori*, why it is valuable to possess the concept of translation and therefore the concept of meaning; hence it accounts for our having those concepts. In other words, there is a pragmatic rationale for our deploying the notions of meaning and translation that are characterized by my initial theses (I), (II), and (III). Since these use-theoretic notions are valuable for us to deploy, they are notions we can be expected to have. Thus the use theory explains the fact that we possess the concept of meaning.

...

Objections to the Use Theory of Meaning

Let me continue to flesh out the theory, and the above reasons for maintaining it, by saying something in response to each of the numerous difficulties that have been thought to preclude use-theoretic accounts of meaning....

The complaints, in brief, are as follows:

1   The notion of 'use' is too obscure for there to be such a thing as the so-called 'use theory' of meaning. (Quine)

2   If meaning were use, then any change in what we say, no matter how minor (for example, our coming to accept a single sentence that we once denied), would entail at least *some* change of meaning – which is absurd. (Fodor and LePore)

...

5   The use of a predicate cannot fix its extension, but its meaning can and does. (Kripke)

...

13   A word's usage may vary radically from one person to another, whereas its meaning is fixed by the linguistic community. (Putnam, Burge)

14   A scientifically valuable account of meaning would have to be internalistic – the alleged meaning-constituting properties would have to be neural (or something like that); but use properties sometimes make reference to the environment – to the fact that certain sentences are asserted in certain external conditions. (Chomsky)

...

17   Any alleged meaning-constituting use for a word (any postulates containing it) can be coherently doubted, and even rejected, without affecting the word's meaning. (Carnap)

...

20   A sound may be produced in accordance with some definite regularity, and yet none the less have no conceptual content.

21   In so far as the uses of words are characterized by reference to sentences containing them that are *accepted* (asserted, held true), then use is not fully explicable in non-semantic terms; for *acceptance* is a semantic notion.

...

23   The meaning of an utterance is the mental state it expresses, which is obviously not a use.

1   *Obscurity*

It is often said that the trouble with the use theory is not so much *falsity* as *unintelligibility*, on the grounds that it is completely unclear what is meant by the "use" of a word. But this complaint is surely an exaggeration. After all, expressions of the form "the use of X" and "how x is used" are common bits of ordinary language (applied, for example, to tools or to pieces in a game); and there is no particular difficulty in understanding someone who says he is going to tell us how some unfamiliar word is used. Moreover, I can be quite specific about what sort of thing is intended, in the present theoretical context, by the "use" of a word.

To begin, I have in mind some property of a word *type*. This property is specified by a generalization about tokens of that type – by the claim that they are all explained in terms of a certain acceptance property, a property specifying the circumstances in which designated sentences containing the word are held true. A couple of examples of such explanatorily basic acceptance properties, already mentioned, are (a) that we have the disposition to assert "That is red" in the presence of evidently red things; and (b) that we have the tendency to accept instances of the schema, "The proposition *that p* is true if and only if *p*". Notice that what I am taking to be the meaning-constituting use of a word is not merely that the word *possesses* a certain acceptance property, but that this fact about it is *explanatorily basic* – that it accounts for all uses of the word.[4] Thus w's meaning what it does is constituted by a regularity of the form, 'All uses of w stem from the fact that $A(w)$' – where $A(x)$ is an acceptance property.

Second, one should refrain from referring to such regularities as *rules*, so as not to encourage the idea that they are explicitly represented and deliberately followed. Such self-conscious following of rules for the use of words may sometimes occur, and may be associated with particular meanings; but it cannot constitute the meanings of *all* words because (as Wittgenstein emphasized) the rules themselves would have to be understood, and we would be faced with an infinite regress.

Third, a use property must be *non-semantic*. In order to specify one it will not do, for example, to say 'Instances of "bachelor" mean UNMARRIED MAN' or ' "Napoleon" is used to refer to Napoleon'. For the whole point is to demystify meaning and affiliated notions by characterising them in such terms that their explanatory relations to verbal behaviour become understandable.

Fourth, a use property should be *readily detectable*. For we can tell whether someone understands a word by the way he uses it. Therefore a property such as 'associated with such-and-such brain activity' could not be a use property; whereas a property such as 'applied in the presence of red things' would be fine.

A fifth point is that uses need not be restricted to inference patterns, or other purely *internal* phenomena. That sort of restriction – which sometimes goes under the name, "narrow conceptual-role (or inferential-role) semantics" – provides a notion of use that is too weak to capture meaning in the ordinary sense of the word.[5] The meanings of certain terms (e.g. "true") may be given by purely internal regularities of use; but others (e.g. "red") will call for reference to the environment. It should be noticed that given the above-mentioned point – namely, that the use regularities are not to be regarded as explicitly formulated, deliberately followed rules – there can be no objection (on grounds of circularity) to the idea that the use regularity of a given term may be characterized using that very term.

Finally, a use regularity for one word relates its occurrence to occurrences of other words. That is to say, the regularities governing the deployment of different words are not entirely separable from one another. In example (b) above, the regularity concerns not merely the word "true" but also the expressions "proposition" and "if and only if".

2   Holism

The fact that the regularities governing our use of any word will inevitably specify the occurrence of other terms (and hence the fact that the meanings of different words are inextricably interconnected with one another) provides one sense in which language is to some extent 'holistic'. But we can imagine a different, and more clearly implausible, form of holism; and it is sometimes alleged against the use theory of meaning that it must be wrong because it entails holism in this bad sense. Here is the argument.

If the meaning of a word were its use, then any discovery, in so far as it leads to the affirmation of previously unaffirmed sentences that contain the word, would give it a slightly new use – and therefore a slightly new meaning. But we do not regard such small changes of use as changes of meaning. So the use theory is false.

In response, it should be pointed out that one would not say, for example, that a hammer is being given a new use when it is used to hammer in a particular nail it has never hammered in before; one would not say that the queen in chess is being given a new use when it happens to be moved into a position that has never before been reached. And similarly, if a planet beyond Pluto were discovered, and we started to say

"There are ten planets", we would not thereby have given the word "planet" a new use. So the objection fails.

But, it will be asked in reply, what is the basis of the distinction that is being assumed here between the use facts (like, perhaps, our disposition to accept "Planets orbit stars") which could plausibly be held to constitute *the use* of "planet", and other use facts (like our disposition to accept "There are nine planets") which surely could not? Are we not committing ourselves (as Fodor and LePore have argued),[6] to some form of the analytic – synthetic distinction which Quine has persuaded us does not exist?

Perhaps. However, the fact that we sometimes do, and sometimes do not, recognize that the use of a word has changed, suggests that we do draw some sort of distinction here. What we have in mind, I would suggest, in differentiating between those use properties which comprise what we call *"the use"* and those which do not is simply the difference between the *explanatorily basic* use property and the rest. In other words, the way to pick out the particular use property of a word that comprises what we call "the use" is to find the use property that provides the best explanation of all the others.

The outcome of this sort of procedure may no doubt be indeterminate. There will sometimes be alternative, equally good ways of finding a simple regularity in the use of a word that (in conjunction with the use regularities of other terms and with general psychological laws) will account for all other aspects of its use. Therefore there will sometimes be no objective fact of the matter as to where the boundary lies between the pattern of use that constitutes the meaning of the expression, and other facts about its deployment. But a distinction with unclear boundaries is a distinction none the less – one that puts us in a position to say of certain novel deployments of a word that they definitely do not amount to changes in its use. Thus the use theory of meaning does not in fact lead to the counterintuitive form of holism.

. . .

5   Reference

. . . It is often said that the meaning of a word cannot be constituted by its use because its meaning determines its reference whereas its use could not do that. It is argued that, fallible finite creatures that we are, the set of things to which we are disposed to apply a predicate will inevitably diverge from its true extension. Thus the use of a predicate does not fix its extension, whereas its meaning obviously does.[7]

However, this reasoning is fallacious, for it equivocates on the sense of "determine". The meaning of a predicate does indeed determine its extension, in the sense that any two expressions with the same meaning must have the same extension (ignoring context sensitivity). But we have been given no reason to think that the use of a predicate fails *in that sense* to determine its extension. On the contrary, in so far as our predicates "*f*" and "*g*" have the same use, we must surely hold true "$(x) (fx \leftrightarrow gx)$", and so cannot suppose that their extensions diverge. What we have been given instead (but irrelevantly) is an argument to show that, in some much stronger sense of "determine" (call it "DETERMINE") the use of a predicate does not DETERMINE its extension.

Let me elaborate the notion of 'DETERMINATION' that appears to be presupposed in this argument. What seems to be understood by saying that the use of a predicate, x, must DETERMINE its extension is that there must be some use relation, '$a(xy)$', linking x with each member of its extension. It must be, in other words, that

x is *true* of y iff $a(xy)$,

where $a(xy)$ is some such relation as

We are disposed to apply predicate x to object y in (ideal) circumstances I.

And this requirement implies that

The extension of x is the set of fs iff $(y)[a(xy) \leftrightarrow y$ is $f]$.

But the meaning of x fixes its extension. The conclusion is therefore drawn that the meaning property

x means F

could be constituted by a certain use property only if that use property were to entail

$(y)[a(xy) \leftrightarrow y$ is $f]$,

for only then would x's extension be DETERMINED by what constitutes its meaning. But it turns out that no such use properties can be found; and that is because we cannot think of any use relation, $a(xy)$, that connects each predicate with the members of its extension. So the use theory of meaning must be wrong.

The obvious response, however, is that in the absence of any initial reason to think that the extension of a predicate should be DETERMINED by the property constituting its meaning, the fact that it is not so DETER-MINED by any use regularity provides no basis for doubting the consti-tution of meaning by use.

But perhaps there *is* some motivation for the DETERMINATION re-quirement? Might one not argue as follows? Since 'x is *true* of y' surely has some sort of analysis – i.e. there is surely some underlying relation, $r(xy)$, such that

x is *true* of $y = r(xy)$

– then whatever constitutes

x means F

must indeed entail something of the form

$(y)[r(xy) \leftrightarrow y$ is $f\,]$.

I suspect that this is indeed the implicit rationale for the DET-ERMINATION requirement. I can think of no other motivation for it. However, it can and should be resisted. For the assumption that the relation

x is *true* of y

has a non-semantic analysis is highly controversial. Indeed, the next chapter elaborates a *deflationist* view of the truth-theoretic properties, according to which there is no such analysis.

Such a view is an instance of what we saw in the previous section: namely, that what constitutes a relational fact need not involve an analy-sis of that relation. From the deflationary perspective, the fact that consti-tutes "dog" being *true* of Fido does not incorporate any analysis of "x is *true* of y"; what constitutes that fact, rather, is simply that Fido is a dog (and that "dog" means DOG). In general, "x is *true* of y" is implicitly defined by a combination of the equivalence schema

$(y)(\text{Concept } F \text{ is } true \text{ of } y \leftrightarrow fy)$

and the definition of "*true* of" for predicates in terms of "true of" for concepts

$$(x)(y)[x \text{ is } true \text{ of } y \leftrightarrow (\exists z)(x \text{ expresses } z \text{ \& } z \text{ is true of } y)].$$

Thus there is no non-semantic reductive analysis of "*x* is *true* of *y*"; so there is no reason to force the properties that constitute meanings into the above mould. Consequently, the fact that the basic regularity of use of a predicate does not DETERMINE an extension provides no ground for denying that it constitutes the meaning property of the predicate....[8]

13   Communal meanings

As Saul Kripke, Hilary Putnam, and Tyler Burge have made clear,[9] members of a linguistic community typically mean exactly the same as one another by a given word, even when their uses of it diverge, not merely in superficial respects (which might be explained away on the basis of differences in evidential circumstances), but also in fundamental respects (stemming from different basic regularities). Thus someone may always be at a loss as to whether to apply "beech" rather than "elm", or may not appreciate that "arthritis" names a disease of the joints; yet he may none the less qualify as an English speaker who means what we do by these words.

This fact about meaning can be dealt with in use-theoretic terms by bringing to bear Putnam's idea of 'the division of linguistic labour'. In order for an individual member of the community to mean a certain thing by a given word, it is not necessary that he himself uses it precisely in accordance with the regularity that fixes the meaning of the word type. What is needed is, first, that there are acknowledged experts in the deployment of the term – experts whose usage is determined by some such regularity; second, that the individual is disposed to defer to the experts – i.e. to accept correction by them; and consequently, third, that his use of the term conforms to that regularity at least to some extent. In these circumstances, even when the speaker's use of a word is fundamentally abnormal, we none the less attribute the normal meaning to him; and that normal meaning is constituted by the regularity that explains the overall use of the word by those 'specialists' to whom the rest of us are prepared to defer.

14 *I-language meanings*

An objection from the opposite direction can well be imagined: namely, that the use theory is not internalistic enough; for the meaning-constituting regularities of use that it postulates sometimes relate the deployment of words to aspects of the environment. But, as Chomsky has argued,[10] the properties that are going to be explanatorily valuable in scientific linguistics are likely to be properties that supervene on internal states of the brain.

Chomsky's view strikes me as quite plausible, but not really to count against the theory under consideration. For the aim of the present use theory is to give an account of 'meaning' in the ordinary, non-scientific sense of the word – to say what we have in mind in our everyday attribution of meanings to expressions in public languages such as English and Spanish. The purpose of the account is not scientific explanation, but rather a demystification of the ordinary concept of meaning, followed by the philosophically beneficial consequences of that demystification: namely, solutions to the numerous problems... that are produced, or at least exacerbated, by confusion about that concept. Thus the use theory is not intended to be a part of science, and so cannot be impugned for failing to meet Chomsky's constraints on an adequate linguistic theory, reasonable as they may be. Moreover, the present account, though perhaps unsuited, as it stands, to the needs of science, might none the less provide a helpful clue to the sort of meaning property that *will* be explanatorily valuable in linguistics. For some of the considerations that favour the use theory of public-language meaning will suggest an analogous account of the meanings of I-language expressions: namely, that they are basic regularities of *internal* use in the conceptual system of the individual.[11]

Some philosophers (for example, Ned Block, Brian Loar, and Colin McGinn)[12] have expressed sympathy for a so-called 'two-factor' theory of meaning according to which the meaning of each term is made up of two distinct components: (1) an internal conceptual role (intended to account for the causal/explanatory power of meaning); and (2) some relation between the term and the external world (intended to account for the reference-determining character of meaning). But this idea seems to me to involve various misconceptions. First, in so far as the aim of the theory is to account for meaning *in the ordinary sense*, then many of the uses of a word that its meaning should help to explain will *not* be internal – they will be uses of the word in relation to the environment. Consequently, the conceptual roles (= basic use regularities) needed to explain them will also have to be not wholly internal. Second, we cannot expect to be able to *split up* the explanatorily basic use regularity of a word into an internal component (which will explain the internal use facts) and an external component (which will explain the relational ones). (How, for example, could such a division be made of the regularity: "Uses of the word 'red' stem from the tendency to apply it to observed surfaces that are determinately red"?) Third, the problem with purely internal conceptual roles is *not* that they are incapable of fixing referential or truth-conditional properties. The problem is rather that purely internal conceptual roles do not constitute the ordinary meanings of our words. Consequently, it will be impossible for us to apply the schema

x has the same conceptual role as our "f" $\rightarrow$ x is *true* of fs

to the terms, x, with purely internal conceptual roles in order to articulate, in ordinary language, the referents and truth conditions of those terms. And fourth, not only is there no *need* to supplement the causal/explanatory aspect of a meaning with something to determine a referent, but there is little likelihood of being able to do so successfully. In light of the plausibility of deflationism about the truth-theoretic notions, we should not expect to find any particular non-semantic relation that is responsible for reference.

...

17   Scepticism

Someone could surely mean what is generally meant by a word, even though he does not endorse the statements that would seem to provide its basic pattern of use. So, for example, we can mean PHLOGISTON by the word "phlogiston" even though we do not maintain the phlogiston theory which supposedly fixes the word's meaning. Similarly, it would seem that a fan of intuitionistic logic might be aware of the meanings of our words "not", "and", etc., despite rejecting the classical principles whose general acceptance implicitly defines these terms.

In order to accommodate this point, which is surely correct, it is necessary to distinguish two closely affiliated acceptance commitments of a word. First, there is the unconditional practice of using that word to formulate one's acceptance of certain substantive principles. Second there is the conditional commitment to use *that* word to articulate those principles *if* they are to be accepted. And it is the second of these commitments that is fundamentally meaning constituting. The first fixes meaning only in so far as it implies the second. Thus the word "phlogis-ton" may be used as the phlogiston theory specifies; and this uncondi-tional regularity of use will indeed be sufficient to fix its meaning – but not necessary. What really constitutes the meaning of "phlogiston" is the conditional acceptance property: of using that word on condition the theory is accepted. In the first of these cases the word is given a meaning and that meaning (i.e. that concept) is canonically deployed; whereas in the second case the assigned meaning is not canonically deployed. It is like the difference between playing a game and merely being aware of the rules, or between employing a tool and merely knowing how to use it. Either way, the word is assigned a function – a conditional acceptance property specifying the circumstances in which certain sentences con-taining the word are accepted. But the resulting linguistic instrument may or may not be found attractive and put to normal work – the unconditional regularity may or may not be actualized.

. . .

20   Regularities without meaning

It seems clear that there are many possible regularities of use that do not coincide with meanings. For example, one might fall into the habit of making a certain noise while sleeping in the afternoon; and this practice would surely not provide that noise with any conceptual content.

We must grant, of course, that not every regularity of use constitutes a meaning of the relevant kind: namely a concept, a constituent of beliefs, desires, and so on. But we have been supposing all along that in order for a type of sound or mark to have the kind of meaning in which we are interested – that is, *conceptual* meaning – the regularity for its use must concern the circumstances in which certain sentences containing it are *accepted* (see the next section for an account of this notion). Moreover the use of a new term must cohere with the regularities that constitute the meanings of the other words. So, for example, in so far as we are disposed (in light of the meaning of "or") to accept instances of "p or not p", then, if "glub" is a new predicate, we must accept "That is glub or it isn't glub". Thus the particular use theory recommended here is not commit-ted to the absurd claim that any old pattern of noise-making is associated with the expression of a concept.

There may be a residual doubt as to whether, even within our *restricted* class of use regularities, every member will constitute a meaning; for it may be thought that not all such regularities could determine a referent or extension. However, this doubt – as we saw in responding to Objection

5 – derives from a misguided, 'inflationary' view of reference. From the deflationary point of view, the conceptually fundamental principle governing the relation 'being *true* of' is the schema

(y)(Predicates meaning F are *true* of $y \leftrightarrow fy$).

And this will trivially fix the extension of any predicate, regardless of how its meaning is constituted.

21 *Acceptance*

The regularities of use that (I am suggesting) constitute the meanings of words concern the circumstances in which specified sentences are privately *accepted* (i.e. uttered assertively to oneself). Therefore, in so far as the aim of the theory is to give a general account of meaning properties through a non-semantic reductive analysis of them, it is essential to make it plausible that the psychological relation 'Person S accepts the sentence "p"' can be explicated in non-semantic terms.[13]

To that end I would like to do two things: first, rebut a popular argument that is supposed to show that the relevant notion of acceptance *is* semantic; and second, sketch a positive account suggesting that it *isn't*.

The argument for the conclusion that 'acceptance' is a semantic concept goes like this. The difference between accepting a sentence and merely uttering it (e.g. as a joke, a linguistic example, etc.) consists in the presence or absence of a commitment to the sentence's being *true*; but *truth* is a semantic notion; therefore so is acceptance.

However, there is a decisive response to this line of thought. Granted, *accepting* a sentence goes hand in hand with accepting its *truth*. But, equally well, *supposing* something goes hand in hand with supposing its *truth*, *doubting* something goes hand in hand with doubting its *truth*, and so on. All of these correlations are fully explained by the obviousness of the schema

"p" is *true* $\leftrightarrow p$.

Consequently, its relationship to truth is not what distinguishes acceptance from other attitudes (such as doubting, conjecturing, etc.) and does not help to constitute its nature. Thus the relevant concept of acceptance does not presuppose the notion of truth.

A reason for thinking, on the contrary, that acceptance is a *non-*semantic notion would be provided by an account of it in purely physical, behavioural, and psychological terms. Let me therefore offer an extremely crude first approximation of such an account: a functional theory that simultaneously characterizes 'acceptance', 'desire', 'observation', and 'action' by means of five principles that relate these notions to one another, to behaviour, and to environmental conditions:

1   For each observable fact O there is a sentence type "o" such that:
    O is instantiated in view of $S \leftrightarrow S$ accepts "o".
2   For each basic action type A there is a sentence type "a" such that:
    S does $A \leftrightarrow S$ wants "a".
3   The set of things S accepts conforms to principles of consistency, simplicity, and conservatism.
4   S accepts "$p \rightarrow q$" iff S is disposed to accept "q" should he come to accept "p".
5   (S wants "q" and S accepts "$p \rightarrow q$") $\rightarrow S$ wants "p".

Thus what S accepts may be inferred, given principles of inference and decision theory, on the basis of what he utters and what he does. No doubt this account is grotesquely over-simple. For one thing, the practical syllogism, expressed in (5), should be replaced with a more sophisticated decision theory, such as the principle of expected utility maximization. However, the theory does appear to capture some of the central characteristics of acceptance – and it does not presuppose any semantic ideas. Therefore one may not unreasonably hope that an adequate account, along roughly these preliminary lines, might be forthcoming. In which case acceptance is indeed a nonsemantic notion and hence legitimate for deployment in a reductive account of meaning.
. . .

23   *Thought*

Language is an expression of thought, a means by which statements are made, questions asked, instructions given, and so on. Therefore, to *understand* a language – to know the significance of its expressions – is to be able to tell which thoughts underlie their use: to know what is being asserted, asked, demanded, and so on. Thus the meaning of a sentence is the propositional character it typically expresses, and the meaning of a word is the element of such a character (i.e. the concept) that it expresses.

    This eminently natural conception of meaning may appear to be quite distinct from, and incompatible with, the conception of meaning as use. But in fact these views are easy to reconcile with one another. For the concept DOG is most directly identified as the concept that is normally expressed in English by using the word "dog" and expressed in other languages by words with the same use as "dog". And on that basis, after the appropriate investigation into the nature of that shared use, we will be led to a characterization of DOG as that entity whose engagement by the speaker's mind is manifested by his deployment of a word with use regularity '$u(x)$'. In other words, we will arrive at a theory of the form

x expresses the concept DOG $= u(x)$

which reduces the meaning property to a basic use regularity. Thus the natural view that the meaning of an expression is the concept it expresses is quite consistent with the further claim that such concepts are identified by means of the use regularities of the words that express them.

Notice that, in so far as 'x means F' implies a correlation between a speaker's use of the term, x, and his engagement with the concept, F, then there must also be a correlation between *acceptance* properties of the term and *belief* properties of the concept. Moreover, if it is explanatorily fundamental, vis-à-vis the overall use of x, that certain specified sentences containing it are accepted in certain specified circumstances, then it will be explanatorily fundamental, vis-à-vis the overall use of the concept F, that the correlated propositions are believed in those circumstances. Thus the use theory of meaning could equally well have been formulated by beginning at the level of thought and maintaining that each concept is individuated by certain explanatorily basic patterns of deployment, and then adding that the meaning of a term is the concept, so individuated, with which it is correlated. This (roughly speaking) is the way things are done by Christopher Peacocke.[14] Similarly, I see no fundamental difference between the use theory and the views of those (such as David Lewis and Frank Jackson)[15] who favour 'functionalist' accounts whereby each mental element is identified as that which plays a certain causal role, and the meaning of a term is then identified with the element it expresses....

Notes

1   See L. Wittgenstein, *Philosophical Investigations* (Oxford: Blackwell, 1953); W. Sellars, "Some Reflections on Language Games", *Philosophy of Science* 21 (1954), 204–8, his "Language as Thought and as Communication", *Philosophy and Phenomenological Research* 29 (1969), 506–27, and his "Empiricism and Abstract Entities", in P. A. Schilpp (ed.), *The Philosophy of Rudolf Carnap* (La

Salle, Ind.: Open Court, 1963), 431–68; H. Field, "Logic, Meaning and Conceptual Role", *Journal of Philosophy* 69 (1977), 379–409; G. Harman, "Conceptual Role Semantics", *Notre Dame Journal of Formal Logic* 23 (1982), 242–56, and his "(Nonsolipsistic) Conceptual Role Semantics", in E. LePore (ed.), *New Directions in Semantics* (London: Academic Press, 1987); N. Block, "Advertisement for a Semantics for Psychology", in P. French, T. Uehling, and H. Wettstein (eds.), *Midwest Studies in Philosophy* 10 (Minneapolis, Minn.: University of Minnesota Press, 1986); C. Peacocke, *A Study of Concepts* (Cambridge, Mass.: MIT Press, 1992); R. Brandom, *Making it Explicit* (Cambridge, Mass.: Harvard University Press, 1994); and C. Cozzo, *Meaning and Argument*, Stockholm Studies in Philosophy no. 17 (Stockholm: Almqvist & Wiksell International, 1994).

2 Belief states are normally categorized in one of two alternative ways. One way is in terms of the proposition believed – e.g. the state of believing *that I have a dog* – a state which anyone who has that belief about me will share, though he might articulate it by thinking to himself, "He has a dog", or "Paul has a dog", etc. The other way is in terms of how the belief is articulated – e.g. the I-have-a-dog belief state which is shared by anyone who thinks to himself either "I have a dog", "Ho un cane", or something else with that meaning. Adapting Kaplan's terminology, the first is a relation to a thought content; the second a relation to a thought character. When I say that concepts are the constituents of belief states, I have in mind the latter kind. More specifically, they are the constituents of the second abstract relatum in such states – a thought character. Although we cannot generally identify the constituents of propositions with concepts, this may be possible for context-insensitive constituents of *de dicto* propositions.

3 For an important refinement of this position see Objection 17.... In a nutshell: a fundamental acceptance property will not imply substantive commitments, but will merely specify how such commitments are to be formulated if they are adopted. For example, what constitutes the meaning of "true" is the conditional commitment to accept instances of 'The proposition *that p* is true iff *p*' *given* a commitment, for some $, to accept instances of "The proposition *that p* is $ iff *p*".

4 The reason for supposing that *w*'s meaning is constituted by a regularity of the form '*w*'s possession of acceptance property $A(x)$ is explanatorily basic', rather than merely '*w* possesses $A(x)$', is that there could be another word, *v*, whose basic acceptance property is '$A(x)$ and $B(x)$', and in that case the second strategy would compel us to conclude, wrongly, that since *w* and *v* both possess $A(x)$, then *v* means the same as *w*.

5 See the response to Objection 14 for discussion of an attempt – known as the 'two-factor theory' – to rectify this weakness.

6 Fodor and Lepore, *Holism*.

7 This reasoning can arguably be extracted from Kripke's *Wittgenstein on Rules and Private Language*.... Kripke's difficulty, which is widely thought to plague all accounts of meaning constitution, is known as 'the problem of error'.

8 Christopher Peacocke, in his *A Study of Concepts*, combines a form of the use theory of meaning with the view that meaning-constituting properties must DETERMINE reference. From our point of view this position falls foul both of Kripke's arguments that no such DETERMINATION is possible, and of the present argument that no such DETERMINATION is necessary.

9 See S. Kripke, *Naming and Necessity* (Cambridge, Mass.: Harvard University Press, 1980); H. Putnam, "The Meaning of 'Meaning'", in his *Mind, Language and Reality: Philosophical Papers* 2 (Cambridge: Cambridge University Press, 1975); T. Burge, "Individualism and the Mental", in P. French, T. Uehling, and H. Wettstein (eds.), *Midwest Studies in Philosophy* 4: 73–121 (Minneapolis, Minn.: University of Minnesota Press, 1979).

10 See, for example, Chomsky's *Knowledge of Language* (New York: Praeger, 1986).

11 For further discussion see my "Meaning and its Place in the Language Faculty".

12 See Block, "Advertisement for a Semantics for Psychology"; B. Loar, "Conceptual Role and Truth Conditions", *Notre Dame Journal of Formal Logic* 23 (1982), 272–83; C. McGinn, "The Structure of Content", in A. Woodfield (ed.), *Thought and Object* (Oxford: Oxford University Press, 1982).

13 In ordinary language the word "acceptance" designates an attitude to *propositions* – one might accept, for example, *that dogs bark*. Here, however, I am using the word in a non-standard sense, to refer to the corresponding attitude to sentences – what Davidson calls "holding true". Thus in the sense deployed here one may 'accept' (i.e. hold true) "dogs bark" and thereby accept (in the ordinary sense) the proposition it expresses.

14 See Peacocke, *A Study of Concepts*. The principal difference between Peacocke's account and what is argued here concerns truth and reference. Peacocke supposes that there must be something he calls a "Determination Theory" whose job it is to explain, given the individuating ("possession") conditions for a concept, why it has the particular extension it does. More specifically, he assumes that if a concept is individuated by the acceptance of certain propositions containing it, then the extension it must have is the one that will render those propositions true. This assumption leads him to suppose that not every pattern of use can constitute a coherent concept (for not every such pattern will, given the Determination Theory, be able to have an extension). And on this basis he concludes that we know certain propositions a priori, in virtue of our possession of their constituent concepts; for when the acceptance of a proposition is an individuating condition for one of its constituents, then that proposition must be true. However, according to the account I am developing here, this line of thought goes wrong at the outset. For...the demand for a Determination Theory presupposes an *inflationary* view of truth and reference – a view that should be rejected. And in that case there will no reason to think certain patterns of acceptance cannot constitute

concepts, and no basis for inferring that concept-possession engenders a priori knowledge. . . .

15 See F. Jackson, *From Metaphysics to Ethics* (Oxford: Clarendon Press, 1998), and D. Lewis, "Reduction of Mind", in S. Guttenplan (ed.), *A Companion to the Philosophy of Mind* (Oxford: Blackwell, 1994).

6

From "Ontological Relativity"

W. V. Quine

I

I listened to Dewey on Art as Experience when I was a graduate student in the spring of 1931. Dewey was then at Harvard as the first William James Lecturer. I am proud now to be at Columbia as the first John Dewey Lecturer.

Philosophically I am bound to Dewey by the naturalism that dominated his last three decades. With Dewey I hold that knowledge, mind, and meaning are part of the same world that they have to do with, and that they are to be studied in the same empirical spirit that animates natural science. There is no place for a prior philosophy.

When a naturalistic philosopher addresses himself to the philosophy of mind, he is apt to talk of language. Meanings are, first and foremost, meanings of language. Language is a social art which we all acquire on the evidence solely of other people's overt behavior under publicly recognizable circumstances. Meanings, therefore, those very models of mental entities, end up as grist for the behaviorist's mill. Dewey was explicit on the point: "Meaning . . . is not a psychic existence; it is primarily a property of behavior."[1]

Once we appreciate the institution of language in these terms, we see that there cannot be, in any useful sense, a private language. This point was stressed by Dewey in the twenties. "Soliloquy," he wrote, "is the product and reflex of converse with others" (170). Farther along he expanded the point thus: "Language is specifically a mode of interaction of at least two beings, a speaker and a hearer; it presupposes an organized group to which these creatures belong, and from whom they have acquired their habits of speech. It is therefore a relationship" (185). Years later, Wittgenstein likewise rejected private language. When Dewey was writing in this naturalistic vein, Wittgenstein still held his copy theory of language.

The copy theory in its various forms stands closer to the main philosophical tradition, and to the attitude of common sense today. Uncritical semantics is the myth of a museum in which the exhibits are meanings and the words are labels. To switch languages is to change the labels. Now the naturalist's primary objection to this view is not an objection to meanings on account of their being mental entities, though that could be objection enough. The primary objection persists even if we take the labeled exhibits not as mental ideas but as Platonic ideas or even as the denoted concrete objects. Semantics is vitiated by a pernicious mentalism as long as we regard a man's semantics as somehow determinate in his mind beyond what might be implicit in his dispositions to overt behavior. It is the very facts about meaning, not the entities meant, that must be construed in terms of behavior.

There are two parts to knowing a word. One part is being familiar with the sound of it and being able to reproduce it. This part, the phonetic part, is achieved by observing and imitating other people's behavior, and there are no important illusions about the process. The other part, the semantic part, is knowing how to use the word. This part, even in the paradigm case, is more complex than the phonetic part. The word refers, in the paradigm case, to some visible object. The learner has now not only to learn the word phonetically, by hearing it from another speaker; he also has to see the object; and in addition to this, in order to capture the relevance of the object to the word, he has to see that the speaker also sees the object. Dewey summed up the point thus: "The characteristic theory about B's understanding of A's sounds is that he responds to the thing from the standpoint of A" (178). Each of us, as he learns his language, is a student of his neighbor's behavior; and conversely, insofar as his tries are approved or corrected, he is a subject of his neighbor's behavioral study.

The semantic part of learning a word is more complex than the phonetic part, therefore, even in simple cases: we have to see what is stimulating the other speaker. In the case of words not directly ascribing observable traits to things, the learning process is increasingly complex and obscure; and obscurity is the breeding place of mentalistic semantics. What the naturalist insists on is that, even in the complex and obscure parts of language learning, the learner has no data to work with but the overt behavior of other speakers.

When with Dewey we turn thus toward a naturalistic view of language and a behavioral view of meaning, what we give up is not just the museum figure of speech. We give up an assurance of determinacy. Seen according to the museum myth, the words and sentences of a language have their determinate meanings. To discover the meanings of the native's words we may have to observe his behavior, but still the meanings of the words are supposed to be determinate in the native's *mind*, his mental museum, even in cases where behavioral criteria are powerless to discover them for us. When on the other hand we recognize with Dewey that "meaning . . . is primarily a property of behavior," we recognize that there are no meanings, nor likenesses nor distinctions of meaning, beyond what are implicit in people's dispositions to overt behavior. For naturalism the question whether two expressions are alike or unlike in meaning has no determinate answer, known or unknown, except insofar as the answer is settled in principle by people's speech dispositions, known or unknown. If by these standards there are indeterminate cases, so much the worse for the terminology of meaning and likeness of meaning.

To see what such indeterminacy would be like, suppose there were an expression in a remote language that could be translated into English equally defensibly in either of two ways, unlike in meaning in English. I am not speaking of ambiguity within the native language. I am supposing that one and the same native use of the expression can be given either of the English translations, each being accommodated by compensating adjustments in the translation of other words. Suppose both translations, along with these accommodations in each case, accord equally well with all observable behavior on the part of speakers of the remote language and speakers of English. Suppose they accord perfectly not only with behavior actually observed, but with all dispositions to behavior on the part of all the speakers concerned. On these assumptions it would be forever impossible to know of one of these translations that it was the right one, and the other wrong. Still, if the museum myth were true, there would be a right and wrong of the matter; it is just that we would never know, not having access to the museum. See language naturalistically, on the other hand, and you have to see the notion of likeness of meaning in such a case simply as nonsense.

I have been keeping to the hypothetical. Turning now to examples, let me begin with a disappointing one and work up. In the French construction 'ne . . . rien' you can translate 'rien' into English as 'anything' or as 'nothing' at will, and then accommodate your choice by translating 'ne' as 'not' or by construing it as pleonastic. This example is disappointing because you can object that I have merely cut the French units too small. You can believe the mentalistic myth of the meaning museum and still grant that 'rien' of itself has no meaning, being no whole label; it is part of 'ne . . . rien', which has its meaning as a whole.

I began with this disappointing example because I think its conspicuous trait – its dependence on cutting language into segments too short to carry meanings – is the secret of the more serious cases as well. What makes other cases more serious is that the segments they involve are seriously long: long enough to be predicates and to be true of things and hence, you would think, to carry meanings.

An artificial example which I have used elsewhere[2] depends on the fact that a whole rabbit is present when and only when an undetached part of a rabbit is present; also when and only when a temporal stage of a rabbit is present. If we are wondering whether to translate a native expression 'gavagai' as 'rabbit' or as 'undetached rabbit part' or as 'rabbit stage', we can never settle the matter simply by ostension – that is, simply by repeatedly querying the expression 'gavagai' for the native's assent or dissent in the presence of assorted stimulations.

Before going on to urge that we cannot settle the matter by nonostensive means either, let me belabor this ostensive predicament a bit. I am not worrying, as Wittgenstein did, about simple cases of ostension. The color word 'sepia', to take one of his examples,[3] can certainly be learned by an ordinary process of conditioning, or induction. One need not even be told that sepia is a color and not a shape or a material or an article. True, barring such hints, many lessons may be needed, so as to eliminate wrong generalizations based on shape, material, etc., rather than color, and so as to eliminate wrong notions as to the intended boundary of an indicated example, and so as to delimit the admissible variations of color itself. Like all conditioning, or induction, the process will depend ultimately also on one's own inborn propensity to find one stimulation qualitatively more akin to a second stimulation than to a third; otherwise there can never be any selective reinforcement and extinction of responses.[4] Still, in principle nothing more is needed in learning 'sepia' than in any conditioning or induction.

But the big difference between 'rabbit' and 'sepia' is that whereas 'sepia' is a mass term like 'water', 'rabbit' is a term of divided reference. As such it cannot be mastered without mastering its principle of individuation: where one rabbit leaves off and another begins. And this cannot be mastered by pure ostension, however persistent.

Such is the quandary over 'gavagai': where one gavagai leaves off and another begins. The only difference between rabbits, undetached rabbit parts, and rabbit stages is in their individuation. If you take the total scattered portion of the spatiotemporal world that is made up of rabbits, and that which is made up of undetached rabbit parts, and that which is made up of rabbit stages, you come out with the same scattered portion of the world each of the three times. The only difference is in how you slice it. And how to slice it is what ostension or simple conditioning, however persistently repeated, cannot teach.

Thus consider specifically the problem of deciding between 'rabbit' and 'undetached rabbit part' as translation of 'gavagai'. No word of the native language is known, except that we have settled on some working hypothesis as to what native words or gestures to construe as assent and dissent in response to our pointings and queryings. Now the trouble is that whenever we point to different parts of the rabbit, even sometimes screening the rest of the rabbit, we are pointing also each time to the rabbit. When, conversely, we indicate the whole rabbit with a sweeping gesture, we are still pointing to a multitude of rabbit parts. And note that we do not have even a native analogue of our plural ending to exploit, in asking 'gavagai?'. It seems clear that no even tentative decision between 'rabbit' and 'undetached rabbit part' is to be sought at this level.

How would we finally decide? My passing mention of plural endings is part of the answer. Our individuating of terms of divided reference, in English, is bound up with a cluster of interrelated grammatical particles and constructions: plural endings, pronouns, numerals, the 'is' of identity, and its adaptations 'same' and 'other'. It is the cluster of interrelated devices in which quantification becomes central when the regimentation of symbolic logic is imposed. If in his language we could ask the native 'Is this *gavagai* the same as that one?' while making appropriate multiple ostensions, then indeed we would be well on our way to deciding between 'rabbit', 'undetached rabbit part', and 'rabbit stage'. And of course the linguist does at length reach the point where he can ask what purports to be that question. He develops a system for translating our pluralizations, pronouns, numerals, identity, and related devices contextually into the native idiom. He develops such a system by abstraction and hypothesis. He abstracts native particles and constructions from observed native sentences, and tries associating these variously with English particles and constructions. Insofar as the native sentences and the thus associated English ones seem to match up in respect of appropriate occasions of use, the linguist feels confirmed in these hypotheses of translation – what I call *analytical hypotheses*.[5]

But it seems that this method, though laudable in practice and the best we can hope for, does not in principle settle the indeterminacy between 'rabbit', 'undetached rabbit part', and 'rabbit stage'. For if one workable over-all system of analytical hypotheses provides for translating a given native expression into 'is the same as', perhaps another equally workable but systematically different system would translate that native expression rather into something like 'belongs with'. Then when in the native language we try to ask 'Is this *gavagai* the same as that?', we could as well be asking 'Does this *gavagai* belong with that?'. Insofar, the native's assent is no objective evidence for translating 'gavagai' as 'rabbit' rather than 'undetached rabbit part' or 'rabbit stage'.

This artificial example shares the structure of the trivial earlier example 'ne...rien'. We were able to translate 'rien' as 'anything' or as 'nothing', thanks to a compensatory adjustment in the handling of 'ne'. And I suggest that we can translate 'gavagai' as 'rabbit' or 'undetached rabbit part' or 'rabbit stage', thanks to compensatory adjustments in the translation of accompanying native locutions. Other adjustments still might accommodate translation of 'gavagai' as 'rabbithood', or in further ways. I find this plausible because of the broadly structural and contextual character of any considerations that could guide us to native translations of the English cluster of interrelated devices of individuation. There seem bound to be systematically very different choices, all of which do justice to all dispositions to verbal behavior on the part of all concerned.

An actual field linguist would of course be sensible enough to equate 'gavagai' with 'rabbit', dismissing such perverse alternatives as 'undetached rabbit part' and 'rabbit stage' out of hand. This sensible choice and others like it would help in turn to determine his subsequent hypotheses as to what native locutions should answer to the English apparatus of individuation, and thus everything would come out all right. The implicit maxim guiding his choice of 'rabbit', and similar choices for other native words, is that an enduring and relatively homogeneous object, moving as a whole against a contrasting background, is a likely reference for a short expression. If he were to become conscious of this maxim, he might celebrate it as one of the linguistic universals, or traits of all languages, and he would have no trouble pointing out its psychological plausibility. But he would be wrong; the maxim is his own imposition, toward settling what is objectively indeterminate. It is a very sensible imposition, and I would recommend no other. But I am making a philosophical point.

It is philosophically interesting, moreover, that what is indeterminate in this artificial example is not just meaning, but extension; reference. My remarks on indeterminacy began as a challenge to likeness of meaning. I had us imagining "an expression that could be translated into English equally defensibly in either of two ways, unlike in meaning in English." Certainly likeness of meaning is a dim notion, repeatedly challenged. Of two predicates which are alike in extension, it has never been clear when to say that they are alike in meaning and when not; it is the old matter of featherless bipeds and rational animals, or of equiangular and equilateral triangles. Reference, extension, has been the firm thing; meaning, intension, the infirm. The indeterminacy of translation now confronting us, however, cuts across extension and intension alike. The terms 'rabbit', 'undetached rabbit part', and 'rabbit stage' differ not only in meaning; they are true of different things. Reference itself proves behaviorally inscrutable.

Within the parochial limits of our own language, we can continue as always to find extensional talk clearer than intensional. For the indeterminacy between 'rabbit', 'rabbit stage', and the rest depended only on a correlative indeterminacy of translation of the English apparatus of individuation – the apparatus of pronouns, pluralization, identity, numerals, and so on. No such indeterminacy obtrudes so long as we think of this apparatus as given and fixed. Given this apparatus, there is no mystery about extension; terms have the same extension when true of the same things. At the level of radical translation, on the other hand, extension itself goes inscrutable.

My example of rabbits and their parts and stages is a contrived example and a perverse one, with which, as I said, the practicing linguist would have no patience. But there are also cases, less bizarre ones, that obtrude in practice. In Japanese there are certain particles, called "classifiers," which may be explained in either of two ways. Commonly they are explained as attaching to numerals, to form compound numerals of distinctive styles. Thus take the numeral for 5. If you attach one classifier to it you get a style of '5' suitable for counting animals; if you attach a different classifier, you get a style of '5' suitable for counting slim things like pencils and chopsticks; and so on. But another way of viewing classifiers is to view them not as constituting part of the numeral, but as constituting part of the term – the term for 'chopsticks' or 'oxen' or whatever. On this view the classifier does the individuative job that is done in English by 'sticks of' as applied to the mass term 'wood', or 'head of' as applied to the mass term 'cattle'.

What we have on either view is a Japanese phrase tantamount say to 'five oxen', but consisting of three words;[6] the first is in effect the neutral numeral '5', the second is a classifier of the animal kind, and the last corresponds in some fashion to 'ox'. On one view the neutral numeral and the classifier go together to constitute a declined numeral in the "animal gender," which then modifies 'ox' to give, in effect, 'five oxen'. On the other view the third Japanese word answers not to the individuative term 'ox' but to the mass term 'cattle'; the classifier applies to this mass term to produce a composite individuative term, in effect 'head of cattle'; and the neutral numeral applies directly to all this without benefit of gender, giving 'five head of cattle', hence again in effect 'five oxen'.

If so simple an example is to serve its expository purpose, it needs your connivance. You have to understand 'cattle' as a mass term covering only bovines, and 'ox' as applying to all bovines. That these usages are not the invariable usages is beside the point. The point is that the Japanese phrase comes out as 'five bovines', as desired, when parsed in either of two ways. The one way treats the third Japanese word as an individuative term true of each bovine, and the other way treats that word rather as a mass term covering the unindividuated totality of beef on the hoof. These are two very different ways of treating the third Japanese word; and the three-word phrase as a whole turns out all right in both cases only because of compensatory differences in our account of the second word, the classifier.

This example is reminiscent in a way of our trivial initial example, 'ne...rien'. We were able to represent 'rien' as 'anything' or as 'nothing', by compensatorily taking 'ne' as negative or as vacuous. We are able now to represent a Japanese word either as an individuative term for bovines or as a mass term for live beef, by compensatorily taking the classifier as declining the numeral or as individuating the mass term. However, the triviality of the one example does not quite carry over to the other. The early example was dismissed on the ground that we had cut too small: 'rien' was too short for significant translation on its own, and 'ne...rien' was the significant unit. But you cannot dismiss the Japanese example by saying that the third word was too short for significant translation on its own and that only the whole three-word phrase, tantamount to 'five oxen', was the significant unit. You cannot take this line unless you are prepared to call a word too short for significant translation even when it is long enough to be a term and carry denotation. For the third Japanese word is, on either approach, a term; on one approach a term of divided reference, and on the other a mass term. If you are indeed prepared thus to call a word too short for significant translation even when it is a denoting term, then in a back-handed way you are granting what I wanted to prove: the inscrutability of reference.

Between the two accounts of Japanese classifiers there is no question of right and wrong. The one account makes for more efficient translation into idiomatic English; the other makes for more of a feeling for the Japanese idiom. Both fit all verbal behavior equally well. All whole sentences, and even component phrases like 'five oxen', admit of the same net over-all English translations on either account. This much is invariant. But what is philosophically interesting is that the reference or extension of shorter terms can fail to be invariant. Whether that third Japanese word is itself true of each ox, or whether on the other hand it is a mass term which needs to be adjoined to the classifier to make a term which is true of each ox – here is a question that remains undecided by the totality of human dispositions to verbal behavior. It is indeterminate in principle; there is no fact of the matter. Either answer can be accommodated by an account of the classifier. Here again, then, is the inscrutability of reference – illustrated this time by a humdrum point of practical translation.

The inscrutability of reference can be brought closer to home by considering the word 'alpha', or again the word 'green'. In our use of these words and others like them there is a systematic ambiguity. Sometimes we use such words as concrete general terms, as when we say the grass is green, or that some inscription begins with an alpha. Sometimes on the other hand we use them as abstract singular terms, as when we say that green is a color and alpha is a letter. Such ambiguity is encouraged by the fact that there is nothing in ostension to distinguish the two uses. The pointing that would be done in teaching the concrete general term 'green', or 'alpha', differs none from the pointing that would be done in teaching the abstract singular term 'green' or 'alpha'. Yet the objects referred to by the word are very different under the two uses; under the one use the word is true of many concrete objects, and under the other use it names a single abstract object.

We can of course tell the two uses apart by seeing how the word turns up in sentences: whether it takes an indefinite article, whether it takes a plural ending, whether it stands as singular subject, whether it stands as modifier, as predicate complement, and so on. But these criteria appeal to our special English grammatical constructions and particles, our special English apparatus of individuation, which, I already urged, is itself subject to indeterminacy of translation. So, from the point of view of translation into a remote language, the distinction between a concrete general and an abstract singular term is in the same predicament as the distinction between 'rabbit', 'rabbit part', and 'rabbit stage'. Here then is another example of the inscrutability of reference, since the difference between the concrete general and the abstract singular is a difference in the objects referred to.

Incidentally we can concede this much indeterminacy also to the 'sepia' example, after all. But this move is not evidently what was worrying Wittgenstein.

The ostensive indistinguishability of the abstract singular from the concrete general turns upon what may be called "deferred ostension," as opposed to direct ostension. First let me define direct ostension. The *ostended point*, as I shall call it, is the point where the line of the pointing finger first meets an opaque surface. What characterizes *direct ostension*, then, is that the term which is being ostensively explained is true of something that contains the ostended point. Even such direct ostension has its uncertainties, of course, and these are familiar. There is the question how wide an environment of the ostended point is meant to be covered by the term that is being ostensively explained. There is the question how considerably an absent thing or substance might be allowed to differ from what is now ostended, and still be covered by the term that is now being ostensively explained. Both of these questions can in principle be settled as well as need be by induction from multiple ostensions. Also, if the term is a term of divided reference like 'apple', there is the question of individuation: the question where one of its objects leaves off and another begins. This can be settled by induction from multiple ostensions of a more elaborate kind, accompanied by expressions like 'same apple' and 'another', if an equivalent of this English apparatus of individuation has been settled on; otherwise the indeterminacy persists that was illustrated by 'rabbit', 'undetached rabbit part', and 'rabbit stage'.

Such, then, is the way of direct ostension. Other ostension I call *deferred*. It occurs when we point at the gauge, and not the gasoline, to show that there is gasoline. Also it occurs when we explain the abstract singular term 'green' or 'alpha' by pointing at grass or a Greek inscription. Such pointing is direct ostension when used to explain the concrete general term 'green' or 'alpha', but it is deferred ostension when used to explain the abstract singular terms; for the abstract object which is the color green or the letter alpha does not contain the ostended point, nor any point.

Deferred ostension occurs very naturally when, as in the case of the gasoline gauge, we have a correspondence in mind. Another such example is afforded by the Gödel numbering of expressions. Thus if 7 has been assigned as Gödel number of the letter alpha, a man conscious of the Gödel numbering would not hesitate to say 'Seven' on pointing to an inscription of the Greek letter in question. This is, on the face of it, a doubly deferred ostension: one step of deferment carries us from the inscription to the letter as abstract object, and a second step carries us thence to the number.

By appeal to our apparatus of individuation, if it is available, we can distinguish between the concrete general and the abstract singular use of the word 'alpha'; this we saw. By appeal again to that apparatus, and in particular to identity, we can evidently settle also whether the word 'alpha' in its abstract singular use is being used really to name the letter or whether, perversely, it is being used to name the Gödel number of the letter. At any rate we can distinguish these alternatives if also we have located the speaker's equivalent of the numeral '7' to our satisfaction; for we can ask him whether alpha *is* 7.

These considerations suggest that deferred ostension adds no essential problem to those presented by direct ostension. Once we have settled upon analytical hypotheses of translation covering identity and the other English particles relating to individuation, we can resolve not only the indecision between 'rabbit' and 'rabbit stage' and the rest, which came of direct ostension, but also any indecision between concrete general and abstract singular, and any indecision between expression and Gödel number, which come of deferred ostension.

However, this conclusion is too sanguine. The inscrutability of reference runs deep, and it persists in a subtle form even if we accept identity and the rest of the apparatus of individuation as fixed and settled; even, indeed, if we forsake radical translation and think only of English.

Consider the case of a thoughtful protosyntactician. He has a formalized system of first-order proof theory, or protosyntax, whose universe comprises just expressions, that is, strings of signs of a specified alphabet. Now just what sorts of things, more specifically, are these expressions? They are types, not tokens. So, one might suppose, each of them is the set of all its tokens. That is, each expression is a set of inscriptions which are variously situated in space-time but are classed together by virtue of a certain similarity in shape. The concatenate xy of two expressions x and y, in a given order, will be the set of all inscriptions each of which has two parts which are tokens respectively of x and y and follow one upon the other in that order. But xy may then be the null set, though x and y are not null; for it may be that inscriptions belonging to x and y happen to turn up head to tail nowhere, in the past, present, or future. This danger increases with the lengths of x and y. But it is easily seen to violate a law of protosyntax which says that $x = z$ whenever $xy = zy$.

Thus it is that our thoughtful protosyntactician will not construe the things in his universe as sets of inscriptions. He can still take his atoms, the single signs, as sets of inscriptions, for there is no risk of nullity in these cases. And then, instead of taking his strings of signs as sets of inscriptions, he can invoke the mathematical notion of sequence and take them as sequences of signs. A familiar way of taking sequences, in turn, is as a mapping of things on numbers. On this approach an expression or string of signs becomes a finite set of pairs each of which is the pair of a sign and a number.

This account of expressions is more artificial and more complex than one is apt to expect who simply says he is letting his variables range over the strings of such and such signs. Moreover, it is not the inevitable choice; the considerations that motivated it can be met also by alternative constructions. One of these constructions is Gödel numbering itself, and it is temptingly simple. It uses just natural numbers, whereas the foregoing construction used sets of one-letter inscriptions and also natural numbers and sets of pairs of these. How clear is it that at just *this* point we have dropped expressions in favor of numbers? What is clearer is merely that in both constructions we were artificially devising models to satisfy laws that expressions in an unexplicated sense had been meant to satisfy.

So much for expressions. Consider now the arithmetician himself, with his elementary number theory. His universe comprises the natural numbers outright. Is it clearer than the protosyntactician's? What, after all, is a natural number? There are Frege's version, Zermelo's, and von Neumann's, and countless further alternatives, all mutually incompatible and equally correct. What we are doing in any one of these explications of natural number is to devise set-theoretic models to satisfy laws which the natural numbers in an unexplicated sense had been meant to satisfy. The case is quite like that of protosyntax.

It will perhaps be felt that any set-theoretic explication of natural number is at best a case of *obscurum per obscurius*; that all explications must assume something, and the natural numbers themselves are an admirable assumption to start with. I must agree that a construction of sets and set theory from natural numbers and arithmetic would be far more desirable than the familiar opposite. On the other hand our impression of the clarity even of the notion of natural number itself has suffered somewhat from Gödel's proof of the impossibility of a complete proof procedure for elementary number theory, or, for that matter, from Skolem's and Henkin's observations that all laws of natural numbers admit nonstandard models.[7]

We are finding no clear difference between *specifying* a universe of discourse – the range of the variables of quantification – and *reducing* that universe to some other. We saw no significant difference between clarifying the notion of expression and supplanting it by that of number.

And now to say more particularly what numbers themselves are is in no evident way different from just dropping numbers and assigning to arithmetic one or another new model, say in set theory.

Expressions are known only by their laws, the laws of concatenation theory, so that any constructs obeying those laws – Gödel numbers, for instance – are *ipso facto* eligible as explications of expression. Numbers in turn are known only by their laws, the laws of arithmetic, so that any constructs obeying those laws – certain sets, for instance – are eligible in turn as explications of number. Sets in turn are known only by their laws, the laws of set theory.

Russell pressed a contrary thesis, long ago. Writing of numbers, he argued that for an understanding of number the laws of arithmetic are not enough; we must know the applications, we must understand numerical discourse embedded in discourse of other matters. In applying number the key notion, he urged, is *Anzahl*: there are n so-and-sos. However, Russell can be answered. First take, specifically, *Anzahl*. We can define 'there are n so-and-sos' without ever deciding what numbers are, apart from their fulfillment of arithmetic. That there are n so-and-sos can be explained simply as meaning that the so-and-sos are in one-to-one correspondence with the numbers up to n.[8]

Russell's more general point about application can be answered too. Always, if the structure is there, the applications will fall into place. As paradigm it is perhaps sufficient to recall again this reflection on expressions and Gödel numbers: that even the pointing out of an inscription is no final evidence that our talk is of expressions and not of Gödel numbers. We can always plead deferred ostension.

It is in this sense true to say, as mathematicians often do, that arithmetic is all there is to number. But it would be a confusion to express this point by saying, as is sometimes said, that numbers are any things fulfilling arithmetic. This formulation is wrong because distinct domains of objects yield distinct models of arithmetic. Any progression can be made to serve; and to identify all progressions with one another, e.g., to identify the progression of odd numbers with the progression of evens, would contradict arithmetic after all.

So, though Russell was wrong in suggesting that numbers need more than their arithmetical properties, he was right in objecting to the definition of numbers as any things fulfilling arithmetic. The subtle point is that any progression will serve as a version of number so long and only so long as we stick to one and the same progression. Arithmetic is, in this sense, all there is to number: there is no saying absolutely what the numbers are; there is only arithmetic.[9]

II

I first urged the inscrutability of reference with the help of examples like the one about rabbits and rabbit parts. These used direct ostension, and the inscrutability of reference hinged on the indeterminacy of translation of identity and other individuative apparatus. The setting of these examples, accordingly, was radical translation: translation from a remote language on behavioral evidence, unaided by prior dictionaries. Moving then to deferred ostension and abstract objects, we found a certain dimness of reference pervading the home language itself.

Now it should be noted that even for the earlier examples the resort to a remote language was not really essential. On deeper reflection, radical translation begins at home. Must we equate our neighbor's English words with the same strings of phonemes in our own mouths? Certainly not; for sometimes we do not thus equate them. Sometimes we find it to be in the interests of communication to recognize that our neighbor's use of some word, such as 'cool' or 'square' or 'hopefully', differs from ours, and so we translate that word of his into a different string of phonemes in our idiolect. Our usual domestic rule of translation is indeed the homophonic one, which simply carries each string of phonemes into itself; but still we are always prepared to temper homophony with what Neil Wilson has called the "principle of charity."[10] We will construe a neighbor's word heterophonically now and again if thereby we see our way to making his message less absurd.

The homophonic rule is a handy one on the whole. That it works so well is no accident, since imitation and feedback are what propagate a language. We acquired a great fund of basic words and phrases in this way, imitating our elders and encouraged by our elders amid external circumstances to which the phrases suitably apply. Homophonic translation is implicit in this social method of learning. Departure from homophonic translation in this quarter would only hinder communication. Then there are the relatively rare instances of opposite kind, due to divergence in dialect or confusion in an individual, where homophonic translation incurs negative feedback. But what tends to escape notice is that there is also a vast mid-region where the homophonic method is indifferent. Here, gratuitously, we can systematically reconstrue our neighbor's apparent references to rabbits as really references to rabbit stages, and his apparent references to formulas as really references to Gödel numbers and vice versa. We can reconcile all this with our neighbor's verbal behavior, by cunningly readjusting our translations of his various connecting predicates so as to compensate for the switch of ontology. In short, we can reproduce the inscrutability of reference at home. It is of no avail to check on this fanciful version of our neighbor's meanings by asking him, say, whether he really means at a certain point to refer to formulas or to their Gödel numbers; for our question and his answer – "By all means, the numbers" – have lost their title to homophonic translation. The problem at home differs none from radical translation ordinarily so called except in the willfulness of this suspension of homophonic translation.

I have urged in defense of the behavioral philosophy of language, Dewey's, that the inscrutability of reference is not the inscrutability of a fact; there is no fact of the matter. But if there is really no fact of the matter, then the inscrutability of reference can be brought even closer to home than the neighbor's case; we can apply it to ourselves. If it is to make sense to say even of oneself that one is referring to rabbits and formulas and not to rabbit stages and Gödel numbers, then it should make sense equally to say it of someone else. After all, as Dewey stressed, there is no private language.

We seem to be maneuvering ourselves into the absurd position that there is no difference on any terms, interlinguistic or intralinguistic, objective or subjective, between referring to rabbits and referring to rabbit parts or stages; or between referring to formulas and referring to their Gödel numbers. Surely this is absurd, for it would imply that there is no difference between the rabbit and each of its parts or stages, and no difference between a formula and its Gödel number. Reference would seem now to become nonsense not just in radical translation, but at home.

Toward resolving this quandary, begin by picturing us at home in our language, with all its predicates and auxiliary devices. This vocabulary includes 'rabbit', 'rabbit part', 'rabbit stage', 'formula', 'number', 'ox', 'cattle'; also the two-place predicates of identity and difference, and other logical particles. In these terms we can say in so many words that this is a formula and that a number, this a rabbit and that a rabbit part, this and that the same rabbit, and this and that different parts. *In just those words.* This network of terms and predicates and auxiliary devices is, in relativity jargon, our frame of reference, or coordinate system. Relative to *it* we can and do talk meaningfully and distinctively of rabbits and parts, numbers and formulas. Next, as in recent paragraphs, we contemplate alternative denotations for our familiar terms. We begin to appreciate that a grand and ingenious permutation of these denotations, along with compensatory adjustments in the interpretations of the auxiliary particles, might still accommodate all existing speech dispositions. This was the inscrutability of reference, applied to ourselves; and it made nonsense of reference. Fair enough; reference *is* nonsense except relative to a coordinate system. In this principle of relativity lies the resolution of our quandary.

It is meaningless to ask whether, in general, our terms 'rabbit', 'rabbit part', 'number', etc., really refer respectively to rabbits, rabbit parts, numbers, etc., rather than to some ingeniously permuted denotations. It is meaningless to ask this absolutely; we can meaningfully ask it only relative to some background language. When we ask, "Does 'rabbit' really refer to rabbits?" someone can counter with the question: "Refer to rabbits in what sense of 'rabbits'?" thus launching a regress; and we need the background language to regress into. The background language gives the query sense, if only relative sense; sense relative in turn to it, this background language. Querying reference in any more absolute way would be like asking absolute position, or absolute velocity, rather than position or velocity relative to a given frame of reference. Also it is very much like asking whether our neighbor may not systematically see everything upside down, or in complementary color, forever undetectably.

We need a background language, I said, to regress into. Are we involved now in an infinite regress? If questions of reference of the sort we are considering make sense only relative to a background language, then evidently questions of reference for the background language make sense in turn only relative to a further background language. In these terms the situation sounds desperate, but in fact it is little different from questions of position and velocity. When we are given position and velocity relative to a given coordinate system, we can always ask in turn about the placing of origin and orientation of axes of that system of coordinates; and there is no end to the succession of further coordinate systems that could be adduced in answering the successive questions thus generated.

In practice of course we end the regress of coordinate systems by something like pointing. And in practice we end the regress of background languages, in discussions of reference, by acquiescing in our mother tongue and taking its words at face value.

Very well; in the case of position and velocity, in practice, pointing breaks the regress. But what of position and velocity apart from practice? what of the regress then? The answer, of course, is the relational doctrine of space; there is no absolute position or velocity; there are just the relations of coordinate systems to one another, and ultimately of things to one another. And I think that the parallel question regarding denotation calls for a parallel answer, a relational theory of what the objects of theories are. What makes sense is to say not what the objects of a theory are, absolutely speaking, but how one theory of objects is interpretable or reinterpretable in another.

The point is not that bare matter is inscrutable: that things are indistinguishable except by their properties. That point does not need making. The present point is reflected better in the riddle about seeing things upside down, or in complementary colors; for it is that things can be inscrutably switched even while carrying their properties with them. Rabbits differ from rabbit parts and rabbit stages not just as bare matter, after all, but in respect of properties; and formulas differ from numbers in respect of properties. What our present reflections are leading us to appreciate is that the riddle about seeing things upside down, or in complementary colors, should be taken seriously and its moral applied widely. The relativistic thesis to which we have come is this, to repeat: it makes no sense to say what the objects of a theory are, beyond saying how to interpret or reinterpret that theory in another. Suppose we are working within a theory and thus treating of its objects. We do so by using the variables of the theory, whose values those objects are, though there be no ultimate sense in which that universe can have been specified. In the language of the theory there are predicates by which to distinguish portions of this universe from other portions, and these predicates differ from one another purely in the roles they play in the laws of the theory. Within this background theory we can show how some subordinate theory, whose universe is some portion of the background universe, can by a reinterpretation be reduced to another subordinate theory whose universe is some lesser portion. Such talk of subordinate theories and their ontologies *is* meaningful, but only relative to the background theory with its own primitively adopted and ultimately inscrutable ontology.

To talk thus of theories raises a problem of formulation. A theory, it will be said, is a set of fully interpreted sentences. (More particularly, it is a deductively closed set: it includes all its own logical consequences, insofar as they are couched in the same notation.) But if the sentences of a theory are fully interpreted, then in particular the range of values of their variables is settled. How then can there be no sense in saying what the objects of a theory are?

My answer is simply that we cannot require theories to be fully interpreted, except in a relative sense, if anything is to count as a theory. In specifying a theory we must indeed fully specify, in our own words, what sentences are to comprise the theory and what things are to be taken as values of the variables and what things are to be taken as satisfying the predicate letters; insofar we do fully interpret the theory, *relative* to our own words and relative to our over-all home theory which lies behind them. But this fixes the objects of the described theory only relative to those of the home theory; and these can, at will, be questioned in turn.

One is tempted to conclude simply that meaninglessness sets in when we try to pronounce on everything in our universe; that universal predication takes on sense only when furnished with the background of a wider universe, where the predication is no longer universal. And this is even a familiar doctrine, the doctrine that no proper predicate is true of everything. We have all heard it claimed that a predicate is meaningful only by contrast with what it excludes, and hence that being true of everything would make a predicate meaningless. But surely this doctrine is wrong. Surely self-identity, for instance, is not to be rejected as meaningless. For that matter, any statement of fact at all, however brutally meaningful, can be put artificially into a form in which it pronounces on everything. To say merely of Jones that he sings, for instance, is to say of everything that it is other than Jones or sings. We had better beware of repudiating universal predication, lest we be tricked into repudiating everything there is to say.

Carnap took an intermediate line in his doctrine of universal words, or *Allwörter*, in *The Logical Syntax of Language*. He did treat the predicating of universal words as "quasi-syntactical" – as a predication only by courtesy, and without empirical content. But universal words were for him not just any universally true predicates, like 'is other than Jones or sings'. They were a special breed of universally true predicates, ones that are universally true by the sheer meanings of their words and no thanks to nature. In his later writing this doctrine of universal words takes the form of a distinction between "internal" questions, in which a theory comes to grips with facts about the world, and "external" questions, in which people come to grips with the relative merits of theories.

Should we look to these distinctions of Carnap's for light on ontological relativity? When we found there was no absolute sense in saying what a theory is about, were we sensing the infactuality of what Carnap calls "external questions"? When we found that saying what a theory is about did make sense against a background theory, were we sensing the factuality of internal questions of the background theory? I see no hope of illumination in this quarter. Carnap's universal words were not just any universally true predicates, but, as I said, a special breed; and what distinguishes this breed is not clear. What I said distinguished them was that they were universally true by sheer meanings and not by nature;

but this is a very questionable distinction. Talking of "internal" and "external" is no better.

Ontological relativity is not to be clarified by any distinction between kinds of universal predication – unfactual and factual, external and internal. It is not a question of universal predication. When questions regarding the ontology of a theory are meaningless absolutely, and become meaningful relative to a background theory, this is not in general because the background theory has a wider universe. One is tempted, as I said a little while back, to suppose that it is; but one is then wrong.

What makes ontological questions meaningless when taken absolutely is not universality, but circularity. A question of the form 'What is an F?' can be answered only by recourse to a further term: 'An F is a G'. The answer makes only relative sense: sense relative to an uncritical acceptance of 'G'.

We may picture the vocabulary of a theory as comprising logical signs such as quantifiers and the signs for the truth functions and identity, and in addition descriptive or nonlogical signs, which, typically, are singular terms, or names, and general terms, or predicates. Suppose next that in the statements which comprise the theory, that is, are true according to the theory, we abstract from the meanings of the nonlogical vocabulary and from the range of the variables. We are left with the logical form of the theory, or, as I shall say, the *theory-form*. Now we may interpret this theory-form anew by picking a new universe for its variables of quantification to range over, and assigning objects from this universe to the names, and choosing subsets of this universe as extensions of the one-place predicates, and so on. Each such interpretation of the theory-form is called a model of it, if it makes it come out true. Which of these models is meant in a given actual theory cannot, of course, be guessed from the theory-form. The intended references of the names and predicates have to be learned rather by ostension, or else by paraphrase in some antecedently familiar vocabulary. But the first of these two ways has proved inconclusive, since, even apart from indeterminacies of translation affecting identity and other logical vocabulary, there is the problem of deferred ostension. Paraphrase in some antecedently familiar vocabulary, then, is our only recourse; and such is ontological relativity. To question the reference of all the terms of our all-inclusive theory becomes meaningless, simply for want of further terms relative to which to ask or answer the question.

It is thus meaningless within the theory to say which of the various possible models of our theory-form is our real or intended model. Yet even here we can make sense still of there being many models. For we might be able to show that for each of the models, however unspecifiable, there is bound to be another which is a permutation or perhaps a diminution of the first.

Suppose for example that our theory is purely numerical. Its objects are just the natural numbers. There is no sense in saying, from within that theory, just which of the various models of number theory is in force. But we can observe even from within the theory that, whatever 0, 1, 2, 3, etc. may be, the theory would still hold true if the 17 of this series were moved into the role of 0, and the 18 moved into the role of 1, and so on.

Ontology is indeed doubly relative. Specifying the universe of a theory makes sense only relative to some background theory, and only relative to some choice of a manual of translation of the one theory into the other. Commonly of course the background theory will simply be a containing theory, and in this case no question of a manual of translation arises. But this is after all just a degenerate case of translation still – the case where the rule of translation is the homophonic one.

A usual occasion for ontological talk is reduction, where it is shown how the universe of some theory can by a reinterpretation be dispensed with in favor of some other universe, perhaps a proper part of the first. I have treated elsewhere[11] of the reduction of one ontology to another with help of a *proxy function*: a function mapping the one universe into part or all of the other. For instance, the function "Gödel number of" is a proxy function. The universe of elementary proof theory or protosyntax, which consists of expressions or strings of signs, is mapped by this function into the universe of elementary number theory, which consists of numbers. The proxy function used in reducing one ontology to another is not necessarily one-to-one. This one is; and note that one ontology is *always* reducible to another when we are given a proxy function f that is one-to-one. The essential reasoning is as follows. Where P is any predicate of the old system, its work can be done in the new system by a new predicate which we interpret as true of just the correlates fx of the old objects x that P was true of. Thus suppose we take fx as the Gödel number of x, and as our old system we take a syntactical system in which one of the predicates is 'is a segment of'. The corresponding predicate of the new, or numerical system, then, would be one which amounts, so far as its extension is concerned, to the words 'is the Gödel number of a segment of that whose Gödel number is'. The numerical predicate would not be given this devious form, of course, but would be rendered as an appropriate purely arithmetical condition.

Our dependence upon a background theory becomes especially evident when we reduce our universe U to another V by appeal to a proxy function. For it is only in a theory with an inclusive universe, embracing U and V, that we can make sense of the proxy function. The function maps U into V and, hence, needs all the old objects of U as well as their new proxies in V.

The proxy function need not exist as an object in the universe even of the background theory. It may do its work merely as what I have called a "virtual class,"[12] and Gödel has called a "notion."[13] That is to say, all that is required toward a function is an open sentence with two free variables, provided that it is fulfilled by exactly one value of the first variable for each object of the old universe as value of the second variable. But the point is that it is only in the background theory, with its inclusive universe, that we can hope to write such a sentence and have the right values at our disposal for its variables.

If the new objects happen to be among the old, so that V is a subclass of U, then the old theory with universe U can itself sometimes qualify as the background theory in which to describe its own ontological reduction. But we cannot do better than that; we cannot declare our new ontological economies without having recourse to the uneconomical old ontology.

This sounds, perhaps, like a predicament: as if no ontological economy is justifiable unless it is a false economy and the repudiated objects really exist after all. But actually this is wrong; there is no more cause for worry here than there is in *reductio ad absurdum*, where we assume a falsehood that we are out to disprove. If what we want to show is that the universe U is excessive and that only a part exists, or need exist, then we are quite within our rights to assume all of U for the space of the argument. We show thereby that if all of U were needed then not all of U would be needed; and so our ontological reduction is sealed by *reductio ad absurdum*.

. . .

Notes

Presented as a pair of lectures of the same title at Columbia University, March 26 and 28, 1968. The lectures are the first series of John Dewey Lectures, which will be delivered biennially and which have been established to honor the late John Dewey, from 1905 to 1930 a professor of philosophy at Columbia. The editors are pleased to have the opportunity to publish them.

1   *Experience and Nature* (La Salle, Ill.: Open Court, 1925, 1958), p. 179.
2   *Word and Object* (Cambridge, Mass.: MIT Press, 1960), §12.
3   *Philosophical Investigations* (New York: Macmillan, 1953), p. 14.

4 Cf. *Word and Object*, §17.

5 *Word and Object*, §15. For a summary of the general point of view see also §I of my "Speaking of Objects," *Proceedings and Addresses of American Philosophical Association*, XXXI (1958): 5ff; reprinted in Y. Krikorian and A. Edel, eds., *Contemporary Philosophical Problems* (New York: Macmillan, 1959), and in J. Fodor and J. Katz, eds., *The Structure of Language* (Englewood Cliffs, N.J.: Prentice-Hall, 1964), and in P. Kurtz, ed., *American Philosophy in the Twentieth Century* (New York: Macmillan, 1966).

6 To keep my account graphic I am counting a certain postpositive particle as a suffix rather than a word.

7 See Leon Henkin, "Completeness in the Theory of Types," *Journal of Symbolic Logic*, XV, 2 (June 1950): 81–91, and references therein.

8 For more on this theme see my *Set Theory and Its Logic* (Cambridge, Mass.: Harvard, 1963, 1968), §11.

9 Paul Benacerraf, "What Numbers Cannot Be," *Philosophical Review*, LXXIV, 1 (January 1965): 47–73, develops this point. His conclusions differ in some ways from those I shall come to.

10 N. L. Wilson, "Substances without Substrata," *Review of Metaphysics*, XII, 4 (June 1959): 521–539, p. 532.

11 *The Ways of Paradox and Other Essays* (New York: Random House, 1966), pp. 204ff. or "Ontological Reduction and the World of Numbers," *Journal of Philosophy*, LXI, 7 (March 26, 1964): 209–215, pp. 214ff.

12 *Set Theory and Its Logic*, §§2f.

13 Kurt Gödel, *The Consistency of the Continuum Hypothesis* (Princeton, N.J.: The University Press, 1940), p. 11.

7

From "The Indeterminacy of Translation and the Inscrutability of Reference"[1]

Scott Soames

W. V. Quine's doctrines of the indeterminacy of translation and the inscrutability of reference are among the most famous and influential theses in philosophy in the past fifty years. Although by no means universally accepted, the arguments for them have been widely regarded as powerful challenges to our most fundamental beliefs about meaning and reference – including the belief that many of our words have meaning and reference in the sense in which we ordinarily understand those notions, as well as beliefs about the particular things meant and referred to in specific cases, such as my belief that in the past my son Brian often referred with affection to his pet rabbit Bigwig. If Quine's doctrines, and the arguments for them, are correct, then beliefs such as these cannot be accepted as true.

One might expect that with consequences like these Quine's theses would widely be regarded as obviously incorrect. That this has not been their fate has, in my opinion, been due in large part to a persistent unclarity about what the theses actually say and what the arguments for them really are. I will try to rectify this situation. My expository task will be to explain the content and consequences of Quine's doctrines, and to reconstruct the main arguments for them. My critical task will be to show that these arguments are not good ones, and to explain why they should be rejected.

In the first section, I lay out Quine's central theses and the arguments for them. I maintain that the plausibility of these arguments depends on systematic equivocation about what it means for one set of truths to determine the truth of another set of claims. Once this equivocation is eliminated, there turns out to be no plausible route to the indeterminacy of translation. In section II, I extend this result to the inscrutability of reference, and argue that Quine's position leads him to a radical form of eliminativism about both meaning and reference, as ordinarily understood. In section III, this position is shown to be not only deeply unpersuasive but also self-defeating.

I

I begin with Quine's discussion of the indeterminacy of translation. Much of that discussion is concerned with the thesis of the underdetermination of translation by data, which is about the relationship between translation theories and the observational evidence for them. The thesis asserts that the totality of empirical evidence bearing on the translation of one language into another fails to determine a unique system of translation; no matter how much data one amasses there will always be incompatible systems of translation equally well supported by the data. This thesis is an instance of Quine's view that empirical theories of all sorts typically are underdetermined by observational evidence.

The Underdetermination of Translation by Data

Let L_1 and L_2 be arbitrary languages, and let D be the set of all observational truths (known and unknown) relevant to translation from one to the other. For any theory of translation T for L_1 and L_2, compatible with D, there is a theory T', incompatible with T, that is equally well supported by D.[2]

The underdetermination thesis can be fleshed out by saying a little about what theories of translation are, and what Quine takes the evidence for them to be. First consider theories of translation. A theory of translation for two languages correlates individual words of each language with words or phrases of the other language; this correlation is then used to correlate the sentences of the two languages.[3] Any system of establishing such correlations can be counted as a translation manual, or a theory of translation. We may take such a theory as yielding (infinitely many) theorems of the form:

Word or phrase w_1 in L_1 means the same as word or phrase w_2 in L_2.
Sentence S_1 in L_1 means the same as sentence S_2 in L_2.

According to Quine, the empirical data relevant to theories of translation are statements about the stimulus meanings of sentences. The stimulus meaning of a sentence S (for a speaker at a time) is a pair of classes – the class of situations in which the speaker would assent to S, and the class in which the speaker would dissent from S. Stimulus meanings are particularly important in evaluating translations of what Quine calls 'occasion sentences' and 'observation sentences.' An occasion sentence is one assent to which, or dissent from which, depends (in part) on the speaker's current observation. An observation sentence is an occasion sentence for which assent or dissent depends only on observation – with no, or only a minimum in the way of, background information required. For example, 'He is a bachelor' is an occasion sentence, since assent or dissent in a given case depends (in part) on whom the subject is observing; but it is not an observation sentence in Quine's sense because whether or not one assents in a particular case depends on having special background information about the person perceived. 'That is red,' on the other hand, does not depend (to the same extent) on having such background information, and so counts as an observation sentence for Quine. Quine's way of approximating this intuitive notion of an observation sentence within his behavioristic framework is to define an observation sentence in a language L to be an occasion sentence for speakers of L the stimulus meaning of which varies little from one speaker to another.

The stimulus meanings of observation and occasion sentences play a prominent role in Quine's conception of the main observational predictions made by translation theories. These predictions are summarized by three principles for extracting testable claims from theories of translation (which otherwise wouldn't entail any such predictions via their form alone).[4] The first principle reflects Quine's requirement that correct translations must preserve the stimulus meanings of observation sentences.

(i)   If a translation theory states that an observation sentence S_1 in L_1 means the same as a sentence S_2 in L_2, then the theory predicts that S_1 and S_2 have the same stimulus meanings in their respective linguistic communities.

The second principle corresponds to Quine's requirement that correct translations must preserve the stimulus synonymy of pairs of occasion sentences.

(ii)   If S_{1a} and S_{1b} are occasion sentences of L_1, and if a translation theory states both that S_{1a} means the same in L_1 as S_{2a} in L_2 and that S_{1b} means the same in L_1 as S_{2b} in L_2, then the theory predicts that S_{1a} and S_{1b} have the same stimulus meaning in L_1 iff S_{2a} and S_{2b} have the same stimulus meaning in L_2.

The third principle relates the translation of truth functional connectives to their effects on stimulus meanings.

(iii)   If a theory translates an expression n of a language L as meaning the same as 'not' in English, then adding n to sentences of L must reverse stimulus meaning; similar claims are made regarding other truth functional operators.

On Quine's conception, the observational data for theories of translation consist mainly of behavioral evidence regarding the stimulus meanings of occasion sentences.[5]

Quine also considers a possible constraint relevant to the translation of what he calls standing sentences – sentences assent to, or dissent from, which is independent of current sensory stimulation. The possible constraint – (iv) – is that sentences assented to (dissented from) in every situation by the community of speakers of L_1 must be translated onto those assented to (dissented from) in every situation by the community of speakers of L_2. But this constraint is itself problematic, since it would require us to treat some sentence which, though universally assented to by the speakers of L_1, may be false (e.g. 'the sun god is mighty') as meaning the same as some sentence of our language that we take to be an obvious truth. Fortunately, the status of this possible constraint is not crucial to Quine's discussion. Whatever one thinks about it, adding the constraint would not significantly change the overall picture. It is clear that if the observational data for theories of translation are restricted to behavioral evidence of the sort Quine has in mind, then profoundly different theories of translation will be supported equally well (in his sense) by all observational data, known and unknown, in virtually all interesting cases.

Quine's most well-known example of this involves translation from his imagined language, Junglese, into English. He argues, quite persuasively, that the set of all behavioral data concerning the stimulus meanings of sentences for speakers of the two languages does not distinguish theories that translate the Jungle word 'gavagai' as meaning the same as the English word 'rabbit' from theories that translate it as meaning the same as the English phrases 'temporal stage of a rabbit' or 'undetached rabbit part.' Moreover, he takes his point not to be limited to translation between different languages in the usual sense, but to apply with equal force to interpreting the words of other English speakers, or even of one's own words at some time in the past.[6] If this is right, then the set of all behavioral data concerning the stimulus meanings of sentences of normal English speakers, past and present, is equally compatible with theories of translation which claim that (i) the term 'rabbit' as used by us in the past means the same as the term 'rabbit' as used by us now, (ii) the term 'rabbit' as used by us in the past means the same as the phrase 'undetached rabbit part' as used by us now, or (iii) the term 'rabbit' as used by us in the past means the same as the phrase 'temporal stage of a rabbit' as used by us now. Since the expressions 'rabbit,' 'undetached rabbit part,' and 'temporal stage of a rabbit,' as used by us now mean, and refer to, different things, alternative translation theories that map these different expressions onto the term 'rabbit' as we used it in the past conflict with one another. Quine concludes from examples like this that theories of translation are underdetermined, in the sense defined above, by the observational data for them.

At this point I would like to clarify something that has sometimes been the source of confusion. The underdetermination thesis tells us that different, and incompatible theories of translation are equally supported by the set of all observational data. What does it mean to call two such theories incompatible? There is a potential problem here. It would be tempting to say that two theories that translate expressions of L_1 onto expressions of L_2 are incompatible if there is some expression α of L_1 such that the translation of α given by one of the theories is an expression β of L_2 that means and refers to something different from the expression γ that is the translation of α given by the other theory. However there is a problem with this characterization; it takes for granted that there are definite facts about whether different expressions in L_2 mean or refer to the same thing. Since this is something that Quine will later call into question, even when L_2 is our own present language, it would be desirable to have some other characterization of what it is for translation theories to be incompatible.

Often what Quine seems to have in mind is that the theories are logically incompatible.[7] However, despite the obvious intuitive difference in meanings between the terms 'rabbit,' 'undetached rabbit part,' and 'temporal stage of a rabbit' as we use them now, the following claims are not logically incompatible:

(i)   The term 'rabbit' as we used it in the past means the same as the term 'rabbit' as we use it now.

(ii) The term 'rabbit' as we used it in the past means the same as the phrase 'undetached rabbit part' as we use it now.

(iii) The term 'rabbit' as we used it in the past means the same as the phrase 'temporal stage of a rabbit' as we use it now.

Consequently, translation theories making these different claims need not be logically incompatible with one another.

Logical incompatibility will result if these translation theories are embedded in larger background theories containing the claims (a)–(d).

(a) Rabbits are not undetached rabbit parts & undetached rabbit parts are not temporal stages of rabbits & rabbits are not temporal stages of rabbits.

(b) 'Rabbit' (as we use it now) refers to an object iff it is a rabbit & 'undetached rabbit part' (as we use it now) refers to an object iff it is an undetached rabbit part & 'temporal stage of a rabbit' (as we use it now) refers to an object iff it is a temporal stage of a rabbit.

(c) If two words refer to different things then they don't mean the same thing.

(d) If a means the same thing as b & a means the same thing as c, then b means the same thing as c.

Let T_1 be a translation theory containing statement (i) above, and T_2 be a translation theory containing statement (ii). The union of T_1, T_2, and a set containing (a)–(d) is logically inconsistent. In light of this we may take Quine's talk about incompatible theories of translation to be talk about theories which when augmented by background claims analogous to (a)–(d) are logically incompatible with one another. The justification for appealing to these auxiliary claims is that (a) states an obvious fact about the world, and (b)–(d) are axiomatic to any overall theory that makes significant use of the concepts of meaning and reference.

Where are we? Given Quine's conception of the observational evidence relevant to translation, we have reached the result that theories of translation are underdetermined by the set of all observational evidence for them. One might object that this conclusion is too hasty, on the grounds that the identification of observational evidence for translation with claims about stimulus meaning is too restricted, and does not exhaust the range of relevant observational data. However, this turns out not to be very important, since it is doubtful that enlarging the class of observational data will change the overall result. Even if we add further observational claims, it is reasonable to suppose that theories of translation will remain underdetermined by the observational data. But this is hardly momentous. Since empirical theories of all sorts are typically underdetermined by the observational evidence bearing on them, the extension of this result to theories of translation is not, in itself, a radical development.

What makes it striking is Quine's use of it as the basis for the truly radical doctrine of the Indeterminacy of Translation.

The Indeterminacy of Translation

Translation is not determined by the set N of all truths of nature, known and unknown. For any pair of languages and theory of translation T for those languages, there are alternative theories of translation, incompatible with T, that accord equally well with N. All such theories are equally true to the facts of nature; there is no objective matter of fact on which they disagree, and no objective sense in which one is true and the other is not.[8]

How does Quine get from the underdetermination of translation by data to the indeterminacy of translation? There are two main routes in his writings. The first route relies on the behaviorist premise that since we learn language by observing the linguistic behavior of others, the only facts relevant to determining linguistic meaning must be publicly observable behavioral facts – in particular facts about stimulus meaning. Quine's discussion of the underdetermination of translation by data is designed to show that these facts do not determine which translations of our words are correct, and so do not determine what our words mean. Thus he is able to deduce the indeterminacy of translation from his behaviorism plus the underdetermination of translation by data.

There are, however, several problems with relying on behaviorism in this way. For one thing, behaviorism is essentially a species of verificationism restricted to the mental and the linguistic. As such it is no more plausible than verificationism in general, the difficulties with which are well known. For another thing, Quine's notion of stimulus meaning is problematic from a behavioristic perspective. Stimulus meaning is, of course, defined in terms of assent and dissent. But what are assent and dissent, from a behaviorist point of view? To assent or dissent is not to utter the English words 'yes' or 'no'; nor is it to utter translations of them, since on Quine's view we don't have any idea of what counts as a translation until after we settle facts about stimulus meaning, and hence facts about assent and dissent. Intuitively, one thinks of assent to a sentence as expressing one's belief that the sentence is true, and of dissent from a sentence as expressing one's belief that the sentence is false. Of course we also recognize that the correlations between assent and belief are not perfect, since all manner of factors may intrude in particular cases – e.g., conversational implicatures, considerations of politeness, the desire not to offend, or a desire to conceal one's true opinion. Quine's use of assent and dissent to characterize the evidence for theories of translation is effective only to the extent that we abstract away from these complicating factors. But, when we do this our notion of the stimulus meaning of a sentence for a speaker becomes essentially that of a pair consisting of the set of circumstances in which the speaker believes the sentence expresses a truth, and the set of circumstances in which the speaker believes the sentence expresses a falsehood. If we understand claims about stimulus meaning in this way, then it is reasonable to take them as providing evidence for theories of translation. But then the evidence for such theories is not itself behavioristic, but rather involves a certain kind of belief. One wonders why, if one species of belief is to be accepted and taken for granted, other beliefs shouldn't be accorded the same status.

In any case, I am not going to concentrate on Quine's problematic behaviorism.[9] Instead, I will focus on a more powerful and more widely influential route to his thesis of the indeterminacy of translation. Quine recognized that many philosophers might agree with his claim that the set of (quasi-behavioral) facts about stimulus meanings does not resolve indeterminacies about meaning, while at the same time disagreeing with his contention that these are the only meaning-determining facts. To these philosophers Quine issued a challenge – namely to show how indeterminacies could be resolved by adding to this set of facts any other physical facts that one likes. Quine was convinced that even when the set of (quasi-behavioral) facts about stimulus meanings was enriched with all other physical facts, indeterminacies about whether a given word means the same as 'rabbit,' or 'temporal stage of a rabbit,' would remain.

It is understandable why he should think this. If I can't deduce from the native's behavior that his world 'gavagai' means the same as my word 'rabbit,' how would it help to add that certain neurons in his brain fire when he uses the word? We can no more read off the contents of a person's words from physiological claims about neurons than we can read off the contents of his words from statements about the noises he makes in certain environments. Consequently, it seems that if we cannot deduce a determinate meaning from a non-intensional description of linguistic behavior, adding facts about neurons won't help. On Quine's view, the same could be said about any other physical fact one might appeal to.

We can now state Quine's second route to the indeterminacy of translation. On this route, he derives it as a consequence of the subsidiary doctrines of physicalism and the underdetermination of translation by physics.

Physicalism

All genuine truths (facts) are determined by physical truths (facts).[10]

The Underdetermination of Translation by Physics

Translation is not determined by the set of all physical truths (facts), known and unknown. For any pair of languages and theory of translation T for those languages, there are alternative theories of translation, incompatible with T, that accord equally well with all physical truths (facts).

If these two doctrines are correct, then claims about what our words mean – e.g. claims like that expressed by *'rabbit' as I used it in the past means the same as 'rabbit' as I use it now* – never state genuine facts, and never count as expressing genuine truths.[11] Moreover, since the only facts and truths are genuine facts and truths, these claims simply do not state facts, and so are not true. Hence, the indeterminacy of translation. This, I believe, is the most influential and challenging argument for the indeterminacy thesis.[12]

What should we say about it? To begin with, the contents of the premises and the conclusion are unclear. Each of Quine's doctrines – physicalism, the underdetermination of translation by physics, and the indeterminacy of translation – speaks of one set of truths as determining, or not determining, another set of claims. However, we are not told what it is for one set of claims to determine another. Because of this, it is unclear precisely what determination relation is invoked in these doctrines. Since there are several possibilities, equivocation threatens. On certain interpretations of what determination means, physicalism is plausible, while on other interpretations the underdetermination of translation by physics is plausible. However, as I will try to show, these interpretations do not make both doctrines plausible. More generally, I will argue that there is no interpretation on which both physicalism and the underdetermination of translation by physics are plausible, and no interpretation in which the indeterminacy of translation can be sustained.

What is it for one set of claims to determine another? It is not for the claims in the second set to be logical consequences of the claims in the first. Certainly translation theories are not logical consequences of the set of all physical truths. But this is trivial, since whenever an empirical theory of any interest includes vocabulary not found in the truths of physics it will fail to be a logical consequence of those truths. For example, not all the truths of biology are logical consequences of the set of true sentences of the language of an ideal physics. But biology is supposed by Quine to be determined by physics; so the determination relation cannot be that of logical consequence. If it were, physicalism would obviously be false.

A different way of specifying the determination relation would be to say that a set P of statements determines a set Q of statements iff it would be (metaphysically) impossible for all the statements in P to be true without all the statements in Q being true – i.e. iff Q is a (metaphysically) necessary consequence of P. On this interpretation, physicalism – in something close to the form I have stated it – is quite plausible; it states that all genuine truths (facts) supervene on the physical truths (facts). However, the underdetermination of translation by physics now turns out to be implausible. Prior to Quine's skeptical attack, we naturally assume that there are facts about meaning and translation of the sort that Quine denies. Moreover, at this stage of the argument we are entitled to assume this, since prior to drawing any conclusions about indeterminacy we have been given no reason to doubt that our most basic pretheoretic convictions about meaning are correct. Given these convictions, we may ask directly whether a physically identical twin – someone (in a physically identical possible world) whose utterances, behavior, brain states, causal and historical relations to the environment, and interactions with other speakers completely and exactly matches mine (in the actual world) – could mean by 'rabbit,' what I mean (in the actual world) by, say, 'temporal stage of a rabbit.' One would think not. If there are such things as meaning and reference as we ordinarily understand them, then they supervene on the totality of physical facts. Hence on this interpretation, the underdetermination of translation by physics should be rejected.

The thesis could, of course, be saved if it could be shown both that theories of translation are not a priori, or conceptual, consequences of the set of physical truths, and that because of this, they are not necessary consequences of those statements either. The first of those claims is reasonably plausible – it is plausible to suppose that theories of transla-tion are not a priori, or conceptual consequences of the set of physical truths. Thus if one were confused about the relationship between neces-sity and a prioricity, or if one failed to distinguish them, one might wrongly conclude that both physicalism and the underdetermination of translation by physics are true, when determination is taken to be [a] necessary consequence. The error here lies in the reliance on the un-argued, and I believe false, assumption that semantic statements are necessary consequences of the physical truths only if they are a priori consequences of those truths.[13] Once this error is removed there is no plausible route to the underdetermination of translation by physics, on the interpretation in which determination is construed as necessary con-sequence.

In light of this, it may be worthwhile to put the notion of necessity aside and examine a more epistemological conception of the determin-ation relation. One might say that a set P of claims determines a set Q iff it is in principle possible, given the claims in P, for one to demonstrate the truth of the claims in Q, appealing only to logic and obvious a priori principles or definitions. The idea here is that for P to determine Q is for P to provide a theoretical basis for establishing Q that is absolutely conclusive, and that rules out any possibility of falsehood. In effect, determination is here construed as a priori consequence.

On this interpretation, the underdetermination of translation by phys-ics is both interesting and plausible. Given the total set of evidence about stimulus meanings of the sort Quine identifies, I cannot absolutely estab-lish that what a speaker means by one of his terms is what I now mean by 'rabbit,' as opposed to what I now mean by 'undetached rabbit part' or 'temporal stage of a rabbit' (even if the speaker is me in the past). The claim that a speaker means one of these things rather than another is not an a priori consequence of the total set of claims about Quinean stimulus meanings. Moreover, it is hard to see how adding more behavioral facts, or even more physical facts – about the neurological events in the per-son's brain or his physical interactions with the environment – would, by themselves, change the situation. Thus, it may well turn out that theories of translation are epistemologically underdetermined by the set of all physical truths.

But how serious would this be? Is there some reason to believe that all truths must be not just necessary consequences, but also purely a priori consequences of the set of all physical truths? Once we are clear about the difference between the two, I can see no reason to believe this; nor has Quine given a theoretical explanation of why it must be maintained.[14]

Hence, if theories of translation do turn out to be underdetermined by physics in this epistemological sense, such a result should be taken to show that the corresponding epistemic version of physicalism is false, even though the metaphysical version of physicalism, in which the determination relation is that of necessary consequence, remains true.

If this is right, then there may be an interesting epistemological interpretation of the determination relation according to which the underdetermination of translation by physics is true, while physicalism and the indeterminacy of translation are false. However, at this point we need to note a complication. In order to derive any empirical theory T from the set of truths of physics, one must appeal to theoretical identifications, or bridge principles, relating the concepts and vocabulary of T to the concepts and vocabulary of the underlying physics. What conditions must these identifications or bridge principles satisfy in order to be available for such derivations? Is it enough that they be true, or must they also be a priori (and/or necessary)? In my epistemic characterization of the determination relation, I allowed only a priori truths and definitions. With this understanding the underdetermination of translation by physics is plausible.

However, with this same understanding, physicalism is threatened, not just by theories of meaning or translation, but by a wide variety of empirical theories and claims. Consider, for example, ordinary instances of theoretical reduction, such as the reduction of the biological concept of a gene to a physical construction involving the concept DNA. The relevant theoretical statement relating the two seems to be an empirical, a posteriori truth. Thus if bridge principles relating the biological vocabulary to the physical vocabulary are restricted to a priori definitions, then our theoretical statement will be excluded, and the derivation of genetics from physical theory will be placed in jeopardy. Surely no one would conclude from this that genetics in particular, or biology in general, fail to state genuine truths; rather, if a choice has to be made, we will reject the (strong) epistemological version of physicalism.[15]

In light of this, one could opt to weaken the epistemological determination relation so as to allow P to determine Q provided that Q is a logical consequence of P together with bridge principles, or theoretical identifications, consisting of any truths – contingent, a posteriori, or otherwise – that relate the vocabulary of P to that of Q.[16] This is essentially the classical concept of reduction.[17] On this weakened conception, the usual reduction of the notion of a gene to DNA will pose no difficulty for physicalism. However, this weakened conception is too weak; according to it even theories of translation may turn out to be determined by the set of physical truths.

To see this let *Sx* be some formula specifying a set of physical facts satisfied by me and only me – so that *Sx* is true relative to an assignment of me as value of *x*, and is false relative to other assignments. It doesn't matter what this formula looks like – whether it is complex, whether we can identify it as applying just to me, etc. It only matters that it exists. For completeness we may suppose that it includes a specification of all physical facts about me relevant to my use of language. Let *Lx* be a similar formula applying uniquely to a certain Spanish speaker, Luis. (For the sake of simplicity, suppose that I am a monolingual speaker of English and Luis is a monolingual speaker of Spanish.) Now imagine a claim of the following sort, exhaustively listing the translation of the finitely many individual words of my language onto words and phrases of his language.[18]

TSL   ∃x ∃y [Sx & Ly & for all words w (of English) and words or phrases w* (of Spanish), w as used by x means the same as w* as used by y iff (i) w = 'woman' and w* = 'mujer,' or (ii) w = 'headache' and w* = 'dolor de cabeza,' or … …..

A corresponding claim lists the translation of the finitely many individual words of his language onto words and phrases of my language; similar claims may be imagined for each actual pair of language users – past, present and future. Since it is plausible to suppose that there are only finitely many such pairs of speakers, it seems reasonable to assume that there exists some extremely long and complicated general formula of the following sort that encompasses all the individual cases.

GT   For all speakers x and y, and for all words w in x's language and words or phrases w* in y's language, w as used by x means the same as w* as used by y iff (i) Sx & Ly &(w = 'woman' & w* = 'mujer,' or w = 'headache' & w* = 'dolor de cabeza,' or … …..; or (ii) Lx & Sy &(w = 'semaforo' & w* = 'traffic light,' or …; or (iii) Sx & Gy & … … … …..; or ….

GT may be regarded as a bridge principle providing a coextensive physicalistic counterpart of the predicate 'means the same as' applied to words and phrases in theories of translation. Next we need a general bridge principle that encompasses the rules used in theories of translation to combine translations of parts into translations of whole sentences. Presumably there are only finitely many such combinatorial rules for each pair of speakers. If, as we are assuming, there are only finitely many such pairs of actual speakers, these rules can in principle be exhaustively listed. This list together with GT can then be used to formulate another bridge principle that provides a coextensive physicalistic counterpart to the predicate 'means the same as' as used between sentences in theories of translation. But then, theories of translation will be derivable from the set of all physical truths together with these bridge principles, and so will count as determined by physics in our weakened epistemological sense.

The purpose of this exercise is, of course, to show that the version of the epistemic determination according to which P determines Q iff there is some set of truths T which together with P logically entail Q is far too weak to support Quine's indeterminacy thesis. Could stronger conditions be found that would serve Quine's skeptical purposes? Several possibilities suggest themselves. First, it might be claimed that what we want is not just a reduction of theories of translation to physical truths, but rather a single reduction to the set of physical truths of all theories making use of semantic notions such as meaning and reference. Surely, if these notions are legitimate they will have significant theoretical uses well beyond theories of translation in the narrow sense considered here. The fact that a trivial reduction is theoretically possible when translation theories are considered in isolation does not show that such a reduction is possible in a context that is properly more inclusive.

The point is, I think, well taken. But the problem with this suggestion is that it takes us far beyond Quine's own discussion and into uncharted waters. Before we can make any progress on the question of whether a single physicalistic reduction of all legitimate uses of semantic notions is theoretically possible, we need a reasonably precise and exhaustive characterization of the range of theoretical uses of semantic notions. Until we have this, we can't evaluate the case for skepticism about meaning (and reference) because no sufficiently articulated case for skepticism about these notions has been made.

A second possible response to my trivial reduction is to stick to a physicalistic reduction simply of translation theories, but to claim that what is wanted are bridge principles that provide definitions yielding physical formulas coextensive with their nonphysical counterparts in all counterfactual circumstances. The bridge principles in my trivial reduction do not satisfy this demand, and so do not satisfy this strengthened modal constraint on the determination relation. Although I have no quarrel with this strengthened requirement, two points should be noted. First, if, unlike Quine, we grant the legitimacy of modal notions, then we can characterize determination directly in terms of necessary consequence. But then, as I have maintained above, we have been given no reason to doubt that theories of translation are determined by the physical truths. Second, if one insists on characterizing determination in terms of a strengthened reduction relation that requires physicalistic formulas that are necessarily coextensive with the predicates used in the theories undergoing reduction, then it is not clear what our attitude should be towards the resulting strengthened versions of physicalism and the underdetermination of translation by physics. Are there physicalistic formulas that are necessarily coextensive with the relevant semantic predicates employed by a theory of translation? It is hard to be sure. Certainly Quine has given no compelling arguments to think that there aren't. Thus, on this interpretation, the case for the underdetermination of translation by physics has not been made.

A similar point holds for physicalism. On the present strengthened interpretation of the determination relation, it is not evident what we should think of this doctrine. I have already granted the truth of a weaker version of physicalism, which states that all truths must be necessary consequences of the physical truths. Is it obvious that we should add the further requirement that they be logical consequences of the physical truths plus definitions that provide necessarily coextensive physical translations of all vocabulary items used in stating any truth? I should think not. Suppose certain claims are necessary consequences of the set of all physical truths. It is hard to see why we should deny that these claims state genuine facts if it turns out, for example, that there are no finitely long formulas in the language of an ideal physics that are necessarily coextensive with the relevant non-physical predicates. Since this stronger requirement is both implausible and unsupported by argument, the present interpretation of the determination relation is one in which neither of the two premises for the indeterminacy thesis has been secured.

In light of this, the conclusion to be drawn is that Quine's argument for the indeterminacy of translation fails to provide a compelling challenge to our fundamental convictions about meaning and translation. This does not, by itself, foreclose the possibility that something could be done to strengthen, or revive, such a skeptical challenge. But surely the burden of proof is on those who wish to persuade us to adopt a radically skeptical attitude toward our ordinary semantic notions.

II

So far, I haven't said anything about the doctrine of the inscrutability of reference, nor have I made good on my introductory remark that Quine's skeptical theses lead him to a radical and self-undermining form of eliminativism. I now turn to these topics....

... [I]n his essay 'Ontological Relativity'[19] ... [Quine] considers whether his doctrine of the inscrutability of reference applies to ourselves, and whether, if it does, this makes 'nonsense of the notion of reference.' Prior to this point in the essay he has pointed out that the indeterminacy of translation is inextricably linked to the inscrutability of reference. He has argued that if it is indeterminate whether the native's word 'gavagai' means the same as my word 'rabbit,' then it is indeterminate whether the native's word 'gavagai' refers to rabbits. He has also pointed out that if it is indeterminate whether the native's word 'gavagai' refers to rabbits, then it is indeterminate whether my English-speaking neighbor uses the word 'rabbit' to refer to rabbits.

At this point Quine considers the possibility of making the same claim about himself.

> I have urged in defense of the behavioral philosophy of language, Dewey's, that the inscrutability of reference is not the inscrutability of a fact; there is no fact of the matter. But if there is really no fact of the matter, then the inscrutability of reference can be brought even closer to home than the neighbor's case; we can apply it to ourselves. If it is to make sense to say even of oneself that one is referring to rabbits and formulas and not to rabbit stages and Gödel numbers, then it should make sense equally to say it of someone else. After all, as Dewey stressed, there is no private language.
>
> We seem to be maneuvering ourselves into the absurd position that there is no difference on any terms, interlinguistic or intralinguistic, objective or subjective, between referring to rabbits and referring to rabbit parts or stages; or between referring to formulas and referring to their Gödel numbers. Surely this is absurd, for it would imply that there is no difference between the rabbit and each of its parts or stages, and no difference between a formula and its Gödel number. Reference would seem now to become nonsense not just in radical translation but at home.   (47–8)

The argument contained in this passage may be reconstructed as follows:

Quine's Reductio ad Absurdum in 'Ontological Relativity'

R1   It is indeterminate (hence there is no fact of the matter) whether the native uses 'gavagai' to refer to rabbits as opposed to temporal stages of rabbits, undetached rabbit parts, and so on.

R2   If (R1), then it is indeterminate (hence there is no fact of the matter) whether my neighbor uses 'rabbit' to refer to rabbits as opposed to temporal stages of rabbits, undetached rabbit parts, and so on.

R3   Therefore, it is indeterminate (hence there is no fact of the matter) whether my neighbor uses 'rabbit' to refer to rabbits as opposed to temporal stages of rabbits, undetached rabbit parts, and so on.

R4   If (R3), then it is indeterminate (hence there is no fact of the matter) whether I use 'rabbit' to refer to rabbits as opposed to temporal stages of rabbits, undetached rabbit parts, and so on.

R5   Therefore it is indeterminate (hence there is no fact of the matter) whether I use 'rabbit' to refer to rabbits as opposed to temporal stages of rabbits, undetached rabbit parts, and so on.

R6   If (R1), (R3) and (R5), then there is no difference between referring to rabbits and referring to temporal stages of rabbits, undetached rabbit parts, and so on.

R7   If there is no difference between referring to rabbits and referring to temporal stages of rabbits, undetached rabbit parts, and so on, then there is no difference between rabbits, temporal stages of rabbits, undetached rabbit parts, and so on.

R8   Therefore, there is no difference between rabbits, temporal stages of rabbits, undetached rabbit parts, and so on.

Since the conclusion, (R8), is clearly false, and the argument is logically valid, at least one of the premises (R1), (R2), (R4), (R6), or (R7) must be incorrect. The problem is to determine which.

In attacking this problem it is important to be clear about the ontological nature of Quine's underdetermination, indeterminacy, and inscrutability theses. What they claim is that the set of all physical truths does not determine the truth of statements about meaning and reference. Now certainly the set of all physical truths does not distinguish between the native, my neighbor, and me. If physical truths determine reference for any of us, then physical truths determine reference for all of us. So, given the nature of the indeterminacy and inscrutability theses, one cannot avoid the argument's conclusion by rejecting premises (R2) or (R4). If we claim that there is indeterminacy regarding the native, then we must accept the same indeterminacy for ourselves. In short, the only way to block the absurd conclusion (R8) is to reject either (R1), (R6), or (R7). Since (R1) is essential to Quine's position, his only option is to reject (R6) or (R7)....

Consider again (R6). The antecedent is tantamount to the claim that for every speaker x and expression α it is not determinate that α, as used by x, refers to rabbits – i.e., it is not determinate that α, as used by x, refers to an object o iff o is a rabbit (as opposed to referring to an object o iff o is a temporal stage of a rabbit, an undetached rabbit part, and so on). Given this, we may take the consequent of (R6) as saying that for no speaker x and expression α is it true that α, as used by x, refers to an object o iff o is a rabbit *without it being equally true* that α, as used by x, refers to an object o iff o is a temporal stage of a rabbit (and so on for the other potential referents). In other words, the consequent of (R6) specifies that for all speakers x and expressions α, α, as used by x, refers to all and only rabbits, only if it also refers to all and only temporal stages of rabbits, and so on. Thus, the conditional, (R6), tells us that if it is never determinate whether an expression α, as used by a x, refers to all and only rabbits (as opposed to all and only temporal stages of rabbits, and the like), then α, as used by x, refers to all and only rabbits, only if it simultaneously refers to all and only temporal stages of rabbits (and the like).

On this interpretation the content of (R7) and (R8) is clear. (R7) says that if for any person x and expression α, α, as used by x, refers to all and only rabbits, only if it also refers to all and only temporal stages of rabbits, then something is a rabbit iff it is a temporal stage of a rabbit (and similarly for other possible referents). (R8) is the obviously false claim that for any object o, o is a rabbit iff o is a temporal stage of a rabbit iff o is an undetached rabbit part, and so on.

As I have said, there is no doubt that Quine rejects (R8). Our exegetical problem is to find a Quinean basis for rejecting either (R6) or (R7) that fits the moral that Quine draws from the argument – namely that reference, when understood in a certain way, 'is nonsense.' The problem is solved by taking Quine to be an eliminativist about our ordinary notion of reference. For Quine, it is reference as we ordinarily understand it that is indeterminate in the manner chronicled by (R1)–(R5). His claim that the argument shows that this notion of reference is 'nonsense' may be understood as the claim that the argument shows that there is no such thing as reference in this sense – i.e. when reference is understood in the ordinary way, no expression ever refers to any object. Note, if no expression refers to any object, then for no speaker x and expression α is it true that α, as used by x, refers to an object o iff o is a rabbit. But if this is so, then (R6) is true, (R7) is false, and the absurd conclusion (R8) is blocked.[20] Thus, we have found a Quinean response to the reductio ad absurdum that makes sense of the lesson that Quine draws from the argument.

In addition, eliminativism about ordinary reference is quite natural from a Quinean perspective. Given Quine's commitment to the indeterminacy of reference not only for others, but also for oneself, he must reject even such apparently obvious disquotational claims as (D).

> D   It is determinate, and hence a fact, (i) that for any object o, 'rabbit,' as I now use it, refers to o iff o is a rabbit, (ii) that for any object o, the phrase 'temporal stage of a rabbit,' as I now use it, refers to o iff o is a temporal stage of a rabbit, and so on.

But surely, one is inclined to think, if there are any positive facts about reference, as we ordinarily understand it, commonplace disquotational facts must be among them. Thus if one has reason to reject even such disquotational claims as (D), then one has reason to think that words never refer to anything.[21]

The same conclusion can be reached from Quinean premises without the detour through (R6) and (R7). Starting from (R5) one can reason as follows.

> R5a   If (R5), then it is indeterminate whether I use 'rabbit' to refer to rabbits.
> b   So it is indeterminate whether I use 'rabbit' to refer to rabbits.
> c   Thus it is not true that I use 'rabbit' to refer to rabbits.
> d   By parity of reasoning I don't use it to refer to anything else either. Since the same can be said for other speakers and other words, no one's words ever refer to anything (in the ordinary sense in which we understand the notion of reference).

This, I believe, is the most accurate and straight forward interpretation of Quine's position.

It also fits nicely with the positive remarks Quine makes immediately following the quoted passage in which he sets out the reductio ad absurdum. As I have indicated, the lesson he explicitly draws from the argument is that 'reference would seem now to become nonsense not just in radical translation but at home.' In the paragraphs immediately following this remark he tries to explain what this means by propounding a doctrine of the relativity of reference and ontology.[22] The key feature of the doctrine is supposed to be that reference is nonsense, if thought of 'absolutely,' but it is not nonsense if understood as relativized to some sort of background theory or language. One problem is that Quine never makes clear precisely what it means to think of reference 'absolutely.' But whatever it means, he seems to be saying that if we understand reference in that sense, then there is no such thing as reference – no expression ever refers (in that sense) to an object. In other words, Quine claims that the way to block the obviously false conclusion (R8) is to embrace eliminativism about a certain notion of reference. However, this strategy will succeed only if the notion of reference about which one is an eliminativist is the one that appears in steps (R1)–(R5) of the argument; and that is reference as we ordinarily understand it.

For Quine, our ordinary 'absolute' notion of reference is to be contrasted with a different 'relative' notion of reference. On his view, when I use this latter notion, claims I make about the reference of others are relative to some background interpretation, or translation manual. When I say, using Quine's proposed substitute for our ordinary notion of reference, that x's expression α refers to F's, I am saying that according to some underdetermined system T of translation that I am employing, x's expression refers to F's. Moreover, when I claim that x's expression α refers to F's relative to a translation manual T, I am saying that there is some word or phrase p in my present language that satisfies two conditions: (i) according to T, α means the same thing as p (T maps α onto p), and (ii) p, as I now use it, refers to F's.

This invites a further question. What does it mean to say that an expression in my present language refers to F's? The answer is that by reference in my present language I just mean that which is given by the sum of all relevant disquotational axioms:

'N,' as used by me now, refers to an object o iff o is an N.

So on this view there are two kinds of reference: (i) disquotational reference for words and phrases of my own present language, and (ii) translation plus disquotational reference for all words and phrases other than those used by me now. Quine appears to explicitly endorse this view in *Pursuit of Truth*, where he clarifies and modifies his original discussion in 'Ontological Relativity.'[23]

> I can now say what ontological relativity is relative to, more succinctly than I did in the lectures, paper, and book of that title. It is relative to a manual of translation. To say that "gavagai" denotes rabbits is to opt for a manual

of translation in which "gavagai" is translated as "rabbit," instead of opting for any of the alternative manuals.... And does the indeterminacy or relativity also extend somehow to the home language? In "Ontological Relativity" I said it did, for the home language can be translated into itself by permutations that depart materially from the mere identity transformation.... But if we choose as our manual of translation the identity transformation, thus taking the home language at face value, the relativity is resolved. Reference is then explicated in disquotational paradigms analogous to Tarski's truth paradigm (section 33); thus "rabbit" denotes rabbits, whatever *they* are, and "Boston" designates Boston.   (51–2)

As I see it, the way to understand Quine's view is to take it as a proposal as to replace our ordinary notion of reference with two related notions – disquotational reference for one's own present language and translation plus disquotation for everything else. Technicalities aside, one can think of the disquotational reference of one's present words as being defined in the following Tarski-like way:

Disquotational reference of my present words

For all names n of my own present language and objects o, n refers to o iff n = 'Alfred' and o is Alfred, or n = 'Willard' and o is Willard, or ...
For all predicates P of my own present language and objects o, P refers (applies) to o iff P = 'rabbit' and o is a rabbit, or ...

When reference is defined in this way, the disquotational claim

(i)   For all objects o, 'rabbit' refers in my own present language to an object o iff o is a rabbit

has the content

(ii)   For all objects o, either 'rabbit' = 'rabbit' and o is a rabbit, or 'rabbit' = 'dog' and o is a dog, or ..., iff o is a rabbit.

If we assume that the set of physical truths (somehow) includes statements of elementary syntax like *'rabbit' = 'rabbit'* and *'rabbit' ≠ 'dog',*[24] then it is reasonable to suppose that (ii) is a logical consequence of the set of physical truths, and therefore is determinately true.

So, commonplace claims I make about my own present reference – using Quine's disquotational substitute for our ordinary notion – turn out to be determinately true. What about claims I make about the reference of others – using Quine's substitute for these cases? Here the situation is not as clear. Suppose I make a claim about someone else's reference by assertively uttering (i).

(i) α, as used by x, refers to (all and only) rabbits.

One way of construing this along roughly Quinean lines would be to see it as making the claim (ii).

(ii) α, as used by x, means the same as some expression in my language that (disquotationally) refers to (all and only) rabbits.

On this construal my claim about the reference of x's term carries with it a claim about meaning, and therefore it is, on Quine's view, indeterminate.

However, this may not be the only alternative open to Quine. My remark (i) might also be construed as having the content (iii).

(iii) There is a translation theory, or manual, T, that I have adopted for translating x's words onto mine, and there is an expression r in my present language such that (a) T maps α onto r, and (b) r (disquotationally) refers to rabbits.

Here, to say that I have adopted a translation manual T need not mean that I endorse claims of the form *A means the same as B* that arise from T's mapping of A onto B. Rather, Quine might maintain that one can adopt a translation manual as a practical tool for dealing with other speakers, without being committed to the truth of the manual's (implicit) claims about meaning. If this is right, then even a demonstration that these claims are indeterminate would not show that (iii) is indeterminate.[25]

Whether or not (iii) is indeterminate depends on whether the physical truths determine that it is true that I have adopted a translation manual that maps α onto some expression r of my present language. Presumably, to say that a translation manual maps α onto r is to say that according to the translation manual, α means the same as r, which in turn is to specify the meaning, or content, one of the theorems extractable from the manual. This is a type of semantic claim, just as the claim that one has adopted a particular translation manual is a type of psychological claim. Thus, it would seem that (iii) will qualify as determinate only if the physical truths determine the truth of certain claims about linguistic and psychological content. One cannot help but think that, from Quine's perspective, it is doubtful that this will turn out to be so. Thus it seems likely that, on his view, claims like (i), about the reference of expressions used by others, will turn out to be indeterminate when the notion of reference involved is the one that he proposes as a substitute for our ordinary notion.[26]

Suppose we accept this characterization of Quine's position. On this view, claims I make about the reference of others are indeterminate, whereas some claims I make about my own present reference are determinately true. Does this contradict Quine's original statement that the indeterminacy of reference for me is the same as the indeterminacy of reference for others? No, it does not. Quine's original indeterminacy claims were claims about statements involving the ordinary notion of reference. When what is meant by 'refers' is ordinary reference, Quine's view is that no claims to the effect [that] a given word as used by a given speaker refers to a given object are determinate; hence no such claims are true, no matter whether the speaker is me or anyone else. However, when the ordinary interpretation of 'refers' is replaced by the disquotational, or Tarski, interpretation for my own present language, the claim made by *'rabbit' as used by me now refers to x*, relative to an assignment of a particular rabbit to 'x,' is not the claim made by that same formula relative to the same assignment, when 'refers' is given its ordinary interpretation. Since the claims are different, there is no contradiction in supposing that one is trivial, and determined by the physical truths, whereas the other is not. Similarly when my claims about my own reference are understood purely disquotationally, while my claims about the reference of others are analyzed as involving claims about translation from their words onto mine, there is no tension in holding that the former may be determined by the set of physical truths even if the latter are not.

On this interpretation, the indeterminacy of translation leads Quine to eliminativism about meaning, as ordinarily understood. Similarly, the inscrutability of reference leads him to eliminativism about reference, as ordinarily understood. It must be remembered, however, that just as eliminativism about ordinary meaning is compatible with Quine's attempt to construct a limited, behavioristically acceptable substitute notion of meaning, so eliminativism about ordinary reference is compatible with the construction of a limited, physicalistically acceptable substitute notion of reference – namely, disquotational, or Tarski-reference. Disquotational, or Tarski-reference, is much more limited than ordinary reference. For Quine, it is applied only to one's present language, whereas ordinary reference is a relation that purports to hold between expressions, objects, and languages L, for variable 'L.' In addition, the ordinary notion of reference is one that holds in any given case in virtue of the ways in which an expression is used by speakers. It is because speakers use a word in the way they do that the word refers to what it does. By contrast, it is not because of how I use the word 'rabbit' that it Tarski-refers to an object iff it is a rabbit. That is a quasi-logical fact that doesn't depend on anything.[27]

III

To sum up, Quine's theses of the indeterminacy of translation and the inscrutability of reference lead him to be an eliminativist about (i) and (ii).

(i) meaning, as we ordinarily understand it – including putative facts to the effect that a given sentence means that P.

(ii) reference, denotation, and application, as these are ordinarily understood – including putative facts to the effect a given word refers (applies) to an object o iff o is F.

That isn't all. The same considerations that lead to eliminativism about (i) and (ii) lead to eliminativism about (iii) and (iv).

(iii) propositional attitudes; including believing that P, asserting that P, and so on.[28]

(iv) truth, in the sense in which we ordinarily understand it – namely as a property that (a) applies to a sentence of an arbitrary language in virtue of what it is used to say in that language (which in turn is dependent on how speakers of the language use the expressions in the sentence, and what those expressions refer to) and that (b) is conceptually connected to the notion of meaning (as we ordinarily understand it).[29]

Quine tries to soften the blow of all this eliminativism by suggesting replacements for our ordinary notions of meaning, reference, and truth. Ordinary meaning is to be replaced by stimulus meaning, and ordinary reference and truth are to be replaced – in the special case of one's own present language – by Tarski-reference and Tarski-truth, which are disquotational in spirit, and which can, in principle, be defined using list-type definitions.[30]

It should be remembered that Quine's wholesale rejection of these central aspects of our ordinary ways of understanding ourselves and our words is without foundation. His radical skepticism about facts stated by sentences containing our ordinary semantic and intentional notions is based on his argument for indeterminacy. If I am right about that argument, then once equivocation on the determination relation is resolved, the set of premises he appeals to loses virtually all of its independent plausibility. In effect, we are asked to give up central convictions that are vital to our self-understanding on the slenderest of grounds. But that isn't the worst of it. The worst of it is that Quine's position has several consequences that are so unpalatable as to make it reasonable to regard his view as self-undermining.

The first of these consequences involves Quine's proposed rejection of all the normal semantic facts that one might use to identify and individuate languages, and to specify the language one speaks. Normally we think of a language as a set of expressions with certain semantic properties. We identify languages in part by the truth conditions of, and propositions expressed by, their sentences. If these ordinary semantic facts are eliminated, then it is not clear that I can give any informative specification of what language I speak, of how it differs from other languages, or of what languages are. I can give the conditions under which sentences are TARSKI-TRUE-IN-MY-PRESENT-LANGUAGE, but these are not truth conditions, in the ordinary sense, and they provide no information about what my words mean, or about what language I speak.[31] Even the notion of translation becomes questionable, in so far as it presupposes the identification of different languages.

The second unpalatable consequence is that Quine's radical eliminativism runs the risk of rendering his own theses of physicalism, the underdetermination of translation by physics, the indeterminacy of translation, and the inscrutability of reference as either philosophically innocuous, obviously false, or unstatable. Consider, for example, his claim that biology is determined by the physical truths, but semantics is not. In speaking of truths here, Quine has to be speaking of Tarski-truths of the present-Quine-language. So we have a thesis to the effect that a certain set of physical sentences of present-Quine-language determines a certain other set of biological sentences in present-Quine-language, but does not determine a third set of semantic sentences in present-Quine-language. Presumably for Quine determination involves something akin to the Tarski-style, model-theoretic entailment of one set of sentences in present-Quine-language by the Tarski-true physical sentences of that language, plus definitions in the language.

There is reason to think that this cannot capture Quine's philosophical intention. For instance, it may very well turn out that our present physics, biology, and so on, are incomplete in the sense of lacking certain concepts needed for an accurate and comprehensive scientific description of the world. If the physics expressible in the present-Quine-language is incomplete in this way, then the fact that some set of claims is not determined by the Tarski-true physical sentences of that language will not carry the desired ontological implications. Suppose three hundred years ago, before we had the vocabulary needed for atomic theory, or modern biology, someone claimed that the set of Tarski-true physical sentences in his then present language failed to determine the set of Tarski-true biological sentences of his language. Surely no interesting conclusion would follow from this.

There are two cases to consider: First, if the set of physical truths appealed to in the statement of physicalism is conceptually impoverished, then physicalism itself will be unacceptable – for surely the fact that some claim is not determined by a conceptually incomplete physics establishes nothing about whether or not the claim is true.[32] Second, if the theory to be determined is impoverished, then even if it does turn out to be determined by the physical truths, this won't carry the needed guarantee that there aren't further facts of the sort that a correct theory would include, but which are nevertheless underdetermined by physics. For these reasons Quine's theses of physicalism, underdetermination, indeterminacy, and inscrutability cannot be given their intended force if they are stated using only semantic notions restricted to his present language.

One feels like saying that Quine's theses concern claims about the relationship between the totality of physical truths – in the sense of the totality of true propositions about the subject matter of physics, or the totality of true physical sentences in some possible language – on the one hand, and the totality of truths about anything else, on the other. But such formulations of Quine's theses presuppose that the truths in question are not limited to those expressible in one's present language – and this is incompatible with his semantic eliminativism. The problem is that there seems to be no way to give his theses the needed generality without appealing to semantic and other intentional facts that those theses are meant to eliminate. If this is right, then Quine faces a dilemma. Either his theses state something about the totality of physical truths in the ordinary sense, in which case they are inconsistent with the radical eliminativism to which he is driven, or they state something only about the totality of Tarski-truths in his present language, in which case the underdetermination thesis does not have its intended philosophical import, physicalism is obviously unacceptable, and the indeterminacy and inscrutability theses are nonstarters.[33]

Finally, there is an additional way in which Quine's position is self-undermining. Consider the following illustrations.

(i)   Quine says, or asserts, something – namely the conjunction of physicalism and his indeterminacy theses – which has the consequence that no one ever says or asserts anything.

(ii) Similarly, Quine believes something which has the consequence that no one ever believes anything.

(iii) By producing a sequence of meaningful sentences, Quine argues for something that has the consequence that there are no meaningful sentences.

It follows from these illustrations that the existence of Quine's own assertions, his own beliefs, and his own arguments is sufficient to falsify that which he asserted, believed and argued for. What he asserted, believed, and argued for has the character that the very act of asserting, believing, or arguing for it is itself sufficient to falsify it.[34]

Can Quine avoid this kind of self undermining? Well, it is tempting to think that he may do so by claiming that he didn't state, assert, believe, or argue for his theses. But even this won't help, since if he claims that he didn't state, believe, or argue for anything, then he still will have claimed something, and that is enough to falsify his theses. The problem is this: Quine writes a book that contains lots of sentences. We see the book; we want to know what it says, and what Quine was trying to tell us. However, all the concepts we would ordinarily use to describe this are forbidden to us by his eliminativist theses. Could we invent some technical notions to replace those eliminated that would allow us to answer our questions, without reintroducing the allegedly objectionable features of our ordinary notions? There is no reason to think so. Thus it seems that Quine's position really is self-undermining in this sense.[35]

...

Notes

1   The material in section I of this paper is a slightly expanded and reshaped version of the final section of my 'Skepticism about Meaning: Indeterminacy, Normativity, and the Rule-Following Paradox,' in Ali A. Kazmi, ed., *Meaning and Reference, The Canadian Journal of Philosophy Supplement* **23** (1998). Sections II–IV have not appeared in print before. They are based on seminars given at Princeton in 1993 and 1996. The first three sections of the paper were given as a talk at Tufts University, March 13, 1998.

I am indebted to Ali Akhtar Kazmi and Michael Thau for many useful comments on, and extensive discussion of, an earlier draft of this paper.

2 The strength of this thesis, as well as the more general thesis of the under-determination of empirical theories by observational data, depends on one's conception of what it is for a class of data statements to support a theory. For present purposes I will follow what appears to be Quine's latitudinarianism on this subject. Theories, together with auxiliary observational statements, make (entail) observational predictions. (Which statements count as observational for this purpose will not be an issue here.) A set of such observational predictions supports a theory to the extent that the theory, supplemented by true auxiliary observation statements, entails the members of the set. Two theories (appropriately supplemented with auxiliary observational statements) that entail the same members of the set, are equally well supported by the set.

3 I am assuming, in order to simplify the argument, that words are the minimal meaning bearing units, that languages contain finitely many such words, and that the translation of the infinitely many phrases and sentences of the two languages is the result of (i) the translation of the words that make them up plus (ii) combinatorial principles specifying the translations of syntactically complex expressions in terms of the translations of their parts.

4 See chapter 2 of Willard V. Quine, *Word and Object* (Cambridge, MA: The MIT Press 1960).

5 The importance that Quine attaches to stimulus meanings in testing theories of translation seems to reflect the importance one would intuitively place on information about the circumstances in which speakers would regard sentences of their language as expressing truths vs. the circumstances in which they would regard their sentences as expressing falsehoods. The circumstances in which speakers would assent to S seem intended by Quine to approximate the circumstances in which speakers would take S to express a truth; the case is similar with dissent and falsehood. It is worth remembering, however, that these are only approximations. Various nonsemantic factors – conversational implicatures, politeness, etc. – may bring it about in particular cases that one is unwilling to assent to S even though one believes it to be true, or that one is willing to assent to S even though one does not believe it to be true. Once this is realized, principles like Quine's (i) may seem less plausible than corresponding principles in which reference to stimulus meanings is replaced by reference to the circumstances in which speakers believe sentences to express truths and those in which they believe them to express falsehoods.

This also raises a question about the precise content of the claim that one sentence means the same as another. Nowadays talk about meaning typically involves carefully distinguishing content, character, and conventional impli-cature from one another, and all three from nonsemantic factors like conver-sational implicature. Quine's discussion, which predates the development of some of these ideas, is less precise and operates at a much higher level of abstraction. Since this does not affect the main lessons I want to draw from Quine, I will follow him in this.

6   See page 78 of *Word and Object* and pages 46–8 of Willard V. Quine, 'Ontological Relativity,' in *Ontological Relativity and Other Essays* (New York: Columbia University Press 1969).

7   See W. V. Quine, 'On the Reasons for Indeterminacy of Translation,' *Journal of Philosophy* **67** (1970) 178–83; and 'On Empirically Equivalent Systems of the World,' *Erkenntnis* **9** (1975) 313–28, at 322. By *logical incompatibility* I mean (and I assume Quine also means) the relation standardly defined – either model-theoretically or substitutionally – in logic books, as opposed to looser notions of 'conceptual incompatibility' or 'analytic incompatibility.'

8   See W. V. Quine, 'Reply to Chomsky,' in *Words and Objections*, D. Davidson and J. Hintikka, eds. (Dordrecht: Reidel 1969), 303.

9   In speaking of 'Quine's behaviorism,' one should distinguish several different theses that Quine himself is not at pains to separate. One thesis is that all linguistic facts are determined by purely behavioral facts, nonintentionally described. Since claims about Quinean stimulus meanings themselves appear implicitly to invoke intentional notions, facts about stimulus meanings may not be among the meaning-determining facts recognized by this thesis. A second thesis – which is not really a version of behaviorism in the strict sense – expands the range of facts that are alleged to determine linguistic facts so as to include both purely behavioral facts and facts about Quinean stimulus meanings. A third thesis maintains that facts about stimulus meanings alone determine all linguistic facts. The first of these theses – which may not be able to accommodate even facts about stimulus meanings – is not of much use to Quine, whereas the second and third lack any principled motivation. In addition, in my view all three theses are false (on any reasonable interpretation of what it means for one set of facts, or truths, to determine another).

Although I will not here give an extended argument for this position, I take the following considerations to be relevant. (i) Behaviorism shares the difficulties of verificationism in general, including certain forms of self-undermining. (ii) In addition, although Quine is sympathetic to one general version of verificationism – holistic verificationism – an attempt to ground the move from the underdetermination of translation by data to the indeterminacy of translation in a general version of verificationism would rob the indeterminacy thesis of what Quine takes to be its unique status. Since for Quine all significant empirical theories are underdetermined by data, an appeal to generalized verificationism would lead to indeterminacy doctrines for all such theories, obliterating Quine's special concerns about the linguistic and the mental. (iii) In the case of language, meaning and reference determining facts are not limited to the behavioral reactions of present speakers, but include historical facts relating present speakers to past speakers, and to the circumstances in which various individual words were introduced.

10   This is a preliminary statement of Quinean physicalism. In section IV [not reprinted here] I will take a closer look at several questions regarding how the doctrine should be formulated.

11   I use italics as a form of (single) quotation for sentences and phrases, especially when the quoted sentence or phrase itself includes single quotes.

12   The connection between the two Quinean routes to the indeterminacy of translation – one appealing to behaviorism and one appealing to physicalism – may be thought of as follows. Quine seems to assume that facts about stimulus meanings are determined by the physical truths. (This assumption could be questioned, due to the apparently intentional character of assent and dissent, but let it pass.) He also thinks that truths about stimulus meanings do not determine claims about meaning made by theories of translation. If his version of behaviorism is correct, then it follows that theories of translation aren't determined by any facts. Suppose, however, that one rejects his version of behaviorism while still accepting physicalism. One could then appeal to additional physical facts, over and above facts about stimulus meanings or the physical facts allegedly determining stimulus meanings, in an attempt to specify the totality of facts that determine the claims made by theories of translation. Quine's thesis of the underdetermination of translation by physics is aimed at defeating this strategy.

13   David Chalmers and Frank Jackson are two philosophers who seem to believe that (certain) physicalists may be on solid ground at least to the extent of claiming that semantic statements are necessary consequences of the physical truths only if they are a priori consequences of those truths. See Chalmers, *The Conscious Mind* (Oxford: Oxford University Press 1996), and Jackson, 'Armchair Metaphysics,' in *Philosophy of Mind*, M. Michael and J. O'Leary-Hawthorne, eds. (Dordrecht: Kluwer Academic Publishers 1994); Jackson, 'Postscript to "What Mary didn't Know,"' in *Materialism*, P. K. Moser and J. D. Trout, eds. (London: Routledge 1994); Jackson, 'Finding the Mind in the Natural World,' reprinted in *The Nature of Consciousness*, N. Block, O. Flanagan, and G. Guzeldere, eds. (Cambridge, MA: The MIT Press 1994); and Jackson, *From Metaphysics to Ethics: A Defense of Conceptual Analysis* (Oxford: Oxford University Press 1998). For a good critical discussion of Chalmers and Jackson, see Alex Byrne, 'Cosmic Hermeneutics,' *Philosophical Perspectives* **13** (1999).

14   It is important not to confuse the obvious fact that we know what our words, and those of our neighbors, mean with the utterly implausible claim that we arrive at this knowledge by deriving true claims about the meanings of our words, and those of our neighbors, as a priori consequences of purely physical truths. In the case of translation, it is clear that evidence involving speakers' assent to and dissent from sentences in various situations does constitute part of the evidence that bears on our acceptance of one or another system of translation. Thus Quinean stimulus meanings do have a genuine epistemic bearing on translation. However, (i) as we have seen, it is doubtful

that claims about stimulus meanings are themselves epistemic consequences of the set of purely physical truths, (ii) claims about stimulus meanings, and other current behavior of speakers, do not exhaust the evidence bearing on translation (see note 9), and (iii) the relationship between theories of translation we accept and our evidential base for such theories is not one of a priori consequence.

15 This result could be avoided if it could be shown that there are genuinely a priori semantic definitions of 'gene' and 'DNA' from which, together with the set of purely physical truths, the theoretical identification of genes with DNA could be derived. I am doubtful that such definitions exist. However, I will not attempt to prove this. By the same token, I offer no conclusive proof that there aren't genuinely a priori semantic definitions of meaning and reference from which, together with all physical truths, our ordinary claims about meaning and reference can be derived.

16 Here, when determination is defined in terms of logical consequence (plus auxiliary truths) it is natural to take 'P' and 'Q' to range over sets of sentences, rather than sets of propositions (statements). Although this, presumably, would be congenial to Quine, it contrasts with my favored way of understanding previous construals of the determination relation. When determination is construed as necessary consequence, or a priori consequence, it is natural [to] take it to be a relation between sets of propositions. Fortunately, at this stage of the discussion the choice between sentences and propositions is not crucial, and we may consider candidates for the determination relation involving either one. Later, in sections III and IV [the latter not included here], significant issues related to this choice will be discussed.

17 This conception of determination is closely related to familiar conceptions of theoretical reduction, which are used by Michael Friedman in 'Physicalism and the Indeterminacy of Translation,' *Noûs* 9 (1975) 353–73 to characterize Quine's theses of physicalism and the indeterminacy of translation.

18 In this discussion I ignore certain practical complications such as the fact that some speakers speak more than one language, the fact that words of the language may be ambiguous, and the possibility that sometimes there may be no translation of a word in one language onto a word or phrase of the other language. Although these are real factors in translation, they are peripheral to Quine's philosophical claims about translation.

19 In *Ontological Relativity and Other Essays* (New York: Columbia University Press 1969).

20 (R6) is true, on this account, because its consequent – *for all speakers x and expressions α, α, as used by x, refers to all and only rabbits, only if it also refers to all and only temporal stages of rabbits, and so on* – is vacuously true. (R7) is false because its antecedent, which is the same as the consequent of (R6), is vacuously true and its consequent is false. A slightly different rendering of the argument could be given by building into the consequent of (R6) (and antecedent of (R7)) the existential claim that some expression does refer to all

and only rabbits. On this reading, (R6) turns out to be false, on Quine's view, while (R7) comes out true. A point in favor of this reading is that it fits Quine's comment in the quoted passage to the effect that the consequent of (R6) is 'absurd.'

21 In section IV [not reprinted here] I examine the possibility of rejecting all claims, including disquotational ones, that purport to specify which objects words refer to, in the ordinary sense, while nevertheless accepting – as true – the thesis that one's words, and those of others, refer to some objects or other. For the moment, however, I will put aside this unusual possibility in order to examine the consequences of the more natural interpretation of Quine, according to which he is a complete eliminativist about ordinary reference. Once this position is shown to be self-undermining I will turn to the alternative possibility in order to determine whether or not it is viable.

22 Quine, 'Ontological Relativity,' 48–9.

23 W. V. Quine, *Pursuit of Truth* (Cambridge, MA: Harvard University Press 1992).

24 Quine seems to intend to include such statements.

25 It should be noted that (iii) is not very plausible, as it stands. As formulated at present, it does not require the translation manual T I have adopted to satisfy any conditions of empirical adequacy. For example, if I have adopted a translation manual T that translates your word 'rabbit' onto my phrase 'prime number,' then, according to (iii) my remark *You use 'rabbit' to refer to prime numbers* will be counted as true. But that seems unreasonable.

One might address this problem by modifying (iii) so that it requires the translation manual T that I have adopted to meet all Quinean conditions on empirical adequacy – i.e. to be compatible with all relevant facts about stimulus meaning. However, then a different problem arises. Suppose that T maps your word 'rabbit' onto my word 'rabbit,' but also maps your word 'dog' onto my phrase 'prime number.' Suppose further that because of this bizarre linking of your talk about dogs with my talk about numbers, T fails to meet Quinean conditions of empirical adequacy. Then, on the proposed modification of (iii), this fact alone will be sufficient to guarantee that my claim *Your word 'rabbit' refers to rabbits* is false. But this also seems unreasonable.

I leave it here as an open question whether these problems can be solved from a Quinean perspective. I am indebted to Anil Gupta for bringing these issues to my attention.

26 Because there are several Quinean options for interpreting claims like (i), and no clear specification of a determination relation that would allow us to settle precisely what is determined in Quine's sense and what is not, the conclusion that, on his view, claims like (i) are indeterminate should be regarded as plausible, but not absolutely conclusive. Should it turn out that there is a way of construing these claims as determinate in his sense the argument that follows would not be significantly affected.

27   For more on the difference between ordinary reference and disquotational, or Tarski-reference, as well as the related difference between ordinary truth and Tarski-truth, see chapters 3 and 4 of Soames, *Understanding Truth* (New York: Oxford University Press 1999).

28   See pp. 220–1 of *Word and Object*.

29   For an extended discussion of the difference between Tarski's truth predicate and our ordinary notion of truth see Chapter 4 of *Understanding Truth*.

30   Quine routinely uses the term 'refers' both for the relation between a singular term and its extension and for the relation between a predicate and individuals to which the predicate applies. (Sometimes in the semantic literature 'refers' is used only with singular terms, and 'applies' is reserved for the relation between predicates and individuals.) In this discussion I follow Quine's broad use of 'refers'; similarly for 'Tarski-refers' and related notions.

31   See chapter 4 of *Understanding Truth*.

32   Note, the problem is not that the theorems of the physical theory adopted at a given time may leave out some physical truths, but that the physical language in which that theory is formulated is not capable of expressing all the physical facts.

33   In my seminar at Princeton in the fall of 1996, David Lewis raised the possibility that the thing that does the determining might not have to be a set of sentences, but rather might be construed as something non-linguistic – e.g. an arrangement of elementary particles. Perhaps. But when we try to say what an arrangement is, and what it is for various claims to be determined by the arrangement, it is difficult to avoid appealing to ordinary semantic and intentional notions that Quine's theses are meant to eliminate. For example, an arrangement might be identified with a set of (physically identical) possible worlds, and a proposition might be declared to be determined by such a set iff it is true at each member of the set. But then we have appealed to a notion of truth that goes beyond Quine's eliminativism. Depending on what possible worlds are taken to be – e.g. maximally complete sets of propositions, or maximal properties that the universe might have had – mere reference to such worlds may also be inconsistent with his eliminativism.

34   A nice discussion of this sort of self-undermining eliminativism can be found in chapter 4 of Alex Byrne, 'The Emergent Mind,' unpublished dissertation, Princeton University (1993).

35   In section IV, which is not reprinted here, I take up the question of whether something can be salvaged from Quine's skeptical vision. To that end, I develop a more nuanced version of Quineanism that holds out the prospect of escaping some of the most damaging criticisms of the previous section. Although it can be argued that this modified Quinean position represents some improvement over the original view, in the end it too succumbs to internal difficulties.

8

Individuation, Causal Relations, and Quine[1]

Jody Azzouni

Introduction

Noun-phrases seem useful at picking out bits and pieces of the world: this much is beyond doubt. A natural question, though, is *how* the world gets chunked: are we the grateful recipients of the world's individuating largesse; or do we impose divisions upon it? And if the chunking *is* our doing, how is the trick done: are these divisions projections of our language or thought with the frightening corollary that there is nothing more to facts about how the world divides than how our language or thought projects divisions onto it? The idealist- and relativist-sounding view that *we* individuate the world, *we* project divisions into it the way a cookie cutter shapes and cuts homogenous dough, is one with a long pedigree, stretching all the way from Parmenides – on some interpretations of him anyway – up until Putnam (and beyond): shock value alone, I suspect, does much to explain its millennia-long appeal for philosophers.

One way to get past the false dichotomy the above considerations push us towards is to recognize, first, that *relations* are every bit as objective as properties are. It may be that our way of chunking the world is undeniably due to the special relations *we have* to certain chunks of it and not to others, and that other beings with different relations to the world may chunk it differently. Indeed, perhaps there is no particularly unique way the world chunks – in itself – but that doesn't have to mean that the bite-size bits we refer to the way we do are *merely* projections of our language or thought, and ones easily discarded by a mere change in vocabulary. This relational perspective denies the pernicious dichotomy that either the world supplies its own *objective* divisions (which we discover) or such divisions are *subjective* projections of our all-too-human constructions which tell us nothing about the world-in-itself.

I understand one version of the causal theory of reference (for kind terms) to be urging the relation-perspective of causes on us: it is *relations*, our causal relations to the world, that are offered as the most significant factor in how we individuate the world into parts. So, it is claimed, there is no surprise that we individuate rabbits differently than we individuate water: it is our causal relations to water (as opposed to rabbits) that explains why water-as-fusion is the appropriate relata of our references to water and rabbits (not rabbit-fusion) which are the appropriate relata of our references to rabbits. Those beings – if there be such – who causally interact with water molecules (who have eyes to see them, say) will individuate water the way we individuate rabbits. That is, the differences between us and them in how the world is individuated are due to objective differences in the causal relations to water we and such beings have.

My aim in this paper is to defend the causal view so understood against the influential arguments Quine parlays against it. Quine is a good target precisely because he first introduces in the contemporary setting most of the weapons so many have subsequently used against the causal view, and because he is far more explicit than others that it is a causal view that he is out to undermine. The two strategies raised against the causal theorist that I will discuss here are (i) *permutation arguments*, the use in one way or another of the claim that the terms of languages – given certain very natural assumptions – can be permuted in role without a resulting change in the usefulness of that language or a change in the truth values of any of its sentences,[2] and (ii) the claim that causal relations are too weak to replicate the implicit individuation conditions of our terms, what I will call the *ICR strategy*.[3]

Be forewarned: I am only a temporary ally of the causal theorist. I thus close the paper with some brief remarks on why the causal theory of reference must fail, and what the resulting alternative view looks like. My general point, however, is that this alternative view – discussed at length in KRE – is nothing akin to the views currently thought to follow from the failure of causal relations to underwrite the individuation requirements of our terms; and that we can only see this provided we honestly allow the causal theorist to demonstrate how far causality actually reaches as opposed to illegitimately cheating her of her just resources: *how* the causal theory of reference for kind terms fails to handle implicit term-individuation is crucial to understanding what the alternative view on such individuation has to be.

II

Logical preliminaries

Any countable consistent first-order theory has a countable model. Moreover, given any uncountable model of such a theory, a countable model may be extracted from it. This is one version of the Löwenheim–Skolem theorem. It is sensitive to the resources of the underlying logic, vanishing if we go second-order, modify quantificational power, or alter the upper cardinal boundary on sentence length. *But* it is a deep result for all that, since such modifications can be costly.[4]

Given any countable consistent first-order theory and a model of that theory, consider *any* permutation of the domain of the model onto itself. By similarly permuting the referential relations of the names and predicates of the theory, we can construct another model of the same theory. This property *is* humdrum: it generalizes to second-order logic and the other logics mentioned, though the Löwenheim–Skolem theorem doesn't.[5]

Some technicalities

Given an arbitrary permutation $f(x)$ of the domain of the model onto itself (or a 1–1 mapping of the domain of the model M onto another set), a new model M' is defined thus: if the name **c** is mapped by M to the object c, then M' maps c to $f(c)$. Similarly, if M maps an n-place predicate $\mathbf{P}^n$ to a set of n-tuples $(p_1, \ldots, p_n)$, then M' maps $\mathbf{P}^n$ to a set of n-tuples $(f(p_1), \ldots, f(p_n))$.[6] Each sentence of the language is true in M iff it is true in M'.

We may consider certain generalizations. The above 1–1 mappings always guarantee the desired sort of model can be defined on the target set. But in certain cases the mappings need not be 1–1 and a model can still be forthcoming.[7] We can also consider mappings that fail to be defined on the entire domain of M. In particular we can consider a mapping determined by the Löwenheim–Skolem theorem which is an identity mapping on that part of M retained in the construction of the countable submodel M' of M, and which is not defined on the remaining elements of M.

For historical reasons, call the permutation function a "proxy function," and call the so-described humdrum theorem "the humdrum theorem." Also, call any mapping determined by the Löwenheim–Skolem theorem as above a "proxy function."

What philosophical implications do proxy functions have? Start with the Löwenheim–Skolem theorem case: if we have no more resources for linking our terms to the world than those supplied by asserting truths in countable first-order languages then (for all we know) our predicates – such as "is a real number" – hold at most of countable numbers of things even if we think they don't; and a model for our truths can be defined on any countable collection of items. This may be regarded as an argument for Pythagoreanism.

The antecedent of this conditional is dubious; *why* do we have no more resources for linking our terms to the world than those afforded by first-order languages? Why couldn't it be, for example, that we have second-order resources?[8] An argument based on the humdrum theorem cannot be escaped this way. Nevertheless, *prima facie*, such arguments seem to bear, if at all, only on our capacity to refer to *mathematical objects*, but to have no effect whatsoever on our capacity to refer to empirical objects. This is because it is natural to assume that we have additional resources for referring to empirical objects: the causal connections forged and exploited between ourselves and such objects – while such connections are patently absent in the mathematical case. The expressive resources afforded by a logic are purely formal: *anything* fitting the conditions of a set of truths will do. But causal relations are *material*: they *nail* our usage to *certain* particulars, even if *other* things have the same formal properties.

This shows that permutations cannot do it alone: it takes, or *should take*, auxiliary argument to show we have no additional (causal) resources to help fix the references of our terms to natural kinds and concrete individuals. *And* the general form of such an argument should look like this: proxy functions provide admissible alternative interpretations for our kind terms and proper names because..., where what follows "because" are considerations ruling out other possible resources for fixing the references of our terms. I show in what follows that the Quine of *Word and Object* and *Ontological Relativity* mounts arguments of just this sort: careful considerations meant to infirm the causal resources the causal theorist takes herself to have are given first, and the possibility of permutations of the language consistent with this infirming come second. But the later Quine of *Things and Their Place in Nature* has changed strategies: instead of this acceptable argument-form against the causal theorist, the mere *existence* of proxy functions is offered as an *argument* for the claim that there are multiple interpretations possible for such terms.

III

I start with Quine's *Ontological Relativity*, where he first applies proxy functions in a nonmathematical context. Quine begins by reviewing the *gavagai* example from his *Word and Object*. A rabbit hops by, a native exclaims "Gavagai," and we wonder what's being referred to.[9] The famous problem, found in Quine (1969, p. 30), is "that a whole rabbit is present when and only when an undetached part of a rabbit is present; also when and only when a temporal stage of a rabbit is present." As a result (Quine 1969, pp. 30–1), "we can never settle the matter simply by ostension...simply by repeatedly querying the expression 'gavagai' for the native's assent or dissent in the presence of assorted stimulations." Why not? Because (Quine 1969, p. 32) "the only difference is in how you slice it. And how to slice it is what ostension or simple conditioning, however persistently repeated, cannot teach."

It is worth stressing that up until now causal connections between word-usage and the world *have been* Quine's focus. Factors such as salience (1969, p. 31), "one's own inborn propensity to find one stimulation qualitatively more akin to a second stimulation than to a third," have not been excluded from our tools to individuate what natives talk about: it's just that Quine thinks such resources won't do the job. Consequently, he despairs of looking to the native's interaction with the world to fix the reference of the native vis-à-vis the various rabbity options. All that's left to decide the issue is the projection of certain *grammatical forms* onto native utterances: the individuation of native words must be handled by *our* quantificational devices, and a residue of arbitrary choice in the imposition of such devices on native speech remains.[10]

Those planning to couch the referential attributions they make to natives via causal connections they see natives make to the world should be justly puzzled. *How did we get here so fast?* One popular diagnosis blames Quine's linguistic behaviorism: he thinks we only have access to *surfaces*: verbal and non-verbal behavior against backgrounds. This exegetical gloss is refuted by Quine's explicit acknowledgment of psychological dispositions. No, what is going on is rather that Quine has neatly excluded the causal relations themselves that the causal theorist hoped to rely on to fix reference: given Quine's set-up of the situation of radical translation, such relations are not perusable.

The crucial move is not explicit in *Ontological Relativity*, however; one must travel back to chapter 2 of *Word and Object*. Quine, good physicalist that he is, thinks that during radical translation – contexts, that is, where field linguists or anthropologists are attempting to translate the language of natives with whom we've had no previous contact nor cultural exchanges of any sort[11] – such linguists must focus on the sensory stimulations of natives: the excitement that external events cause in the native's nerve-endings. This requires an antecedent _modulus of stimulation_: a decision on the appropriate lengths of the time-slices of nerve-excitement which is to demarcate relevant causal (and referential) factors when natives utter sounds.

Precisely this move, however, unjustifiably deprives the causal theorist of what she needs. Talk of sensory stimulations, physicalistically acceptable though it may be, is talk neither field linguists nor anyone else, for that matter, have access to. One can speak _in general_, as Quine does, of sensory stimulations. But without an explicit vocabulary in terms of such stimulations _the scope of which extends easily to natives_, this is useless. Such a vocabulary would require labels for each nerve-ending (or significant groups of nerve-endings); and the linguist would need methods (instruments) to tell in each circumstance _which_ nerve-endings were "on" or "off." Nothing like this is available.[12]

What tools _does_ the field linguist have? Perception plus a few additional instrumental aids, such as recording devices, video cameras, etc.; theoretically: whatever from the human sciences (biology, linguistics, etc.) that can be brought to bear. That is, as in the stereotypical picture of radical translation, he faces (or is within hearing of) natives, jungle plants, rabbits, lions, etc. all of which he can refer to in enough detail to mark out observable regularities in the native's experiences which are simultaneously observable regularities _for him_. Given his rudimentary technology (from the point of view of an experimental physicist), his vocabulary is largely restricted to commonsense terminology and what such terms refer to: the stimulations relevant to what the native is referring to, therefore, _must be_ expressible in these terms. Nerve-endings simply can't come up.[13]

IV

Having sketched the causal theorist's objection to Quine's construal of the radical translation context, let's ask what the causal theorist's approach requires, and whether the resources I've described as present suffice. There are three assumptions clearly at work.

Assumption 1   Referential relations are constituted out of causal ones.
Assumption 2   There exists a rich enough set of causal relations to give *individuation conditions* for the causal *relata* of native utterances; they distinguish among candidate items such as *undetached rabbit stuff, rabbits, rabbit-fusion*, etc.
Assumption 3   These rich causal relations are epistemically accessible to the field linguist given the tools (and science) at his disposal.

All *three* assumptions can (and have) been attacked. Our focus is on Quine's arguments, however, and it is important to realize that Quine officially objects only to Assumption 2, and his objection – in pretty much his version – continues to attract philosophers, even those otherwise alien to his viewpoint.[14] Following suit, our main concern will be with Assumption 2; I will discuss Assumption 3, and why the causal theorist should not be worried about it, in §VI. Assumption 1 is the problematical assumption; here is where I part ways with the causal theorist; I sketch how in §VIII.

So let's consider Assumption 2 more closely. Where are the causal relations that can *individuate* the object being causally interacted with in a way the causal theorist needs? If we're restricted to perceptual relations available in the immediate context, we'll never find *any*: the causal relations needed are ones at work during the *entire history* of the interaction of a speaker (and his community) with a kind of thing.

If I point at the ocean (or at a rabbit), my causal relations at that moment are pretty limited in both cases; on the basis of these alone, there's nothing to reveal whether my interaction with the ocean is with *one big thing* or with *lots of little things* (and the same is true of rabbits as opposed to rabbit-fusion). Once my interactional capacities to make distinctions among things is brought to bear on the situation, and my causal history and capacities with respect to the ocean (and rabbits) are perused, it can be seen that the ocean – causally speaking – is one big thing for me, and that rabbits are not.[15]

This should make clear that the causal relations beings have to things – if seen from a broad enough context – are rich enough to individuate things in quite different ways – and it's easy to see that creatures with different powers individuate things differently.[16]

By the way, it is worth stressing again that the causal theorist need not be committed to a metaphysical claim about there being a fact in nature about how things – the things anyone refers to – are individuated. She only has to say that – in most cases – the causal relations between a speaker (and her community) and a kind of thing provide individuation conditions: they tell us the causally relevant units the speaker interacts with.

V

Quine's particular way of employing the ICR strategy turns on offering competing referential candidates for a term (*rabbits, rabbit-fusion, rabbit-stages,...*) and arguing that (perceptual) causal relations fail to distinguish among them. Variants of the ICR strategy do something similar: they argue that, given what we are in fact causally related to, there are too many candidates for the referential relata of our terms. I distinguish between *cross-grained* and *long-grained* strategies, allowing, of course, the possibility of blends.

Cross-grained strategies focus on the richness of our environment and how much is going on during any one time. What impinges on us causally is, as it were, a "blooming, buzzing, confusion," and so much is at work that we cannot – causally, anyway – single out particular items to the detriment of other candidates. I point to a dog, and hope the other person knows what I am pointing at. What causally impinges on my interlocutor (and me) is far too rich and varied for causality alone to enable him to know what I mean to point to (the surface of the dog? the dog, some of the sidewalk he's on, and a bit of murky air? the dog and the fire engine sounds in the background?).

The response to this concern is to point out (again) that causal effects on us are *relational* – and we have dispositions to weigh impacts on us differently: we push some items into the foreground and others in the background, and otherwise single out what information is pertinent. And, I must stress, one should not restrict the causal relations to one sense modality. Surprisingly, this doesn't give the cross-grained strategy more grist for its mill (even *more* is going on that the agent has to handle – information coming in through *all* the senses): rather, certain choices that seem natural if we restrict ourselves to what is perceived visually – the surface of the dog, the surface of the dog and some of the grass in the background – become obviously terrible choices if we include how people interact with dogs using their other senses (although, arguably, we only *see* surfaces, we don't *pet* surfaces; the mass of the dog exerts pressure back on our hand when we touch him; so too, items visually contiguous are not so with regard to the other senses).

Secondly, (therefore) these dispositions to prioritize imputs are not (or not entirely) a matter of language: they are matters of brute saliencies, biological dispositions in us to chunk the world in certain ways. The world may be a blur of activity, *in itself*, but that isn't relevent since it is not a blur *to us*, and it is causal relations between us *and* the world which enable us to indicate aspects of it to ourselves or to others (whose causal relations to the world are like ours), and to overlook or delegate into the background other aspects of it which we are causally insensitive to in the same way.[17]

The long-grained strategy seems more threatening to the causal theorist if only because it does not overlook the relational nature of causality. What it stresses, however, is that causal relations between us and the objects we refer to are invariably *segmental*; there are always mediating objects in the causal chain from agent to object which are not (usually) referred to. I see the table (that's a causal relation between me and the table) but I do so because of the surface of the table, intervening photons and because of my retinas, all of which I *also* have causal relations to. So, as far as causality is concerned – the long-grained strategist asks – why is the table distinguished, and not the image on the retina, the retina itself (or photons, etc.) instead?[18]

The long-grained strategy only flourishes (like the cross-grained strategy) in artificial environments, ones where we – for the sake of argument – focus on each sense modality separately. For only then is it even plausible to think that more proximate causal factors can be treated as the relata of the causal relations we have to the world. In practice, of course, as I've already intimated, we bring *all* our senses to bear on something (I call this *triangulation*[19]) and because of this, we bundle numerous causal relations – over time, as I stressed in the last section – from various different sensory modalities. Included are also interventions of various sorts with what we take ourselves to be interacting with. Once *this* setting is in place – as opposed to starkly artificial ones, like merely perceiving something visually – simple proximate candidates (images on one's retinas, photons, eardrums, the surface of the table) vanish as competing causal relata. I not only see the table, I pick it up, bang on it, and so on.

This response to the long-grained strategy brings in its wake another worry: in avoiding the artificiality the long-grained strategy implicitly presupposes, the causal theorist replaces one causal relation in one sensory modality with a family of them in various modalities. Exactly how are these (various) causal relations unified? The causal theorist again invokes the fact that what's involved are causal relations with an agent at one end of them, and it is (biological) dispositions in that agent that bundle them this way (the baby picks up the toy, tries to break it, sniffs at it, and then puts it in her mouth; a dog, by the way, does something similar). Furthermore, that the agent is (or is not) bundling causal relations as relations to the same object is something that can be *detected*: we can imagine cases where the agent fails to realize that the person she hears is the person she sees.

VI

I raised the point in the last section that how causal relations are bundled, which ones are taken as relations to the same items, is something we can detect. Let's pursue this a little (and in doing so, defend the causal theorist against those who mean to undermine her third assumption) by considering again Quine's favorite scenario: the situation of radical translation, where the field linguist attempts to learn the language of native speakers by watching and interacting with them in their natural habitat. Causal relations between natives and their world are amenable to scientific study, and Quine, of course, would be the last to deny this. Because he is a confirmation holist, he recognizes – in principle – that data can come from anywhere. But his narrow view of the pertinent causal relations between, say, native speakers and objects referred to makes it easy for him overlook how much information the field linguist has access to, information (1) that bears on the actual causal relations between speakers and objects, and (2) which is from *outside* the speech situation. Evolutionary considerations provide constraints; anatomical studies do something similar: we know what bats are and are not sensitive to in just this way.

Imagine the field linguist in search of data for the reference of "gavagai," and consider the two (empirical) candidates "rabbit" and "undetached rabbit-parts." How might careful investigation of the relationship between natives and these rabbity things incline him towards rabbits as the appropriate causal *relata* of "gavagai" rather than towards their undetached parts? One needs a feel for the texture of native life. Imagine, for example, that the interaction of the natives with rabbits is quite complex – they not only eat rabbits, but keep them as pets. They act as if rabbits have awareness, where this is understood in the ordinary way:

the thing reacts, eats, notices what's going on around it, must be hunted, sometimes tricked, etc.[20] The native, in this case, is clearly not merely (or even, sometimes, at all) concerned with the parts the rabbit carries along when it travels, but how the creature as a whole is operating.

How might we come to know this? *Not* by translating or interpreting native-sentences, and not by imposing an apparatus of quantification on their utterances. Rather, by getting a grip on what their actual (causal) interaction with rabbits amounts to.

What's been described so far doesn't quite exclude "undetached rabbit-parts" because it's still possible that the causal *relatum* of the term is a complex kind that includes the entire rabbit itself among the undetached rabbit-parts; for what we can see of native interactions is satisfied either by assuming the term "gavagai" relates only to rabbits, or by assuming that the term actually relates in addition to all the further instances of undetached rabbit-parts that lie buried in each rabbit. Here a quite justifiable version of Occam's razor is called for. If a full description of the causal relations between someone and the world is possible in terms of a *simple* kind then we should exclude more complicated but causally idle kinds.[21]

A similar argument can be used to rule out rabbit-stages, if natives are not causally interacting with them. However, the field linguist might conclude rabbit-stages *are* the appropriate causal *relata*. This can happen because the native interactions in question are *minimal*. Suppose natives *only* see a particular kind of antelope at dusk when it's particularly misty (because of the animal's shy and nocturnal habits). And suppose they've a label for it. The natural first reaction is that they have a name for the *animal*. But that is to confuse *our* causal relations with the animal with *their* causal relations. Their causal interactions with it, we might discover, are not like their causal interactions with animals but more like causal interactions with dreams or group hallucinations. In this case, we're likely to attribute to them the belief that an antelope isn't an animal but a kind of hallucination or a deity – perhaps their causal interactions with separate appearances of the same animal are not even bundled together by them – in this case sightings of *the same animal* would have to be individuated differently for them – possibly as *stages* (for example).[22]

Contrary to Quine, insight into the causal interactions that determine native principles of individuation do not (usually) require translation of their idioms of identity into ours. Rather, we can often *just see* when natives think they're facing the same thing and when they don't. Also, we can tell a lovely evolutionary story for why their survival turned on recognizing identity in certain cases (bundling causal relations a certain way). And here our own perceptual procedures, and scientific theories, when relevant and when applicable, offer both strong constraints and an implicit understanding of which causal relations are involved.

Consider rabbit-fusion. We're forced to treat this as the appropriate causal *relatum* if native causal interactions with rabbits are so meager that rabbit-fusion *is* the causal *relatum*; this again is by the causal version of Occam's razor.

Here are some details. The difference between "rabbit-fusion" and "rabbit" is that the former is a mass noun, and the latter is not. This grammatical distinction translates (causally) into counting practices; that is, the distinction between the causal *relata* of count as opposed to mass nouns manifests as different ways our practices associated with these words impinge on the world.

Suppose natives hoard certain discrete food stuffs (such as apples), and that stealing sometimes takes place. Furthermore, suppose we see that natives often do something that *looks like* counting (they go through a process of picking up each item and putting it down in a different pile), and that they usually recognize when something is missing *even though* the number of items can be quite large.

That they are *counting* is an empirical thesis, of course, and other hypotheses must be ruled out. For example, perhaps they are actually measuring volume or mass. We can test these alternatives if the items are generally irregular in size or mass by making appropriate substitutions in their hoards and seeing if and when they notice differences. It is exactly the sorts of causal relations natives have to collections of foodstuffs that tell us what individuation conditions they're using; and it's nice to be able to say that this can be recognized for what it is without having any grasp of their language at all.

Our ability to understand details of native practice (i.e. counting) enables us to determine, in certain cases, on the basis of the causal *relata*, whether the terms so causally related to the world are count or mass nouns; in particular, we have a principled way to exclude *rabbit-fusion* as a candidate for "gavagai," if, indeed, that is not what they causally interact with. And this procedure does not rely on translation – but precedes it, and can be used as data *for* translation.

"Gavagai," of course, is *not* a term but a *sentence*. As Quine points out, its translation is, perhaps, "Lo, a rabbit," or perhaps "Lo, undetached rabbit-parts." In a translation context, one is faced with *whole* sentences and *whole* chunks of the world, and *both* must be analyzed into their significant parts. I've argued that the field linguist has ways of recognizing how the native cuts up her world. And I've argued that these insights are to be (largely) procured independently of how one translates native sentences. Although it's *not* unreasonable for the way the world is sliced up by natives to *bear on* what suitable grammatical units the sentences should be divided into, it doesn't follow, because of Assumption 1, that the *semantic* units of the sentences are the same as the referential ones.

An example will make clear why: imagine the natives are pantheists and that this belief is so ancient that it has impinged on the grammar of their language so that most of their sentences must be *translated* adverbally: "Gavagai," in particular, as "It's rabbiting" (in analogy to our "It's raining"). *This* has *no* impact on referential facts about their terms because *we* are not pantheists and reject their ontology. We will, of course, have to talk about the things their *adverbs* are causally connected to, but this is because we take their adverbs to be the significant units of speech – at least as far as reference is concerned.[23]

I've presented a best-case scenario for learning about natives, but there are several ways that circumstances can prevent us from getting the data we need to decide among alternative hypotheses. I wrote earlier of switching items in native hoards without the natives realizing what we're doing. Such "experiments" may not always be possible.[24] Nevertheless, there can still be a "fact of the matter" about what natives are referring to in such cases.

There's another way in which *precise* characterization of what natives refer to may elude us: there really may be no fact of the matter about reference in certain cases. This is because procedures for interacting in the world are sloppy in any case,[25] and language, ours or the native's, always seems to divide the world in ways more precise than the procedures we associate with our terms can keep up with. In a certain sense, there are always referential promissory notes involved with language. Imagine we are faced with a native term we're fairly sure refers to rabbit-parts. As natives become more refined at hacking rabbits apart – we sell them metal knives that replace stone ones – we may notice they continue to apply the same word to the new parts they are now able to chop rabbits into. This clues us into how the word can be extended – what the native term can be taken to cover.

But terminology can really outstrip mere matter here. Does the native term corresponding to "rabbit-part" cover those parts *we* can cut the rabbit into that natives can't? Probably. Certainly this hypothesis is easy to test: present such a piece of rabbit to the native and see what he says once he overcomes his disgust.[26] What about those nonmeasurable parts we can remove from the rabbit by the axiom of choice? Hard to say. There are also puzzles about peripheral molecules hovering about rabbit parts –

how many of these should be included or excluded? Hard to say; and not just with respect to native speech.

There are limits to how far our understanding of causal relations of natives to their world can help fix what they refer to, since we always have the problem that causal procedures do not quite divide the world neatly into what fits a term and what doesn't. The resulting slack however is nothing even akin to Quinean inscrutability.[27]

Quine writes of his *gavagai* example that it "has figured too centrally in discussions of the indeterminacy of translation,"[28] but the argument then given doesn't affect the issue of reference as posed here. Also, what he says on "gavagai" later in that article supports my interpretation of how he is undercutting the causal theorist's resources. He (1970, p. 181) complains that attempts to settle the reference of "Gavagai" suffer from vagueness of purpose, for "the purpose cannot be to drive a wedge between stimulus meanings of observation sentences, thereby linking *Gavagai* rather to 'Rabbit' than to 'Rabbit stage' or 'Undetached rabbit part'; for the stimulus meanings of all these sentences are incontestably identical. They comprise the stimulations that would make people think a rabbit was present. The purpose can only be to settle what *gavagai* denotes for the native as a term. But the whole notion of terms and their denotation is bound up with our own grammatical analysis of the sentences of our own language."

VII

Let's pick up the thread of the argument in Quine's *Ontological Relativity*. Even if we concede the conclusions Quine wants to draw from his *gavagai* example to him, it seems we're faced only with tame inscrutability: "gavagai" is indeterminate among rabbits, rabbit-stages, or rabbit-fusion, but not grass (because salience considerations rule that out), nor certain rocks on Pluto (for salience considerations rule that out too). Inscrutability (with its accompanying factlessness) rampages only within fairly limited parameters.

This is *not* Quine's position. Admissible reinterpretation is far wilder than the *gavagai* example reveals; and unrestrained proxy functions indicate this. But before proxy functions are given full play, Quine softens us up with deferred ostension.

The idea is straightforward enough: one can indicate amounts of gasoline by pointing to a gasoline gauge, or refer to a number via a material token of a sentence it's the Gödel number of. Anything may stand referential stead for anything else. How, then, can we possibly decide *what* is being referred to by a particular act of reference?

Quine claims our general incapacity to decide is inscrutability at second intension (1969, p. 41): "The inscrutability of reference runs deep, and it persists in a subtle form even if we accept identity and the rest of the apparatus of individuation as fixed and settled; even, indeed, if we forsake radical translation and think only of English."

But what's the argument? The alert causal theorist concedes problems with mathematical objects. But she sets such cases aside, and claims that the explanation for deferred ostension in the case of gasoline, subatomic particles, or anything else out of reach of direct ostension is possible via the causal relations forged to such objects. (Relations, again, that are recognized not by looking at the deferred ostension situation alone, but by an examination of the whole history of our causal interactions.) And such causal connections, if required of what we refer to, do not justify the suggestion that our use of a term to refer is one that can be reinterpreted at will. It's just rhetoric to run cases where causal resources are available together with mathematical ones where such resources are absent: it's to deny the importance of causal mechanisms in all cases of reference merely because they're absent in the mathematical ones.

If we accept the causal theorist's claim that the practice of deferred ostension, like any other referential practice, is one which we can study by examining causal relations between referrers and referred, deferred ostension poses no special problem.[29]

In any case, once Quine has the concession that deferred ostension is open to arbitrary reinterpretation (even after fixing the apparatus of quantification), a congenial setting for proxy functions is in place. For the force of causality has been ruled out altogether. Consider, once again, "gavagai." Perhaps the term *does* refer to rocks on Pluto, via deferred ostension.

Quine's argument fits the required pattern for the use of proxy functions, and this despite my protests against every one of his moves. For proxy functions come at the end of a lengthy argument (although some of the premises for that argument are supported in a different book). But the Quine of *Things and Their Place in Theories*, I'm convinced, has lost sight of this, for he offers proxy functions *alone* to show ontological relativity.[30] First he discusses abstract objects: he notes one could permute the entire set-theoretic universe by exchanging the referential roles played by sets and their complements, and nothing in our linguistic practice would change. One can grant the example because one, in any case, has no idea how to cement words to *mathematical* objects. And although Quine concedes there seems to be a difference between mathematical objects and concrete objects, in this respect, he writes (1981a, p. 16): "But I am persuaded that this contrast is illusory."

Why? What follows, *by way of argument*, are permutations: of material objects with the portions of space-time they inhabit and the various permutations of a coordinate system laid on the universe. But without a justification that such permutations bear on *reference*, and no such justification is found in the discussion at hand, Quine is open to the objection that he is pushing permutations *on their own* against the causal theorist, despite the illegitimacy of this.

VIII

The causal theorist and I have been congenial philosophical companions up until now. But divorce is imminent: I conclude this paper with some indications of what the problems are with her view and what the view we must replace it with looks like. What follows is only a sketch, and probably an inadequate one: I refer the reader to KRE for amplification and elucidation.

Let's start with what can be called the *challenge of normativity*. Many philosophers may feel that all of the foregoing considerations have failed to indicate that the most significant problem for the project of underwriting referential relations with causal relations is this: we can always be mistaken in what we take to be an *A*: this shows that any purported causal relation can fail to underwrite the referential relation we take it to underwrite: my dispositions – let them be as causally rich as you like – may nevertheless incline me to regard (certain) cats as dogs. But it is part of how we understand reference that in those cases it is not the causal relation that dictates that such things *are* dogs: I am wrong (no doubt about it) – those are cats *despite* my causal dispositions.

When the issue is put this way it seems as if the referential relation has certain properties: it is a normative relation, and since causality lacks those properties, we can see – at a glance, as it were – that the causal theorist's project is doomed from the start. The referential relation, and what it is a relation to, involve logical presuppositions that the causal theorist's purely descriptive resources cannot handle.

There is a temptation at this point to presume the existence of a referential relation from us to items in the world, and then – based on its purported normative qualities – to project that normativity *into the world*. But this is a mistake: the normativity involved in reference is a verbal device designed to facilitate our adjudication among causal relations we have to items in the world – it is not an indication of either a special relation to the world, or of special things, of any sort.

The problem *talk* of reference is meant to solve is with the causal relations themselves. As my talk of "bundling" in §V indicated – there never is *one* simple causal relation users have with objects or kinds, what is involved is always an open-ended, and constantly changing variety of such causal relations. Indeed, a major aspect of scientific practice is the development and implementation of *new* causal relations to kinds which cannot be easily assimilated to already-in-place causal relations. So, for example, our original simple observational methods for determining the presence of lead have been progressively supplemented with a giant collection of various chemical and physical methods for recognizing the presence of lead in minute amounts in all sorts of places we – at one time – would never even have considered as possible locations for lead. An examination of this ongoing process of modification and refinement of our causal relations to the world shows, first, that our causal relations do not extend far enough to cover all the instances of the kinds, that we take ourselves as referring to, and second, that we are willing to subsequently desert particular causal relations (to certain instances) while denying that our referential relations to the kinds have changed at all.

Interestingly, acknowledging all this does not lead to anything drastic – at least as far as the causal theorist is concerned. Normativity – talk of mistakes – is restricted to the *language* we use: instead of wedding our terminology to causal relations so that each time our causal relations change, so does our terminology, we introduce the *myth* of terms with never-changing referential relations to what is out there. Of course we are always in vigorous contact with what is out there (*causally*, just as the causal theorist insists): indeed, at any one time, we can always (more or less) measure exactly how far our causal reach into the world is. It is just that our talk of reference always extends beyond what we can do causally at any time; and in relation to this talk about reference, we treat our causal relations as *epistemically suspect*. This is a matter of verbal convenience: it does *not* mean that somehow there is a normatively-thick relation between us and what we refer to which goes beyond the mere descriptive capacities of the causal theorist. There is no such *relation*. Nor does it mean that normatively-thick objects, in some sense, are constituted from a norm-rich pattern which we impose on our interactions with the world.[31] Rather (to repeat), what is going on is that all the *genuine* relations we have to the world – relations we can explicitly study – are causal ones and only causal ones. How we *talk about* those relations, however, introduces elements of normativity (talk of mistakes), and presupposes the *language* of a referential relation that is partly (and robustly) underwritten by causality, and the remainder of which is sheer promissory note, some of which (admittedly) will never be fulfilled.

Notes

1 This paper owes its existence to an invitation by Mark Richard to include the chapter on Quine's version of the permutation argument from my book *Knowledge and Reference in Empirical Science* (hereafter KRE). Part III, §§ 2 and 3 (pp. 144–159) of that book have been combined and augmented – somewhat substantially – to make the resulting article self-contained.

2 Permutations are plied by a large number of philosophers: Davidson, Field, Putnam, Quine, Wallace, to name some. I discuss here only Quine's original use of this style of argument. For its mutations in other hands, see KRE.

3 This strategy takes many forms, and is even more popular than permutation arguments: I cannot begin to list citations nor will I be able to describe *all* its mutations. Examples of its proponents include, however, the permutation pliers cited in note 2 as well as philosophers as different as Haugeland (1998) and Richard (1997).

4 A precise statement of the theorem, its proof, and interesting strengthenings may be found in Chang and Keisler (1973). They call it the Löweinheim–Skolem–Tarski theorem for obvious reasons. I retain the shorter nomenclature because that's how the theorem is commonly referred to by philosophers. One or another version of the result can also be found in most logic textbooks, e.g. Shoenfeld (1967), Enderton (1972), or Boolos and Jeffrey (1989). See Barwise and Feferman (1985) and Van Benthem and Doets (1983) for details on those logics where versions of this theorem vanish.

5 It is easy to design logics where this otherwise trivial theorem *doesn't* hold. See Azzouni (1991). But that is an unusual case where there's a two-place device present with truth conditions including that the constant appearing in its first place is mapped to the sentence appearing in its second place.

6 If the language contains function symbols, a similar definition is available for them.

7 For some examples in the first-order case, see Chang and Keisler (1973). Also see Quine (1969, pp. 56–7).

8 Quine considers various ways to avoid Pythagoreanism in his 1964 and his 1969, but never considers going second-order. His main strategic move against the Pythagorean is simply to require proxy functions to be defined on the *entire* domain of M. This amounts to allowing in as referential resources not only first-order logic, but, in addition, relations among items in the intended model M (e.g. relations among the real numbers) – regardless of whether these relations can be expressed in the first-order theory of M: such relations

provide additional constraints on admissible proxy functions. But what entitles Quine to this? One may think that if we only have first-order resources (plus whatever causal resources are left after Quine's undermining of causality) one should drop relations among items in the intended model as an initial assumption on our referential powers, and simply determine what sorts of models are compatible with our resources for fixing what we refer to. Proxy functions, depending as they do on the presence of an initial intended model *M*, then drop out of the strategy. This is how Putnam proceeds, and on his view nothing precludes countable models for any first-order theory we hold (via a sophisticated application of the Löwen-heim–Skolem theorem); for the causal theorist's response to Putnam, see KRE, Part III, §5.

9 I separate, on the causal theorist's behalf, issues about what the native is referring to from questions of how to translate "gavagai." Translation involves concerns beyond those raised by reference, as I explain in §IV.

10 We see this maneuver again and again in the subsequent literature. The philosopher raises considerations – all too often just in passing – to show that causality is ill-equipped to fix the references of our terms or thought, and then trots out his or her alternative which is to fix reference "from above." Davidson, Haugeland, Katz, Putnam, Richard and Soames are all examples. The alternatives that are supposed to fix reference in the stead of causality are things like *a priori* constraints on translation, previous translation practices, special-science constraints on meaning, imposition of a norm-rich pattern on the world, and so on. The interesting fact is that many philosophers balk at Quine's approach not because of its premature infirmation of causality but because the resulting picture introduces inscrutability of reference – the existence of numerous equally-good alternatives in how reference is to be fixed. It is this inscrutability that (some) philosophers distrust and attempt to eliminate by the introduction of other (non-causal) constraints. Although I cannot pursue specific objections to these alternatives now, the usual result, once the bond of causality from term to world is gone, is a kind of linguistic idealism: if alternative projections of referential divisions onto the world *are* eliminated, the result is *still* linguistic idealism, but of a Kantian sort.

11 See note 9. Our concern, I repeat, is with determining what the causal relata to natives is, not with translating their language. I continue to use Quine's language, but the reader should transpose our concerns with his. See §IV where this is sorted out.

12 Davidson (1973, p. 136, note 16) repudiates Quine's stimulations for "reference to the objective features of the world which alter in conjunction with changes in attitude towards the truth of sentences."

13 I have suppressed certain subtleties and complications in my description of the field linguist's resources in the interests of making the discussion self-contained. See KRE for details. Be assured that adding in the subtleties will not be helpful to Quine.

14 Richard (1997, p. 166): "Some would appeal to causal considerations to defeat inscrutability: reference, we are told, is grounded in causal contacts between applications of word and object referred to. It is not clear that this is much help. Touch a cat and you touch an undetached cat part. Smell a dog and you are causally in touch with the dog fusion.... Once this occurs to one, it becomes somewhat plausible that there may not be *any* physical fact that distinguishes one of two incompatible reference schemes as *the* correct scheme. If we think that the physical facts determine all the facts, we will then find inscrutability a plausible if unsettling doctrine" (italics his).

15 If I had *really* fine-tuned senses *and* really fine-tuned physical powers to act on the distinctions my senses could make – I would be able to causally interact with *water molecules*. In that case, my causal relations with the ocean would be similar to my relations with rabbits: my causal powers would individuate both rabbits and water molecules.

16 Consider a fish being attacked by *Pfiesteria* – single-celled aquatic organisms (see Burkholder 1999). The fish interacts with *Pfiesteria*-fusion because it does not have the causal powers to distinguish single-celled items. We too, until recently, were in the same boat with the fish when *It* attacked *us*. But we now have instrumental access to the separate organisms, and can individuate *Pfiesteria* differently.

17 This is why pointing is, at best, only ambiguous in *finitely* many ways; it's not infinitely open-ended, open to infinitely many possibilities of interpretation as philosophers often assume. No doubt, if I were trying to point something out to someone with "bee-eyes," or someone who was visually sensitive to heat-radiation, I would have trouble. He or she (or it) would have senses that chunk the world in ways that I would, at least initially, have a lot of trouble getting onto: I might need to use *instruments* to get a grip on the causal relations my interlocutor was biologically advantaged to handle.

18 Haugeland (1998, pp. 242–6) employs this strategy, and discusses Dretske's response to it. Davidson invokes it as well.

19 The reader should take care not to confuse my use of "triangulation" with Davidson's (very different) use.

20 Watching someone hunt rabbits tells us volumes about the kind of thing he's interacting with. Do we need a *theory* of natives here; a *psychology* of natives? Not in any scientifically respectable sense: we do need to be able to recognize when the hunter is sneaking up on the rabbit (why he thinks it's necessary to sneak up on the animal), and we need to be able to tell when the hunter thinks he's made a mistake: we need gross regularities about natives. (See KRE, Part I, §6.) Does the success of this knowledge-gathering endeavor call for translation or interpretation of native sentences? Hardly – pretty much the same sort of insights are needed to understand what dogs, cats, and snakes are up to when *they* hunt.

It's now palpable why Quine's (1960) talk of "moduli of stimulations" seems so artificial. Make the modulus short and enormous amounts of causally-relevant historical information are lost; make the modulus long and we're overwhelmed with *irrelevancies* which we have no means of picking through. In practice we're selective and picky about what we look for as candidates for what natives causally interact with, and we're guided in this by our grasp of observational regularities.

21 This principle must be applied with care because even the causal theorist admits that speakers need not have causal connections with *all* the members of a kind. Eventually this last observation causes trouble for the causal theorist, as I indicate briefly at the end of this paper – but the resolution of these troubles will not resurrect the Quinean view of these matters.

22 Given that the presence of an antelope is recognized only through one sensory modality, why can't we draw the conclusion that perhaps natives are (causally) interacting with retinal images? The answer to this is that what they see is generally triangulated with what comes through their other senses, and so there is no more reason to take the causal relata to be *this* proximate in this case than there is to do so in other cases. (This of course doesn't *always* exclude retinal images as causal relata, as the existence of optometrists makes clear. But optometrists do quite specific things – *instrumentally* – that natives, in this case, do not do, and so the former can causally interact with retinas (even their own) – and the images upon them – although natives cannot.)

23 There's strain due to our translation of their language treating them as referring to only one object (the *relatum* of "It") but our treating the causal *relata* as what we in fact see the native as causally interacting with. I assume, of course, that a translation treating natives as getting things this wrong is cogent, which many disagree with. Granting this, however, Assumption 1 poses a problem because referential relations construed causally come apart from referential relations construed translationally. The causal theorist either denies the cogency of this kind of translation or claims that "refers" as it occurs within the parameters of translation is not the same notion as the one pertinent to Assumption 1.

24 The anthropologist or linguist tricking humans in their own habitats, in fact, is far less likely than their tricking the anthropologist or linguist instead.

25 See Part II, §3 of KRE.

26 *Contra* Quine, letting the native *see* how the part was cut from the rabbit is probably pertinent.

27 Quine (1981b) is unjustly neglected (even by Quine!). It delineates nicely the kind of problem in fixing reference by means of procedures I am talking about here. But conceding this (and no more) leads to the position I indicate in §VIII rather than anything as radical as, say, Quine's inscrutability of reference.

28 Quine (1970, p. 178). Even so, the real disagreement is that Quine thinks you can't tell how the thing is sliced by using simple ostension and querying. I agree, but claim that scientific theory and ordinary observation *can* tell us

how the native slices things up if we have access to her slicing history, and some scientific theory. This makes the various options for the reference of "gavagai" empirical options, as I've indicated.

29 Unfortunately, deferred ostension is more than the causal theorist *can* handle, as I show in Part III, §7 of KRE. Despite this, *Quine* can't use deferred ostension to establish ontological relativity because deferred ostension, as we intuitively understand it, largely requires explicit conventions: if I point to something *A*, and by means of that, refer to something else *B*, this only works if an understanding is already in place which enables us to so interpret the gesture. Thus deferred ostension is a poor tool for *Quine* since he understands ontological relativity to apply *despite* our practices, and not by means of them. No *argument* is given that his is a reasonable way to interpret deferred ostension; but without one, the causal theorist simply denies that deferred ostension can operate freely outside of explicit conventions, as Quine needs it to.

30 Quine (1986) writes approvingly of the newer discussion over that in his *Ontological Relativity* since proxy functions are latterly presented independently of considerations of indeterminacy of translation. But if my analysis is right, this is a mistake. What arguments Quine has to infirm the causal relations the causal theorist claims are present occur in his discussion of indeterminacy. To present proxy-functions shorn of these supporting considerations is thus illegitimate.

31 The reader is meant to recognize descriptions of views held by, say, McDowell or Haugeland.

References

Azzouni, Jody 1991. "A Simple Axiomatizable Theory of Truth," *Notre Dame Journal of Formal Logic* 32: 458–93.

Azzouni, Jody 2000. *Knowledge and Reference in Empirical Science*. London: Routledge.

Barwise, J. and Feferman, S. (eds) 1985. *Model-Theoretic Logics*. Berlin: Springer-Verlag.

Boolos, George S. and Jeffrey, Richard C. 1989. *Computability and Logic* (3rd edn). Cambridge: Cambridge University Press.

Burkholder, JoAnn M. 1999. "The Lurking Perils of *Pfiesteria*," *Scientific American*, August: 42–9.

Chang, C. C. and Keisler, Jerome H. 1973. *Model Theory*. Amsterdam: North Holland.

Davidson, Donald 1973. "Radical Interpretation," *Inquiries into Truth and Interpretation* (1980). Oxford: Clarendon Press, 125–39.

Enderton, Herbert 1972. *A Mathematical Introduction to Logic*. New York: Academic Press.

Haugeland, John 1998. *Having Thought*. Cambridge, MA: Harvard University Press.

Quine, W. V. 1960. *Word and Object*. Cambridge, MA: MIT Press.

Quine, W. V. 1964. "Ontological Reduction and the World of Numbers," *The Ways of Paradox and Other Essays* (rev. edn, 1976). Cambridge: Cambridge University Press, 212–20.

Quine, W. V. 1969. "Ontological Relativity," *Ontological Relativity and Other Essays*. New York: Columbia University Press, 69–90.

Quine, W. V. 1970. "On the Reasons for Indeterminacy of Translation," *Journal of Philosophy* 67: 178–83.

Quine, W. V. 1981a. "Things and Their Place in Theories," *Theories and Things*. Cambridge, MA: Harvard University Press, 31–7.

Quine, W. V. 1981b. "What Price Bivalence?", *Theories and Things*. Cambridge: Cambridge University Press, 31–7.

Quine, W. V. 1986. "Reply to Paul A. Roth," in Lewis Edwin Hahn and Paul Arthur Schilpp (eds.), *The Philosophy of W. V. O. Quine*. La Salle, IL: Open Court, 459–61.

Richard, Mark 1997. "Inscrutability," *Canadian Journal of Philosophy* 23: (supplementary volume) 165–209.

Shoenfeld, Joseph R. 1967. *Mathematical Logic*. Reading, MA: Addison-Wesley.

Van Benthem, Johan and Doets, Kees 1983. "Higher-Order Logic," in D. Gabbay and F. Guenthner (eds.), *Handbook of Philosophical Logic*, vol. I. Dordrecht: D. Reidel, 275–330.

9

Radical Interpretation

Donald Davidson

Kurt utters the words 'Es regnet' and under the right conditions we know that he has said that it is raining. Having identified his utterance as intentional and linguistic, we are able to go on to interpret his words: we can say what his words, on that occasion, meant. What could we know that would enable us to do this? How could we come to know it? The first of these questions is not the same as the question what we *do* know that enables us to interpret the words of others. For there may easily be something we could know and don't, knowledge of which would suffice for interpretation, while on the other hand it is not altogether obvious that there is anything we actually know which plays an essential role in interpretation. The second question, how we could come to have knowledge that would serve to yield interpretations, does not, of course, concern the actual history of language acquisition. It is thus a doubly hypothetical question: given a theory that would make interpretation possible, what evidence plausibly available to a potential interpreter would support the theory to a reasonable degree? In what follows I shall try to sharpen these questions and suggest answers.

The problem of interpretation is domestic as well as foreign: it surfaces for speakers of the same language in the form of the question, how can it be determined that the language is the same? Speakers of the same language can go on the assumption that for them the same expressions are to be interpreted in the same way, but this does not indicate what justifies the assumption. All understanding of the speech of another involves radical interpretation. But it will help keep assumptions from going unnoticed to focus on cases where interpretation is most clearly called for: interpretation in one idiom of talk in another.[1]

What knowledge would serve for interpretation? A short answer would be, knowledge of what each meaningful expression means. In

German, those words Kurt spoke mean that it is raining and Kurt was speaking German. So in uttering the words 'Es regnet', Kurt said that it was raining. This reply does not, as might first be thought, merely restate the problem. For it suggests that in passing from a description that does not interpret (his uttering of the words 'Es regnet') to interpreting description (his saying that it is raining) we must introduce a machinery of words and expressions (which may or may not be exemplified in actual utterances), and this suggestion is important. But the reply is no further help, for it does not say what it is to know what an expression means.

There is indeed also the hint that corresponding to each meaningful expression that is an entity, its meaning. This idea, even if not wrong, has proven to be very little help: at best it hypostasizes the problem.

Disenchantment with meanings as implementing a viable account of communication or interpretation helps explain why some philosophers have tried to get along without, not only meanings, but any serious theory at all. It is tempting, when the concepts we summon up to try to explain interpretation turn out to be more baffling than the explanandum, to reflect that after all verbal communication consists in nothing more than elaborate disturbances in the air which form a causal link between the non-linguistic activities of human agents. But although interpretable speeches are nothing but (that is, identical with) actions performed with assorted non-linguistic intentions (to warn, control, amuse, distract, insult), and these actions are in turn nothing but (identical with) intentional movements of the lips and larynx, this observation takes us no distance towards an intelligible general account of what we might know that would allow us to redescribe uninterpreted utterances as the right interpreted ones.

Appeal to meanings leaves us stranded further than we started from the non-linguistic goings-on that must supply the evidential base for interpretation; the 'nothing but' attitude provides no clue as to how the evidence is related to what it surely is evident for.

Other proposals for bridging the gap fall short in various ways. The 'causal' theories of Ogden and Richards and of Charles Morris attempted to analyse the meaning of sentences, taken one at a time, on the basis of behaviouristic data. Even if these theories had worked for the simplest sentences (which they clearly did not), they did not touch the problem of extending the method to sentences of greater complexity and abstractness. Theories of another kind start by trying to connect words rather than sentences with non-linguistic facts. This is promising because words are finite in number while sentences are not, and yet each sentence is no more than a concatenation of words: this offers the chance of a theory that interprets each of an infinity of sentences using only finite resources. But such theories fail to reach the evidence, for it seems clear that the semantic features of words cannot be explained directly on the basis of non-linguistic phenomena. The reason is simple. The phenomena to which we must turn are the extra-linguistic interests and activities that language serves, and these are served by words only in so far as the words are incorporated in (or on occasion happen to be) sentences. But then there is no chance of giving a foundational account of words before giving one of sentences.

For quite different reasons, radical interpretation cannot hope to take as evidence for the meaning of a sentence an account of the complex and delicately discriminated intentions with which the sentence is typically uttered. It is not easy to see how such an approach can deal with the structural, recursive feature of language that is essential to explaining how new sentences can be understood. But the central difficulty is that we cannot hope to attach a sense to the attribution of finely discriminated intentions independently of interpreting speech. The reason is not that we cannot ask necessary questions, but that interpreting an agent's intentions, his beliefs and his words are parts of a single project, no part of which can be assumed to be complete before the rest is. If this is right, we cannot make the full panoply of intentions and beliefs the evidential base for a theory of radical interpretation.

We are now in a position to say something more about what would serve to make interpretation possible. The interpreter must be able to understand any of the infinity of sentences the speaker might utter. If we are to state explicitly what the interpreter might know that would enable him to do this, we must put it in finite form.[2] If this requirement is to be met, any hope of a universal method of interpretation must be abandoned. The most that can be expected is to explain how an interpreter could interpret the utterances of speakers of a single language (or a finite number of languages): it makes no sense to ask for a theory that would yield an explicit interpretation for any utterance in any (possible) language.

It is still not clear, of course, what it is for a theory to yield an explicit interpretation of an utterance. The formulation of the problem seems to invite us to think of the theory as the specification of a function taking utterances as arguments and having interpretations as values. But then interpretations would be no better than meanings and just as surely entities of some mysterious kind. So it seems wise to describe what is wanted of the theory without apparent reference to meanings or interpretations: someone who knows the theory can interpret the utterances to which the theory applies.

The second general requirement on a theory of interpretation is that it can be supported or verified by evidence plausibly available to an interpreter. Since the theory is general – it must apply to a potential infinity of utterances – it would be natural to think of evidence in its behalf as instances of particular interpretations recognized as correct. And this case does, of course, arise for the interpreter dealing with a language he already knows. The speaker of a language normally cannot produce an explicit finite theory for his own language, but he can test a proposed theory since he can tell whether it yields correct interpretations when applied to particular utterances.

In radical interpretation, however, the theory is supposed to supply an understanding of particular utterances that is not given in advance, so the ultimate evidence for the theory cannot be correct sample interpretations. To deal with the general case, the evidence must be of a sort that would be available to someone who does not already know how to interpret utterances the theory is designed to cover: it must be evidence that can be stated without essential use of such linguistic concepts as meaning, interpretation, synonymy, and the like.

Before saying what kind of theory I think will do the trick, I want to discuss a last alternative suggestion, namely that a method of translation, from the language to be interpreted into the language of the interpreter, is all the theory that is needed. Such a theory would consist in the statement of an effective method for going from an arbitrary sentence of the alien tongue to a sentence of a familiar language; thus it would satisfy the demand for a finitely stated method applicable to any sentence. But I do not think a translation manual is the best form for a theory of interpretation to take.[3]

When interpretation is our aim, a method of translation deals with a wrong topic, a relation between two languages, where what is wanted is an interpretation of one (in another, of course, but that goes without saying since any theory is in some language). We cannot without confusion count the language used in stating the theory as part of the subject matter of the theory unless we explicitly make it so. In the general case, a theory of translation involves three languages: the object language, the subject language, and the metalanguage (the languages from and into which translation proceeds, and the language of the theory, which says what expressions of the subject language translate which expressions of the object language). And in this general case, we can know which sentences of the subject language translate which sentences of the object language without knowing what any of the sentences of either language mean (in any sense, anyway, that would let someone who understood the theory interpret sentences of the object language). If the subject language happens to be identical with the language of the theory, then someone who understands the theory can no doubt use the translation manual to interpret alien utterances; but this is because he brings to bear two things he knows and that the theory does not state: the fact that the subject language is his own, and his knowledge of how to interpet utterances in his own language.

It is awkward to try to make explicit the assumption that a mentioned sentence belongs to one's own language. We could try, for example, ' "Es regnet" in Kurt's language is translated as "It is raining" in mine', but the indexical self-reference is out of place in a theory that ought to work for any interpreter. If we decide to accept this difficulty, there remains the fact that the method of translation leaves tacit and beyond the reach of theory what we need to know that allows us to interpret our own language. A theory of translation must read some sort of structure into sentences, but there is no reason to expect that it will provide any insight into how the meanings of sentences depend on their structure.

A satisfactory theory for interpreting the utterances of a language, our own included, will reveal significant semantic structure: the interpretation of utterances of complex sentences will systematically depend on the interpretation of utterances of simpler sentences, for example. Suppose we were to add to a theory of translation a satisfactory theory of interpretation for our own language. Then we would have exactly what we want, but in an unnecessarily bulky form. The translation manual churns out, for each sentence of the language to be translated, a sentence of the translator's language; the theory of interpretation then gives the interpretation of these familiar sentences. Clearly the reference to the home language is superfluous; it is an unneeded intermediary between interpretation and alien idiom. The only expressions a theory of interpretation has to mention are those belonging to the language to be interpreted.

A theory of interpretation for an object language may then be viewed as the result of the merger of a structurally revealing theory of interpretation for a known language, and a system of translation from the unknown language into the known. The merger makes all reference to the known language otiose; when this reference is dropped, what is left is a structurally revealing theory of interpretation for the object language – couched, of course, in familiar words. We have such theories, I suggest, in theories of truth of the kind Tarski first showed how to give.[4]

What characterizes a theory of truth in Tarski's style is that it entails, for every sentence *s* of the object language, a sentence of the form:

s is true (in the object language) if and only if *p*.

Instances of the form (which we shall call T-sentences) are obtained by replacing '*s*' by a canonical description of *s*, and '*p*' by a translation of *s*. The important undefined semantical notion in the theory is that of *satisfaction* which relates sentences, open or closed, to infinite sequences of objects, which may be taken to belong to the range of the variables of the object language. The axioms, which are finite in number, are of two kinds: some give the conditions under which a sequence satisfies a complex sentence on the basis of the conditions of satisfaction of simpler sentences, others give the conditions under which the simplest (open) sentences are satisfied. Truth is defined for closed sentences in terms of the notion of satisfaction. A recursive theory like this can be turned into an explicit definition along familiar lines, as Tarski shows, provided the language of the theory contains enough set theory; but we shall not be concerned with this extra step.

Further complexities enter if proper names and functional expressions are irreducible features of the object language. A trickier matter concerns indexical devices. Tarski was interested in formalized languages containing no indexical or demonstrative aspects. He could therefore treat sentences as vehicles of truth; the extension of the theory to utterances is in this case trivial. But natural languages are indispensably replete with indexical features, like tense, and so their sentences may vary in truth according to time and speaker. The remedy is to characterize truth for a language relative to a time and a speaker. The extension to utterances is again straightforward.[5]

What follows is a defence of the claim that a theory of truth, modified to apply to a natural language, can be used as a theory of interpretation. The defence will consist in attempts to answer three questions:

1 Is it reasonable to think that a theory of truth of the sort described can be given for a natural language?
2 Would it be possible to tell that such a theory was correct on the basis of evidence plausibly available to an interpreter with no prior knowledge of the language to be interpreted?
3 If the theory were known to be true, would it be possible to interpret utterances of speakers of the language?

The first question is addressed to the assumption that a theory of truth can be given for a natural language; the second and third questions ask whether such a theory would satisfy the further demands we have made on a theory of interpretation.

1   Can a theory of truth be given for a natural language?

It will help us to appreciate the problem to consider briefly the case where a significant fragment of a language (plus one or two semantical predicates) is used to state its own theory of truth. According to Tarski's Convention T, it is a test of the adequacy of a theory that it entails all the T-sentences. This test apparently cannot be met without assigning something very much like a standard quantificational form to the sentences of the language, and appealing, in the theory, to a relational notion of satisfaction.[6] But the striking thing about T-sentences is that whatever machinery must operate to produce them, and whatever ontological wheels must turn, in the end a T-sentence states the truth conditions of a sentence using resources no richer than, because the same as, those of the sentence itself. Unless the original sentence mentions possible worlds, intensional entities, properties, or propositions, the statement of its truth conditions does not.

There is no equally simple way to make the analogous point about an alien language without appealing, as Tarski does, to an unanalysed notion of translation. But what we can do for our own language we ought to be able to do for another; the problem, it will turn out, will be to know that we are doing it.

The restriction imposed by demanding a theory that satisfies Convention T seems to be considerable: there is no generally accepted method now known for dealing, within the restriction, with a host of problems, for example, sentences that attribute attitudes, modalities, general causal statements, counterfactuals, attributive adjectives, quantifiers like 'most', and so on. On the other hand, there is what seems to me to be fairly impressive progress. To mention some examples, there is the work of Tyler Burge on proper names,[7] Gilbert Harman on 'ought',[8] John Wallace on mass terms and comparatives,[9] and there is my own work on attributions of attitudes and performatives,[10] on adverbs, events, and singular causal statements,[11] and on quotation.[12]

If we are inclined to be pessimistic about what remains to be done (or some of what has been done!), we should think of Frege's magnificent accomplishment in bringing what Dummett calls 'multiple generality' under control.[13] Frege did not have a theory of truth in Tarski's sense in mind, but it is obvious that he sought, and found, structures of a kind for which a theory of truth can be given.

The work of applying a theory of truth in detail to a natural language will in practice almost certainly divide into two stages. In the first stage, truth will be characterized, not for the whole language, but for a carefully gerrymandered part of the language. This part, though no doubt clumsy grammatically, will contain an infinity of sentences which exhaust the expressive power of the whole language. The second part will match each of the remaining sentences to one or (in the case of ambiguity) more than one of the sentences for which truth has been characterized. We may think of the sentences to which the first stage of the theory applies as giving the logical form, or deep structure, of all sentences.

2 Can a theory of truth be verified by appeal to evidence available before interpretation has begun?

Convention T says that a theory of truth is satisfactory if it generates a T-sentence for each sentence of the object language. It is enough to demonstrate that a theory of truth is empirically correct, then, to verify that the T-sentences are true (in practice, an adequate sample will confirm the theory to a reasonable degree). T-sentences mention only the closed sentences of the language, so the relevant evidence can consist entirely of facts about the behaviour and attitudes of speakers in relation to sentences (no doubt by way of utterances). A workable theory must, of course, treat sentences as concatenations of expressions of less than sentential length, it must introduce semantical notions like satisfaction and reference, and it must appeal to an ontology of sequences and the objects ordered by the sequences. All this apparatus is properly viewed as theoretical construction, beyond the reach of direct verification. It has done its work provided only it entails testable results in the form of T-sentences, and these make no mention of the machinery. A theory of truth thus reconciles the demand for a theory that articulates grammatical structure with the demand for a theory that can be tested only by what it says about sentences.

In Tarski's work, T-sentences are taken to be true because the right branch of the biconditional is assumed to be a translation of the sentence truth conditions for which are being given. But we cannot assume in advance that correct translation can be recognized without pre-empting the point of radical interpretation; in empirical applications, we must abandon the assumption. What I propose is to reverse the direction of explanation: assuming translation, Tarski was able to define truth; the present idea is to take truth as basic and to extract an account of translation or interpretation. The advantages, from the point of view of radical interpretation, are obvious. Truth is a single property which attaches, or fails to attach, to utterances, while each utterance has its own interpretation; and truth is more apt to connect with fairly simple attitudes of speakers.

There is no difficulty in rephrasing Convention T without appeal to the concept of translation: an acceptable theory of truth must entail, for every sentence s of the object language, a sentence of the form: s is true if and only if p, where 'p' is replaced by any sentence that is true if and only if s is. Given this formulation, the theory is tested by evidence that T-sentences are simply true; we have given up the idea that we must also tell whether what replaces 'p' translates s. It might seem that there is no chance that if we demand so little of T-sentences, a theory of interpretation will emerge. And of course this would be so if we took the T-sentences in isolation. But the hope is that by putting appropriate formal and empirical restrictions on the theory as a whole, individual T-sentences will in fact serve to yield interpretations.[14]

We have still to say what evidence is available to an interpreter – evidence, we now see, that T-sentences are true. The evidence cannot consist in detailed descriptions of the speaker's beliefs and intentions, since attributions of attitudes, at least where subtlety is required, demand a theory that must rest on much the same evidence as interpretation. The interdependence of belief and meaning is evident in this way: a speaker holds a sentence to be true because of what the sentence (in his language) means, and because of what he believes. Knowing that he holds the sentence to be true, and knowing the meaning, we can infer his belief; given enough information about his beliefs, we could perhaps infer the meaning. But radical interpretation should rest on evidence that does not assume knowledge of meanings or detailed knowledge of beliefs.

A good place to begin is with the attitude of holding a sentence true, of accepting it as true. This is, of course, a belief, but it is a single attitude applicable to all sentences, and so does not ask us to be able to make finely discriminated distinctions among beliefs. It is an attitude an interpreter may plausibly be taken to be able to identify before he can interpret, since he may know that a person intends to express a truth in uttering a sentence without having any idea *what* truth. Not that sincere assertion is the only reason to suppose that a person holds a sentence to be true. Lies, commands, stories, irony, if they are detected as attitudes, can reveal whether a speaker holds his sentences to be true. There is no reason to rule out other attitudes towards sentences, such as wishing true, wanting to make true, believing one is going to make true, and so on, but I am inclined to think that all evidence of this kind may be summed up in terms of holding sentences to be true.

Suppose, then, that the evidence available is just that speakers of the language to be interpreted hold various sentences to be true at certain times and under specified circumstances. How can this evidence be used to support a theory of truth? On the one hand, we have T-sentences, in the form:

(T) 'Es regnet' is true-in-German when spoken by x at time t if and only if it is raining near x at t.

On the other hand, we have the evidence, in the form:

(E) Kurt belongs to the German speech community and Kurt holds true 'Es regnet' on Saturday at noon and it is raining near Kurt on Saturday at noon.

We should, I think, consider (E) as evidence that (T) is true. Since (T) is a universally quantified conditional, the first step would be to gather more evidence to support the claim that:

(GE) $(x)(t)$ (if x belongs to the German speech community then (x holds true 'Es regnet' at t if and only if it is raining near x at t)).

The appeal to a speech community cuts a corner but begs no question: speakers belong to the same speech community if the same theories of interpretation work for them.

The obvious objection is that Kurt, or anyone else, may be wrong about whether it is raining near him. And this is of course a reason for not taking (E) as conclusive evidence for (GE) or for (T); and a reason not to expect generalizations like (GE) to be more than generally true. The method is rather one of getting a best fit. We want a theory that satisfies the formal constraints on a theory of truth, and that maximizes agreement, in the sense of making Kurt (and others) right, as far as we can tell, as often as possible. The concept of maximization cannot be taken literally here, since sentences are infinite in number, and anyway once the theory begins to take shape it makes sense to accept intelligible error and to make allowance for the relative likelihood of various kinds of mistake.[15]

The process of devising a theory of truth for an unknown native tongue might in crude outline go as follows. First we look for the best way to fit our logic, to the extent required to get a theory satisfying Convention T, on to the new language; this may mean reading the logical structure of first-order quantification theory (plus identity) into the language, not taking the logical constants one by one, but treating this much of logic as a grid to be fitted on to the language in one fell swoop. The evidence here is classes of sentences always held true or always held false by almost everyone almost all of the time (potential logical truths) and patterns of inference. The first step identifies predicates, singular terms, quantifiers, connectives, and identity; in theory, it settles matters of logical form. The second step concentrates on sentences with indexicals; those sentences sometimes held true and sometimes false according to discoverable changes in the world. This step in conjunction with the first limits the possibilities for interpreting individual predicates. The last step deals with the remaining sentences, those on which there is not uniform agreement, or whose held truth value does not depend systematically on changes in the environment.[16]

This method is intended to solve the problem of the interdependence of belief and meaning by holding belief constant as far as possible while solving for meaning. This is accomplished by assigning truth conditions to alien sentences that make native speakers right when plausibly possible, according, of course, to our own view of what is right. What justifies the procedure is the fact that disagreement and agreement alike are intelligible only against a background of massive agreement. Applied to language, this principle reads: the more sentences we conspire to accept or reject (whether or not through a medium of interpretation), the better we understand the rest, whether or not we agree about them.

The methodological advice to interpret in a way that optimizes agreement should not be conceived as resting on a charitable assumption about human intelligence that might turn out to be false. If we cannot find a way to interpret the utterances and other behaviour of a creature as revealing a set of beliefs largely consistent and true by our own standards, we have no reason to count that creature as rational, as having beliefs, or as saying anything.

Here I would like to insert a remark about the methodology of my proposal. In philosophy we are used to definitions, analyses, reductions. Typically these are intended to carry us from concepts better understood, or clear, or more basic epistemologically or ontologically, to others we want to understand. The method I have suggested fits none of these categories. I have proposed a looser relation between concepts to be illuminated and the relatively more basic. At the centre stands a formal theory, a theory of truth, which imposes a complex structure on sentences containing the primitive notions of truth and satisfaction. These notions are given application by the form of the theory and the nature of the evidence. The result is a partially interpreted theory. The advantage of the method lies not in its free-style appeal to the notion of evidential support but in the idea of a powerful theory interpreted at the most advantageous point. This allows us to reconcile the need for a semantically articulated structure with a theory testable only at the sentential level. The more subtle gain is that very thin evidence in support of each of a potential infinity of points can yield rich results, even with respect to the points. By knowing only the conditions under which speakers hold sentences true, we can come out, given a satisfactory theory, with an interpretation of each sentence. It remains to make good on this last claim. The theory itself at best gives truth conditions. What we need to show is that if such a theory satisfies the constraints we have specified, it may be used to yield interpretations.

3   *If we know that a theory of truth satisfies the formal and empirical criteria described, can we interpret utterances of the language for which it is a theory?*

A theory of truth entails a T-sentence for each sentence of the object language, and a T-sentence gives truth conditions. It is tempting, therefore, simply to say that a T-sentence 'gives the meaning' of a sentence. Not, of course, by naming or describing an entity that is a meaning, but simply by saying under what conditions an utterance of the sentence is true.

But on reflection it is clear that a T-sentence does not give the meaning of the sentence it concerns: the T-sentence does fix the truth value relative to certain conditions, but it does not say the object language sentence is true *because* the conditions hold. Yet if truth values were all that mattered, the T-sentence for 'Snow is white' could as well say that it is true if and only if grass is green or $2 + 2 = 4$ as say that it is true if and only if snow is white. We may be confident, perhaps, that no satisfactory theory of truth will produce such anomalous T-sentences, but this confidence does not license us to make more of T-sentences.

A move that might seem helpful is to claim that it is not the T-sentence alone, but the canonical proof of a T-sentence, that permits us to interpret the alien sentence. A canonical proof, given a theory of truth, is easy to construct, moving as it does through a string of biconditionals, and requiring for uniqueness only occasional decisions to govern left and right precedence. The proof does reflect the logical form the theory assigns to the sentence, and so might be thought to reveal something about meaning. But in fact we would know no more than before about how to interpret if all we knew was that a certain sequence of sentences was the proof, from some true theory, of a particular T-sentence.

A final suggestion along these lines is that we can interpret a particular sentence provided we know a correct theory of truth that deals with the language of the sentence. For then we know not only the T-sentence for the sentence to be interpreted, but we also 'know' the T-sentences for all other sentences; and of course, all the proofs. Then we would see the place of the sentence in the language as a whole, we would know the role of each significant part of the sentence, and we would know about the logical connections between this sentence and others.

If we knew that a T-sentence satisfied Tarski's Convention T, we would know that it was true, and we could use it to interpret a sentence because we would know that the right branch of the biconditional translated the sentence to be interpreted. Our present trouble springs from the fact that in radical interpretation we cannot assume that a T-sentence satisfies the translation criterion. What we have been overlooking, however, is that we have supplied an alternative criterion: this criterion is that the totality of T-sentences should (in the sense described above) optimally fit evidence about sentences held true by native speakers. The present idea is that what Tarski assumed outright for each T-sentence can be indirectly elicited by a holistic constraint. If that constraint is adequate, each T-sentence will in fact yield an acceptable interpretation.

A T-sentence of an empirical theory of truth can be used to interpret a sentence, then, provided we also know the theory that entails it, and know that it is a theory that meets the formal and empirical criteria.[17] For if the constraints are adequate, the range of acceptable theories will be such that any of them yields some correct interpretation for each potential utterance. To see how it might work, accept for a moment the absurd hypothesis that the constraints narrow down the possible theories to one, and this one implies the T-sentence (T) discussed previously. Then we are justified in using this T-sentence to interpret Kurt's utterance of 'Es regnet' as his saying that it is raining. It is not likely, given the flexible nature of the constraints, that all acceptable theories will be identical. When all the evidence is in, there will remain, as Quine has emphasized, the trade-offs between the beliefs we attribute to a speaker and the interpretations we give his words. But the resulting indeterminacy cannot be so great but that any theory that passes the tests will serve to yield interpretations.

Notes

1 The term 'radical interpretation' is meant to suggest strong kinship with Quine's 'radical translation'. Kinship is not identity, however, and 'interpretation' in place of 'translation' marks one of the differences: a greater emphasis on the explicitly semantical in the former.

2 See Essay 1 in Donald Davidson (1984) *Inquiries into Truth and Interpretation*. Oxford: Clarendon Press.

3 The idea of a translation manual with appropriate empirical constraints as a device for studying problems in the philosophy of language is, of course, Quine's. This idea inspired much of my thinking on the present subject, and my proposal is in important respects very close to Quine's. Since Quine did not intend to answer the questions I have set, the claim that the method of translation is not adequate as a solution to the problem of radical interpretation is not a criticism of any doctrine of Quine's.

4 A. Tarski, 'The Concept of Truth in Formalized Languages', in *Logic, Semantics, Metamathematics*. Oxford: Clarendon Press, 1956.

5 For a discussion of how a theory of truth can handle demonstratives and how Convention T must be modified, see S. Weinstein, 'Truth and Demonstratives', *Noûs*, 8 (1974), 179–84.

6 See J. Wallace. 'On the Frame of Reference', *Synthèse*, 2 (1970), 61–94, and Essay 3 in Davidson (1984) op. cit.

7 T. Burge, 'Reference and Proper Names', *Journal of Philosophy*, 70 (1973), 425–39.

8 G. Harman, 'Moral Relativism Defended', *Philosophical Review*, 84 (1976), 3–22.

9 J. Wallace, 'Positive, Comparative, Superlative', *Journal of Philosophy*, 69 (1972), 773–82.

10 See Essays 7 and 8 in Davidson (1984) op. cit.

11 See Essays 6–10 in D. Davidson, *Essays on Actions and Events* (Oxford: Clarendon Press, 1980).

12 See Essay 6 in Davidson (1984) op. cit.

13 M. Dummett, *Frege: Philosophy of Language* (London: Duckworth, 1973).

14 For essential qualifications, see note 11 of Essay 2 of Davidson (1984) op. cit.

15 For more on getting a 'best fit' see Essays 10–12 in Davidson (1984) op. cit.

16 Readers who appreciate the extent to which this account parallels Quine's account of radical translation in Chapter 2 of *Word and Object* will also notice the differences: the semantic constraint in my method forces quantificational structure on the language to be interpreted, which probably does not leave room for indeterminacy of logical form; the notion of stimulus meaning plays no role in my method, but its place is taken by reference to the objective features of the world which alter in conjunction with changes in attitude towards the truth of sentences; the principle of charity, which Quine emphasizes only in connection with the identification of the (pure) sentential connectives, I apply across the board.

17 See note 11 of Essay 2 and Essay 12 of Davidsen (1984) op. cit.

10

Semantics and Semantic Competence

Scott Soames

The central semantic fact about language is that it carries information about the world. The central psycho-semantic fact about speakers is that they understand the claims about the world made by sentences of their language. This parallel suggests an intimate connection between semantic theories and theories of semantic competence. A semantic theory should tell us what information is encoded by sentences relative to contexts. Since competent speakers seem to grasp this information, and since the ability to correctly pair sentences with their contents seems to be the essence of semantic competence, it might appear that a semantic theory is itself a theory of competence.

Such a view has, I think, been quite common. We are all familiar with syntacticians who tell us that their grammars are attempts to specify the grammatical knowledge in virtue of which speakers are syntactically competent. This knowledge is generally thought to include, though perhaps not be limited to, knowledge of which strings of words are genuine (or grammatical) sentences of the language. By extension, it would seem that a semantic theory ought to specify the semantic knowledge in virtue of which speakers are semantically competent. Presumably, this knowledge will include, though perhaps not be limited to, knowledge of the truth conditions of sentences.

The reason for focusing on truth conditions arises from the representational character of semantic information. A sentence that represents the world as being a certain way implicitly imposes conditions that must be satisfied if the world is to conform to the way it is represented to be. Thus, the semantic information encoded by a sentence determines the conditions under which it is true. There may be more to semantic information than truth conditions, but there is no information without them. Thus, if semantic competence consists in grasping the information semantically encoded by sentence, then it would seem that it must involve knowledge of truth conditions.

The view that linguistic theories of syntax and semantics may double as psychological theories of competence comes in two main forms. The more modest form requires theories of syntax and semantics to provide theorems knowledge of which explains competence; however, it does not require these theories to specify the cognitive states and processes causally responsible for this knowledge. In particular, it does not require the theoretical machinery used in linguistic theories to derive theorems about grammaticality or truth conditions to be internally represented components of any psychologically real system. It simply leaves open the question of how the knowledge characterized by correct linguistic theories is psychologically realized.

The more robust form of the view that linguistic theories may double as psychological theories of linguistic competence tries to answer this question. According to this view, syntactic and semantic theories are required not only to characterize the linguistically significant properties of sentences, but also to do so on the basis of whatever internally represented cognitive apparatus is responsible for speakers' recognition of these properties. In short, linguistic theories are required to specify both the knowledge needed for linguistic competence, and the mechanisms from which that knowledge arises.

Although the robust approach has been accepted by many syntacticians, it has also been highly controversial. I believe it should be rejected for syntax as well as semantics.[1] However, it is not my present target. What I would like to argue is that, at least in the case of semantics, the modest approach is also incorrect. Semantic theories do not state that which a speaker knows in virtue of which he or she is semantically competent. Semantic competence does not arise from knowledge of the semantic properties of expressions characterized by a correct semantic theory.

Knowledge of Truth Conditions

Let us begin with the basics. The job of semantics is to specify the principles by which sentences represent the world. It is impossible to represent the world as being a certain way without implicitly imposing conditions that must be satisfied if the world is to conform to the representation. Thus, whatever else a semantic theory must do, it must at least characterize truth conditions. For certain languages, there are two standard ways of doing this. One involves the construction of a Davidson-style theory of truth for the language. The other involves the construction of a theory, or definition, of a relativized notion of truth for the language, truth-with-respect-to a world w. Both theories can be thought of as entailing statements that give the truth conditions of sentences. In one case, these statements are instances of schema T; in the other they are instances of schema T_W. (Instances are formed by replacing 'P' with a paraphrase of the sentence replacing 'S'.)

Schema T: 'S' is true (in L) iff P
Schema T_W: 'S' is true (in L) w.r.t. w iff in w, P

Now it might be thought that knowledge of truth conditions is the key to semantic competence, and hence that competence is the result of knowing that which is stated by each instance of one or the other of these schemas. But this is false. Knowledge of truth conditions (in this sense) is neither necessary nor sufficient for understanding a language.

It is not sufficient since it is possible for even the logically omniscient to know that

(1)   'Firenze é una bella città' is true in Italian (w.r.t. w) iff (in w) Florence is a beautiful city

while failing to believe that

(2)   'Firenze é una bella città' means in Italian that Florence is a beautiful city

and believing instead that

(3)   'Firenze é una bella città' means in Italian that Florence is a beautiful city and arithmetic is incomplete.

All that is necessary for this is for the agent to believe that (for any w) Florence is a beautiful city (in w) iff (in w) Florence is a beautiful city and arithmetic is incomplete. In short, true beliefs about truth conditions are compatible with false beliefs about meaning.

One sometimes sees it suggested that this problem can be avoided by requiring the agent's knowledge of truth conditions to encompass everything forthcoming from a finitely axiomatized theory of truth for the entire language. But this is not so. Given a first order language, one can always construct extensionally correct, finitely axiomatizable truth theories each of whose theorems resembles (4) in correctly giving the truth conditions of an object language sentence, while failing to provide a basis for paraphrase or interpretation.

(4) 'Firenze é una bella città' is true in Italian (w.r.t. w) iff (in w) Florence is a beautiful city and arithmetic is incomplete.

Now imagine a person ignorant of the object language being given a finitely axiomatized theory of truth. Unless he is also given information about meaning, he will have no way of knowing whether it can be used to paraphrase and interpret object language sentences. In particular, he will have no way of knowing whether the result of substituting 'means that' for 'is true iff' in its theorems will produce truths, as in (2), or falsehoods, as in (3). Knowledge of truth conditions, even of this systematic sort, is simply not sufficient for knowledge of meaning, or semantic competence.[2]

It is also not necessary. Knowledge of truth conditions, as I have described it, presupposes possession of a metalinguistic concept of truth. Thus, the claim that such knowledge is necessary for understanding meaning entails that no one can learn or understand a language without first having such a concept. But this consequence seems false. Certainly, young children and unsophisticated adults can understand lots of sentences without understanding 'true', or any corresponding predicate.

Must they, nevertheless, possess a metalinguistic concept of truth, even though they have no word for it? I don't see why. Perhaps it will be suggested that a person who lacked such a concept couldn't be a language user, since to use language one must realize that assertive utterances aim at truth and seek to avoid falsity. But this suggestion is confused. The child will get along fine so long as he knows that 'Momma is working' is to be assertively uttered only if Momma is working; 'Daddy is asleep' is to be assertively uttered only if Daddy is asleep; and so on. The child doesn't have to say or think to himself, "There is a general (but defeasible) expectation that for all x, if x is a sentence, then one is to assertively utter x only if x is true." It is enough if he says or thinks to himself, "There is a general (but defeasible) expectation that one should assertively utter 'Mommy is working' only if Mommy is working; assertively utter 'Daddy is asleep' only if Daddy is asleep; and so on for every sentence." For this, no notion of truth is needed.[3]

The point here is not that this truthless substitute says exactly the same thing as its truth-containing counterpart. In general, metalinguistic truth is not eliminable without loss of expressive power, and practical utility. The point is that it is not necessary to have such a concept in order to learn and understand a language. Thus, knowledge of that which is expressed by instances of schemas T and T_W is neither necessary nor sufficient for semantic competence.

Beyond Truth Conditions

The problem with such accounts of semantic competence can be expressed as follows: Even if the sentence replacing 'P' is a strict paraphrase of the sentence replacing 'S', the "connective"

(5)　'...' is true (in w) iff (in w)...

used to relate them is too loose to provide the information needed for understanding, or knowing the meaning of, a sentence. Thus, knowledge of truth conditions (in this sense) cannot explain semantic competence.

How might knowledge of meaning be expressed? A natural suggestion is that what one knows when one knows the meaning of a sentence is something of the form

(6)　'S' means that P

or

(7)　'S' says that P.

However, two qualifications must be noted.

First, in general if x means or says that P&Q, then x means or says that P and x means or says that Q. For example, if Reagan meant or said that defense spending would increase and taxes would be cut, then he meant or said that defense spending would increase, and he meant or said that taxes would be cut. However, the sentence 'Defense spending will increase and taxes will be cut' does not mean in English that defense spending will increase; nor does it mean in English that taxes will be cut. When we say that a sentence means in English that so-and-so, we are, I think, saying that it expresses the proposition that so-and-so. An unambiguous conjunction expresses a single, conjunctive, proposition; it does not also express the propositions that its conjuncts do.

Second, when an object language sentence contains an indexical element, we don't want to identify its meaning with any of the different propositions it may be used to express. For example, I don't want to say that 'I live in New Jersey' means (says) that I (S. S.) live in New Jersey. The sentence doesn't mean something specifically about me, any more than it means something about anyone else. Rather, its meaning is what allows it to be used in different contexts to express different (but systematically related) propositions.

These qualifications can be accommodated by suggestion (8).

(8)a The meaning of a sentence is a function from contexts of utterance to propositions expressed by the sentence in those contexts.
   b   Knowledge of meaning is knowledge of that which is expressed by instances of schema K. (Instances are obtained by replacing 'C' with a description of a context of utterance, and 'P' with a sentence that expresses the proposition that the sentence replacing 'S' expresses in the context described.) Schema K: 'S' expresses the proposition that P relative to the context C.

In formulating this schema, we take 'express' to be a three-place predicate relating sentences, contexts, and propositions. A semantic theory utilizing this predicate will assign propositions to sentences, relative to contexts, while deriving the truth conditions of a sentence from the proposition it expresses. The suggestion for relating semantics to semantic competence, then, is that a correct semantic theory will entail instances of schema K, knowledge of which explains semantic competence.

But what are propositions, and how are they assigned to sentences? One familiar suggestion is that propositions are sets of metaphysically possible worlds assigned to sentences by recursive characterizations of truth with respect to a world. Given such a truth characterization, one can define the proposition expressed by a sentence S to be the set of worlds w such that S is true in w.

However, this won't do. On this approach, necessarily equivalent propositions are identified – e.g. the proposition that Florence is a beautiful city is identified with the proposition that Florence is a beautiful city and arithmetic is incomplete. Thus, the approach predicts that anyone who believes the one believes the other, that any sentence which expresses the one expresses the other, and that anyone who knows that a sentence expresses the one knows that it expresses the other. These results are unacceptable.

It is important to note that the problem does not arise from the selection of metaphysically possible worlds as the truth-supporting circumstances in terms of which truth conditions are explicated, and propositions constructed. Given a background of relatively modest and plausible assumptions, one can reconstruct essentially the same problem for any fine-grained conception of truth-supporting circumstances that allows one to maintain the standard recursive clauses in a truth characterization for constructions like conjunction, quantification, and descriptions.[4] This means that no matter what one takes truth-supporting circumstances to be, one cannot identify the proposition expressed by a sentence with the set of circumstances in which it is true; nor can one identify a semantic theory with a characterization of truth with respect to a circumstance.

What is needed is a reversal of familiar semantic priorities. Instead of viewing propositions as artifacts of conceptually prior truth characterizations, we should construct semantic theories that directly assign propositions to sentences, and derive truth conditions of sentences from theories of truth for the propositions they express. In order for these propositions to serve as fine-grained objects of the attitudes they should encode both the structure of the sentences that express them and the semantic contents of subsentential constituents. In this way, sentences with significantly different structures may express different propositions even though they are true in the same truth-supporting circumstances.

I believe that these ideas can best be implemented by an essentially Russellian conception of semantics and semantic content.[5] This approach can be illustrated by considering an elementary first order language with lambda abstraction, a belief operator, and a stock of semantically simple singular terms, all of which are directly referential.[6] On the Russellian account, the semantic content of a variable relative to an assignment is just the object assigned as value of the variable; the semantic content of a closed (directly referential) term, relative to a context, is its referent relative to the context. The contents of n-place predicates are n-place properties and relations. The contents of '&' and '~' are functions, CONJ and NEG, from truth values to truth values.

Variable-binding operations, like lambda abstraction and existential quantification, can be handled by using propositional functions to play the role of complex properties corresponding to certain compound expressions.[7] On this approach, the semantic content of $\lceil[\lambda xRx, x]\rceil$ is the function g from individuals o to propositions that attribute the relation expressed by R to the pair $< o, o >$. $\lceil[\lambda xRx, x]t\rceil$ can then be thought of as attributing the property of bearing R to oneself to the referent of t; and $\lceil\exists x Rx, x\rceil$ can be thought of as "saying" that g assigns a true proposition to at least one object.

The recursive assignment of propositions to sentences is given in (9).[8]

(9)a The proposition expressed by an atomic formula $\lceil Pt_1, \ldots, t_n\rceil$ relative to a context C and assignment f is $<< o_1, \ldots, o_n >$, $P^* >$, where P^* is the property expressed by P, and o_i is the content of t_i relative to C and f.

b The proposition expressed by formula $\lceil[\lambda v\ S]t\rceil$ relative to C and f is $<< o >, g >$, where o is the content of t relative to C and f, and g is the function from individuals o' to propositions expressed by S relative to C and an assignment f' that differs from f at most in assigning o' as the value of v.[9]

c The propositions expressed by $\lceil\sim S\rceil$ and $\lceil S\ \&\ R\rceil$ relative to C and f are $< NEG,\ Prop\ S >$ and $< CONJ, < Prop\ S,\ Prop\ R >>$ respectively, where Prop S and Prop R are the propositions expressed by S and R relative to C and f, and NEG and CONJ are the truth functions for negation and conjunction.

d The proposition expressed by $\lceil\exists v S\rceil$ relative to C and f is $< SOME,\ g >$, where SOME is the property of being a non-empty set, and g is as in (b).

e The proposition expressed by $\lceil t$ believes that $S\rceil$ relative to C and f is $<< o,\ Prop\ S >,\ B >$, where B is the belief relation, o is the content of t relative to C and f, and Prop S is the proposition expressed by S relative to C and f.

f The proposition expressed by a sentence (with no free variables) relative to a context C is the proposition it expresses relative to C and every assignment f.

On this approach, the meaning of an expression is a function from contexts to propositional constituents. The meaning of a sentence is a compositional function from contexts to structured propositions. Intensions (and extensions) of sentences and expressions relative to contexts (and circumstances) derive from intensions (and extensions) of propositions and propositional constituents. These, in turn, can be gotten from a recursive characterization of truth with respect to a circumstance, for propositions.

For this purpose, we let the intension of an n-place property be a function from circumstances to sets of n-tuples of individuals that instantiate the property in the circumstances; we let the intension of an individual be a constant function from circumstances to that individual; and we let the intension of a one-place propositional function g be a function from circumstances E to sets of individuals in E that g assigns propositions true in E. Extension is related to intension in the normal way, with the extension of a proposition relative to a circumstance being its truth value in the circumstance, and its intension being the set of circumstances in which it is true (or, equivalently, the characteristic function of that set). Truth relative to a circumstance is defined in (10).

(10)a A proposition $<< o_1, \ldots, o_n >, P^* >$ is true relative to a circumstance E iff the extension of P^* in E contains $< o_1, \ldots, o_n >$.

 b A proposition $<< o >, g >$ is true relative to E (where g is a one-place propositional function) iff o is a member of the extension of g in E (i.e. iff g(o) is true relative to E).

 c A proposition $< NEG, Prop\ S >$ is true relative to E iff the value of NEG at the extension of Prop S in E is truth (i.e. iff Prop S is not true relative to E).
 A proposition $< CONJ, < Prop\ S, Prop\ R >>$ is true relative to E iff the value of CONJ at the pair consisting of the extension of Prop S in E and the extension of Prop R in E is truth (i.e. iff Prop S and Prop R are true relative to E).

 d A proposition $< SOME, g >$ is true relative to E (where g is as in (b)) iff the extension of g in E is non-empty (i.e. iff g(o) is true relative to E for some o in E).

 e A proposition $<< o, Prop\ S >, B >$ is true relative to E iff $< o, Prop\ S >$ is a member of the extension of B in E (i.e. iff o believes Prop S in E).

Earlier we considered the suggestion that a semantic theory issues in instances of schema K, and that knowledge of that which is expressed by these instances explains semantic competence. The key idea behind this suggestion is that it is knowledge of the propositions expressed by sentences, rather than knowledge of truth conditions, that is fundamental to understanding a language. We now have a conception of semantics that pairs object language sentences with propositions of the right sort. Does this mean that we have a semantic theory that entails instances of schema K?

No, it does not. Instead, the above theory, when supplemented with a theory of object language syntax and an interpretation of its vocabulary, will issue in theorems of the kind shown in (11).

(11) '∃xLx, n' expresses (with respect to every context) the proposition which is the ordered pair whose first coordinate is the property

SOME, of being a non-empty set, and whose second coordinate is the function g which assigns to any object o the proposition which is the ordered pair whose second coordinate is the relation of loving and whose first coordinate is the ordered pair the first coordinate of which is o and the second coordinate of which is Nixon.

Let us suppose, for the sake of argument, that (11) is true, and hence that the description it gives of the proposition expressed by '∃xLx, n' is accurate. Still, the theorem is not an instance of schema K. Moreover, knowledge of that which it expresses is neither necessary nor sufficient for knowing the meaning of the sentence, let alone for explaining speakers' understanding of it.

In essence the situation is this: We think of the instance (12) of schema K as containing a singular term t which denotes the proposition expressed by '∃xLx, n'.

(12) '∃xLx, n' expresses the proposition that something loves Nixon (with respect to every context C).

Corresponding to this, the semantic theory issues theorem (11), which contains a singular term t' that refers to the same proposition as t. However, t and t' are distinct, non-synonymous expressions; t is 'the proposition that something loves Nixon', whereas t' is the complicated definite description given in (11). As a result, (11) and (12) "say" different things. Thus, even if knowledge of meaning amounted to knowledge of that which is expressed by the latter, it would not amount to knowledge of that which is expressed by the former. Semantic competence is not the result of knowing these semantic theorems.

Suppose, however, that one were to make the assumptions in (13).

(13)a The expression ⌈the proposition that P⌉ is a directly referential singular term that refers to the proposition expressed by P.
   b 'Dthat' is an operator which can be prefixed to any definite description D to form a directly referential singular term ⌈dthatD⌉ whose semantic content is the referent of D.[10]
   c A proper semantic theory can be formulated so as to entail theorems analogous to (11) in which 'dthat' is prefixed to the description of the proposition expressed.
   d If t and t' are directly referential singular terms that refer to the same thing, then substitution of one for the other in a sentence (outside of quotes) does not affect what proposition is

expressed. Moreover, substitution of one for the other in propositional attitude constructions preserves truth-value; if ⌜x knows (believes) that ... t ... ⌝ is true, then so is ⌜x knows (believes) that ... t' ... ⌝.

From these assumptions it follows that knowledge of that which is expressed by (the newly formulated) semantic theorems just is knowledge of that which is expressed by instances of schema K.

In my opinion, these assumptions are more reasonable than commonly thought. Indeed, I am willing to accept them. However, even if they are accepted, they cannot be used to connect semantics with semantic competence. The reason they can't is that although they allow semantic theorems to be assimilated to instances of schema K, they make it possible to know that which is expressed by these instances without understanding object language sentences.

I take it that if propositions can be referents of directly referential singular terms, then they can be labeled using directly referential proper names. Suppose, then, that the proposition that mathematics is reducible to logic is labeled 'logicism'. Using the assumptions in (13), we can then conclude that (14) and (15) "say" the same thing, and that (16) and (17) have the same truth value.

(14) Logicism is expressed by s.
(15) The proposition that mathematics is reducible to logic is expressed by s.
(16) x believes (knows) that logicism is expressed by s.
(17) x believes (knows) that the proposition that mathematics is reducible to logic is expressed by s.

Thus, if it is possible to believe or know that logicism is expressed by a certain sentence without understanding that sentence, then it will be possible to believe or know the corresponding instance of schema K – namely (15) – without being semantically competent.

But this is possible. The case is analogous to one in which someone believes that a particular person authored certain axioms without knowing very much about the person. For example, someone being introduced to elementary number theory might be told that certain axioms were first formulated by Peano. On the basis of this, he may come to believe that Peano first formulated those axioms, even though he is not able to identify Peano, distinguish him from other mathematicians, or to accurately characterize him using any uniquely identifying description.

Now consider a student attending his first lecture in the philosophy of mathematics. He may be told that logicism is a proposition about the relationship between logic and mathematics, that formalism is a doctrine about the interpretation of mathematics, and so on. At this stage, the student may not be able to distinguish logicism from other propositions about the relationship between logic and mathematics; or to describe it in any informative way. Nevertheless, he may acquire beliefs about logicism. For example, he may be told, "Russell was a defender of logicism", and thereby come to believe that Russell defended logicism. He might even be told, "Logicism is expressed by sentence s", and thereby come to believe that logicism is expressed by sentence s. In order to acquire this belief, it is not necessary that he understand s. It might, for example, be written on the board and labeled 's', but contain unfamiliar terminology. In such a case, the student's knowledge that s expresses logicism does not make him a linguistically competent user of s.

When combined with the assumptions noted above, this observation leads to the conclusion that one can know that which is expressed by an instance

(18) 'S' expresses the proposition that P (relative to C)

of schema K without understanding the object language sentence that replaces 'S'. It would seem, therefore, that knowledge of semantic theorems is not necessary and sufficient for semantic competence, even under the most favorable assumptions.

To recapitulate: If one doesn't adopt the assumptions in (13), then one's semantic theory will not provide instances of schema K; if one does adopt the assumptions in (13), then one can construct a semantic theory whose theorems express the propositions expressed by instances of schema K – however, under these assumptions knowledge of those propositions does not ensure understanding the object language. Either way, knowledge of semantic theorems is not necessary and sufficient for semantic competence.

Semantic Competence and "The Augustinian Picture"[11]

If this is right, then a familiar strategy for explaining semantic competence won't work. The strategy is based on the idea that competent speakers understand sentences in virtue of knowing precisely the information that a semantic theory provides – namely, the truth conditions of, and propositions expressed by, object language sentences. In attacking this idea I have argued that semantic knowledge and linguistic competence do not always coincide; the presence of one does not guarantee the presence of the other. Thus, semantic knowledge cannot, in general, explain linguistic competence.

There is, however, a more fundamental point to be made. Even in cases in which a linguistically competent speaker is semantically knowledgeable, his competence may not derive from his knowledge; rather, his knowledge may derive from his competence.

The examples in (19) provide a case in point.

(19)a   Pluto is a distant planet.
   b   'Pluto' refers to Pluto.
   c   'Pluto is a distant plant' is true (in English) iff Pluto is a distant planet.
   d   'Pluto is a distant planet' expresses (in English) the proposition that Pluto is a distant planet.

I believe all of these things. The reason I believe them is not that I have seen or had direct contact with Pluto. On the contrary, my only contact with the planet has been an indirect one, mediated by representations of it. In my case, the most important of these has been the name 'Pluto'.

My beliefs about Pluto are similarly mediated. I believe that Pluto is a distant planet because I have read or been told that it is. I have read or been told "Pluto is a distant planet"; I have understood the sentence; and I have accepted it. It is important to note that this understanding did not consist in associating an identifying description with the name 'Pluto', and a descriptive proposition with the entire sentence. In acquiring the belief, I may or may not have associated a description with the name, and I may or may not have come to believe descriptive propositions as a result of accepting the sentence. Still, my belief that Pluto is a distant planet cannot be identified with any such descriptive belief. Even if the description I associate with the name is inaccurate and doesn't, in fact, pick out Pluto, my belief that Pluto is a distant planet is about Pluto (though the descriptive beliefs acquired at the same time may not be). Similarly, even if the descriptive beliefs turn out to be false, my belief that Pluto is a distant planet may remain true. Finally, the proposition I express by 'Pluto is a distant planet' is the same as the proposition that others express by the sentence, even if the descriptions we associate with the name are different.

In short, the explanation of my belief that Pluto is a distant planet involves the fact that, (i) I accept the sentence 'Pluto is a distant planet'; (ii) the sentence expresses the proposition that Pluto is a distant planet; and (iii) I am a competent speaker, and thereby understand the sentence. Moreover, my understanding the sentence is not a matter of my using it to express descriptive propositions that I might have come to believe on independent grounds.

Analogous points can be made regarding other attitudes I might have taken toward the proposition. If I had come to wonder whether Pluto was a distant planet, or to doubt that it was, my having that propositional attitude would have involved my having a certain attitude toward a sentence that expressed it. In short, the only epistemic connection I have with certain propositions is mediated through sentences that express them.

These considerations can be extended to the other examples (19b–d). For instance, I believe the propositions expressed by (c) and (d). However, these beliefs do not explain my understanding of (a). I don't understand the sentence because I have those beliefs. If anything, it is the other way around. My belief in the propositions expressed by (c) and (d) is (in large part) due to my understanding and accepting sentences (c) and (d), and to the fact that they mean what they do. Moreover, part of what it is for me to understand these sentences is for me to understand (a), which is a constituent of both. Thus, the direction of explanation in this case is not from beliefs to competence, but from competence to beliefs.

If this is right, then a natural and seductive picture of language acquisition and linguistic competence is fundamentally mistaken. According to this picture, we have the ability, prior to the acquisition of language, to form beliefs and entertain propositions. In setting up a language, we adopt certain conventions according to which sentences come to express these antecedently apprehended propositions. Learning the language amounts to learning for each sentence, which antecedently apprehended proposition it expresses.

The most fundamental thing wrong with this picture is that in the case of many sentences, we do not grasp the propositions they express prior to understanding the sentences themselves. As a result, coming to understand these sentences does not consist in searching through our stock of propositions to find the ones assigned to them. Rather, coming to understand the sentences is a matter of satisfying conventional standards regarding their use. Just what these standards are is not well understood. However, whatever they are, once they are satisfied, one is counted not only as understanding new sentences, but also as grasping new propositions. As a result, learning a language is not just a matter of acquiring a new tool for manipulating information one already possesses; it is also a means of expanding one's cognitive reach.[12]

This point is potentially more far-reaching than the examples I have used might indicate. Although my beliefs about Pluto are linguistically mediated, they need not have been. They could, presumably, have been acquired through direct, non-linguistic contact with the planet. Many of my beliefs about individuals are like this. For example, my beliefs about Plato are linguistically mediated; but they are also dependent on the fact that others have had direct contact with the man and have passed his name down to me.

In other cases, I have linguistically mediated beliefs about objects with which no one is, or could be, in direct epistemic contact – for example, beliefs about quarks, the addition function, and the cardinal aleph null. In my opinion, there are such objects; we do succeed in referring to them; and we acquire beliefs about them in virtue of understanding and accepting sentences about them.

How this all comes about is a large and unanswered question. Somehow, using the word 'plus' in a certain way counts as referring to the addition function, despite the fact that our use is logically consistent with alternative hypotheses, as well as the fact that there is no direct apprehension of the function.[13] Certainly, we do not say to ourselves, "There is this particular arithmetical function that we have been thinking about which has so far remained nameless; let's call it 'plus'". The reason we don't is that our epistemic access to the function does not precede our ability to represent it linguistically; rather, the two are simultaneous.

These considerations dramatically undermine the "Augustinian" picture of language acquisition and linguistic competence given in (20).

(20)a There are objects, properties, and propositions that we apprehend prior to understanding a language.
   b Linguistic expressions stand for these independently apprehended objects, properties, and propositions.
   c Understanding a language is the result of knowing which expressions stand for which objects – e.g. of knowing that 'Pluto' refers to Pluto, that '+' stands for the addition function, and that 'Quarks are subatomic particles' expresses the proposition that quarks are subatomic particles.

Clause (a) is true but incomplete, since there are objects we apprehend only through linguistic mediation. Clause (b) is false, if taken as a claim about linguistic expressions in general. However, the result of deleting the words "these independently apprehended" from it is true. Clause (c) is objectionable on two grounds. First, it has the dubious consequence that understanding an expression always coincides with knowing that the expression has certain semantic properties. Second, it wrongly suggests that semantic knowledge about what expressions stand for is conceptually prior to, and explains, semantic competence.

Semantics

Where does this leave semantics? I have suggested that a semantic theory must pair sentences with the propositions they express, and derive the truth conditions of sentences from those propositions. I have also noted that the knowledge provided by such a theory is not necessary and sufficient for semantic competence. However, I have argued that this is no defect, since the attempt to explain semantic competence as arising from semantic knowledge rests on an inadequate conception of the role of language in our cognitive lives – a conception that ignores the linguistic basis of many of our semantic and non-semantic beliefs. If this is correct, then one should not look to semantics for an account of semantic competence.

Instead, one should look to it for an explication of the representational character of language. The central semantic fact about language is that it is used to represent the world. Sentences do this by systematically encoding information that characterizes the world as being one way or another. Semantics is the study of this information, and the principles by which it is encoded.

A theory of this sort can be seen as accomplishing three main tasks. First, it tells us what sentences say relative to different contexts of utterance, and thereby provides the basis for interpreting what speakers say when they assertively utter sentences in various contexts, and what they believe when they believe that which is said by one or another assertive utterance. Second, the semantic account of truth conditions explicates a fundamental aspect of the relationship between language and the world. Third, the model-theoretic machinery in the theory provides a semantic account of meaning-determined logical properties and relations holding among sentences.

Theories of semantic competence are responsive to different concerns. Whereas semantic theories focus on the fact that sentences encode information that represents the world, theories of semantic competence focus on the fact that languages are things that people understand. This focus on understanding can be developed in two ways. On the one hand, one may ask for a conceptual analysis (in terms of social, behavioral, mental, or verificationist notions) of what it means to understand an expression, a sentence, or a language. On the other hand, one may want an empirical theory that identifies the cognitive structures and processes that are causally responsible for the linguistic understanding of a particular person or group. Both types of concern with understanding are legitimate, and deserve to be developed. However, neither is essentially semantic, in the sense I have sketched.

This does not mean that there are no interesting connections between semantic theories of information encoding and psychological, or philosophical, theories of linguistic understanding. In fact, they complement one another. Semantic theories specify contents of expressions, but say nothing about the empirical factors that are causally responsible for their coming to have these contents. For certain words, it is plausible to suppose that they got their content from a causal-historical chain connecting tokens produced by different speakers to a real-world referent. This sort of foundational view has been an important supplement to recent semantic theories, even though particular causal-historical chains have no place in semantic theories themselves.

A similar point might be made about mental representations associated with sentences by speakers. A number of cognitive scientists believe that understanding a sentence involves the recovery, manipulation, and storage of abstract representational structures. This belief has led to the attempt to develop theories about how these representational structures are connected to sentences, and how they interact with other cognitive systems. Typically these theories posit rules that take syntactic structures as input and produce different linguistic objects as output, where these latter are thought of as playing some significant role in explaining speakers' understanding, their semantic judgements, or both. If they do play such a role, then they may also be important causal factors in explaining why the natural language sentences they are associated with encode the information that they do.

It must be remembered, however, that these mental representations are not themselves semantic contents. Rather, they are things that have content. Thus, a theory of the cognitive structures associated with sentences is no substitute for a semantics. Indeed, such theories tacitly presuppose a semantics; for to say of an abstract mental structure that it represents so-and-so is to say that it bears information that characterizes things as being a certain way, and thereby imposes truth conditions that must be satisfied if things are to conform to the representation. Making this explicit is the job of semantics.

Thus, there is a sense in which theories of mental representation are incomplete without an accompanying semantics. However, there may also be a sense in which semantics is dependent on theories of mental representation. It is not just that theories of mental representation may be needed to explain how expressions come to have the contents associated with them by a correct semantic theory. Such theories may also be needed to decide what semantic content a sentence has, and hence what semantic theory is correct. The crucial point involves the introduction of structure into semantic content. I have argued, both here and on other occasions, that the semantic content of a sentence cannot be analyzed solely in terms of truth conditions, but rather must be seen as a complex with a structure that parallels that of the sentence itself.[14] But this raises a question. What level, or levels, of sentence structure does semantic information incorporate?

In the case of the simple first order language used to illustrate my propositional semantics, the answer is obvious – surface structure, since that is all the structure there is. However, in the case of natural language the matter is more complicated. Perhaps speakers of natural languages associate sentences with psychologically real underlying representations. If they do, then perhaps the propositions expressed by these sentences encode not their surface syntax, but rather the syntax of their underlying psycho-semantic representations. I don't know whether these possibilities will be born out; but the idea behind them is not unreasonable. It may very well be that cognitive structures involved in understanding sentences are closely related to propositional structures involved in explicating attitudes like saying, asserting, and believing. If they are, then semantic theories of information and psychological theories of semantic competence may turn out to be theories which, though different, have a lot in common after all.

Notes

1 See my "Linguistics and Psychology," *Linguistics and Philosophy*, volume 7, number 2, 1984, pp. 155–179; and my "Semantics and Psychology," in *The Philosophy of Linguistics*, edited by J. J. Katz, Oxford University Press, 1985, pp. 204–26.
2 For a more extended discussion of this point, as it applies to Davidsonian truth theories, see J. A. Foster, "Meaning and Truth Theory," in *Truth and Meaning*, edited by Gareth Evans and John McDowell, Oxford University Press, 1976, pp. 1–32. Although Foster presses the point forcefully against Davidson, he exempts approaches based on theories of truth-with-respect-to a possible world from his criticism. This, in my opinion, is a mistake. In addition to extending to

such theories, the basic argument can be made to apply to any attempt to found meaning, or knowledge of meaning, on theories of truth with respect to a circumstance – no matter how fine grained we make the circumstances (provided standard recursive clauses in the truth theory are maintained).

3   I am not here suggesting that the child really must repeat or represent the latter (truthless) instruction to himself. Thus, I am not claiming that the child must have the notion assertive utterance in order to learn a language. My point is a negative one. If there is anything to the suggestion that language learners must realize that assertive utterances aim at truth, that realization need not involve possession of a concept of truth. It may be that the child ultimately must come to realize something like the following: One is to say that Mommy is working only if Mommy is working, that Daddy is asleep only if Daddy is asleep; and so on. A truth predicate comes in handy in stating such a rule, for it allows one to eliminate the 'and so on' in favor of quantification over assertions plus predications of truth. But handy or not, this logical technology is not necessary for learning.

4   See my "Lost Innocence," *Linguistics and Philosophy*, volume 8, number 1, 1985, pp. 59–71; my "Direct Reference and Propositional Attitudes," in *Themes from Kaplan*, edited by J. Almog, J. Perry, and H. Wettstein, Oxford University Press, 1988; and my "Direct Reference, Propositional Attitudes, and Semantic Content," *Philosophical Topics*, volume 15, number 1, 1987, pp. 47–87, reprinted in *Propositions and Attitudes*, edited by N. Salmon and S. Soames, Oxford University Press, 1988.

5   See the articles mentioned in the preceding note, plus N. Salmon, *Frege's Puzzle*, MIT Press, 1986.

6   A directly referential singular term is one whose semantic content (relative to a context and assignment of values to variables) is its referent (relative to the context and assignment). It is this semantic content that such a term contributes to the information encoded (proposition expressed) by a sentence containing it.

7   Although this Russellian method is, I think, essentially on the right track, it does lead to certain technical problems in special cases. For example, as Nathan Salmon has pointed out to me, Russellian propositional functions must be defined on possible, as well as actual, individuals, in order to assign correct extensions to expressions in different possible worlds. This means that these functions cannot be thought of as set theoretic constructions involving only actually existing objects. Another problem involves non-well-foundedness. As Terence Parsons has observed, in order for the self-referential, but unparadoxical, (i) and (ii) to have their intended interpretations, the propositional functions corresponding to the matrices in these examples must be defined on the propositions expressed by (i) and (ii).

i. (x) (I assert $x \to$ I believe x)
ii. (x) (I assert x today $\to x$ is expressible in English)

This is impossible, if the set theoretic conception of propositions and propositional functions is maintained.

These problems can, I believe, be avoided by taking the semantic contents of compound expressions to be complex attributes rather than propositional functions. For example, the content of ⌈λvS⌉, w.r.t. a context C and assignment f, might be taken to be the property P of being an object o such that dthat [the proposition expressed by S w.r.t. C and an assignment f′ that differs from f at most in assigning o to v] is true. The extension of P at a world w will then be the set of objects o such that the relevant propositions containing them are true with respect to w (provided that a proposition has the one place property of being true, at a world w, iff the two place relation of being true-with-respect-to holds between it and w).

Other ways of assigning attributes to expressions (compound predicates) may also be found. For present purposes, I will leave the final resolution of this issue open, and continue in the text to use familiar Russellian propositional functions as contents of compound predicates.

8   This system is presented in my "Direct Reference, Propositional Attitudes, and Semantic Content", where it is explained more fully.

9   Nathan Salmon has suggested using this lambda construction to distinguish the propositions expressed by the complement clauses of (i–iii) from those expressed by the complements of (iv–v).

    i.   Pierre says (believes) that London is both pretty and not pretty.
    ii. Pierre says (believes) that London is non-self-identical.
    iii. Pierre says (believes) that London is not identical with itself.
    iv. Pierre says (believes) that London is pretty and London is not pretty.
    v. Pierre says (believes) that London is not identical with London.

This suggestion has the important virtue of allowing us to characterize (iv–v) as true while recognizing that (i–iii) are false. For more discussion, see N. Salmon, "Reflexivity," *Notre Dame Journal of Formal Logic*, volume 27, number 3, 1986, pp. 401–29, and my "Direct Reference, Propositional Attitudes, and Semantic Content" – both reprinted in *Propositions and Attitudes*.

10   See David Kaplan, "On the Logic of Demonstratives," *Journal of Philosophical Logic*, volume 8, 1979, pp. 81–98; reprinted in *Propositions and Attitudes*.

11   The allusion to Augustine refers to the passage quoted by Wittgenstein that opens *The Philosophical Investigations*:

When they (my elders) named some object, and accordingly moved towards something, I saw this and I grasped that the thing was called by the sound they uttered when they meant to point it out. Their intention was shewn by their bodily movements, as it were the natural language of all peoples: the expression of the face, the play of the eyes, the movement of other parts of the body, and the tone of voice which expresses our state of mind in seeking, having, rejecting, or avoiding something. Thus, as I heard words repeatedly used in their proper places in various sentences, I gradually learnt to understand what objects they signified; and after I had trained my mouth to form these signs, I used them to express my own desires.

The "Augustinian Picture" criticized below may be seen as an unwarranted extension of these remarks about language acquisition to cover all aspects of language.

12   I am speaking here primarily about first language acquisition (though the point applies, with less force, to some cases of second language acquisition as well).

13   See S. Kripke, *Wittgenstein on Rules and Private Language*, Harvard University Press, 1982.

14   See note 4.

11

Truth and Understanding[1]

James Higginbotham

1 Introduction

The chief problem about semantics comes at the beginning. What is the theory of meaning a theory of? What are the facts that it is supposed to account for? As the variety of recent and contemporary work in linguistic semantics will attest, the answers to these questions exert a mighty influence on subsequent theory. I won't canvass this variety here, but call attention to a line of reasoning that seems to me attractive, and in harmony with semantic theory as it is actually practiced, if not always with the interpretation of that practice.

Consider the simplest possible answer to our question, namely that the theory of meaning is charged with accounting for facts about meaning. The notion of meaning is at least initially given in our everyday vocabulary: we speak of people knowing the meaning of something, or not knowing it, of their failure to appreciate the full meaning of something, and of what certain signs mean in such-and-such conventional systems. Moreover, it is not difficult in practice to distinguish between the kind of meaning appropriate to language, the kind of meaning appropriate to symptoms and portents (Grice's "natural" meaning), and the kind of meaning or significance with which artworks are said to be fraught. The kind of meaning that a *sentence* has, however, is determined by what it may be used to *say*, and the kind of meaning that words and phrases have is determined by their contributions to the meanings of the sentences in which they occur. It could therefore be proposed that semantic theory is charged with establishing, formally, all of the facts to the effect that so-and-so means such-and-such, or at least all such facts as come readily to the lips of native speakers, hoping in this way to clarify the nature and extent of the human capacity for language.

I think that this simple answer is correct. It turns out, however, that research directed to the end of describing the facts about meaning requires the intervention of other concepts. The reason is that the notion of meaning applies in the first instance only to sentences, and whereas the meanings of sentences must be constructed somehow out of the meanings of words and the meanings of modes of syntactic combination, we are given nothing to go on about the meanings of either except that they "contribute" somehow to the meanings of the sentences in which they figure.[2]

Enter reference. Reference, unlike meaning, attaches to expressions of all syntactic categories, and all modes of syntactic combination, in the latter case as conditions on how the reference of compounds depends on the reference of their parts. Moreover, the reference of an expression is *isolable*, in the sense that the expression carries its reference with it wherever it occurs. Because a theory of meaning requires a concept of this nature, reference is indispensable; it is the backbone of meaning.

But reference, however understood, blurs semantic distinctions. Whether reference is given by sets of possible worlds, or sets of small possible worlds, or objects still further refined, the content of an assertion does not reduce to the reference of the sentence asserted; or so it appears. The reason, I believe, is that content, but not reference, is as fine-grained as the notation used to express it; whereas reference must allow different notations to end up at the same place.[3]

There have been attempts to preserve a standard truth-based conception of content against obvious counterexamples. It has also been suggested that the sensitivity of content to notation may be acknowledged by seeing content as *structured*, so that not just the reference of whole sentences, but also the way in which that reference is built up from the reference of their notational pieces is crucial to their content.[4] Structured content can go only so far, since there can't be any difference between the structured content of...*A*...and...*B*...where *A* and *B* simple expressions with the same content (for example, synonymous words). Then one would have to explain why a person says aye to the question whether... *A*...and nay to the question whether...*B*...without saying that she believes that...*A*...but not that...*B*...A supplement is thus needed in any case.[5]

Assuming that content should be understood in accordance with naive intuitions, and that so understood it cannot reduce to reference, what is the link between the indispensable concept of reference and the target concept of linguistic meaning? I think that the link is the psychological state of the language user, his or her *knowledge* of reference. The facts that semantics must account for comprise the context-independent features of the meaning of expressions that persons must know if they are to be competent speakers of the languages to which those features are assigned. What they must know, I suggest, consists of: facts about the reference of expressions, about what other people know and are expected to know about the reference of expressions, about what they know about what one knows and is expected to know about the reference of expressions, and so on up.[6]

From this point of view, meaning does not reduce to reference, but knowledge of meaning reduces to the norms of knowledge of reference. Such norms are *iterated*, because knowledge of meaning requires knowledge of what others know, including what they know about one's own knowledge. To a first approximation, the meaning of an expression is what you are expected, simply as a speaker, to know about its reference. As a speaker of English, you are expected, for example, to know that 'snow is white' is true if and only if snow is white; to know that 'snow' refers to snow, and that 'is white' is true of just the white things; and to know quite generally that the result of combining a singular term NP with a predicate in the form of an intransitive adjective is a sentence true just in case the predicate is true of the reference of the term. If, and only if, you know these things do you know that the sentence 'snow is white' means that snow is white.

The view that I have sketched forges what seems to me the strongest tenable link between truth and the other concepts of reference on the one hand and understanding on the other. It is weaker than the view that knowledge by the theorist of the truth conditions of a person's potential utterances would suffice for understanding that person; and it differs from various emendations to this view, in that it makes use of the information that a person tacitly possesses about the truth conditions of her own utterances. However, if I am right that knowledge of meaning reduces to the norms of knowledge of reference, then arguments to the effect that linguistic meaning simply cannot be captured in terms of reference must fail; and such arguments appear very powerful. In the next section I will consider some points against the strong view that meaning reduces to truth conditions, or truth conditions plus some supplementary facts, inquiring whether these points bite against the conception that I am advancing. Then in section 3 I will return to questions about the nature of linguistic data, and review some aspects of the psychological program.

2   Can Truth Lead to Meaning?

Considerations of a type due to John Foster have been advanced to show that theories of truth cannot go proxy for theories of meaning.[7] Certainly, to know that for a person *A* the sentences *S* is true if and only if *p* is not to know that it means that *p* (even if it does mean this). One argument growing out of Foster's work, which has been advanced in several versions by different authors, purports to show that the gap between meaning and truth conditions persists even when other data or theoretical parameters are taken into account, including the fact that a projectible theory of truth for a person will have to harmonize with the facts about the person's mental and physical states, and our position with respect to interpreting him. Must a theory of truth, arrived at on the basis of a rational procedure of interpretation, with the proper conception of public evidence, and known to be an adequate theory, serve as an adequate basis for understanding?

How the argument is to be formulated will depend upon how we think of evidence, the nature of psychological plausibility, and much else. We might try to cut through the fog here, as Soames does, by considering a test case.[8] In the test case, we have, or at least have gestured toward, a theory of reference that is acknowledged to be adequate for some person, and we also have what will unexceptionably pass for truth about what that person means. Then if knowledge of the theory of reference is compatible with mistaken beliefs about meaning, that will be a demonstration that knowledge of the one does not bring knowledge of the other.

Gianni is a native speaker of Italian. Hence

(1)   'Firenze è una bella città' is true for Gianni (in the possible world *w*) if and only if Florence is a beautiful city (in *w*)

and also

(2)   'Firenze è una bella città' means for Gianni that Florence is a beautiful city.

I, the theorist, might know (1) and fail to believe (2), because I mistakenly believe (3):

(3)   'Firenze è una bella città' means for Gianni that Florence is a beautiful city and *p*

where 'p' is replaced by something necessary that I believe, for instance "Arithmetic is incomplete."

I distinguish two types of response to the argument, which I will call *immanent* and *transcendent*. The immanent response has been recently and usefully elaborated by Ernie LePore and Barry Loewer.[9] This response grants the argument, but then suggests that certain other knowledge, not itself of an intensional semantic nature, will when taken together with knowledge of truth conditions suffice for understanding.

The transcedent response, which may be considered by itself or in conjunction with an immanent response, is that once we recognize that what we have to go on in interpretation may admit more than one possible correct ascription of a language to a person, then we may conclude that linguistic reality does not really offer counterexamples to the thesis that knowledge of truth conditions suffices to confer under-standing.[10] An allegedly mistaken attribution of meaning to Gianni will either disrupt communication with him, or it will not. If it will not, then where is the alleged mistake? But if it will, then the mistake should come to light.

Gianni interacts with people back home, and also with tourists like me. Holding as I do (3), I am bound to find that a rather ordinary sentence, suitable for insertion in travel brochures, is going on about the incom-pleteness of arithmetic. In Florence, Gianni gestures toward the Duomo, volunteering "Firenze è una bella città." Is he trying to impress me with his knowledge of logic? Surely I'll find out that (3) is false, and latch on instead to (2). In my coming to see the falsehood of (3), however, the truth theory played no role (this can be seen indirectly from the fact that, when I correct my hypothesis about what Gianni means, I need not revise the truth theory at all). The transcendent response therefore has the feature that mistakes like (3) are corrected on the basis of coming better to understand Gianni's meanings, not the truth conditions of his utterances.

For the purposes of the present discussion, it is assumed that *some* materially adequate theory of truth for Gianni, together with *some* con-ception of what is canonically provable within it, will have the property that the canonically provable truth conditions of an arbitrary sentence (the "target" equivalences, in some formulations) constitute a translation of that sentence. The considerations derived from Foster, and advanced in Soames's example, do not question this assumption, but ask instead how such a theory may be chosen without adverting to the concept of meaning. The choice of a conception of canonical proof (which includes the form of the axioms) can readily depend upon psychological hypotheses, or "constraints," governing reference and satisfaction, It cannot, however, depend directly upon assumptions about what people intend, by virtue of the linguistic forms they use, to be saying; for if it did, then it would depend upon meaning by another name. In my fanciful illustration, I guessed at Gianni's meaning based upon my beliefs about what he would be likely to be interested in telling me. If getting at theories of truth that are revelatory of meaning goes like that, then the transcendent response does not provide a conception of meaning based on truth. By taking in the contents of speech acts, it swallows meaning whole.

Consider now the immanent response, taken in isolation from the transcendent one. According to LePore and Loewer, the knowledge that supplements knowledge of truth conditions is the knowledge of when utterances match in content, or stand in the samesaying relation.[11] Now, knowledge of when utterances would match in content obviously is required for understanding. But LePore and Loewer's defense of truth-theoretic semantics is not in any evident way different from the proposal that interpretation should proceed by translation into one's own speech. In terms of our example, suppose I come to know that Gianni's 'Firenze è una bella città' matches my 'Florence is a beautiful city' in content. Then I come to know that (3) is false, and that (2) is true. With a theory of truth for my own language, I can then infer (1) with or without a theory of truth for Gianni.

If I am right to suggest that LePore and Loewer's view amounts to the thesis that translation into one's own speech, supplemented with a theory of truth for that speech, is sufficient for understanding, then it appears that the theory of truth can be jettisoned too. For I know routinely all the disquotational facts about meaning in my own speech, and if I add these to my translation I will know about meaning in Gianni's.

Our original question was: can a theory T for L, all of whose semantic concepts are drawn from the theory of reference, have the property that knowledge of T, and knowledge that it is correct for L, confers under-standing of L? The immanent response is that the answer is positive, provided that besides the semantic concepts T contains information about when utterances of L and utterances in the language used in expounding T have the same content. But then the latter information alone confers understanding.[12] The transcendent response is that the answer is negative, but the theory of reference and truth has a role to play in clarifying interpretive practice. That thesis can hardly be false, since meaning is tied to truth conditions in the weak sense that if s means that p, then s is true if and only if p.

On the conception that I am proposing, what replaces (1) is something like (4):

(4) (Gianni knows that) one is expected to know that 'Firenze è una bella città' is true for one (in the possible world w) if and only if Florence is a beautiful city (in w).

To complete the picuture, we have to add that (4) is the strongest thing that one is expected to know about the truth conditions of the particular sentence in question. Thus Gianni knows that one is not in general expected to know about the incompleteness of arithmetic. That is enough for him to know, and for me to discover, that (3) is false.

My response to Foster's considerations has perhaps changed the subject. As originally conceived within Davidson's approach, the problem was to find some information not itself of a linguistic semantic character that, when it embedded a translational theory of truth for a person such as Gianni, would bring understanding of Gianni. What I have offered is the view that one will understand Gianni when one knows what he, Gianni, knows and is expected to know about reference and truth. The general principles and certain theorems of a theory of truth for Gianni will figure in one's knowledge about him. But the theory of truth for Gianni's speech is not something that one starts with, augmenting it with conditions or constraints so as to make it acceptable as a theory of meaning. Rather, truth comes in as something Gianni knows about, and the deliverancess of the theory are of interest only insofar as knowledge of them is part of Gianni's linguistic competence.

What rules out (3), I have suggested, is the fact that Gianni knows that one is not expected to know about the incompleteness of arithmetic. This and similar facts are part of a theory of what Gianni is expected to know about truth and reference, and about the extent to which Gianni actually knows what he is expected to know, and knows that he is expected to know it. I am supposing that a theory of this kind will exhaustively answer any questions about what Gianni means by his words. The theory of Gianni's competence will incorporate a theory of truth. But even an ideally competent Gianni will know only some of the consequences of that theory, and there will be others perhaps that he knows but does not think it right to expect others to know. Statements of truth conditions that go beyond these bounds are irrelevant to understanding, resting as it does on common knowledge, and so irrelevant to meaning as well.[13]

There are plenty of things we know and expect others to know that are not pertinent to language: that two and three make five, that when it rains the streets become wet, and so forth. Gianni's competence about the reference of 'Firenze' or the truth conditions of 'Firenze è bella' doesn't include such information. On the other hand, it arguably does include the information that Florence – the reference of 'Firenze' – is a city, and there is no more language involved in the cityhood of Florence than in the disposition of the streets to become wet after rain. Thus some notion of linguistically relevant knowledge has to be built into our picture of Gianni's competence. However, I don't see this fact as a limitation of the theory. For the attempt is not first to form a conception of linguistic knowledge properly so called, and then within that conception to articulate a proper theory of Gianni's grasp of it. Rather, one formulates a theory of what Gianni knows and expects others to know about truth and reference, and counts as pertinent to language whatever that knowledge comprises.[14] Thus it is not to be assumed that linguistically pertinent knowledge is restricted to the sort recorded in the usual, elementary basis clauses of the theory of truth, or that it may not include knowledge of contingent matters of fact.[15]

3   Semantic Facts

A person can know something without being in full command of the concepts that may be used to characterize what she knows. I know that atoms are very small, but I am not in full command of the concept *atom*. I also know that 'atom' is true of x if and only if x is an atom, and that to say of a thing 'It is an atom' is to say of it that it is an atom, again without being in full command of the concept *atom*.

Considering these and similar examples, I think that we should conclude that knowledge of the disquotational facts about truth, satisfaction, reference, meaning, and saying should not be overrated. Knowing them is knowing something all right, but not very much. If so, then the disquotational facts about meaning are not more robust than the corresponding facts about truth. In fact, as I have argued elsewhere, we can go further. Suppose that clausal complements make a self-referential semantic contribution; i.e., that they denote themselves, or things similar to themselves, viewed not merely as strings of marks, but rather as syntactic structures with an interpretation, they and their parts having all the referential properties that they would have if occurring in isolation. In that case (5) becomes (6):

(5) 'Snow is white' means that snow is white
(6) 'Snow is white' means something similar to 'snow is white', understood as if uttered.

But (6) cannot fail to be true. So (5) is true.[16]

If (5) is not robust, since one can know it without knowing what snow is, or what it is for something to be white, it is not exactly trivial either. As I conceive it, a monolingual speaker of Chinese, who happened to have got a hold of the information that 'snow is white' was an English sentence, would not know (5). That person would know that 'snow is white' means (in English) something similar to itself (the first part of (6)), but would be unable to utter it as a sentence of his own, thus failing the second part. So the Chinese speaker would not know (6). On the other hand, your power and mine to utter 'snow is white' as a sentence understood as it in fact is does not depend on our having knowledge of snow or whiteness. Similarly, I know that 'atoms are very small' means that atoms are very small, despite my comparative ignorance about atoms.[17]

The central part of the argument derived from Foster uses the fact that, as we understand the notion of meaning, tiny adjustments in the complement sentence may turn a truth '*S* means that *p*' into a falsehood '*S* means that *q*'. That is what leads Soames to suggest (Soames, *op. cit.*, 594 (fn. 2)) that "the basic argument can be made to apply to any attempt to found meaning, or knowledge of meaning, on theories of truth with respect to a circumstance ... (provided standard recursive clauses in the truth theory are maintained)." The conclusion seems hard to escape; on the self-referential view of complement clauses, it is to be expected.

I have said that although content is not reducible to truth conditions, it is reducible to the knowledge of what one is expected to know about them. In this sense, the account of content will be based on truth. The application can be illustrated by means of elucidations of the meaning of ordinary words for perceptual things. I want to consider here, however, its application to the logical constants, which seems to me again to reveal problems both with the view that content reduces to reference and with the view that content should be taken as primitive.

When the account of propositions, the contents of sentences, is not based on truth, there is a certain underdetermination of meaning of the logical constants that appears objectionable. Suppose, for example, that negation and conjunction are functions carrying propositions and ordered pairs of propositions respectively into other propositions. In the setting of possible worlds semantics, whatever the independent difficulties with its conception of a proposition, we know exactly what functions these are: negation maps a proposition into its complement, and conjunction maps an ordered pair of propositions into their intersection. Negation and conjunction might be given to us in various ways, but we are clearly entitled to speak of *the* negation of the proposition *p*, or *the* conjunction of *p* and *q*. Since the identities of *p* and *q* are fixed in terms of truth in possible worlds, the identities of negation and conjunction are fixed as well.

However, if propositions are cut loose from truth conditions, and negation is a function from propositions to propositions, then for all the theory says the negation of a proposition can be any proposition whatever that is true when the argument is false, and false when its argument is true. Similar remarks go for conjunction and, mutatis mutandis, for the quantifiers.[18] But shouldn't the nature of negation be exhausted by the condition that it maps truth into falsehood and falsehood into truth? When prepositions are primitive, it isn't. There will be many, equally good, candidates.[19]

The point that I have raised comes out also in a setting where propositions are taken to be structured contents. Soames, for example, takes the sign '¬' of negation as contributing its own truth function, NEG. The negation of a proposition P is the ordered pair $\langle NEG, P \rangle$. The characterization of truth makes $\langle NEG, P \rangle$ false if P is a true proposition, true if P is a false proposition. But the choice of NEG for '¬' was inessential.[20]

On the view that I am taking, you know what the simple sign for negation expresses if you know what one is expected to know about its effects on truth. But that is just (7):

(7)   ¬ S is true if S is false and false if S is true.

(In this case, what you have to know does not actually assign '¬' a reference, but rather treats it syncategorematically.) Thus we have a conception of what the negation of something is, and that it is unique. I would apply the above conception to knowledge of the meanings of the quantifiers as well.

I am applying to semantics a research program that goes forward in syntax and phonology, asking, "What do you know when you know a language, and how do you come to know it?" I have supposed that the central notion that figures in knowledge of meaning is knowledge of reference, in particular knowledge of the truth conditions of sentences. If this is right, then Gianni speaks Italian because he knows a certain theory, which he applies and expects others to apply in speech and understanding, and in his other significant uses of language, and you know English because you know a certain theory of reference which you apply, and expect others to apply.

How is the theory acquired, and in what specific form is it made available to the mature speaker? There is reason to believe that semantic competence exploits domain-specific patterns of learning and cognitive development; in short, a language faculty. Our grasp of the particular modes of correlation of form and meaning typical of human first languages, and the convergence of intuitive judgments among persons of diverse experience (and little or no relevant experience) both support this presumption. Our specialized cognitive faculties need not be restricted to the motor and perceptual, as though everything outside this realm, including thought about the objective world and ourselves and other people as both members of it and observers of it, were an undifferentiated mass of general knowledge. On the contrary, such knowledge, including knowledge of meaning, may be in Chomsky's sense highly modular in character.

In closing, I will briefly consider an objection to the picture that I have been presenting of language learning as an intellectual achievement. The objection is that language learning seen in this way necessarily attributes to the learner a prior grasp of concepts that have to be brought to bear in framing hypotheses about reference, and therefore distorts our relation to content. Again, Soames expresses the objection well: in a semantic theory that ties reference to understanding, and both to knowledge, we seem to invoke an antecedent grasp of propositions, so that language learning is reduced to learning which proposition a sentence stands for. And Soames objects to this picture on the grounds that knowing about propositions is often not distinct from getting ahold of the sentences that in fact express them.

I intend the view that I have outlined of the nature of contents and our often partial knowledge of them explicitly to allow for the possession of a belief in partial ignorance of its content; indeed, the view positively embraces the phenomenon of partial knowledge, and a certain distance between our conceptual grasp and the things we can have beliefs about. There is no assumption that in coming to know that atoms are very small, or that the sentence 'atoms are very small' means that atoms are very small, I had to already know tacitly or unconsciously what the MIT undergraduates explicitly know about atoms. In this respect, the view agrees with Soames that we need not picture all of language learning in terms of the labelling of concepts antecedently available (although many studies of language acquisition do suggest that much of language learning really is like this).

Nevertheless, there is a real clash between the view that Soames and many others take and the one that I am defending. Soames holds that coming to understand the sentences of a language is a matter of "satisfying conventional standards regarding their use."[21] I am saying that coming to satisfy conventional standards regarding the use of sentences depends upon coming to know about reference.

Notes

1   This article was written for an American Philosophical Association Symposium of the same title held in San Francisco, March 1991, with Scott Soames as cosymposiast and Mark Richard commenting; a longer version has appeared in *Iyyun*. It is also a descendant of a paper given under the title "Semantics Past and Future" at a meeting of the Bar-Hillel Colloquium, Jerusalem, Israel, in January 1991, Tanya Reinhart commenting. The comments of Reinhart and of Richard, and Soames's contribution to the symposium, have prompted some revisions in the text; but because of the occasional nature of their drafts I have not cited them explicitly. For other comments on this article and its antecedent I am indebted particularly to Noam Chomsky, Martin Davies, Alexander George, Gabriel Segal, and Robert Stalnaker.

2   Mark Johnston in "The End of the Theory of Meaning," *Mind and Language 3*, 1 (1989): 28–42 proposes what he calls a "minimalist" theory of meaning, which has no substantive conception of the contribution of the meaning of a word to the meaning of a sentence. In the minimalist theory, for example, we can say of the meaning of 'is white' only that it is such that, when combined with the meaning of 'snow,' it yields the meaning of 'snow is white' – that is, that snow is white. The explanatory vacuity of the minimalist theory suggests to Johnston that meaning has been overrated. I think that Johnston's conclusion can be accepted without undermining a conception of semantics that puts at the center, not meaning itself, but rather people's knowledge of and beliefs about truth and reference, knowledge that determines knowledge of meaning.

3   It has been argued, particularly by Brian Loar, that the notion of content needed for psychological explanation is still more refined than the notation of our common language: see Loar, "Social Content and Psychological Content," in R. Grimm and D. Merrill (eds.), *Contents of Thought* (Tucson: University of Arizona Press, 1988): 99–110. Although Loar's thesis does imply that reference in our common language is not adequate for getting at content, it does not imply that reference in a tailor-made psychological language is inadequate. However, I am inclined to believe that our common language already contains the means for getting at what Loar calls

psychological content; if so, then his considerations make no essential difference to the present point of discussion.

4 I have taken the phrase from Max Cresswell, *Structured Meanings* (Cambridge, Mass.: MIT Press, 1985).

5 Similar problems for the structured meaning idea arise from the tacit use of combinatorial semantic rules that are not themselves represented in the meanings assigned; I elaborate on this theme in work in preparation.

6 The features of common knowledge that I allude to here have figured prominently in accounts of language as conventional, articulated prominently in David Lewis, *Convention* (Cambridge, Mass.: Harvard University Press, 1969) and "Languages and Language," in K. Gunderson (ed.), *Minnesota Studies in the Philosophy of Science*, vol. 7 (Minneapolis: University of Minnesota Press, 1975), reprinted in Lewis, *Philosophical Papers*, vol. I (Oxford: Oxford University Press, 1983): 163–188; and in Stephen Schiffer, *Remnants of Meaning* (Cambridge, Mass.: MIT Press, 1987).

7 Foster, "Meaning and Truth Theory," in G. Evans and J. McDowell (eds.), *Truth and Meaning* (Oxford University Press, 1976): 3–32.

8 The example below is taken from Scott Soames, "Semantics and Semantic Competence," in J. Tomberlin (ed.), *Philosophical Perspectives 3: Philosophy of Mind and Action Theory* (Altascadero, California: Ridgeview, 1989): 575–596.

9 "What Davidson Should Have Said," in E. Villanueva (ed.), *Information, Semantics, and Epistemology* (Oxford: Basil Blackwell, 1990): 190–199.

10 I identify the transcendent response with certain suggestions of Donald Davidson, going back to some remarks in Davidson's *Inquiries into Truth and Interpretation* (Oxford: Clarendon Press, 1984). I do not mean to tie the response as I sketch it here to Davidson's own views, however.

11 LePore and Loewer, *op. cit.*, 197. I am abstracting here from the question whether it is utterances or sentence types in their contexts of utterance that are to match in content.

12 The difficulty I am pressing for the immanent response depends crucially on the assumption that disquotational knowledge of meaning is routine, a point I discuss below but do not defend here (see Higginbotham, "Knowledge of Reference," in A. George (ed.), *Reflections on Chomsky* (Oxford: Basil Blackwell, 1989): 153–174 for some discussion). Even if the difficulty is waived, and samesaying is not regarded as a "semantic" relation, the theory of reference for *L* becomes on the immanent response an idle wheel; moreover, questions crowd in about what it is to understand one's *own* language, if the knowledge that, say, 'snow is white' means that snow is white is so substantial.

13 The last three paragraphs were prompted by critical discussion by Scott Soames.

14 A point that has emerged with particular clarity in some recent studies is that material knowledge enters into the acceptability conditions for a variety of syntactic types, including the formation of middle verbs (e.g., the word 'read' in 'the books read quickly') and the absolute 'with' (as in: 'With John in the

hospital, we'll have to go without our best player'), the latter being discussed especially in Gregory Stump, *The Semantic Variability of Absolute Constructions* (Dordrecht, Holland: D. Reidel, 1985).

15   For some further discussion, see Higginbotham, "Elucidations of Meaning," *Linguistics and Philosophy* 12, 3 (1989): 465–517; p. 470.

16   This point is elaborated in my "Knowledge of Reference." The formula "understood as if uttered" is taken from Tyler Burge, "Self-Reference and Translation," in F. Guenthner and M. Geunthner-Reutter (eds.), *Meaning and Translation* (New York: New York University Press, 1978): 137–153.

17   I am indebted here to comments by Mark Richard.

18   I am indebted here to comments by Tanya Reinhart.

19   The point arises in particular if propositions are added as a primitive type to intensional logic. See Richmond Thomason, "A Model Theory for Propositional Attitudes," *Linguistics and Philosophy* 4, 1: 47–70; 50 *passim*.

20   For example, we could have taken '$\urcorner$' to express $\langle\langle$ NEG*, NEG $+\rangle$, NEG $\rangle$ where $(\text{NEG} + (f))(x) = \text{NEG}(f(x))$ and $(\text{NEG} * (F))(x) = \text{NEG}(F(f(x)))$. With a certain latitude in the form of a definition of truth, still more outlandish interpretations of '$\urcorner$' are possible.

21   Soames, *op. cit.*, 589.

12

From "Indexicals and Demonstratives"

John Perry

1 Introduction

When you use the word "I" it designates you; when I use the same word, it designates me. If you use "you" talking to me, it designates me; when I use it talking to you, it designates you. "I" and "you" are *indexicals*. The designation of an indexical *shifts* from speaker to speaker, time to time, place to place. Different utterances of the same indexical designate different things, because what is designated depends not only on the meaning associated with the expression, but also on facts about the utterance. An utterance of "I" designates the person who utters it; an utterance of "you" designates the person to whom it is addressed, an utterance of "here" designates the place at which the utterance is made, and so forth. Because indexicals shift their designation in this way, sentences containing indexicals can be used to say different things on different occasions. Suppose you say to me, "You are wrong and I am right about reference," and I reply with the same sentence. We have used the same sentence, with the same meaning, but said quite different and incompatible things.

In addition to "I" and "you", the standard list of indexicals includes the personal pronouns "my", "he", "his", "she", "it", the demonstrative pronouns "that" and "this", the adverbs "here", "now", "today", "yesterday", and "tomorrow" and the adjectives "actual" and "present". This list is from David Kaplan (1989a), whose work on the "logic of demonstratives" is responsible for much of the increased attention given to indexicals by philosophers of language in recent years. The words and aspects of words that indicate tense are also indexicals. And many other words, like "local", seem to have an indexical element.

Philosophers have found indexicals interesting for at least two reasons. First, such words as "I", "now", and "this" play crucial roles in arguments and paradoxes about such philosophically rich subjects as the self, the nature of time, and the nature of perception. Second, although the meanings of these words seem relatively straightforward, it has not been so obvious how to incorporate these meanings into semantical theory. I will focus on the second issue in this essay and, even with respect to that issue, will discuss only a few of the many topics that deserve attention. Among other things, I won't consider tense, or plurals,[1] or the relation of indexicality to anaphora,[2] or Castañeda's concept of quasi-indication.[3] I'll focus on the words Kaplan listed, and among those on singular terms.

In section 2 I fix some concepts and terms. In section 3 I develop a treatment of indexicals that I call the "Reflexive-referential theory". It is based on an account by Arthur Burks, and also incorporates ideas from Reichenbach, Kaplan, and a number of other authors.

2   Meaning, Content and Propositions

Meaning, as I shall use the term, is a property of expressions – that is, of *types* rather than tokens or utterances. Meaning is what is fixed by the conventions for the use of expressions that we learn when we learn a language. In contrast, *content* is a property of individual utterances. Content is tied to truth-conditions. The content of a statement – a specific use of a declarative sentence – is a proposition that embodies its truth-conditions. The contents of utterances of sub-sentential expressions – terms and predicates – is the contribution they make to truth-conditions; it's the things that utterances of names designate, and the conditions expressed by utterances of predicates and definite descriptions.

Any part of speech can have an indexical element, but I'll focus on the role of such expressions as "I", "you" and "that man" in simple statements. This will allow us to compare indexicals with the categories of expression most studied in the philosophy of language: proper names and definite descriptions – phrases of the form *the so-and-so*.

First I need to make some distinctions and develop some concepts about propositions. I will not need to adopt a specific and detailed ontology of propositions and their components for the purposes of this chapter. There are two main approaches to propositions in the literature today, the classic conception of a proposition as a set of possible worlds, and a number of conceptions of structured propositions....I'll think of propositions structurally, but borrow the possible-worlds conception when convenient to get clear about things. The distinctions I need can be made in any number of more detailed approaches.

Consider:

(1) Jim was born in Lincoln

(1) is a statement of mine, referring to my son Jim Perry and to Lincoln, Nebraska. On the now-standard view of proper names (which I'll discuss below), (1) expresses a *singular* proposition, a proposition that is about Jim himself and Lincoln itself, rather than any descriptions or attributes of them. In some of the possible worlds in which this proposition is true Jim will not be named "Jim"; in some he will look different than he in fact does, act differently than he in fact does, have a different job than he in fact has, and so forth. And in some of the worlds Lincoln may be named "Davis" or "McClellan" and may not be the capital of Nebraska. As long as Jim was born in Lincoln in a given world then the proposition is true in that world, whatever he is like and whatever he is called in that world, and whatever Lincoln is like and whatever it is called.

On the possible-worlds conception of propositions, this proposition just *is* the set of worlds in which Jim was born in Lincoln. On a structural conception of propositions, one could think of the proposition expressed by (1) as an ordered pair of a sequence of objects and a condition:

$\langle\langle$Jim Perry, Lincoln$\rangle, x$ was born in $y\rangle$

Such propositions are true if the sequences of objects in the first member of the pair meets the condition that is the second member. It is natural to say that Jim himself is a constituent of the proposition, on the structural conception. Although on this conception we don't identify the proposition with a set of worlds, it is still natural to talk about the worlds in which it is true.

In fact, Jim is the manager of Kinko's,[4] and Lincoln is the capital of Nebraska. So consider,

(2) The manager of Kinko's was born in the capital of Nebraska.

On the standard account of definite descriptions, (2) expresses a *general* proposition, a proposition that is not specifically about Jim and Lincoln, but about being the manager of Kinko's, and being the capital of Nebraska. This proposition is true in worlds in which someone – it doesn't have to be Jim – is the manager of Kinko's, and some city – it doesn't have to be Lincoln – is the capital of Nebraska, and the someone was born in the city. Consider the possible world in which Omaha is the capital of

Nebraska, and Marlon Brando or Henry Fonda or Saul Kripke or some other native Omahan[5] manages the Kinko's in Lincoln. In these worlds (2) would be true, wherever my son might be born.

Let a *mode of presentation* be a condition that has uniqueness built into it, so that at most one thing can meet it, such as *x is the manager of Kinko's* or *x is the capital of Nebraska*. We can think of the proposition expressed by (2) as an ordered pair of a sequence of modes of presentation and a condition:

$\langle\langle x$ is the manager of Kinko's, y is the capital of Nebraska$\rangle$, x was born in $y\rangle$

The distinction between singular and general propositions is helpful, but a bit too simple. Consider,

(3)   Jim was born in the capital of Nebraska.

This would usually be called a singular proposition; being singular is sort of a dominant characteristic, so that if at least one argument role of a condition is filled by an object, the result is singular even if the other argument roles are filled by modes of presentation. I will speak this way, but we have to keep in mind that the basic concept is that of an argument role being filled either by an object or by a mode of presentation of an object.

Now consider,

(4)   *x was born in Lincoln.*
(5)   *x was born in the capital of Nebraska.*

Conditions (4) and (5) express conditions rather than propositions. But we need to draw a distinction between them: (4) is a singular condition, because it incorporates the city, Lincoln, as a constituent, while (5) is a general condition, with the mode of presentation *y is the capital of Nebraska* as a constituent.

For our final point, look closely at (2). It expresses a general proposition – both argument roles of the condition *x was born in y* are filled by modes of presentation. But these modes of presentation themselves are singular, involving Kinko's and Nebraska as constituents respectively. I'll say that a proposition or condition is *purely qualitative* if, as one goes down through the hierarchy of conditions involved in it, one never encounters an object, only more conditions. I'll call it *lumpy* if one encounters an object. The proposition expressed by (2), though general, is lumpy.

Now compare

(1)   Jim was born in Lincoln.
(6)   The manager of Kinko's was born in Lincoln.

I use "designate" as a general word for the relations between singular terms and the objects they stand for. Thus the subject terms of both (1) and (6) *designate* the same person, Jim Perry. Both (1) and (6) assert the same thing of the same person, and in that sense (1) and (6) have the same truth conditions.

In spite of this, (1) and (6) are quite different, because the singular terms in them work quite differently. I'll express this difference by saying "Jim", the name in (1), *names* and *refers* to Jim Perry, but neither *denotes* nor *describes* him. "The manager of Kinko's" *denotes* and *describes* him, but neither *names* him nor *refers* to him. Let me explain these terms.[6]

Denoting versus naming

Definite descriptions and names have quite different sorts of meaning. Language associates definite descriptions with modes of presentation. Definite descriptions are only indirectly associated with the objects they designate, as the objects that meet the mode of presentation associated by meaning. So, in virtue of its meaning, "The manager of Kinko's" is associated with a certain mode of presentation. It designates Jim Perry not simply in virtue of its meaning, but in virtue of its meaning and his job.

With names it is quite different. The convention I invoke when I use "Jim" to refer to my oldest son, is not a convention that associates the name with a condition which, as it happens, he fulfills. It's just a convention that says that "Jim" is his name – a convention established when he was born and that name was used on the birth certificate.[7]

There are then two quite different forms in answer to the question "Why does term *t* designate object *a*?" may take:

(i)   The meaning of *t* associates it with a certain mode of presentation
      C, and
(ii)   *a* is the object that satisfies *C*

or,

The meaning of *t* associates it directly with *a*.

I use the terms *denoting* for the form of designation corresponding to the first, two-part, answer, and the term *naming* for the form of designation corresponding to the second, one-part, answer.

Describing versus referring

Our second distinction has to do with the contribution terms make to what I shall call "the official content" of a statement. The official content of a statement is what we would take the speaker as having asserted or said, or, as it is sometimes put, "what is said" by the statement.

On standard accounts, at least, the official contents of (1) and (6) are different. The proposition expressed by (1) is a singular proposition about Jim, while that expressed by (6) is a general proposition about being the manager of Kinko's. As we saw above, these are different propositions, true in different possible worlds.

I use "refers" and "describes" to mark this distinction. These terms pertain to the contribution a term makes to the official content of statements of which it is a part. Names *refer*; that is, they contribute to official content the individual they designate. Definite descriptions *describe*; that is, they contribute to official content the mode of presentation their meaning associates with them.[8]

If we ignore indexicals, confining our attention to names and definite descriptions, our two distinctions line up, and may seem to amount to the same thing.[9] Definite descriptions denote and describe, names name and refer. But in the case of indexicals the distinction is needed. For, as we shall see, indexicals are like definite descriptions in that they denote, but like names in that they refer.

3   The Reflexive-Referential Theory

3.1   Burks's framework

In his pioneering work, Arthur Burks (1949) distinguishes the following aspects of an utterance containing indexicals:

(i)   The sign itself, which is a token that occurs at a spatio-temporal location and which belongs to a certain linguistic type.

(ii)   The existential relations of the token to other objects.

(iii)   The meaning associated with the type.

(iv) The indexical meaning of the token, which, in the case of tokens involving indexicals, goes beyond the type meaning.[10]
(v) The information conveyed by the sign.

Suppose, for example, Burks tells me, pointing to a house on Monroe Street in Ann Arbor: "I live in that house." (i) The sign itself is the token or burst of sound that Burks utters; it is a token of an English sentence of a certain type, namely, "I live in that house", and it occurs at a certain spatio-temporal location. (ii) This token has "existential relations" to other objects. That is, *there is* a person who uttered it (Burks), *there is* a house at which that person was pointing at the time of utterance, and so forth. (iii) English associates a meaning with the type, the same for every token of it. Any token of "I live in that house" will be true if the speaker of that token lives in the house he or she points to at the time they produce the token. This is what all tokens of the type have in common. (iv) Each token also has an *indexical meaning*, which results from the combination of the type-meaning and the particular token. Call the token Burks produced t. Imagine David Kaplan pointing to a house in Pacific Palasaides at some other time and producing a token t'. Tokens t and t' have the same type-meaning, but different indexical meanings. Token t will be true if the house Burks points to is the one he lives in, while t' will be true if the house Kaplan points at is the one he lives in.

Aspect (v) is the information conveyed by the sign. Let's add a third token to our example. Let t'' be my token of "You live in that house", said to Burks, pointing to the house on Monroe Street. My token doesn't have the same symbolic meaning or the same indexical meaning as t, Burks's token of "I live in that house". But there is something important that my token and Burks's have in common. Each of them will be true if a certain person, Burks, lives in a certain house, the one on Monroe Street. Once we factor in the contextual or "existential" facts that are relevant to each token, they have the same truth-conditions. Their truth places the same conditions on the same objects. Burks calls this "conveying the same information".

The reflexive-referential theory that I advocate builds on Burks's basic framework. . . .

3.2 *Signs, tokens and utterances*

For Burks, the sign itself is simply the token. But the term "token" is used in two ways in the literature. Sometimes it is used for the *act* of speaking, writing, or otherwise using language. At other times, it is used for an object that is produced by, or at least used in, such an act. Reichenbach, for example, says that tokens are acts of speaking, but then talks about the position of a token on a page.

I use "utterance" for the first sense. Utterances are intentional acts. The term "utterance" often connotes spoken language, but as I use it an utterance may involve speech, writing, typing, gestures, or any other sort of linguistic activity.

I use "token" in the second sense, in the way Reichenbach used it when he said that a certain token was to be found on a certain page of a certain copy of a book. Tokens, in this sense, are traces left by utterances. They can be perceived when the utterances cannot, and can be used as evidence for them. Modern technology allows for their reproduction. The paradigm tokens are the ink marks produced in writing or typing. When we read, tokens are epistemically basic, and the utterances that produced them hardly thought of. But the utterances are semantically basic; it is from the intentional acts of speakers and writers that the content derives.

. . .

3.3   Context

What Burks calls the "existential relations" of a token or utterance is now usually referred to as its "context". The "context-dependence" of indexicals is often taken as their defining feature: what an indexical designates *shifts* from context to context. But there are many kinds of shiftiness, with corresponding conceptions of context. Until we clarify what we mean by "context", this defining feature remains unclear.

The key distinction is between pre-semantic and semantic uses of context. Sometimes we use context to figure out with which meaning a word is being used, or which of several words that look or sound alike is being used, or even which language is being spoken. These are *pre-semantic* uses of context. In the case of indexicals, however, context is used *semantically*. It remains relevant after the language, words, and meaning are all known; the meaning directs us to certain aspects of context.

Consider these utterances:

(7)   Ich! (said by several teenagers at camp in response to the question, "Who would like some sauerkraut?").
(8)   I forgot how good beer tastes.
(9)   I saw her duck under the table.[11]

With (7), knowing that the utterance occurred in Frankfurt rather than San Francisco might help us determine that it was German teenagers expressing enthusiasm and not American teenagers expressing disgust.

With (8), knowing whether our speaker has just arrived from Germany or just arrived from Saudi Arabia might help us to decide what the syntactic structure of the sentence is, and whether "good" was being used as an adjective or an adverb.

With (9), knowing a little about the situation that this utterance is describing will help us to decide whether the person in question had lost her pet or was seeking security in an earthquake, and whether "duck" is a noun or a verb.

In each of these cases, the context, the environment of the utterance, the larger situation in which it occurs, helps us to determine what is said. But these cases differ from indexicals. In these cases it is a sort of accident, external to the utterance, that context is needed. We need the context to identify which name, syntactic structure, or meaning is used because the very same shapes and sounds happen to be shared by other words, structures, or meanings. In the case of indexicals we still need context *after* we determine which words, syntactic structures, and meanings are being used. The meanings *exploit* the context to perform their function. The meaning of the indexical "directs us" to certain features of the context, in order to fix the designation.

It seems, then, that a defining feature of indexicals is that the meanings of these words fix the designation of specific utterances of them in terms of facts about those specific utterances. The facts that the meaning of a particular indexical deems relevant are the contextual facts for particular uses of it. . . .

3.3.1 *Types of indexical contexts*
With respect to contexts for indexicals I need to emphasize two distinctions, . . .

- Does designation depend on narrow or wide context?
- Is designation "automatic" given meaning and public contextual facts, or does it depend in part on the intentions of the speaker?

. . .

3.3.2 *Narrow and wide context*
The narrow context consists of the constitutive facts about the utterance, which I will take to be the agent, time, and position. These roles are filled

with every utterance. The clearest case of an indexical that relies only on the narrow context is "I", whose designation depends on the agent and nothing else.

The wider context consists of those facts, plus anything else that might be relevant, according to the workings of a particular indexical.

The sorts of factors on which an indexical can be made to depend seem, in principle, limitless. For example,

It is yea big.

means that it is as big as the space between the outstretched hands of the speaker, so this space is a contextual factor in the required sense for the indexical "yea".

3.3.3 *Automatic versus intentional indexicals*

When Rip Van Winkle says, "I fell asleep yesterday," he intended to designate (let us suppose) July 3, 1766. He in fact designated July 2, 1786, for he awoke 20 years to the day after he fell asleep. An utterance of "yesterday" designates the day before the utterance occurs, no matter what the speaker intends. Given the meaning and context, the designation is automatic. No further intention than that of using the words with their ordinary meaning is relevant.

The designation of an utterance of "that man", however, is not automatic. The speaker's intention is relevant. There may be several men standing across the street when I say, "That man stole my wallet." Which of them I refer to depends on my intention.

However, we need to be careful here. Suppose there are two men across the street, Harold, dressed in brown, and Fred, in blue. I think that Harold stole my wallet and I also think wrongly that the man dressed in blue is Harold. I intend to designate Harold *by* designating the man in blue. So I point towards the man in blue as I say "that man". In this case I designate the man in blue – even if my pointing is a bit off-target. My intention to point to the man in blue is relevant to the issue of whom I designate and what I say, but my intention to refer to Harold is not. In this case, I say something I don't intend to say: that Fred, the man in blue, stole my wallet; and fail to say what I intended to, that Harold did. So it is not just any referential intention that is relevant to demonstratives, but only the more basic ones, which I will call *directing intentions*, following Kaplan (1989b).

In a case like this I will typically perceive the man I refer to, and may often point to or otherwise demonstrate that person. But neither perceiving nor pointing seems necessary to referring with a demonstrative.

...

3.4 Meaning

To repeat: as I use the terms, *meaning* is what the rules of language associate with simple and complex expressions; *content* is an attribute of individual utterances. The simple theory into which I am trying to incorporate indexicals focuses on the contents of utterances of four kinds. The content of a statement is a proposition, incorporating the conditions of truth of the statement. The content of an utterance of a predicate (for our purposes, a declarative sentence with some of its terms replaced by variables) is a condition on objects. The content of an utterance of a definite description will be a mode of presentation. The content of the utterance of a name will be an individual. The contents of utterances of terms combine with the contents of utterances of predicates to yield propositions.

The contents of utterances derive from the meaning which language associates with expressions. The simplest way for this to happen is equisignificance: the meaning of an expression assigns the same content to each and every utterance of the expression.

But, as I explained in section 3.3, indexicals don't work this way. The meaning directs us to certain aspects of the context of the utterance, which are needed to determine the content. The object designated by an indexical will be the object that bears some more or less complicated relation to the utterance. Instead of the usual twofold distinction – *Sinn* and *Bedeutung*, meaning and denotation, intension and extension – we have a threefold one:

The meaning provides us with a binary condition on objects and utterances, the condition of designation.
The utterance itself fills the utterance parameter of this condition, yielding a unary condition on objects, or a mode of presentation.
The object that meets this condition is the object designated by the indexical, or the *designatum*.

The *reflexivity* apparent in the second level has long been one of the major themes in the study of indexicals. Reichenbach put forward a *token-reflexive* theory in his *Introduction to Symbolic Logic* (1947).

Reichenbach claimed that token-reflexive words could be defined in terms of the token-reflexive phrase "this token", and in particular, as he put it, 'The word "I" ... means the same as "the person who utters this token"' (p. 284).

If we take Reichenbach's claim as a literal claim of synonymy between "I" and "the person who utters this token", it is wrong. The two terms may be assigned the same condition, but "I" refers, whereas "the person who utters this token" describes. But Reichenbach was clearly on to something. There is an intimate connection between the meanings of "I" and "the person who utters this token", even if it falls short of synonymy. The second phrase does not *have* the meaning of "I", but it *gives* part of the meaning of "I". It supplies the condition of designation that English associates with "I". We can put this in a rule that brings out the reflexivity:

If *u* is an utterance of "I", the condition of designation for *u* is *being the speaker of u*.

Here we see that the condition of designation assigned to an utterance *u* has that very utterance as a constituent, hence it is reflexive. (I discussed the reasons for using "utterance" rather than "token" above, in section 3.2.)

This rule does two things. First, it assigns a binary condition to the type, "I". The condition is that *x is the speaker of u*. This condition has a parameter for the object designated and one for utterances. Second, the rule assigns a unary condition, on objects, to each utterance of "I", by specifying that the utterance parameter is to be filled with that very utterance. To state this sort of rule in English, we would naturally make use of a reflexive pronoun:

The designation of every utterance of "I" is the speaker of the utterance *itself*.

Here are the conditions of designation for some familiar indexicals, in line with the discussion in section 3.3.

I: *u* designates x iff x is the speaker of u
you: *u* designates y iff $\exists x(x$ is the speaker of u & x addresses y with $u)$
now: *u* designates t iff $\exists x(x$ is the speaker of u & x directs u at t during part of $t)$
that: *u* designates y iff $\exists x(x$ is the speaker of u & x directs u towards $y)$

In considering the meanings of sentences, it is helpful to think of propositions as 0-ary conditions. English assigns 0-ary conditions, propositions, to indexical-free sentences, but assigns unary conditions on utterances to sentences with indexicals in them.

So our conditions of designation give rise to *conditions of truth* that are also reflexive. Meaning does not associate a proposition or 0-ary condition with a sentence containing an indexical, but a unary condition on utterances:

An utterance u of the form $\phi(\alpha)$, where u' is the subutterance of an indexical α, is true iff $\exists y(u'$ designates y & $\phi(y))$.

So, for example,

An utterance u of "You were born in Los Angeles", where u' is the subutterance of "you", is true iff $\exists y(u'$ designates y & y was born in Los Angeles);

that is, iff

$\exists y \, \exists x(x$ is the speaker of u' & x addresses y with u & y was born in Los Angeles).

On David Kaplan's approach, the meanings of expressions in languages with indexicals are regarded as characters. Characters are functions from contexts to contents. So the meaning of "I" is a function, whose value is a for contexts in which a is the speaker and the meaning of "I am sitting" is a function whose value is the singular proposition that a is sitting for such contexts. This theory neatly captures what is special about *context* in the case of indexicality; that it plays a semantic role, rather than merely a pre-semantic one. I don't think Kaplan's view does as well with what is special about *content* in the case of indexicals, however. Kaplan provides only one level of content – official content – where I agree with Burks that more than one level of content is needed in the case of indexical utterances. In the next two sections I will defend Burks's perspective.

3.5 Content$_M$

Reichenbach analyzed Luther's utterance, "Here I stand," in terms of the relation speaks(x, θ, z)

where x is a person, θ is a token and z is a place. In

stands[(the x)($\exists z$(speaks (x, θ, z), (the z)$\exists x$(speaks(x, θ, z)]

θ is Reichenbach's term for Luther's utterance; his analysis amounts to:

(12)   The speaker of θ stands in the place where θ is made.[12]

In our scheme, we have here a general proposition about two modes of presentation, *being the speaker of* θ and *being the place of* θ. Each of these modes is a singular condition, with θ as a constituent.

This proposition fits pretty well Burks's description of his fourth aspect, as what results from combining the meaning with the token or utterance. On the reflexive-referential account, the meaning of a sentence like Luther's is a condition on utterances, and Reichenbach's analysis fills the parameter of that condition with the utterance itself. It seems that Reichenbach's proposition, or something like it, deserves a central place in our account.

However, (12) is clearly not what Luther said. He didn't say anything about his own utterance, and he referred to himself with "I", rather than describing himself. (12) is not a good candidate for the official content of Luther's remark. Where, then, does it fit in?

On Kaplan's approach, the level of analysis represented by (12) and by Burks's fourth aspect is bypassed (1989a, 1989b). The meaning, or *character*, of an indexical is, on Kaplan's theory, a function from context to official content, to what is said. The approach Barwise and I took in *Situations and Attitudes* (1983) was similar, although we did compensate somewhat with what we called "inverse interpretation". Stalnaker complained that something was missing from such approaches (1981), and I have come to think that he and Burks were correct.[13] In fact, we need a variety of contents.

3.5.1   *Varieties of truth-conditions*
A problem that underlies the simple picture of meaning and content is now going to come to the surface. The problem is that the concept of "truth-conditions of an utterance" is a *relative concept*, although it is often treated as if it were absolute. Instead of thinking in terms of *the* truth-conditions of an utterance, we should think of the truth conditions

of an utterance *given* various facts about it. And when we do this we are led to see that talking about *the* content of an utterance is an over-simplification.

. . .

As I mentioned above, I use three different kinds of content in the account of indexicals. These correspond to three kinds of facts one might take as fixed in assessing truth-conditions:

> The content$_M$ of an utterance corresponds to the truth-conditions of the utterance given the facts that fix the language of the utterance, the words involved, their syntax and their *meaning*.[14]
>
> The content$_C$ of an utterance corresponds to the truth-conditions given all of these factors, plus the facts about the *context* of the utterance that are needed to fix the designation of indexicals.
>
> The content$_D$ of an utterance corresponds to the truth-conditions given all of these factors, plus the additional facts that are needed to fix the *designation* of the terms that remain (definite descriptions in particular, but also possessives, etc.).

We shall see below that we need all three kinds of content to adequately describe the epistemology of indexicals and other terms.

3.5.2 *Content$_M$ as cognitively relevant content*
As we saw in section 3.4, the meaning of an indexical or sentence containing indexicals provides a condition on utterances. We move from this condition to the content$_M$ of an utterance of that type by filling the parameter of that condition with the utterance itself. In the case of indexical terms, we go from binary conditions on objects and utterances to 1-ary conditions on objects. In the case of sentences containing indexicals, we go from 1-ary conditions on utterances to 0-ary conditions, propositions. These are propositions *about* utterances.

Consider,

(13) You were born in the capital of Nebraska.

The content$_M$ of (13) is a proposition about (13) itself:

$\exists x \, \exists y (x$ is the addressee of (13) & y is the capital of Nebraska & x was born in y).

As we noted, this proposition certainly does not seem to be the official content of (13), what the speaker said when he uttered (13) – a point I will emphasize in the next section.

Nevertheless, content$_M$ is very important in understanding the connection between meaning and cognition, how we use language to express our beliefs, and influence the beliefs of others. It is *cognitively relevant* content.

Imagine that I am standing next to W. V. Quine at a party. Consider the difference between my saying "I would like to shake your hand" and "John Perry would like to shake your hand." In response to the first, we would expect Quine to extend his hand; in response to the second, he might well ask, "Well, where is he?" (See Castañeda (1966), Perry (1979), Stalnaker (1981), and Perry (1993).)

If we ask what I hoped to accomplish by saying, "I'd like to shake your hand," we might just say that I wanted to make him aware that I wanted to shake his hand, so I said that I wanted to. This would be accurate, but incomplete. It leaves out many of my subgoals and my plans for achieving them. I spoke the sentence, rather than including it in a letter or email, because I realized that he was standing where he could hear me. I said it in English because I thought that he understood English. I wanted him to be aware of that, in order to get him to turn and offer his hand for me to shake. In order to get that effect, I wanted to produce a certain kind of thought in him. I wanted him to think that the person in front of him wanted to shake his hand. My plan might be summarized as follows:

Goal: To get Quine to turn towards me and offer his hand for me to shake.

Given: Quine knows English; he can hear me if I speak; he can see me and will recognize that the person he sees is the speaker of the utterance he hears; he knows how to shake hands with a person in front of him; he is goodnatured and will try to shake the hand of someone next to him if he knows that this person would like him to.

Plan: (i)   Direct an utterance **u** of "I'd like to shake your hand" at Quine.

         (ii) Quine will hear **u** and grasp its content$_M$, thinking, "That utterance is spoken by someone who wants to shake the hand of the person he or she is addressing."

         (iii) Quine will think, "That person I see in front of me is the speaker of that utterance."

> (iv) Quine will think, "I am the person the person I see in front of me is addressing."
>
> (v) Quine will think, "That person I see in front of me wants to shake my hand."
>
> (vi) Quine will extend his hand.

Now the content$_M$ of my utterance is the key to this plan. The content$_C$ of my utterance is simply the singular proposition that John Perry wants to shake W. V. Quine's hand. This is the same as the content$_C$ of "John Perry wants to shake your hand".[15] But there would be no reason to expect this utterance to have the desired effect, given my assumptions. The difference between them comes out at the level of content$_M$.

3.6 Official content

3.6.1 Content$_C$ as official content

Content$_M$ is a useful tool for understanding the motivation and impact of utterances. But it is not our ordinary concept of content. It is not what I have called official content, the content that corresponds to what the speaker says. There are two main arguments for this; the reader may be convinced by and familiar with the arguments, but I want to highlight them to help us reflect on just what they show.

The first and simplest I'll call the "samesaying argument". Consider my utterance, directed at my son Jim:

(14) You were born in Lincoln.

The content$_M$ of (14) is a proposition about (14). But we would ordinarily count me as having said the same thing to him as he said to me with his utterance:

(15) I was born in Lincoln.

And the same thing I say to a third party with my utterance

(1) Jim was born in Lincoln.

But these two utterances have quite different contents$_M$ than (14). The content$_M$ of (15) is a proposition about (15) itself, and the content$_M$ of (1) is just a singular proposition about Jim (since names name, their designation is fixed by their meaning). It seems, then, that it is the individual designated by the subutterance of "you", and not the condition of being the addressee of that subutterance, that makes it into the official content of (14).

The second argument I call the "counterfactual circumstances argument". To understand it, one needs to keep clearly in mind the difference between the conditions under which an utterance is true, and conditions under which *what is said by the utterance* (or perhaps better, *what the speaker says*, in virtue of making the utterance) is true. We can separate these, by considering counterfactual circumstances in which the utterance is false, but what is said by the utterance is true (Kaplan, 1989a).

Now suppose, contrary to fact, that when I uttered (14) I was mistaken, and was talking to my son Joe rather than Jim. In those circumstances, my utterance would have been false, since Joe was born in California. And what I would have said in those circumstances, that Joe was born in Lincoln, is false. But what I *actually* said, since I *actually* was talking to Jim, was that he was born in Lincoln. And that proposition, that Jim was born in Lincoln, would have been true, even if, when I uttered (14), I was talking to Joe.

The upshot of these arguments is that the official content of (14) is a singular proposition about Jim. This is the same proposition that Jim expressed with (15), and that I expressed with (1). And it is a proposition that would still be true even if I were talking to Joe rather than Jim, although of course then I would not have expressed this proposition, but a quite different and false one about Joe.

Our other two kinds of content, content$_C$ and content$_D$, both assign this proposition to (14), (15), and (1). But these differ with respect to

(6)   The manager of Kinko's was born in Lincoln.

Content$_C$, recall, corresponds to truth-conditions with the contextual facts fixed. The content$_C$ of (6) is not a singular proposition about Jim. The first argument-role of *x was born in y* gets filled with a mode of presentation of Jim, not Jim himself.

Content$_D$ corresponds to truth-conditions with *all* the facts that determine designation of terms fixed, including, in this case, the fact that Jim is the manager of Kinko's. So the content$_D$ of (6) is our singular proposition about Jim.

Content$_D$ corresponds to Burks's concept of "information conveyed". On this concept (14), (1), and (6) all convey the same information, "for they both refer to the same object and predicate the same property of it".

Which corresponds to official content, content$_C$ or content$_D$? It depends on whether we think of definite descriptions as referring or describing. If they refer, then they contribute the objects they designate to official content, and the right answer is that content$_D$ is official content. If they describe, then content$_C$ is the right answer. For the purposes of this chapter, I have accepted the traditional account of definite descriptions as describing.[16]

With this understanding of definite descriptions, it seems that content$_C$ corresponds to official content. When we compare what people say, and consider the counterfactual circumstances in which what they say is true, we fix the meaning and context, but let other facts vary, even the ones that fix the designation of definite descriptions. Consider,

(16)   You were born in the capital of Nebraska

said to Jim. When we think of the possible worlds in which this is true, what do we require of them? Worlds in which Jim was born in Iowa, but "You were born in the capital of Nebraska" means that $2 + 2 = 4$ don't get in. We fix the meaning, before we consider the world. Worlds in which Jim was born in Iowa, but I am talking to Sue, who was born in the capital of Nebraska, don't get in. We fix the contextual facts, and so the designation of indexicals, before we consider the worlds. But worlds in which Jim was born in Omaha, and Omaha is the capital of Nebraska, do get in. We consider the worlds, before we fix the facts that determine the designation of definite descriptions.

3.6.2   Referentialism

In maintaining that content$_C$ is official content, I agree with a movement in the philosophy of language I call "referentialism". The referentialist thinks that names and indexicals refer, and statements containing them express singular propositions. This set of views constitutes a movement because it had to overthrow an opposing orthodoxy, which dated back to Frege and Russell.

Frege was troubled by singular propositions.[17] How can a proposition have an object in it? Won't there always be different ways of thinking about the object? So won't a belief or desire or hope about an object always involve some specific way of thinking about it? Shouldn't the propositions we are worried about be ones that incorporate those ways of thinking – shouldn't propositions always have modes of presentation, not objects, as constituents?

This line of thinking led Frege and Russell away from singular propositions; Frege didn't have them at all, and Russell made less and less use of them as time went on. Both concluded that names were something like hidden definite descriptions; in our terminology, ordinary names denote and describe rather than name and refer.[18] And this became the standard view for the first two-thirds of the century, with some dissenters, like Burks and Ruth Marcus (Marcus, 1961, pp. 309–10). When Donnellan and Kripke attacked description-theories of names and argued that names referred and statements containing them expressed singular propositions, the feeling was that something like a conceptual revolution was occurring. And Kaplan's "direct reference" theory of indexicals seemed to turn the revolutionary doctrine into unassailable common sense. . . .

It seems to me that the referentialist movement was basically correct. Names and indexicals refer; they do not describe. Singular propositions may be sort of fishy, but they play a central role in the way that we classify content for the purpose of describing minds and utterances. Our concept of what is said is, as such things go, fairly robust.

Still, it is not entirely clear how far-reaching the philosophical consequences of this revolution are. There are three attitudes towards the referentialist treatment of "what is said" or official content:

The skeptic.   Something is wrong with official content, for the reasons sketched above. The whole idea was really refuted by Frege, with his puzzles about identity. Consider the two cases we looked at in section 3.5. One can simply not give a coherent account of these cases, if one sticks to content$_C$ or content$_D$. So the true contents must be something else.

The true believer.   Referentialist arguments show what the true content of a statement is. We just have to live with any epistemological difficulties it raises. The proposition expressed by an utterance is its "semantic value", that which a competent speaker and hearer must grasp, and all the information that is semantically conveyed by the utterance is to be found in, or implied or implicated by, this proposition.

The moderate.   Official content gets at an aspect of statements that is important for describing utterances, one that has shaped the concepts of "folk psychology" – but no more than that. There is no reason to postulate that an utterance has a unique "semantic content" that encapsulates all of the information it semantically conveys.

The third, reasonable-sounding view is, of course, my own. I call it "critical referentialism" – a term so ugly only moderates could like it. The critical referentialist believes that one commits "the fallacy of misplaced information" (Barwise and Perry, 1983) when one expects that all of the content a meaningful utterance carries can be found at the level of official content. Critical referentialism is simply referentialism without the fallacy. Free of the fallacy, the referentialist can employ other aspects of content, such as content$_M$, to explain the motivations and impact of language on semantically competent speakers and listeners, without having to elevate it to official content.

According to critical referentialism, the counterfactual test and samesaying tests identify the proposition that best fits our intuitive conception of *what is said* by an utterance or *what the speaker says* in making an utterance. There are many other propositions systematically associated with an utterance in virtue of the meaning of the words used in it, which can and must enter into the explanation of the significance the utterance has for competent speakers and listeners.

The "reflexive-referential" account of indexicals developed in this essay is an example of critical referentialism. We need to consider the content$_M$ of statements containing indexicals to deal with the sorts of cases that bothered Frege, such as our example of meeting Quine. But for other purposes, including those enshrined in our everyday concepts for describing utterances, the referentialist concept of what is said is useful and legitimate. Burks's original account was also critically referentialist; he recognized the importance of content$_D$ for certain purposes, and of content$_M$ for others.

The importance of the contextual or official level of content stems from the basic facts of communication and the purposes for which our ordinary tools for classifying and reporting content are adapted.

In the paradigm communicative situation, the speaker suits the message to the listener's knowledge of the context of utterance and the impact on belief he hopes to achieve. That is, he assumes the listener to know the relevant contextual facts, and tries to convey the incremental content. I assume that Quine will recognize the speaker of "I'd like to shake your hand," ("that person in front of me") and the addressee ("me"). Given this knowledge, the additional information he receives is: *that person* would like to shake *my* hand. The incremental content of my utterance, given the facts about context – the singular proposition that John Perry would like to shake Quine's hand – does a good job of characterizing what *additional* fact I am trying to convey to Quine, given what he knows and what will be obvious to him.

In a non-philosophical moment someone might explain Quine's action, of turning and extending his hand to me, by simply saying:

(17)   Perry told Quine that he wanted to shake his hand.

The embedded sentence here, "he wanted to shake his hand", does not seem to identify any of the modes of presentation that were crucial to my plan and Quine's understanding, as explored in section 3.5. And yet (17) is a perfectly adequate explanation.

We have to see this as a *situated* explanation. In the background is the assumption that Quine and I were engaged in a normal case of face-to-face communication. The explainer tells what I was trying to *add to* what Quine knew and could easily perceive, and to do this it suffices to identify the singular proposition that is the content$_C$ of my utterance. This is what the ordinary report does.

Frege's insight was that there are multiple ways to cognize any object. Any utterance that adds to a listener's knowledge in a significant way will connect to the modes of presentation by which the listener already cognizes the object, or can easily do so, and the modes of presentation that connect with the ways the listener has for acting on the object or dealing with information about the object. To trace these interactions in a completely unsituated way, making no assumptions, dealing with the listener's thought-processes in a way that doesn't rely on the external world to suggest internal connections, would require what we might call completely "Fregean" content, totally without lumps. For practical purposes, what we need is "Fregean-enough" content. That is, we must specify the modes of presentation that are actually involved in cognition and the ways they are linked in the mind in so far as there is something in the context of explanation that suggests that the ordinary links might be broken.[19]

Thus when I raised, in section 3.5, the question of the difference between "I'd like to shake your hand" and "John Perry would like to shake your hand", I undermined the assumptions that make (17) an adequate explanation of Quine's action. I asked for an account of exactly what is taken for granted by (17), the planned connections between the modes of presentation involved in the utterance (being the speaker of it, being the addressee), and those involved in the cognitions that led to Quine's action (being the man he sees, being himself).[20]

When we retreat from the content$_C$ of my utterance to its content$_M$, to provide an explanation for the links now brought into question, we retreat to more Fregean, less lumpy content, in the sense that I and Quine are replaced by modes of presentation. But note that the content is not without lumps. For the content$_M$ of an utterance is also a singular proposition, about the utterance itself. The explanation I gave in section 3.5 is also situated; the assumption is that Quine hears my utterance in the usual way, as it comes out of my mouth. If we asked why I could get him to shake my hand by talking *to* him, but not by saying the same thing in such a manner that his first perception of my utterance was of an echo from a far room (details left to reader), we would have to revert to even more Fregean content, with modes of presentations of the utterance, rather than the utterance itself, appearing in the contents.

. . .

Notes

1   See Nunberg (1992, 1993), Vallee (1996).
2   See Partee (1989), Condoravdi and Gawron (1996).
3   See Castañeda (1967), Corazza (1995).
4   I use 'Kinko's' as a name for the Kinko's store on P street in Lincoln.
5   Actually, I'm not sure these famous people who grew up in Omaha were all born there.
6   The following distinctions, although not the terminology, I owe to Genoveva Marti, who presents them forcefully in Marti (1996). On this topic and elsewhere I also owe a great debt to Recanati's *Direct Reference* (1993), a work that can be profitably consulted on virtually any topic connected with indexicality and reference.
7   It is easy to be led astray here. Suppose you see Jim at a party, and ask him what his name is. I tell you, and thus disclose to you a certain naming convention. Now you will be thinking of Jim Perry in a certain way at that point, perhaps as 'the man I am looking at and just asked the name of and heard saying something interesting about computers a minute ago'. So, when I tell you that man's name is 'Jim', the association in your mind may be between the name and a certain mode of presentation of him. This does not mean that the *convention* I have disclosed to you is one linking the name with the mode of presentation. The convention links the name with Jim; it has been around since he was born, and so long before he had anything interesting to say about computers; the mode of presentation comes in only because that is how you happen to be thinking of him; the mode of presentation is involved in your way of thinking of the convention, but not the convention itself.
8   More accurately, in terms introduced below, definite descriptions contribute the condition associated with them by meaning and context, their content$_C$.

9   Keith Donnellan's famous distinction between referential and attributive uses of definite descriptions could be interpreted as the claim that definite descriptions do sometimes refer. I'll basically ignore this idea in this chapter, simply to keep the focus on indexicals, but see also note 16.

10 Burks also uses the term 'symbolic meaning' for a property of tokens determined by the meaning of their type.

11 Thanks to Ivan Sag for the examples.

12 More literally: The person such that there is a place where that person speaks q there stands at the place such that there is a person who speaks q there.

13 For a discussion of Stalnaker's approach and its relation to Reichenbach's approach and the current approach, see Perry (1993, pp. 51ff.). Evans's complaints (1981) about Perry (1977) are related. See Perry (1993, pp. 26ff.).

14 Note that, given our assumption that names name rather than denote, this means that the designata of names is fixed at the level of content$_M$.

15 See note 14.

16 As noted in note 9, I am offically ignoring Donnellan's distinction between attributive and referential uses of definite descriptions. This is not to imply that there is anything absurd about the idea that definite descriptions refer. Recanati has a clear conception of this. He sees terms as having or lacking a certain feature, 'ref'. In my terms, a term that has this feature contributes the object it designates to official content, whether the term names or denotes. Indexicals have this feature in virtue of their meaning. On Recanati's view, definite descriptions do not have this feature built into their meaning, but it can be added at a pragmatic level in particular cases (1993). One can surmise that David Kaplan's 'dthat' operator (1979, 1989a) is a way of making the ref feature syntactially explicit; 'dthat' itself is, of course, open to various interpretations, even by its inventor (1989b).

17 See the discussion in Perry (1990).

18 Russell continued to recognize a category of 'logically proper names' that referred, but ordinary proper names weren't among them. Interestingly, they comprised such indexicals as 'this' and 'I'.

19 Compare what David Israel and I say (1991) on the issue of having 'narrow' enough content.

20 For more on these themes, see Israel, Perry, and Tutiya (1993).

References

Almog, Joseph, John Perry and Howard Wettstein (eds) 1989. *Themes from Kaplan*. New York: Oxford University Press.

Barwise, Jon and John Perry 1983. *Situations and Attitudes*. Cambridge, MA: MIT-Bradford.

Burks, Arthur 1949. Icon, Index and Symbol. *Philosophical and Phenomenological Research*, 9 (4), June: 673–89.

Castañeda, Hector-Neri 1966. 'He': A study in the logic of self-consciousness. *Ratio*, 8, 130–57.

Castañeda, Hector-Neri 1967. Indicators and Quasi-Indicators. *American Philosophical Quarterly*, 4, 85–100.

Condoravdi, Cleo and Mark Gawron, 1996. The context dependency of implicit arguments. In *Quantifiers, Deduction and Context*, eds Makoto Kanazawa, Christopher Piñon, and Henriette de Swart. Stanford: CSLI.

Corazza, Eros, 1995. *Référence, Contexte et Attitudes*, Paris: Vrin.

Donnellan, Keith 1966. Reference and Definite Descriptions. *Philosophical Review*, 75, 281–304.

Donnellan, Keith 1970. Proper Names and Identifying Descriptions. *Synthese*, 21, pp. 335–58.

Evans, Gareth 1981. Understanding Demonstratives. In Herman Parret and Jacques Bouveresse (eds), *Meaning and Understanding*. Berlin and New York: Walter de Gruyter, 280–303.

Frege, Gottlob 1960a. *Translations from the Philosophical Writings of Gottlob Frege*. Edited and translated by Peter Geach and Max Black. Oxford: Basil Blackwell.

Frege, Gottlob 1960b. On Sense and Reference. In Frege (1960a), 56–78.

French, Peter A., Theodore E. Uehuling, Jr., and Howard K. Wettstein (eds) 1979. *Contemporary Perspectives in the Philosophy of Language*. Minneapolis: University of Minnesota Press.

Israel, David, John Perry, and Syun Tutiya 1993. Executions, Motivations and Accomplishments. *Philosophical Review*, 102 (October): 515–40.

Israel, David and John Perry 1990. What is information? In *Information, Language and Cognition*, ed. by Philip Hanson. Vancouver: University of British Columbia Press, 1–19.

Kaplan, David 1978. Dthat. In French et al. (1979), 383–400. Reprinted in Yourgrau (1990), 11–33.

Kaplan, David 1979. On the logic of demonstratives. *Journal of Philosophical Logic*, 8, 81–98. Reprinted in French et al. (1979), 401–12.

Kaplan, David 1989a. Demonstratives. In Almog (1989), 481–563.

Kaplan, David 1989b. Afterthoughts. In Almog (1989), 565–614.

Kripke, Saul 1980. *Naming and Necessity*. Cambridge, MA: Harvard University Press.

Marcus, Ruth 1961. Modalities and Intensional Languages. *Synthese*, 13, 303–22.

Marti, Genoveva 1995. The essence of genuine reference. *Journal of Philosophical Logic*, 24, 375–89.

Nunberg, Geoffrey 1992. Two kinds of indexicality. In Chris Barker and David Dowty (eds), *Proceedings of the Second Conference on Semantics and Linguistic Theory*. Columbus: Ohio State University, 283–301.

Nunberg, Geoffrey 1993. Indexicality and deixis. *Linguistics and Philosophy*, 16, 1–43.

Partee, Barbara 1989: Binding implicit variables in quantified contexts. *Papers of the Chicago Linguistic Society*, 25, 342–65.

Perry, John 1970. The Same F. *Philosophical Review*, 79 (2), 181–200.

Perry, John 1977. Frege on Demonstratives. *Philosophical Review*, 86 (4), 474–97. Reprinted in Perry (1993, pp. 3–25).

Perry, John 1979. The problem of the essential indexical. *Noûs*, 13 (1), 3–21. Reprinted in Perry (1993, 3–49).

Perry, John 1980. A problem about continued belief. *Pacific Philosophical Quarterly*, 61(4), 317–22. Reprinted in Perry (1993, pp. 69–90).

Perry, John 1990. Individuals in informational and intentional content. In Enrique Villaneueva (ed.), *Information, Semantics and Epistemology*. Oxford: Basil Blackwell, 172–89. Reprinted in Perry (1993, pp. 279–300).

Perry, John 1993. *The Problem of the Essential Indexical and Other Essays*. New York: Oxford University Press.

Perry, John and David Israel 1991. Fodor and Psychological Explanation. In *Meaning and Mind*, ed. Barry Loewer and Georges Rey. Oxford: Basil Blackwell, 1991, 165–80. Reprinted in Perry (1993, pp. 301–21).

Recanati, François 1993. *Direct Reference: From Language to Thought*. Oxford: Blackwell.

Reichenbach, Hans 1947. Section 50: token-reflexive words. In *Elements of Symbolic Logic*. New York: Free Press, 284ff.

Stalnaker, Robert 1981. Indexical Belief. *Synthese*, 49, 129–51.

Vallee, Richard 1996. Who Are We? *Canadian Journal of Philosophy*, 26 (2), 211–30.

Yourgrau, Palle (ed.) 1990. *Demonstratives*. Oxford: Oxford University Press.

Wettstein, Howard 1986. Has Semantics Rested on a Mistake? *Journal of Philosophy*, 83 (4), 185–209.

13

Two Dogmas of Empiricism

W. V. Quine

Modern empiricism has been conditioned in large part by two dogmas. One is a belief in some fundamental cleavage between truths which are *analytic*, or grounded in meanings independently of matters of fact, and truths which are *synthetic*, or grounded in fact. The other dogma is *reductionism*: the belief that each meaningful statement is equivalent to some logical construct upon terms which refer to immediate experience. Both dogmas, I shall argue, are ill-founded. One effect of abandoning them is, as we shall see, a blurring of the supposed boundary between speculative metaphysics and natural science. Another effect is a shift toward pragmatism.

1 Background for Analyticity

Kant's cleavage between analytic and synthetic truths was foreshadowed in Hume's distinction between relations of ideas and matters of fact, and in Leibniz's distinction between truths of reason and truths of fact. Leibniz spoke of the truths of reason as true in all possible worlds. Picturesqueness aside, this is to say that the truths of reason are those which could not possibly be false. In the same vein we hear analytic statements defined as statements whose denials are self-contradictory. But this definition has small explanatory value; for the notion of self-contradictoriness, in the quite broad sense needed for this definition of analyticity, stands in exactly the same need of clarification as does the notion of analyticity itself. The two notions are the two sides of a single dubious coin.

Kant conceived of an analytic statement as one that attributes to its subject no more than is already conceptually contained in the subject.

This formulation has two shortcomings: it limits itself to statements of subject-predicate form, and it appeals to a notion of containment which is left at a metaphorical level. But Kant's intent, evident more from the use he makes of the notion of analyticity than from his definition of it, can be restated thus: a statement is analytic when it is true by virtue of meanings and independently of fact. Pursuing this line, let us examine the concept of *meaning* which is presupposed.

Meaning, let us remember, is not to be identified with naming. Frege's example of 'Evening Star' and 'Morning Star', and Russell's of 'Scott' and 'the author of *Waverley*', illustrate that terms can name the same thing but differ in meaning. The distinction between meaning and naming is no less important at the level of abstract terms. The terms '9' and 'the number of the planets' name one and the same abstract entity but presumably must be regarded as unlike in meaning; for astronomical observation was needed, and not mere reflection on meanings, to determine the sameness of the entity in question.

The above examples consist of singular terms, concrete and abstract. With general terms, or predicates, the situation is somewhat different but parallel. Whereas a singular term purports to name an entity, abstract or concrete, a general term does not; but a general term is *true of* an entity, or of each of many or of none. The class of all entities of which a general term is true is called the *extension* of the term. Now paralleling the contrast between the meaning of a singular term and the entity named, we must distinguish equally between the meaning of a general term and its extension. The general terms 'creature with a heart' and 'creature with kidneys', for example, are perhaps alike in extension but unlike in meaning.

Confusion of meaning with extension, in the case of general terms, is less common than confusion of meaning with naming in the case of singular terms. It is indeed a commonplace in philosophy to oppose intension (or meaning) to extension, or, in a variant vocabulary, connotation to denotation.

The Aristotelian notion of essence was the forerunner, no doubt, of the modern notion of intension or meaning. For Aristotle it was essential in men to be rational, accidental to be two-legged. But there is an important difference between this attitude and the doctrine of meaning. From the latter point of view it may indeed be conceded (if only for the sake of argument) that rationality is involved in the meaning of the word 'man' while two-leggedness is not; but two-leggedness may at the same time be viewed as involved in the meaning of 'biped' while rationality is not. Thus from the point of view of the doctrine of meaning it makes no sense to say of the actual individual, who is at once a man and a biped, that his rationality is essential and his two-leggedness accidental or vice versa. Things had essences, for Aristotle, but only linguistic forms have meanings. Meaning is what essence becomes when it is divorced from the object of reference and wedded to the word.

For the theory of meaning a conspicuous question is the nature of its objects: what sort of things are meanings? A felt need for meant entities may derive from an earlier failure to appreciate that meaning and reference are distinct. Once the theory of meaning is sharply separated from the theory of reference, it is a short step to recognizing as the primary business of the theory of meaning simply the synonymy of linguistic forms and the analyticity of statements; meanings themselves, as obscure intermediary entities, may well be abandoned.

The problem of analyticity then confronts us anew. Statements which are analytic by general philosophical acclaim are not, indeed, far to seek. They fall into two classes. Those of the first class, which may be called *logically true*, are typified by:

(1)   No unmarried man is married.

The relevant feature of this example is that it not merely is true as it stands, but remains true under any and all reinterpretations of 'man' and 'married'. If we suppose a prior inventory of *logical* particles, comprising 'no', 'un-', 'not', 'if', 'then', 'and', etc., then in general a logical truth is a statement which is true and remains true under all reinterpretations of its components other than the logical particles.

But there is also a second class of analytic statements, typified by:

(2)   No bachelor is married.

The characteristic of such a statement is that it can be turned into a logical truth by putting synonyms for synonyms; thus (2) can be turned into (1) by putting 'unmarried man' for its synonym 'bachelor'. We still lack a proper characterization of this second class of analytic statements, and therewith of analyticity generally, inasmuch as we have had in the above description to lean on a notion of "synonymy" which is no less in need of clarification than analyticity itself.

In recent years Carnap has tended to explain analyticity by appeal to what he calls state-descriptions.[1] A state-description is any exhaustive assignment of truth values to the atomic, or noncompound, statements of the language. All other statements of the language are, Carnap assumes, built up of their component clauses by means of the familiar logical devices, in such a way that the truth value of any complex statement is fixed for each state-description by specifiable logical laws. A statement is then explained as analytic when it comes out true under every state description. This account is an adaptation of Leibniz's "true in all possible worlds." But note that this version of analyticity serves its purpose only if the atomic statements of the language are, unlike 'John is a bachelor' and 'John is married', mutually independent. Otherwise there would be a state-description which assigned truth to 'John is a bachelor' and to 'John is married', and consequently 'No bachelors are married' would turn out synthetic rather than analytic under the proposed criterion. Thus the criterion of analyticity in terms of state-descriptions serves only for languages devoid of extra-logical synonym-pairs, such as 'bachelor' and 'unmarried man' – synonym-pairs of the type which give rise to the "second class" of analytic statements. The criterion in terms of state-descriptions is a reconstruction at best of logical truth, not of analyticity.

I do not mean to suggest that Carnap is under any illusions on this point. His simplified model language with its state-descriptions is aimed primarily not at the general problem of analyticity but at another purpose, the clarification of probability and induction. Our problem, however, is analyticity; and here the major difficulty lies not in the first class of analytic statements, the logical truths, but rather in the second class, which depends on the notion of synonymy.

2   Definition

There are those who find it soothing to say that the analytic statements of the second class reduce to those of the first class, the logical truths, by *definition*; 'bachelor', for example, is *defined* as 'unmarried man'. But how de we find that 'bachelor' is defined as 'unmarried man'? Who defined it thus, and when? Are we to appeal to the nearest dictionary, and accept the lexicographer's formulation as law? Clearly this would be to put the cart before the horse. The lexicographer is an empirical scientist, whose business is the recording of antecedent facts; and if he glosses 'bachelor' as 'unmarried man' it is because of his belief that there is a relation of synonymy between those forms, implicit in general or preferred usage prior to his own work. The notion of synonymy presupposed here has still to be clarified, presumably in terms relating to linguistic behavior. Certainly the "definition" which is the lexicographer's report of an observed synonymy cannot be taken as the ground of the synonymy.

Definition is not, indeed, an activity exclusively of philologists. Philosophers and scientists frequently have occasion to "define" a recondite term by paraphrasing it into terms of a more familiar vocabulary. But ordinarily such a definition, like the philologist's, is pure lexicography, affirming a relation of synonymy antecedent to the exposition in hand.

Just what it means to affirm synonymy, just what the interconnections may be which are necessary and sufficient in order that two linguistic forms be properly describable as synonymous, is far from clear; but, whatever these interconnections may be, ordinarily they are grounded in usage. Definitions reporting selected instances of synonymy come then as reports upon usage.

There is also, however, a variant type of definitional activity which does not limit itself to the reporting of preëxisting synonymies. I have in mind what Carnap calls *explication* – an activity to which philosophers are given, and scientists also in their more philosophical moments. In explication the purpose is not merely to paraphrase the definiendum into an outright synonym, but actually to improve upon the definiendum by refining or supplementing its meaning. But even explication, though not merely reporting a preëxisting synonymy between definiendum and definiens, does rest nevertheless on *other* preexisting synonymies. The matter may be viewed as follows. Any word worth explicating has some contexts which, as wholes, are clear and precise enough to be useful; and the purpose of explication is to preserve the usage of these favored contexts while sharpening the usage of other contexts. In order that a given definition be suitable for purposes of explication, therefore, what is required is not that the definiendum in its antecedent usage be synonymous with the definiens, but just that each of these favored contexts of the definiendum, taken as a whole in its antecedent usage, be synonymous with the corresponding context of the definiens.

Two alternative definientia may be equally appropriate for the purposes of a given task of explication and yet not be synonymous with each other; for they may serve interchangeably within the favored contexts but diverge elsewhere. By cleaving to one of these definientia rather than the other, a definition of explicative kind generates, by fiat, a relation of synonymy between definiendum and definiens which did not hold before. But such a definition still owes its explicative function, as seen, to preexisting synonymies.

There does, however, remain still an extreme sort of definition which does not hark back to prior synonymies at all: namely, the explicitly conventional introduction of novel notations for purposes of sheer abbreviation. Here the definiendum becomes synonymous with the definiens simply because it has been created expressly for the purpose of being synonymous with the definiens. Here we have a really transparent case of synonymy created by definition; would that all species of synonymy were as intelligible. For the rest, definition rests on synonymy rather than explaining it.

The word 'definition' has come to have a dangerously reassuring sound, owing no doubt to its frequent occurrence in logical and mathematical writings. We shall do well to digress now into a brief appraisal of the role of definition in formal work.

In logical and mathematical systems either of two mutually antagonistic types of economy may be striven for, and each has its peculiar practical utility. On the one hand we may seek economy of practical expression – ease and brevity in the statement of multifarious relations. This sort of economy calls usually for distinctive concise notations for a wealth of concepts. Second, however, and oppositely, we may seek economy in grammar and vocabulary; we may try to find a minimum of basic concepts such that, once a distinctive notation has been appropriated to each of them, it becomes possible to express any desired further concept by mere combination and iteration of our basic notations. This second sort of economy is impractical in one way, since a poverty in basic idioms tends to a necessary lengthening of discourse. But it is practical in another way: it greatly simplifies theoretical discourse *about* the language, through minimizing the terms and the forms of construction wherein the language consists.

Both sorts of economy, though prima facie incompatible, are valuable in their separate ways. The custom has consequently arisen of combining both sorts of economy by forging in effect two languages, the one a part of the other. The inclusive language, though redundant in grammar and vocabulary, is economical in message lengths, while the part, called primitive notation, is economical in grammar and vocabulary. Whole and part are correlated by rules of translation whereby each idiom not in primitive notation is equated to some complex built up of primitive notation. These rules of translation are the so-called *definitions* which appear in formalized systems. They are best viewed not as adjuncts to one language but as correlations between two languages, the one a part of the other.

But these correlations are not arbitrary. They are supposed to show how the primitive notations can accomplish all purposes, save brevity and convenience, of the redundant language. Hence the definiendum and its definiens may be expected, in each case, to be related in one or another of the three ways lately noted. The definiens may be a faithful paraphrase of the definiendum into the narrower notation, preserving a direct synonymy² as of antecedent usage; or the definiens may, in the spirit of explication, improve upon the antecedent usage of the definiendum; or finally, the definiendum may be a newly created notation, newly endowed with meaning here and now.

In formal and informal work alike, thus, we find that definition – except in the extreme case of the explicitly conventional introduction of new notations – hinges on prior relations of synonymy. Recognizing then that the notion of definition does not hold the key to synonymy and analyticity, let us look further into synonymy and say no more of definition.

3 Interchangeability

A natural suggestion, deserving close examination, is that the synonymy of two linguistic forms consists simply in their interchangeability in all contexts without change of truth value – interchangeability, in Leibniz's phrase, *salva veritate*.³ Note that synonyms so conceived need not even be free from vagueness, as long as the vaguenesses match.

But it is not quite true that the synonyms 'bachelor' and 'unmarried man' are everywhere interchangeable *salva veritate*. Truths which become false under substitution of 'unmarried man' for 'bachelor' are easily constructed with the help of 'bachelor of arts' or 'bachelor's buttons'; also with the help of quotation, thus:

'Bachelor' has less than ten letters.

Such counterinstances can, however, perhaps be set aside by treating the phrases 'bachelor of arts' and 'bachelor's buttons' and the quotation ''bachelor'' each as a single indivisible word and then stipulating that the interchangeability *salva veritate* which is to be the touchstone of synonymy is not supposed to apply to fragmentary occurrences inside of a word. This account of synonymy, supposing it acceptable on other counts, has indeed the drawback of appealing to a prior conception of ''word'' which can be counted on to present difficulties of formulation in its turn. Nevertheless some progress might be claimed in having reduced the problem of synonymy to a problem of wordhood. Let us pursue this line a bit, taking ''word'' for granted.

The question remains whether interchangeability *salva veritate* (apart from occurrences within words) is a strong enough condition for synonymy, or whether, on the contrary, some heteronymous expressions might be thus interchangeable. Now let us be clear that we are not concerned here with synonymy in the sense of complete identity in psychological associations or poetic quality; indeed no two expressions are synonymous in such a sense. We are concerned only with what may be called *cognitive* synonymy. Just what this is cannot be said without successfully finishing the present study; but we know something about it from the need which arose for it in connection with analyticity in §1. The sort of synonymy needed there was merely such that any analytic statement could be turned into a logical truth by putting synonyms for synonyms. Turning the tables and assuming analyticity, indeed, we could explain cognitive synonymy of terms as follows (keeping to the familiar example): to say that 'bachelor' and 'unmarried man' are cognitively synonymous is to say no more nor less than that the statement:

(3)   All and only bachelors are unmarried men

is analytic.[4]

What we need is an account of cognitive synonymy not presupposing analyticity – if we are to explain analyticity conversely with help of cognitive synonymy as undertaken in §1. And indeed such an independent account of cognitive synonymy is at present up for consideration, namely, interchangeability *salva veritate* everywhere except within words. The question before us, to resume the thread at last, is whether such interchangeability is a sufficient condition for cognitive synonymy. We can quickly assure ourselves that it is, by examples of the following sort. The statement:

(4)   Necessarily all and only bachelors are bachelors

is evidently true, even supposing 'necessarily' so narrowly construed as to be truly applicable only to analytic statements. Then, if 'bachelor' and 'unmarried man' are interchangeable *salva veritate*, the result:

(5)   Necessarily all and only bachelors are unmarried men

of putting 'unmarried man' for an occurrence of 'bachelor' in (4) must, like (4), be true. But to say that (5) is true is to say that (3) is analytic, and hence that 'bachelor' and 'unmarried man' are cognitively synonymous.

Let us see what there is about the above argument that gives it its air of hocus-pocus. The condition of interchangeability *salva veritate* varies in its force with variations in the richness of the language at hand. The above argument supposes we are working with a language rich enough to contain the adverb 'necessarily', this adverb being so construed as to yield truth when and only when applied to an analytic statement. But can we condone a language which contains such an adverb? Does the adverb really make sense? To suppose that it does is to suppose that we have already made satisfactory sense of 'analytic'. Then what are we so hard at work on right now?

Our argument is not flatly circular, but something like it. It has the form, figuratively speaking, of a closed curve in space.

Interchangeability *salva veritate* is meaningless until relativized to a language whose extent is specified in relevant respects. Suppose now we consider a language containing just the following materials. There is an indefinitely large stock of one-place predicates (for example, 'F' where 'Fx' means that x is a man) and many-place predicates (for example, 'G' where 'Gxy' means that x loves y), mostly having to do with extralogical subject matter. The rest of the language is logical. The atomic sentences consist each of a predicate followed by one or more variables 'x', 'y', etc.; and the complex sentences are built up of the atomic ones by truth functions ('not', 'and', 'or', etc.) and quantification. In effect such a language enjoys the benefits also of descriptions and indeed singular terms generally, these being contextually definable in known ways. Even abstract singular terms naming classes, classes of classes, etc., are contextually definable in case the assumed stock of predicates includes the two-place predicate of class membership. Such a language can be adequate to classical mathematics and indeed to scientific discourse generally, except in so far as the latter involves debatable devices such as contrary-to-fact conditionals or modal adverbs like 'necessarily'.[5] Now a language of this type is extensional, in this sense: any two predicates which agree extensionally (that is, are true of the same objects) are interchangeable *salva veritate*.[6]

In an extensional language, therefore, interchangeability *salva veritate* is no assurance of cognitive synonymy of the desired type. That 'bachelor' and 'unmarried man' are interchangeable *salva veritate* in an extensional language assures us of no more than that (3) is true. There is no assurance here that the extensional agreement of 'bachelor' and 'unmarried man' rests on meaning rather than merely on accidental matters of fact, as does the extensional agreement of 'creature with a heart' and 'creature with kidneys'.

For most purposes extensional agreement is the nearest approximation to synonymy we need care about. But the fact remains that extensional agreement falls far short of cognitive synonymy of the type required for

explaining analyticity in the manner of §1. The type of cognitive synonymy required there is such as to equate the synonymy of 'bachelor'
and 'unmarried man' with the analyticity of (3), not merely with the truth
of (3).

So we must recognize that interchangeability *salva veritate*, if construed
in relation to an extensional language, is not a sufficient condition of
cognitive synonymy in the sense needed for deriving analyticity in the
manner of §1. If a language contains an intensional adverb 'necessarily' in
the sense lately noted, or other particles to the same effect, then interchangeability *salva veritate* in such a language does afford a sufficient
condition of cognitive synonymy; but such a language is intelligible only
in so far as the notion of analyticity is already understood in advance.

The effort to explain cognitive synonymy first, for the sake of deriving
analyticity from it afterward as in §1, is perhaps the wrong approach.
Instead we might try explaining analyticity somehow without appeal to
cognitive synonymy. Afterward we could doubtless derive cognitive
synonymy from analyticity satisfactorily enough if desired. We have
seen that cognitive synonymy of 'bachelor' and 'unmarried man' can be
explained as analyticity of (3). The same explanation works for any pair
of one-place predicates, of course, and it can be extended in obvious
fashion to many-place predicates. Other syntactical categories can also
be accommodated in fairly parallel fashion. Singular terms may be said to
be cognitively synonymous when the statement of identity formed by
putting '=' between them is analytic. Statements may be said simply to be
cognitively synonymous when their biconditional (the result of joining
them by 'if and only if') is analytic.[7] If we care to lump all categories into
a single formulation, at the expense of assuming again the notion of
"word" which was appealed to early in this section, we can describe
any two linguistic forms as cognitively synonymous when the two forms
are interchangeable (apart from occurrences within "words") *salva* (no
longer *veritate* but) *analyticitate*. Certain technical questions arise, indeed,
over cases of ambiguity or homonymy; let us not pause for them, however, for we are already digressing. Let us rather turn our backs on the
problem of synonymy and address ourselves anew to that of analyticity.

4   Semantical Rules

Analyticity at first seemed most naturally definable by appeal to a realm
of meanings. On refinement, the appeal to meanings gave way to an
appeal to synonymy or definition. But definition turned out to be a

will-o'-the-wisp, and synonymy turned out to be best understood only by dint of a prior appeal to analyticity itself. So we are back at the problem of analyticity.

I do not know whether the statement 'Everything green is extended' is analytic. Now does my indecision over this example really betray an incomplete understanding, an incomplete grasp of the "meanings", of 'green' and 'extended'? I think not. The trouble is not with 'green' or 'extended', but with 'analytic'.

It is often hinted that the difficulty in separating analytic statements from synthetic ones in ordinary language is due to the vagueness of ordinary language and that the distinction is clear when we have a precise artificial language with explicit "semantical rules." This, however, as I shall now attempt to show, is a confusion.

The notion of analyticity about which we are worrying is a purported relation between statements and languages: a statement S is said to be *analytic for* a language L, and the problem is to make sense of this relation generally, that is, for variable 'S' and 'L'. The gravity of this problem is not perceptibly less for artificial languages than for natural ones. The problem of making sense of the idiom 'S is analytic for L', with variable 'S' and 'L', retains its stubbornness even if we limit the range of the variable 'L' to artificial languages. Let me now try to make this point evident.

For artificial languages and semantical rules we look naturally to the writings of Carnap. His semantical rules take various forms, and to make my point I shall have to distinguish certain of the forms. Let us suppose, to begin with, an artificial language L_0 whose semantical rules have the form explicitly of a specification, by recursion or otherwise, of all the analytic statements of L_0. The rules tell us that such and such statements, and only those, are the analytic statements of L_0. Now here the difficulty is simply that the rules contain the word 'analytic', which we do not understand! We understand what expressions the rules attribute analyticity to, but we do not understand what the rules attribute to those expressions. In short, before we can understand a rule which begins 'A statement S is analytic for language L_0 if and only if . . .', we must understand the general relative term 'analytic for'; we must understand 'S is analytic for L' where 'S' and 'L' are variables.

Alternatively we may, indeed, view the so-called rule as a conventional definition of a new simple symbol 'analytic-for-L_0', which might better be written unintendentiously as 'K' so as not to seem to throw light on the interesting word 'analytic'. Obviously any number of classes K, M, N etc. of statements of L_0 can be specified for various purposes or for no purpose; what does it mean to say that K, as against M, N, etc., is the class of the "analytic" statements of L_0?

By saying what statements are analytic for L_0 we explain 'analytic-for-L_0' but not 'analytic', not 'analytic for'. We do not begin to explain the idiom 'S is analytic for L' with variable 'S' and 'L', even if we are content to limit the range of 'L' to the realm of artificial languages.

Actually we do know enough about the intended significance of 'analytic' to know that analytic statements are supposed to be true. Let us then turn to a second form of semantical rule, which says not that such and such statements are analytic but simply that such and such statements are included among the truths. Such a rule is not subject to the criticism of containing the un-understood word 'analytic'; and we may grant for the sake of argument that there is no difficulty over the broader term 'true'. A semantical rule of this second type, a rule of truth, is not supposed to specify all the truths of the language; it merely stipulates, recursively or otherwise, a certain multitude of statements which, along with others unspecified, are to count as true. Such a rule may be conceded to be quite clear. Derivatively, afterward, analyticity can be demarcated thus: a statement is analytic if it is (not merely true but) true according to the semantical rule.

Still there is really no progress. Instead of appealing to an unexplained word 'analytic', we are now appealing to an unexplained phrase 'semantical rule'. Not every true statement which says that the statements of some class are true can count as a semantical rule – otherwise *all* truths would be "analytic" in the sense of being true according to semantical rules. Semantical rules are distinguishable, apparently, only by the fact of appearing on a page under the heading 'Semantical Rules'; and this heading is itself then meaningless.

We can say indeed that a statement is *analytic-for-L_0* if and only if it is true according to such and such specifically appended "semantical rules," but then we find ourselves back at essentially the same case which was originally discussed: 'S is analytic-for-L_0 if and only if....' Once we seek to explain 'S is analytic for L' generally for variable 'L' (even allowing limitation of 'L' to artificial languages), the explanation 'true according to the semantical rules of L' is unavailing; for the relative term 'semantical rule of' is as much in need of clarification, at least, as 'analytic for'.

It may be instructive to compare the notion of semantical rule with that of postulate. Relative to a given set of postulates, it is easy to say what a postulate is: it is a member of the set. Relative to a given set of semantical rules, it is equally easy to say what a semantical rule is. But given simply a notation, mathematical or otherwise, and indeed as thoroughly understood a notation as you please in point of the translations or truth conditions of its statements, who can say which of its true statements rank as postulates? Obviously the question is meaningless – as meaningless as asking which points in Ohio are starting points. Any finite (or effectively specifiable infinite) selection of statements (preferably true ones, perhaps) is as much *a* set of postulates as any other. The word 'postulate' is significant only relative to an act of inquiry; we apply the word to a set of statements just in so far as we happen, for the year or the moment, to be thinking of those statements in relation to the statements which can be reached from them by some set of transformations to which we have seen fit to direct our attention. Now the notion of semantical rule is as sensible and meaningful as that of postulate, if conceived in a similarly relative spirit – relative, this time, to one or another particular enterprise of schooling unconversant persons in sufficient conditions for truth of statements of some natural or artificial language L. But from this point of view no one signalization of a subclass of the truths of L is intrinsically more a semantical rule than another; and, if 'analytic' means 'true by semantical rules', no one truth of L is analytic to the exclusion of another.[8]

It might conceivably be protested that an artificial language L (unlike a natural one) is a language in the ordinary sense *plus* a set of explicit semantical rules – the whole constituting, let us say, an ordered pair; and that the semantical rules of L then are specifiable simply as the second component of the pair L. But, by the same token and more simply, we might construe an artificial language L outright as an ordered pair whose second component is the class of its analytic statements; and then the analytic statements of L become specifiable simply as the statements in the second component of L. Or better still, we might just stop tugging at our bootstraps altogether.

Not all the explanations of analyticity known to Carnap and his readers have been covered explicitly in the above considerations, but the extension to other forms is not hard to see. Just one additional factor should be mentioned which sometimes enters: sometimes the semantical rules are in effect rules of translation into ordinary language, in which case the analytic statements of the artificial language are in effect recognized as such from the analyticity of their specified translations in ordinary language. Here certainly there can be no thought of an illumination of the problem of analyticity from the side of the artificial language.

From the point of view of the problem of analyticity the notion of an artificial language with semantical rules is a *feu follet par excellence*. Semantical rules determining the analytic statements of an artificial language are of interest only in so far as we already understand the notion of analyticity; they are of no help in gaining this understanding.

Appeal to hypothetical languages of an artificially simple kind could conceivably be useful in clarifying analyticity, if the mental or behavioral or cultural factors relevant to analyticity – whatever they may be – were somehow sketched into the simplified model. But a model which takes analyticity merely as an irreducible character is unlikely to throw light on the problem of explicating analyticity.

It is obvious that truth in general depends on both language and extralinguistic fact. The statement 'Brutus killed Caesar' would be false if the world had been different in certain ways, but it would also be false if the word 'killed' happened rather to have the sense of 'begat'. Thus one is tempted to suppose in general that the truth of a statement is somehow analyzable into a linguistic component and a factual component. Given this supposition, it next seems reasonable that in some statements the factual component should be null; and these are the analytic statements. But, for all its a priori reasonableness, a boundary between analytic and synthetic statements simply has not been drawn. That there is such a distinction to be drawn at all is an unempirical dogma of empiricists, a metaphysical article of faith.

5   The Verification Theory and Reductionism

In the course of these somber reflections we have taken a dim view first of the notion of meaning, then of the notion of cognitive synonymy, and finally of the notion of analyticity. But what, it may be asked, of the verification theory of meaning? This phrase has established itself so firmly as a catchword of empiricism that we should be very unscientific indeed not to look beneath it for a possible key to the problem of meaning and the associated problems.

The verification theory of meaning, which has been conspicuous in the literature from Peirce onward, is that the meaning of a statement is the method of empirically confirming or infirming it. An analytic statement is that limiting case which is confirmed no matter what.

As urged in §1, we can as well pass over the question of meanings as entities and move straight to sameness of meaning, or synonymy. Then what the verification theory says is that statements are synonymous if and only if they are alike in point of method of empirical confirmation or infirmation.

This is an account of cognitive synonymy not of linguistic forms generally, but of statements.[9] However, from the concept of synonymy of statements we could derive the concept of synonymy for other linguistic forms, by considerations somewhat similar to those at the end of §3. Assuming the notion of "word," indeed, we could explain any two forms as synonymous when the putting of the one form for an occurrence of the other in any statement (apart from occurrences within "words") yields a synonymous statement. Finally, given the concept of synonymy thus for linguistic forms generally, we could define analyticity in terms of synonymy and logical truth as in §1. For that matter, we could define analyticity more simply in terms of just synonymy of statements together with logical truth; it is not necessary to appeal to synonymy of linguistic forms other than statements. For a statement may be described as analytic simply when it is synonymous with a logically true statement.

So, if the verification theory can be accepted as an adequate account of statement synonymy, the notion of analyticity is saved after all. However, let us reflect. Statement synonymy is said to be likeness of method of empirical confirmation or infirmation. Just what are these methods which are to be compared for likeness? What, in other words, is the nature of the relation between a statement and the experiences which contribute to or detract from its confirmation?

The most naïve view of the relation is that it is one of direct report. This is *radical reductionism*. Every meaningful statement is held to be translatable into a statement (true or false) about immediate experience. Radical reductionism, in one form or another, well antedates the verification theory of meaning explicitly so called. Thus Locke and Hume held that every idea must either originate directly in sense experience or else be compounded of ideas thus originating; and taking a hint from Tooke we might rephrase this doctrine in semantical jargon by saying that a term, to be significant at all, must be either a name of a sense datum or a compound of such names or an abbreviation of such a compound. So stated, the doctrine remains ambiguous as between sense data as sensory events and sense data as sensory qualities; and it remains vague as to the admissible ways of compounding. Moreover, the doctrine is unnecessarily and intolerably restrictive in the term-by-term critique which it imposes. More reasonably, and without yet exceeding the limits of what I have called radical reductionism, we may take full statements as our significant units – thus demanding that our statements as wholes be translatable into sense-datum language, but not that they be translatable term by term.

This emendation would unquestionably have been welcome to Locke and Hume and Tooke, but historically it had to await an important reorientation in semantics – the reorientation whereby the primary vehicle of meaning came to be seen no longer in the term but in the statement. This reorientation, seen in Bentham and Frege, underlies Russell's concept of incomplete symbols defined in use; also it is implicit in the verification theory of meaning, since the objects of verification are statements.

Radical reductionism, conceived now with statements as units, set itself the task of specifying a sense-datum language and showing how to translate the rest of significant discourse, statement by statement, into it. Carnap embarked on this project in the *Aufbau*.

The language which Carnap adopted as his starting point was not a sense-datum language in the narrowest conceivable sense, for it included also the notations of logic, up through higher set theory. In effect it included the whole language of pure mathematics. The ontology implicit in it (that is, the range of values of its variables) embraced not only sensory events but classes, classes of classes, and so on. Empiricists there are who would boggle at such prodigality. Carnap's starting point is very parsimonious, however, in its extralogical or sensory part. In a series of constructions in which he exploits the resources of modern logic with much ingenuity, Carnap succeeds in defining a wide array of important additional sensory concepts which, but for his constructions, one would not have dreamed were definable on so slender a basis. He was the first empiricist who, not content with asserting the reducibility of science to terms of immediate experience, took serious steps toward carrying out the reduction.

If Carnap's starting point is satisfactory, still his constructions were, as he himself stressed, only a fragment of the full program. The construction of even the simplest statements about the physical world was left in a sketchy state. Carnap's suggestions on this subject were, despite their sketchiness, very suggestive. He explained spatio-temporal point-instants as quad-ruples of real numbers and envisaged assignment of sense qualities to point-instants according to certain canons. Roughly summarized, the plan was that qualities should be assigned to point-instants in such a way as to achieve the laziest world compatible with our experience. The principle of least action was to be our guide in construct-ing a world from experience.

Carnap did not seem to recognize, however, that his treatment of physical objects fell short of reduction not merely through sketchiness, but in principle. Statements of the form 'Quality q is at point-instant x; y;

z; t' were, according to his canons, to be apportioned truth values in such a way as to maximize and minimize certain over-all features, and with growth of experience the truth values were to be progressively revised in the same spirit. I think this is a good schematization (deliberately over-simplified, to be sure) of what science really does; but it provides no indication, not even the sketchiest, of how a statement of the form 'Quality q is at x; y; z; t' could ever be translated into Carnap's initial language of sense data and logic. The connective 'is at' remains an added undefined connective; the canons counsel us in its use but not in its elimination.

Carnap seems to have appreciated this point afterward; for in his later writings he abandoned all notion of the translatability of statements about the physical world into statements about immediate experience. Reductionism in its radical form has long since ceased to figure in Carnap's philosophy.

But the dogma of reductionism has, in a subtler and more tenuous form, continued to influence the thought of empiricists. The notion lingers that to each statement, or each synthetic statement, there is associated a unique range of possible sensory events such that the occurrence of any of them would add to the likelihood of truth of the statement, and that there is associated also another unique range of possible sensory events whose occurrence would detract from that likelihood. This notion is of course implicit in the verification theory of meaning.

The dogma of reductionism survives in the supposition that each statement, taken in isolation from its fellows, can admit of confirmation or infirmation at all. My countersuggestion, issuing essentially from Carnap's doctrine of the physical world in the *Aufbau*, is that our statements about the external world face the tribunal of sense experience not individually but only as a corporate body.[10]

The dogma of reductionism, even in its attenuated form, is intimately connected with the other dogma – that there is a cleavage between the analytic and the synthetic. We have found ourselves led, indeed, from the latter problem to the former through the verification theory of meaning. More directly, the one dogma clearly supports the other in this way: as long as it is taken to be significant in general to speak of the confirmation and infirmation of a statement, it seems significant to speak also of a limiting kind of statement which is vacuously confirmed, *ipso facto*, come what may; and such a statement is analytic.

The two dogmas are, indeed, at root identical. We lately reflected that in general the truth of statements does obviously depend both upon language and upon extralinguistic fact; and we noted that this obvious circumstance carries in its train, not logically but all too naturally, a feeling that the truth of a statement is somehow analyzable into a linguistic component and a factual component. The factual component must, if we are empiricists, boil down to a range of confirmatory experiences. In the extreme case where the linguistic component is all that matters, a true statement is analytic. But I hope we are now impressed with how stubbornly the distinction between analytic and synthetic has resisted any straightforward drawing. I am impressed also, apart from prefabricated examples of black and white balls in an urn, with how baffling the problem has always been of arriving at any explicit theory of the empirical confirmation of a synthetic statement. My present suggestion is that it is nonsense, and the root of much nonsense, to speak of a linguistic component and a factual component in the truth of any individual statement. Taken collectively, science has its double dependence upon language and experience; but this duality is not significantly traceable into the statements of science taken one by one.

The idea of defining a symbol in use was, as remarked, an advance over the impossible term-by-term empiricism of Locke and Hume. The statement, rather than the term, came with Bentham to be recognized as the unit accountable to an empiricist critique. But what I am now urging is that even in taking the statement as unit we have drawn our grid too finely. The unit of empirical significance is the whole of science.

6   Empiricism without the Dogmas

The totality of our so-called knowledge or beliefs, from the most casual matters of geography and history to the profoundest laws of atomic physics or even of pure mathematics and logic, is a man-made fabric which impinges on experience only along the edges. Or, to change the figure, total science is like a field of force whose boundary conditions are experience. A conflict with experience at the periphery occasions readjustments in the interior of the field. Truth values have to be redistributed over some of our statements. Reëvaluation of some statements entails reëvaluation of others, because of their logical interconnections – the logical laws being in turn simply certain further statements of the system, certain further elements of the field. Having reëvaluated one statement we must reëvaluate some others, which may be statements logically connected with the first or may be the statements of logical connections themselves. But the total field is so underdetermined by its boundary conditions, experience, that there is much latitude of choice as to what statements to reëvaluate in the light of any single contrary experience. No particular experiences are linked with any particular statements in the interior of the field, except indirectly through considerations of equilibrium affecting the field as a whole.

If this view is right, it is misleading to speak of the empirical content of an individual statement – especially if it is a statement at all remote from the experiential periphery of the field. Furthermore it becomes folly to seek a boundary between synthetic statements, which hold contingently on experience, and analytic statements, which hold come what may. Any statement can be held true come what may, if we make drastic enough adjustments elsewhere in the system. Even a statement very close to the periphery can be held true in the face of recalcitrant experience by pleading hallucination or by amending certain statements of the kind called logical laws. Conversely, by the same token, no statement is immune to revision. Revision even of the logical law of the excluded middle has been proposed as a means of simplifying quantum mechanics; and what difference is there in principle between such a shift and the shift whereby Kepler superseded Ptolemy, or Einstein Newton, or Darwin Aristotle?

For vividness I have been speaking in terms of varying distances from a sensory periphery. Let me try now to clarify this notion without metaphor. Certain statements, though *about* physical objects and not sense experience, seem peculiarly germane to sense experience – and in a selective way: some statements to some experiences, others to others. Such statements, especially germane to particular experiences, I picture as near the periphery. But in this relation of "germaneness" I envisage nothing more than a loose association reflecting the relative likelihood, in practice, of our choosing one statement rather than another for revision in the event of recalcitrant experience. For example, we can imagine recalcitrant experiences to which we would surely be inclined to accommodate our system by reëvaluating just the statement that there are brick houses on Elm Street, together with related statements on the same topic. We can imagine other recalcitrant experiences to which we would be inclined to accommodate our system by reëvaluating just the statement that there are no centaurs, along with kindred statements. A recalcitrant experience can, I have urged, be accommodated by any of various alternative reëvaluations in various alternative quarters of the total system; but, in the cases which we are now imagining, our natural tendency to disturb the total system as little as possible would lead us to focus our revisions upon these specific statements concerning brick houses or centaurs. These statements are felt, therefore, to have a sharper empirical reference than highly theoretical statements of physics or logic or ontology. The latter statements may be thought of as relatively centrally located within the total network, meaning merely that little preferential connection with any particular sense data obtrudes itself.

As an empiricist I continue to think of the conceptual scheme of science as a tool, ultimately, for predicting future experience in the light of past experience. Physical objects are conceptually imported into the situation as convenient intermediaries – not by definition in terms of experience, but simply as irreducible posits comparable, epistemologically, to the gods of Homer. For my part I do, qua lay physicist, believe in physical objects and not in Homer's gods; and I consider it a scientific error to believe otherwise. But in point of epistemological footing the physical objects and the gods differ only in degree and not in kind. Both sorts of entities enter our conception only as cultural posits. The myth of physical objects is epistemologically superior to most in that it has proved more efficacious than other myths as a device for working a manageable structure into the flux of experience.

Positing does not stop with macroscopic physical objects. Objects at the atomic level are posited to make the laws of macroscopic objects, and ultimately the laws of experience, simpler and more manageable; and we need not expect or demand full definition of atomic and subatomic entities in terms of macroscopic ones, any more than definition of macroscopic things in terms of sense data. Science is a continuation of common sense, and it continues the common-sense expedient of swelling ontology to simplify theory.

Physical objects, small and large, are not the only posits. Forces are another example; and indeed we are told nowadays that the boundary between energy and matter is obsolete. Moreover, the abstract entities which are the substance of mathematics – ultimately classes and classes of classes and so on up – are another posit in the same spirit. Epistemologically these are myths on the same footing with physical objects and gods, neither better nor worse except for differences in the degree to which they expedite our dealings with sense experiences.

The over-all algebra of rational and irrational numbers is underdetermined by the algebra of rational numbers, but is smoother and more convenient; and it includes the algebra of rational numbers as a jagged or gerrymandered part. Total science, mathematical and natural and human, is similarly but more extremely underdetermined by experience. The edge of the system must be kept squared with experience; the rest, with all its elaborate myths or fictions, has as its objective the simplicity of laws.

Ontological questions, under this view, are on a par with questions of natural science.[11] Consider the question whether to countenance classes as entities. This, as I have argued elsewhere, is the question whether to quantify with respect to variables which take classes as values. Now Carnap[12] has maintained that this is a question not of matters of fact but of choosing a convenient language form, a convenient conceptual scheme or framework for science. With this I agree, but only on the proviso that the same be conceded regarding scientific hypotheses generally. Carnap has recognized that he is able to preserve a double standard for ontological questions and scientific hypotheses only by assuming an absolute distinction between the analytic and the synthetic; and I need not say again that this is a distinction which I reject.[13]

The issue over there being classes seems more a question of convenient conceptual scheme; the issue over there being centaurs, or brick houses on Elm Street, seems more a question of fact. But I have been urging that this difference is only one of degree, and that it turns upon our vaguely pragmatic inclination to adjust one strand of the fabric of science rather than another in accommodating some particular recalcitrant experience. Conservatism figures in such choices, and so does the quest for simplicity.

Carnap, Lewis, and others take a pragmatic stand on the question of choosing between language forms, scientific frameworks; but their pragmatism leaves off at the imagined boundary between the analytic and the synthetic. In repudiating such a boundary I espouse a more thorough pragmatism. Each man is given a scientific heritage plus a continuing barrage of sensory stimulation; and the considerations which guide him in warping his scientific heritage to fit his continuing sensory promptings are, where rational, pragmatic.

Notes

1 Rudolf Carnap, *Meaning and Necessity* (Chicago: University of Chicago Press, 1947), pp. 9ff.; Rudolf Carnap, *Logical Foundations of Probability* (Chicago: University of Chicago Press, 1950), pp. 70ff.

2 According to an important variant sense of 'definition', the relation preserved may be the weaker relation of mere agreement in reference. But definition in this sense is better ignored in the present connection, being irrelevant to the question of synonymy.

3 Cf. C. I. Lewis, *A Survey of Symbolic Logic* (Berkerley, CA: University of California Press, 1918), p. 373.

4   This is cognitive synonymy in a primary, broad sense. Carnap (*Meaning and Necessity*, pp. 56 ff.) and C. I. Lewis, (*An Analysis of Knowledge and Valuation* (LaSalle, IL: Open Court, 1946), p. 88) have suggested how, once this notion is at hand, a narrower sense of cognitive synonymy which is preferable for some purposes can in turn be derived. But this special ramification of concept-building lies aside from the present purposes and must not be confused with the broad sort of cognitive synonymy here concerned.

5   On such devices see also Essay VIII, 'Reference and Modality', in Quine, *From a Logical Point of View* (Cambridge, MA: Harvard University Press, 1980).

6   This is the substance of Quine, *Mathematical Logic* (New York: W. W. Norton, 1940; Cambridge, MA: Harvard University Press, 1947), p. 121.

7   The 'if and only if' itself is intended in the truth functional sense. See Carnap, *Meaning and Necessity*, p. 14.

8   The foregoing paragraph was not part of the present essay as originally published. It was prompted by Martin, 'On "analytic" ', *Philosophical Studies*, 3 (1952), 42–7, as was the end of Essay VII in Quine, *From a Logical Point of View*.

9   The doctrine can indeed be formulated with terms rather than statements as the units. Thus Lewis describes the meaning of a term as "*a criterion in mind, by reference to which one is able to apply or refuse to apply the expression in question in the case of presented, or imagined, things or situations*" (Lewis, *An Analysis of Knowledge and Valuation*, p. 133). For an instructive account of the vicissitudes of the verification theory of meaning, centered however on the question of meaning*fulness* rather than synonymy and analyticity, see C. G. Hempel, 'The concept of cognitive significance: a reconsideration', *Proceedings of the American Academy of Arts and Sciences*, 80 (1951), 61–77.

10 This doctrine was well argued by Pierce Duhem, La *Théorie Physique: son objet et sa structure* (Paris, 1906), pp. 303–28. Or see Armand Lowinger, *The Methodology of Pierce Duhem* (New York: Columbia University Press, 1941), pp. 132–40.

11 'L'ontologie fait corps avec la science elle-même et ne peut en être separée' (Émile Meyerson, *Identité et realité*, Paris, 1908; 4th edn 1932).

12 Rudolf Carnap, 'Empiricism, semantics, and ontolog', *Revue internationale de philosophie*, 4 (1950), pp. 20–40.

13 For an effective expression of further misgivings over this distinction, see Morton White, 'The analytic and the synthetic: an untenable dualism', in Sidney Hook (ed.), *John Dewey: Philosopher of Science and Freedom* (New York: Dial Press, 1950), pp. 316–30.

14

Armchair Metaphysics

Frank Jackson

What role, if any, is there for conceptual analysis in metaphysics? On the face of it, very little. Metaphysics is to do with what is in the world and what it is like, not with concepts and semantics.[1] We would expect science in the wide sense to be highly relevant, but not the armchair deliberations of the philosopher concerned with the analysis of concepts. However, traditionally metaphysicians have paid at least as much attention to questions of conceptual analysis, and to related questions of logical interconnections (to what entails or fails to entail what) as they have to what science tells us about the world. David Armstrong, for example, while rightly and famously insisting that what is said in the philosophy of mind must be answerable to what science tells us about the role of the brain in the causation of behaviour, spends most of *A Materialist Theory of the Mind* doing conceptual analysis.[2] It is understandable that recently many philosophers writing under the banner of 'naturalism' have declared the traditional preoccupations of metaphysicians with such armchair matters as conceptual analysis and entailments to be a mistake.

Naturalism comes in an extreme and in a moderate form. The extreme form rejects conceptual analysis and its ilk altogether. The extremists sometimes describe the history of conceptual analysis as the history of failure. I think that they are forgetting about biased samples. True, the well-known and much discussed examples of putative analyses in the philosophy journals are highly controversial, but *that* is why they are much discussed. The more moderate form of naturalism accepts that there is a legitimate activity properly called 'conceptual analysis': for example, conceptual analysis is what mathematicians did when they elucidated the notions of infinity, convergence on a limit, irrational numbers, and so on, and that was a good thing to do.

The moderate naturalist view is that conceptual analysis and its ilk are all very well in their place, but their place is not in metaphysics (*qua* speculative cosmology), or at least not at the heart of metaphysics. Questions of analysis and of what entails what belong to semantics and logic, not to ontology and metaphysics. Here is a characteristically straightforward statement by Kim Sterelny of moderate naturalism as it applies to the metaphysics of mind:

> My approach [to the mind] is not just physicalist, it is naturalist.... Naturalists are physicalists...but naturalists have methodological views about philosophy as well; we think philosophy is continuous with the natural sciences. On this view, philosophical theories are conjectures whose fate is ultimately determined by empirical investigation.... An alternative conception is to see philosophy as an investigation into conceptual truths proceeding by thought experiments that probe the way we understand our own concepts.... There very likely are 'conceptual truths'; truths that depend only on the way we understand concepts and thus depend not at all on how the world is. But I doubt that there are any very interesting conceptual truths about the mind, or about thinking.[3]

This chapter is a reply to moderate naturalism. I will argue that issues to do with conceptual analysis broadly conceived are inevitably central to any serious metaphysics. I will start by explaining what I mean by a 'serious metaphysics' and why any such metaphysics brings with it a problem I will call the *placement problem*. I will then argue that there is only one way to solve that problem, namely, by embracing a doctrine I will call *the entry by entailment* doctrine. But this doctrine, I will argue, inevitably makes matters of conceptual analysis central in metaphysics.

1   Serious Metaphysics and the Placement Problem

Some physical objects are true. For example, if I were to utter a token of the type 'Snow is white', the object I would thereby bring into existence would be true. The object I would thereby bring into existence would also: have a certain mass, be caused in a certain way, be of a type the other tokens of which have characteristic causes and effects in my mouth and from my pen, and in the mouths and from the pens of my language community, have a certain structure the parts of which have typical causes and effects, and so on and so forth. How is the first property, the semantic property of being true, related to the host of non-semantic properties of the sentence? How can we find a place or location for the semantic in the physical story about the sentence?

Some who have puzzled about this question have been tempted by a sceptical position on truth, and, correspondingly, on meaning and reference. They feel that the list of non-semantic properties – suitably expanded, of course – is an in principle complete one. Sentences are, when all is said and done, a species of physical object, and we know that science can in principle tell us the whole story about physical objects. And though we are not yet, and may never be, in a position actually to give that whole story, we know enough, as of now, to be able to say (a) that it will look something like the story I gave a glimpse of, and (b) that, in any case, it will not contain terms for truth, reference and meaning. But if the whole story does not contain truth, reference and meaning, then so much the worse for truth, reference and meaning.[4]

A quite different response is to distinguish what appears explicitly in a story from what appears implicitly in a story. I tell you that Jones weighs 70 kilos and Smith weighs 80 kilos. That is something I tell you explicitly. Do I also tell you that Jones weighs less than Smith? Not in so many words, but, of course, it is implicit in what I said in the following sense: what I said entails that Jones weighs less than Smith. Likewise, runs the alternative response, truth, reference and meaning are implicit in the story completed science will tell about our sentence and the world in which it is produced: that story will entail that the sentence is true, that it has a certain meaning, and that its parts refer to certain things, including snow. This response locates the semantic properties of sentences within the picture completed science tells about sentences and the world by arguing that they are entailed by that story. The semantic gets a place in the physical story by being entailed by the physical story.

I have just described a familiar example of the placement problem, and two responses to it. But we can generalise. Metaphysics, we said, is about what there is and what it is like. But of course it is concerned not with any old shopping list of what there is and what it is like. Metaphysicians seek a comprehensive account of some subject matter – the mind, the semantic, or, most ambitiously, everything – in terms of a limited number of more or less basic notions. In doing this they are following the good example of physicists. The methodology is not that of letting a thousand flowers bloom but rather that of making do with as meagre a diet as possible. Some who discuss the debate in the philosophy of mind between dualism and monism complain that each position is equally absurd. We should be *pluralists*. Of course we should be pluralists in some sense or other. However, if the thought is that any attempt to explain it all, or to explain it all as far as the mind is concerned, in terms of some limited set of fundamental ingredients is mistaken in principle, then it seems to me that we are being in effect invited to abandon serious metaphysics in favour of drawing up big lists. But if metaphysics seeks comprehension in terms of limited ingredients, it is continually going to be faced with the problem of location. Because the ingredients *are* limited, some putative features of the world are not going to appear explicitly in the story. The question then will be whether they, nevertheless, figure implicitly in the story. Serious metaphysics is simultaneously discriminatory and putatively complete, and the combination of these two facts means that there is bound to be a whole range of putative features of our world up for either elimination or location.

What is it for some putative feature to have a place in the story some metaphysic tells in its favoured terms? One answer, already mentioned, is for the feature to be entailed by the story told in the favoured terms. I take it that few will quarrel with this as a sufficient condition. One good way to get a place in the story is by entailment. I will argue that not only is it one way, it is the only way. The one and only entry ticket into the story told in the preferred terms is by being entailed by that story.

In order to focus and make familiar the discussion, I am going to develop the argument for the entry by entailment view in terms of the particular example of physicalism and the psychological. I will be arguing, that is, that the psychological appears in the physicalists' story about our world if and only if that story entails the psychological. Similarly, when I discuss the connection between entry by entailment and conceptual analysis, I will focus on the example of physicalism and the psychological. It may help in following the argument that is to come to assume the truth of physicalism. Although the considerations will be deployed in this familiar and particular context, it will be clear, I trust, that they would apply generally.

2   Placing the Psychological in the Physicalists' Picture

Physicalism is the very opposite of a 'big list' metaphysics. It is highly discriminatory, operating in terms of a small set of favoured properties and relations, typically dubbed 'physical'; and it claims that a complete story, or anyway a complete story of everything contingent, about our world can in principle be told in terms of these properties and relations alone. It is miserly in its basic resources while being as bold as can be in what it claims.

A fair question is how to specify precisely the notion of a physical property. I am not going to answer this fair question. Roughly, I will mean what is typically meant: the kinds of properties that figure in, or are explicitly definable in terms of, those that figure in physics, chemistry, biology, and neuroscience. This rough characterisation leaves it open why those sciences, rather than say psychology or politics, are chosen to settle the favoured class, and it says nothing about how committed this approach is to those sciences being roughly right in the kinds of properties they need for their own internal purposes. Nevertheless, I think that the rough characterisation will do for our purposes here. As far as I can see, nothing in what follows turns on the answers to these two controversial matters.[5] What is important here is that there is a favoured list, not how a property or relation gets to be on that favoured list.[6]

What will be important is the notion of a complete story. Our argument for the entry by entailment thesis, as it applies to physicalism and the psychological, will be that it is the physicalists' claim to have a complete story about the nature of our world which commits them to our world having a psychological nature if and only if that nature is entailed by the world's physical nature.

Physicalists variously express their central contention as: that the world is entirely physical; that when you have said all there is to say about physical properties and relations, you have said all there is to say about everything, or anyway everything contingent including psychology; that the world is nothing but, or nothing over and above, the physical world; that a full inventory of the instantiated physical properties and relations would be a full inventory *simpliciter*; and so on and so forth. What does all this come to?

We can make a start by noting that one particularly clear way of showing *incompleteness* is by appeal to independent variation. What shows that three co-ordinates do not provide a complete account of location in space–time is that we can vary position in space–time while keeping any three co-ordinates constant. Hence, an obvious way to approach completeness is in terms of the lack of independent variation. Four co-ordinates completely specify position in space–time because you cannot have two different positions with the same four co-ordinates. But, of course, lack of independent variation is supervenience: position in space–time supervenes on the four co-ordinates. So the place to look when looking for illumination regarding the sense in which physicalism claims to be complete, and, in particular, to be complete with respect to the psychological, is at various supervenience theses.[7]

Now physicalism is not just a claim about the completeness of the physical story concerning the individuals in our world. It claims completeness concerning the world itself. Accordingly, we need to think of the supervenience base as consisting of worlds, not merely of individuals in them. *Intra*-world supervenience theses will not capture what the physicalists have in mind. We need to look to *inter*-world *global* supervenience theses, an example of which is

(A)   Any two possible worlds that are physical duplicates (physical property, relation and law for physical property, relation and law identical) are duplicates *simpliciter*.[8]

(A), however, does not express the physicalists' thesis. Physicalism is a claim about the nature of *our* world. It is perfectly consistent with physicalism that there be a possible world exactly like ours which contains as an *addition* lots of mental life sustained in non-material stuff. This would simply be one of the worlds where physicalism was false. So physicalism does *not* say that every physical duplicate of our world is a duplicate *simpliciter*, and, therefore, does not say that all worlds that are physical duplicates are duplicates *simpliciter*. For the same reason

(B)   Any world that is a physical duplicate of our (the actual) world is identical *simpliciter* with our world.

does not capture physicalism. But it points us in the right direction. For it makes it clear that the trouble is being generated by the fact that (B) makes claims about worlds which are 'bigger' than our world, whereas physicalism is simply a claim that the physical nature of our world exhausts the nature of our world. It is not saying that there cannot be bigger worlds than ours which are bigger partly in virtue of having some non-physical 'stuff'. Accordingly, I suggest

(C)   Any world which is a *minimal* physical duplicate of our world is a duplicate *simpliciter* of our world

as expressing physicalism's essential claim, where we can think of a minimal physical duplicate in terms of what happens when we follow recipes. A recipe tells you what to do, but not what *not* to do. It tells you to add butter to the flour but does not tell you not to add bat wings. Why doesn't it? Part of the reason is that no one would think to add them unless explicitly told to. But part of the reason is logical. It is impossible to list all the things not to do. There are indefinitely many of them. Of necessity, when we follow recipes, we take for granted an implicitly included 'stop' clause. A minimal physical duplicate of our world is what we would get if we – or God, as it is sometimes put – used the physical nature of our world as a recipe with an understood stop clause for making a world.

We noted earlier the physicalists' talk of everything being nothing over and above, nothing more than, the physical; of the full physical story being complete, being the full story *simpliciter*, and so on. The hope has sometimes been that the key notion of, as it is sometimes called, 'nothing buttery' might be susceptible of a precise, non-circular definition in terms of supervenience. If (C), or something like it, is the best we can do by way of specifying what physicalism is committed to in terms of supervenience, then this hope has been dashed. The notion of minimality that features in (C) is too close to nothing buttery. We have, I trust, made matters clearer, but we have not reached what might have been hoped for.

We reached (C) by objecting to (A) and (B). But here is a positive argument to the result that (C) captures the physicalist's claim. Suppose, first, that (C) is false; then there is a difference in nature between our world and some minimal physical duplicate of it. But then either our world contains some nature that the minimal physical duplicate does not, or the minimal physical duplicate contains some nature that our world does not. The second is impossible because the extra nature would have to be non-physical (as our world and the duplicate are physically identical), and the minimal physical duplicate contains no non-physical nature by definition. But if our world contains some nature that the duplicate does not, this nature must be non-physical (as our world and the duplicate are physically identical). But then physicalism would be false, for our world would contain some non-physical nature. Hence, if (C) is false, physicalism is false. We now show that if physicalism is false, (C) is false. If physicalism is false, our world contains some non-physical nature. But that nature cannot be present in any minimal physical duplicate of our world, as any such duplicate is a minimal duplicate. But then any such world is not a duplicate *simpliciter* of our world, and hence (C) is false.

There is a debatable step in this little proof that physicalism is true if and only if (C) is true. At the last stage, I assumed that if our world contains some non-physical nature, there is a minimal physical duplicate which lacks that nature. But suppose that some complex of physical properties in this world is necessarily connected in the strongest sense of 'necessary' to some quite distinct, non-physical property. In that case the assumption will be false. One response to this objection would be to invoke the Humean ban on necessary connections between distinct existences, but a less controversial response is available. I think that we know enough about what the physical properties are like – despite the fact that we ducked the question of how to specify them precisely – to be confident that the connection in question is not possible. The kinds of properties and relations that figure in the physical sciences do not have mysterious *necessary* connections with quite distinct properties and relations. In any case, this is what physicalists should say. To say otherwise is to abandon physicalism (in favour of something far more mysterious than interactionist dualism). So physicalists must, it seems to me, accept (C).

3   A Side Issue: Supervenience and Singular Thought

To accept (C) is *ipso facto* to accept

(C*)   Any world which is a minimal physical duplicate of our world is a psychological duplicate of our world.

Consider a minimal physical duplicate of the actual world. It will contain a duplicate of Bush. It might be urged that our Bush's psychology, while being very similar to his doppelgänger's, will not be quite the same as his doppelgänger's. Their singular thoughts will be different by virtue of being directed to different objects. Only our Bush is thinking about our Clinton. Thus, if physicalism is committed to (C*), physicalism is false.[9]

One response to this putative disproof of physicalism would be to challenge the view about singular thought that lies behind it, but I think we can steer clear of that issue for our purposes here.[10] The disproof as stated is trading on the counterpart way of thinking about objects in possible worlds: the way according to which no object appears in more than one world, and what makes it the case that an object which is F might have failed to be F is the fact that its counterpart in some possible world is not F.[11] However, the duplicate of our Bush is thinking about the very same person as our Bush in the only sense that the counterpart theorist can take seriously. If I had scratched my nose a moment ago, I would still have had the very same nose that I actually have. Noses are not that easy to remove and replace. The counterpart theorist has to say that what makes that true are certain facts about the nose of my counterpart in a world where my counterpart scratched his nose a moment ago. If that is good enough for being the very same nose, then the corresponding facts about Bush's counterpart are good enough for it to be true that he is thinking about the very same person, and hence having the same singular thought.

The putative disproof might be developed without trading on the counterpart way of looking at matters. A believer in transworld identity typically holds that whether an object in our world is literally identical with an object in another is not a qualitative matter. Such a believer might well hold that though Bush, our Bush, and Clinton, our Clinton, eyeball each other in more worlds than this one, it is nevertheless true that in some minimal physical duplicates of our world, our Bush thinks about a qualitative duplicate of our Clinton who nevertheless is not our Clinton. On some views about singular thought, Bush will count as having a different thought in such a world from the thought he has in our world. In this case the steering clear requires a modification of (C). The physicalist will need to require that minimal physical duplicates of our world be ones which, in addition to being physical property and relation identical with our world, are haecceity-associated-with-physical-property-and-relation identical with our world.

4   From (C) to Entry by Entailment

Given that (C) follows from physicalism, there is a straightforward and familiar argument to show that if physicalism is true, then the psychological story about our world is entailed by the physical story about our world. (C) entails that any psychological fact about our world is entailed by the physical nature of our world.

We can think of a statement as telling a story about the way the world is, and as being true inasmuch as the world is the way the story says it is. Let Φ be the statement (an infinite disjunction of very long conjunctions) which tells the rich, complex and detailed physical story which is true at the actual world and all the minimal physical duplicates of the actual world, and false elsewhere. Let Ψ be any true statement entirely about the psychological nature of our world: Ψ is true at our world, and every world at which Ψ is false differs in some psychological way from our world. If (C) is true, every world at which Φ is true is a duplicate *simpliciter* of our world, and so *a fortiori* a psychological duplicate of our world. But then every world at which Φ is true is a world at which Ψ is true – that is, Φ entails Ψ.

We have thus derived the entry by entailment thesis for the special case of physicalism and the psychological. A putative psychological fact has a place in the physicalists' world view if and only if it is entailed by some true, purely physical statement. Any putative psychological fact which is not so entailed must be regarded by the physicalist as either a refutation of physicalism or as *merely* putative. Although the argument was developed for the special case of physicalism and the psychological, the argument did not depend crucially on matters local to that special case. We could have argued in the same general way in the case of physicalism and the semantic, or in the case of Cartesian dualism and the semantic, or in the case of Berkelean idealism and physical objects.[12] Our argument essentially turned on just two facts about any serious metaphysics: it is discriminatory, and it claims completeness. It is those two features of serious metaphysics which mean that it is committed to views about what entails what.

How does entry by entailment show the importance of conceptual analysis? If Φ entails Ψ, what makes Φ true also makes Ψ true (at least when Φ and Ψ are contingent). But what makes Φ true is the physical way our world is. Φ needs nothing more than that. Hence, the physicalist is committed to each and every psychological statement being made true by a purely physical way our world is. The analytical functionalist has a story about how this could be. It comes in two stages. One stage – the most discussed stage – is about how certain functional-cum-causal facts make it true that a subject is in one or another psychological state. The other stage is about how certain physical facts make it true that the appropriate functional-cum-causal states obtain. The story is a piece of conceptual analysis. Analytical functionalism is defended by the a priori methods characteristic of conceptual analysis. For us the important point is that the physicalist must have *some* story to tell; otherwise how the purely physical makes psychological statements true is rendered an impenetrable mystery. But it is the very business of conceptual analysis to explain how matters framed in terms of one set of terms and concepts can make true matters framed in a different set of terms and concepts. When we seek an analysis of knowledge in terms of truth, belief, justification, causation and so on, we seek an account of how matters described in terms of the latter notions can make true matters described in terms of the former. So far we have been unsuccessful (I take it, others disagree). When we seek a causal account of reference, we seek an account of the kinds of causal facts which make it true that a term names an object. When and if we succeed, we will have an account of what makes it true that 'Moses' names Moses in terms of, among other things, causal links between uses of the word and Moses himself. Compatibilists about free will seek accounts of what it is to act freely in terms of facts about the agent's abilities and the causal role of the agent's character. If they have succeeded, they have told us how the way things are described in terms of abilities and causal origins make true the ways things are described in terms of free action. And so on and so forth.

I take the understanding of conceptual analysis just outlined to be pretty much the standard one, but there seems to be another understanding around. For example, some who discuss, and indeed advocate, some version or other of the causal theory of reference also say that they oppose conceptual analysis. But the causal theory of reference *is* a piece of conceptual analysis in our sense. It is defended by a priori reflection on, and intuitions about, possible cases in the manner distinctive of conceptual analysis. And it is hard to see how else one could argue for it. The causal theory of reference is a theory about the conditions under which, say, 'Moses' refers to a certain person. But that is nothing other than a theory about the possible situations in which 'Moses' refers to that person, and the possible situations in which 'Moses' does not refer to that person. Hence, intuitions about various possible situations – the meat and potatoes of conceptual analysis – are bound to hold centre stage simply because it is better to say what is intuitively plausible than what is intuitively implausible. Or consider the book by Sterelny from which we quoted the passages saying that 'an alternative [to the methods of this book] is to see philosophy as an investigation into conceptual truths proceeding by thought experiments' and 'I doubt that there are any very interesting conceptual truths about the mind, or about thinking'. Later in the book we find the following passage:

> Representational notions play a central role in psychology. Yet representational kinds are not individualistic. There is a standard parable that makes this point. Imagine that, far away in space and time, there is a world just like ours, Twin Earth. Twin Earth really is a twin to Earth; the parallel is so exact that each of us have a doppelgänger on Twin Earth, our twinself. A person's twinself is molecule-for-molecule identical to himself or herself you and your twin are individualistically identical, for what is going on inside your heads is molecule-for-molecule the same. But the representational properties of your thoughts are not always the same. For consider your thoughts about your mother. These are about *your* mother. But your twinself has never seen, heard, or thought of your mother. That individual's motherish thoughts are about another individual. An individual amazingly similar to your mother, but none the less a different person. . . . So the representational properties of thoughts about particular people don't supervene on brain states; they are not individualistic. Variations of the Twin Earth theme have been run by Putnam and Burge to show that

thoughts about natural kinds and socio-legal kinds are not individualistic either.   (pp. 82–3)

Surely in this passage we are being offered a defence of a conceptual claim about the representational properties of our thoughts, namely, to the effect that they are not individualistic, and moreover the defence is via a thought experiment (a 'parable')? Clearly Sterelny, and at least some other critics of conceptual analysis, must mean by conceptual analysis something different from what we mean here.

Many will feel that there is a major objection to the argument given from (C) to the conclusion that Φ entails Ψ. The objection is that the argument neglects a crucial distinction between entailment and *fixing* which arises from the recognition of the necessary a posteriori.[13]

5   Entailment and the Necessary a posteriori

'Water $= H_2O$' is necessarily true (modulo worlds where there is no water) despite being a posteriori.[14] This means that conditionals which say that if H_2O has a certain distribution, so does water – for example, 'If H_2O is L-located then water is L-located' – are necessarily true though a posteriori. Does it follow that 'H_2O is L-located' entails 'Water is L-located'? You might say 'yes' on the ground that every world where H_2O is L-located is a world where water is L-located. You might say 'no' on the ground that the conditional is not a priori knowable. The second response might be bolstered by noting that we would not normally assess the argument

H_2O is L-located.
Therefore, water is L-located.

as valid. The second response might be spelt out by insisting on a distinction between fixing and entailment proper.[15] If every P-world is a Q-world, then P fixes Q, but in order for P to entail Q it must in addition be the case that 'If P then Q' is a priori.

The decision between the two responses turns, it seems to me, on the decision between two different ways of looking at the distinction between necessary a posteriori statements like 'Water $= H_2O$' and necessary a priori ones like '$H_2O = H_2O$'. You might say that the latter are analytically or conceptually or logically (in some wide sense not tied to provability in a formal system) necessary, whereas the former are

metaphysically necessary, meaning by the terminology that we are dealing with two senses of 'necessary' in somewhat the way that we are when
we contrast logical necessity with nomic necessity.[16] Thus the class of
nomic possibilities is a proper subset of the class of logical possibilities –
every nomic possibility is a logical possibility, but some logical possibilities (for example, travelling faster than the speed of light) are not nomic
possibilities. Similarly, the idea is that the class of metaphysical possibilities is a proper subset of the class of logical possibilities. Every metaphysically possible world is logically possible, but some logically or
conceptually possible worlds – for instance, those where water is not
H_2O – are metaphysically impossible. On this approach the reason the
necessity of water's being H_2O is not available a priori is that though
what is logically possible and impossible is available in principle to
reason alone given sufficient grasp of the relevant concepts and logical
acumen, what is metaphysically possible and impossible is not so available.

I think, as against this view, that it is a mistake to hold that the
necessity possessed by 'Water = H_2O' is different from that possessed
by 'Water = water' (or that possessed by '2 + 2 = 4'). Just as Quine insists
that numbers and tables exist in the very same sense, and that the
difference between numbers existing and tables existing is a difference
between numbers and tables, I think that we should insist that water's
being H_2O and water's being water are necessary in the very same sense.
The difference lies, not in the kind of necessity possessed, but rather
where the labels 'a priori' and 'a posteriori' suggest it lies: in our epistemic access to the necessity they share.

My reason for holding that there is one sense of necessity here relates to
what it was that convinced us that 'Water = H_2O' is necessarily true.
What convinced us were the arguments of Saul Kripke and Hilary Putnam to the conclusion that the terms 'Water' and 'H_2O' are rigid designators, and so that it follows from the fact that 'Water is H_2O' is true that
it is necessarily true. This was the discovery of a semantic fact about
certain terms, not the discovery of a new sort of necessity. Kripke and
Putnam taught us something important about the semantics of certain
singular terms which means that we must acknowledge a new way for a
statement to be necessary, a way which cannot be known a priori; but it is
a new way to have the old property.[17]

If the relevant statements are necessary in the same sense but differ
with regard to the epistemological status of their shared necessity, there
is an obvious response to the question, Does 'H_2O is *L*-located' entail
'Water is *L*-located'? It is to say 'yes', but hasten to distinguish a priori

from a posteriori entailment, and hold that the entailment in this case is a posteriori. In short, the response is to adopt the following definitions:

P a priori entails *Q* iff (a) every *P*-world is a *Q*-world, and (b) the conditional 'If *P* then *Q*' is a priori.
P entails (or fixes) *Q* iff every *P*-world is a *Q*-world.
P a posteriori entails *Q* iff (a) *P* entails *Q*, and (b) *P* does not a priori entail *Q*.

Hence it seems to me that our result that physicalism is committed to Φ's entailing Ψ stands. (From here on we will think of Ψ as some arbitrary true psychological statement; it might even be the huge one that says all there is to say about our world's psychology.) But there are two objections that moderate naturalists might well make all the same.

First, they might object that our argument assumed that there are psychological facts. The entailment result was obtained from the combination of (C) with the assumption that there are true psychological statements. A physicalist of the eliminativist persuasion can reject one of our premises. This is right, but does not affect the overall issue. Eliminativism about the mental is implausible. Eliminativism across the board about matters described in any terms other than the austerely physical is incredible. We could have developed the argument in terms of the relationship between the physical story and any true statement **S** about our world not framed in the austere terms, in order to show that the physicalist is committed to Φ's entailing **S**. The general point is that a serious metaphysics is committed to there being entailments between the full story told in its favoured terms and each and every truth told in other terms. The only physicalistic eliminativism which would avoid commitment to entailments from Φ to statements in other terms would be one which said that there are *no* truths tellable in other terms. But such a metaphysics would no longer be a serious one in our sense. For it would not effect a partition of the truths acknowledged by it into those pertaining most directly to the properties and relations viewed as the fundamental ingredients of everything, and the others; it would not be discriminating. Also, it would be unbelievable.[18]

Second, they might very reasonably object that the result that Φ entails Ψ is not a result which supports the importance of conceptual analysis in anything like the traditional sense. Conceptual analysis in the traditional sense, as we noted earlier, is constituted by a priori reflection on concepts and possible cases with an aim to elucidating connections between different ways of describing matters. Hence, it might be objected, if we allow that some entailments are a posteriori, to demonstrate an entailment is conspicuously not to demonstrate the importance of conceptual analysis. In order to reply to this objection, I need to say more about the necessary a posteriori.

6 The a priori Part of the Story about the Necessary a posteriori

We urged that the explanation of the a posteriori nature of the necessary a posteriori does not lie in the special necessity possessed; where then does it lie? I think that the answer is best approached if we have before us from the beginning two central facts about the issue. First, the issue is an issue about sentences or, if you like, statements or stories in the sense of assertoric sentences in some possible language, and not about propositions, or at least not propositions thought of as sets of possible worlds.[19] By the argument lately rehearsed, the set of worlds where water is water is the very same set as the set where water is H_2O; so by Leibnitz's Law, there is no question of the proposition that water is water differing from the proposition that water is H_2O in that one is, and one is not, necessary a posteriori. Second, the puzzle about the necessary a posteriori is not how a sentence can be necessary and yet it takes empirical work to find this out. Russians utter plenty of sentences which are necessarily true and yet it takes, or would take, many of us a lot of empirical work to discover the fact. The puzzle is how a sentence can be necessarily true and understood by someone, and yet the fact of its necessity be obscure to that person. And the reason this is a puzzle is because of the way we use sentences to tell people how things are.

Consider what happens when I utter the true sentence 'There is a coin in my pocket'. I tell you something about how things are, and to do that is precisely to tell you which of the various possibilities concerning how things are is actual. My success in conveying this simple bit of information depends on two things: your understanding the sentence, and your taking the sentence to be true. We have here a folk theory that ties together understanding, truth and information about possibilities; and the obvious way to articulate this folk theory is to identify, or at least essentially connect, understanding a sentence with knowing the conditions under which it is true, that is, knowing the possibilities at which it is true and the possibilities at which it is false.[20] Indeed, if we could not connect understanding a sentence, accepting it, and knowing about possibilities in this kind of way, there would be little point in asserting

sentences to one another. There are many possibilities concerning when
the bus leaves. Your uttering a sentence I understand and accept, namely,
'The bus leaves at six', is exactly what I need to tell me which of the many
possibilities is actual, and that fact constitutes the essential point of your
utterance. But it seems, then, that understanding a necessarily true sentence should, at least in principle, be enough to reveal its necessary
status. For understanding it would require knowing the conditions
under which it is true, and how could you know them and yet fail to
notice that they are universal? The puzzle is particularly pressing when,
as in the cases we are concerned with, the statements are about relatively
accessible, contingent features of our world.

I think – unoriginally[21] – that the way out of our puzzle is to allow that
we understand some sentences without knowing the conditions under
which they are true, but to do this in a way which retains the central idea
of the folk theory that the three notions of: understanding a sentence, of a
sentence's being true, and of the information carried by a sentence are
very closely connected. It is just that the connection is not always so
simple as that understanding requires knowledge of the truth conditions
of what is expressed.

Here is an illustrative example, familiar from discussions of two-
dimensional modal logic, of understanding without knowing truth conditions.[22] Suppose I hear someone say 'He has a beard'. I will understand
what is being said without necessarily knowing the conditions under
which what is said is true, because I may not know who is being spoken
of. As it is sometimes put, I may not know which proposition is being
expressed. If I am the person being spoken of, the proposition
being expressed is that Jackson has a beard, and what is said counts as
true if and only if Jackson has a beard; if Jones is the person being spoken
of, the proposition being expressed is that Jones has a beard, and what is
said counts as true if and only if Jones has a beard. Hence, if I don't know
whether it is Jackson, Jones or someone else altogether, I don't
know which proposition is being expressed, and I don't know the conditions under which what is said is true. But obviously I do understand the
sentence. However, granting this does not require us to abandon the folk
theory that understanding, truth and information are very closely connected. For I am much better placed than the Russian speaker who hears
'He has a beard'. Unlike the Russian speaker, I know how context determines the conditions under which what is said is true. I know how to
move from the appropriate contextual information, the information
which in this case determines who is being spoken of, to the truth
conditions of what is said. Thus, uttering the sentence has for me, but

not for the Russian speaker, the potential to convey information about which possibilities are realised, and it has this potential precisely because I understand the sentence.[23]

A similar point can be made about 'water' sentences. The doctrine that meanings 'ain't in the head' means that the truth-conditions of our 'water' sentences depend on matters outside our heads that we may be ignorant of. But someone who does not know that it is H_2O that falls from the sky and all the rest, may, as we have already noted, understand 'water' sentences. Hence, understanding, say, 'There is water hereabouts' does not require knowing the conditions under which it is true, though it does require knowing how the conditions under which it is true depend on context, on how things are outside the head.[24] But this means that although understanding alone does not give truth conditions, under-standing alone does give us the way truth conditions depend on context, and that fact is enough for us to move a priori from, for example, statements about the distribution of H_2O *combined with the right context-giving statements*, to information about the distribution of water. For example, suppose that the right account of the semantics of 'water' is that it is a rigidified definite description meaning roughly 'stuff which actually falls from the sky, fills the oceans, is odourless and colourless, is essential for life, is called 'water' by our experts,... or which satisfies enough of the foregoing', and consider the inference

1   H_2O is *L*-distributed.
2   H_2O is the stuff which falls from the sky, fills the oceans, etc.
3   Therefore, water is *L*-distributed.

Although, as noted earlier, the passage from (1) to (3) is a posteriori – (2) being the a posteriori, contingent fact that needs to be known in order to make the step from (1) to (3) – the passage from (1) *and* (2) to (3) will be a priori. And it will be so because although our understanding of the word 'water' does not determine its reference-conditions, it does determine how the reference-conditions of the word depend on context, and (2) gives that context. It gives the relevant fact about how things are outside the head.[25] Our understanding of the relevant terms plus logical acumen is enough to enable us to go from (1) combined with (2) to (3). Indeed, this is the a priori fact which reveals the a posteriori entailment. We did not know that (1) entailed (3) until we learnt (2). But as soon as we learnt (2), we had the wherewithal to move a priori to (3). We could put it this way. Conceptual analysis tells us that we can move from the combination of (1) and (2) to (3). For conceptual analysis – what is in principle possible a priori from understanding plus logical acumen – tells us how truth-conditions depend on context, and that is all we need to go from the combination of (1) and (2) to (3).

Earlier I drew the connection between the entry by entailment thesis which commits physicalists to holding that Φ entails Ψ, and the centrality of conceptual analysis to physicalism, by saying (a) that physicalism, on pain of making mysteries, had better tell us how physical nature makes true, in the sense of necessitating, psychological nature, and (b) that conceptual analysis tells us how matters framed in one set of terms can make true matters framed in different terms. One way of putting the objection under discussion is that H_2O being L-distributed makes it true that water is L-distributed, but conceptual analysis cannot tell us about this. That H_2O facts make true water facts is a posteriori. Our reply is that there *is* an a priori story to be told about how H_2O facts make true water facts.

More generally, the two-dimensional modal logic way of looking at the necessary a posteriori shows that even if the entailment from Φ to Ψ is a posteriori, there is still an a priori story tellable about how the story in physical terms about our world makes true the story in psychological terms about our world. Although understanding may not even in principle be enough to yield truth-conditions, it is enough to yield how truth-conditions depend on context. But of course the context is, according to the physicalist, entirely physical. Hence, the physicalist is committed to there being an a priori story to tell about how the physical way things are makes true the psychological way things are. But the story may come in two parts. It may be that one part of the story says which physical way things are, Φ_1, makes some psychological statement true; and the other part of the story, the part that tells the context, says which different physical way things are, Φ_2, makes it the case that it is Φ_1 that makes the psychological statement true. What will be a priori accessible is that Φ_1 and Φ_2 together make the psychological statement true.

Notes

1   I mean metaphysics in the sense of speculative cosmology rather than analytic ontology, see D. C. Williams, *Principles of Empirical Realism*, Springfield, IL: Thomas, 1966.

2   D. M. Armstrong, *A Materialist Theory of the Mind*, London, Routledge & Kegan Paul, 1968. Of course, part of the reason that he spends so much of the book doing conceptual analysis is that he thinks (reasonably) that the relevant empirical results are all but in.

3   Kim Sterelny, *The Representational Theory of Mind*, Oxford, Basil Blackwell, 1990, p. xi. I suspect however that Sterelny means (must mean) something different by 'conceptual truths' and 'conceptual analysis' from what we will be meaning by them. I return to this matter later.

4   This line of thought is very clearly presented, but not endorsed, in Michael Devitt, *Realism and Truth*, Oxford, Basil Blackwell, 1984, ch. 6.

5   I discuss some of questions that the notion of a physical property raises in Frank Jackson, *From Metaphysics to Ethics*, Oxford, Oxford University Press, 1998, ch. 1.

6   Physicalists who think that there are irreducibly *de se* truths – for instance, about what a person thinks – will of course include the appropriate physical specification of them in their favoured list. I am indebted here to Richard Holton and David Lewis.

7   What follows is one version of a familiar story, see, e.g., Terence Horgan, 'Supervenience and Microphysics', *Pacific Philosophical Quarterly*, 63 (1982): 29–43, and David Lewis, 'New Work for a Theory of Universals', *Australasian Journal of Philosophy*, 61 (1983): 343–77. I am much indebted to their discussions. Added note: I have sharpened and shortened the discussion of the supervenience theses in what follows.

8   As far as I can see, it does not matter for what follows what view precisely is taken of non-actual possible worlds: perhaps they are concrete entities of the same ontological type as our world, as David Lewis, *On the Plurality of Worlds*, Oxford, Basil Blackwell, 1986, holds; perhaps they are abstract entities as Robert Stalnaker, 'Possible Worlds', *Noûs*, 10 (1976): 65–75, holds; perhaps they are structured universals as Peter Forrest, 'Ways Worlds Could Be', *Australasian Journal of Philosophy*, 64 (1986): 15–24, holds; perhaps they are nothing at all, but talk of 'them' is understandable in terms of combinations of properties and relations, as D. M. Armstrong, *A Combinatorial Theory of Possibility*, Cambridge, Cambridge University Press, 1989, holds. Added note: in the original version of this chapter I omitted the needed reference to law in (A).

9   I am indebted to Rae Langton and David Lewis in what follows.

10 For a survey of various views about singular thought, see Simon Blackburn, *Spreading the Word*, Oxford, Oxford University Press, 1984.

11 See Lewis, *On the Plurality of Worlds*, Oxford, Basil Blackwell, 1986.

12 A traditional objection to idealism has been that no congeries of actual and hypothetical facts about sense impressions, no matter how complex and detailed, *entails* that there is a table in the next room; and so idealists must embrace eliminativism about tables. A contemporary criticism of this traditional objection is that it is confusing the ontological thesis of idealism with the analytical thesis of phenomenalism. If we are right, the traditional objection is very much to the point.

13 The possibility of this objection was forcibly drawn to my attention by Peter Railton, Lloyd Humberstone and Michaelis Michael. I am not sure where

they stand on it however. The terms in which I characterise it are closest to those of Peter Forrest, 'Universals and Universalizability', *Australasian Journal of Philosophy*, 70 (1992): 93–8.

14   I am taking for granted the view that the term 'water' is a rigid designator of (as we discovered) H_2O. I am in fact agnostic on the question of whether 'water' as used by the person in the street is a rigid designator. But clearly it is a rigid designator in the mouths and from the pens of many philosophers alive today, and for the purposes of the discussion here we will give it that meaning. It is clear in any case that 'water' *could* have been a rigid designator.

15   Stephen Yablo, 'Mental Causation', *Philosophical Review*, 101 (1992): 245–80 distinguishes fixing from conceptual entailment, see especially pp. 253–4. His conceptual entailment is, I take it, our a priori entailment below.

16   See, e.g., Peter Forrest, 'Universals and Universalisability'. Saul Kripke, *Naming and Necessity*, Oxford, Basil Blackwell, 1980, p. 125, says that 'statements representing scientific discoveries about what this stuff *is . . .* are *. . .* necessary truths in the strictest possible sense'. This suggests that he does not hold the view in question, though he does not, as far as I know, address the matter explicitly.

17   Saul Kripke, *Naming and Necessity*, Oxford, Basil Blackwell, 1980, and Hilary Putnam, 'The Meaning of "Meaning"' in *Mind, Language and Reality*, Cambridge, Cambridge University Press, 1975, pp. 215–71.

18   I am indebted here to a discussion with John O'Leary Hawthorne.

19   At the end of the preface to *Naming and Necessity*, Oxford, Basil Blackwell, 1980, Kripke insists that his concern is with sentences, not propositions; see pp. 20–1.

20   This kind of theory in its philosophically sophisticated articulations is best known through the work of David Lewis, see, e.g., *On the Plurality of Worlds*, Oxford, Basil Blackwell, 1986, and Robert Stalnaker, *Inquiry*, Cambridge, Mass., MIT Press, 1984. But it would, I think, be wrong to regard the folk theory as being as controversial as these articulations. The folk theory is, it seems to me, a commonplace. The sports section of any newspaper is full of speculations about possible outcomes conveyed by sentences that discriminate among the outcomes in a way we grasp because we understand the sentences. There is, of course, a major problem about what to say concerning mathematical statements within this framework, but our concern will be with sentences about relatively mundane items like water, and with entailments between sentences putatively representing the way things are as a matter of empirical fact.

21   I take it that the account which follows is a thumbnail sketch of the approach naturally suggested by the two-dimensional modal logic treatment of the necessary a posteriori in, for instance, Robert C. Stalnaker, 'Assertion' in P. Cole, ed., *Syntax and Semantics*, vol. 9, New York, Academic Press, 1978, pp. 315–32 and M. K. Davies and I. L. Humberstone, 'Two Notions of Necessity',

Philosophical Studies, 38 (1980): 1–30. They should not be held responsible for my way of putting matters.

22 The example is a variant on one discussed by Stalnaker in 'Assertion'.

23 It might be objected that I do know who is being spoken of: I know something unique about the person being spoken of, namely that he is being spoken of and is designated by a certain utterance of the pronoun 'I'. But this is 'Cambridge' knowing who. It is no more knowing who than Cambridge change is change. I do not know who will win the next election, but I know something unique (and important) about that person, namely, that he or she will be the person who will win the most votes.

24 Thus, there is *a* sense in which understanding 'There is water hereabouts' requires knowing truth-conditions, for it requires knowing a whole lot of things of the form 'If the context is thus and so, then the sentence is true in such and such conditions'. What is not required for understanding is knowledge of the truth-conditions of the proposition expressed. I am indebted here to David Lewis and to Pavel Tichy, 'Kripke on Necessity A Posteriori', *Philosophical Studies*, 43, (1983): 225–41. Added note: this issue is addressed in a little detail in *From Metaphysics to Ethics*, ch. 3.

25 Other views about how the word 'water' gets to pick out H_2O would require appropriately different versions of (2). The view I have used by way of illustration is *roughly* that of Davies and Humberstone, 'Two Notions of Necessity'. If you prefer a causal-historical theory, you would have to replace (2) by something like 'It is H_2O that was the (right kind of) causal origin of our use of the word "water"'. Of course, any view about how 'water' gets to pick out what it does will be controversial. But it is incredible that there is *no* story to tell. It is not a bit of magic that 'water' picks out what it does pick out.

Index